Death and Culture

Series Editors: **Ruth Penfold-Mounce**, University of York, UK,
Kate Woodthorpe, University of Bath, UK and
Erica Borgstrom, The Open University, UK

Mortality is a research theme in evidence across multiple disciplines, but one that is not always explicitly acknowledged. This series provides an outlet for a social science and cross-disciplinary exploration of all aspects of mortality. The aim of the series is to create a forum for the publication of sociologically relevant research that approaches death from a cultural perspective, supported by evidence and framed by theoretical engagement. The series advances cross-disciplinary, international and social discussions about death and culture.

Published in the series

Death's Social and Material Meaning Beyond the Human
Edited by **Jesse D. Peterson**, **Natashe Lemos Dekker** and
Philip R. Olson

Forthcoming in the series

Death, Institutions and Institutionalisation
Edited by **Kate Woodthorpe**, **Helen Frisby** and
Bethan Michael-Fox

Find out more

bristoluniversitypress.co.uk/
death-and-culture

International advisory board

Jacque Lynn Foltyn, National University, US
Margaret Gibson, Griffith Centre for Cultural Research, Australia
Hannah Gould, University of Melbourne, Australia
Tsepang Leuta, University of the Witwatersrand, South Africa
Lisa McCormick, University of Edinburgh, UK
Montse Morcate, University of Barcelona, Spain
Ben Poore, University of York, UK
Melissa Schrift, East Tennessee State University, US
Johanna Sumiala, University of Helsinki, Finland

Find out more

bristoluniversitypress.co.uk/
death-and-culture

DISSECTION PHOTOGRAPHY

Cadavers, Abjection, and the
Formation of Identity

Brandon Zimmerman

First published in Great Britain in 2024 by

Bristol University Press
University of Bristol
1–9 Old Park Hill
Bristol
BS2 8BB
UK
t: +44 (0)117 374 6645
e: bup-info@bristol.ac.uk

Details of international sales and distribution partners are available at bristoluniversitypress.co.uk

© Bristol University Press 2024

British Library Cataloguing in Publication Data
A catalogue record for this book is available from the British Library

ISBN 978-1-5292-2218-0 hardcover
ISBN 978-1-5292-2219-7 ePub
ISBN 978-1-5292-2220-3 ePdf

The right of Brandon Zimmerman to be identified as author of this work has been asserted by him in accordance with the Copyright, Designs and Patents Act 1988.

All rights reserved: no part of this publication may be reproduced, stored in a retrieval system, or transmitted in any form or by any means, electronic, mechanical, photocopying, recording, or otherwise without the prior permission of Bristol University Press.

Every reasonable effort has been made to obtain permission to reproduce copyrighted material. If, however, anyone knows of an oversight, please contact the publisher.

The statements and opinions contained within this publication are solely those of the author and not of the University of Bristol or Bristol University Press. The University of Bristol and Bristol University Press disclaim responsibility for any injury to persons or property resulting from any material published in this publication.

Bristol University Press works to counter discrimination on grounds of gender, race, disability, age and sexuality.

Cover design: Liam Roberts Design
Front cover image: Private collection. "*A Student's Dream.*" Unknown school. Unidentified photographer. Gelatin silver print, circa 1920
Bristol University Press uses environmentally responsible print partners.
Printed and bound in Great Britain by CPI Group (UK) Ltd, Croydon, CR0 4YY

For Rilo

Contents

Series Editors' Preface	x
List of Figures	xii
Note from the Publisher	xiv
Introduction: My Companions in Misery	1
Must be seen to be believed	2
Postmarked postmortems	4
The demise of cameras and cadavers	6
Hiding in plain sight	9
Without looking	10
Dissection photography: an evolving genre	11
1	The Stages of an Evolving Genre	14
	Confusing conventions of counterculture	15
	The three stages of evolution	17
2	Photography Is Dead	21
	Dead machinery	24
	Convincing humanity	27
	A grim reality: "the heart is not satisfied"	29
	Life from lifelessness	30
3	Defining Disgust: Abjection, Photography, and the Cadaver	33
	Exposing the cadaver: on becoming ambiguous and abject	37
	Transcending the rot: turning ritual transgressions into transgressive rituals	39
	An anus by any other name would still excrete: abjection and the limitations of cadaveric objectification	42
	A proper sense of disgust	45
4	Is Dissection Photography *Really* a Genre?	49
	Adapting to life in a moral world	52
	What dreams may come?	54

DISSECTION PHOTOGRAPHY

5	Iconographic Ambiguities	57
	Digging up the past: grave robbing and its relation to the origins of dissection photography	61
	Of shutters and shuddering horror	64
	Dissecting Black identity	66
6	A Necessary Inhumanity	71
	Cruel winter: hazing rituals and the American dissecting room	75
	Let all men be brothers	78
	Waste not want not	81
	Traversing the land of the dead	82
7	No One Ever Did: Dissection Photography and Female Identity	85
	Always the dissected, never the dissector	87
	It's no joke	90
	What's in a name?	92
	When legs and arms won	94
8	Of Sharp Minds and Sharpened Tools: Dissection Photography and the Ambiguity of the Scalpel	96
	The purity of the knife	101
	The hand of nature	106
	The pen is mightier than the scalpel	109
	Adapting to the cut	112
	The authority of the knife	115
	Cutting up while cutting up the cadaver	119
	Over the top, under the knife: photography's use to "appear wicked"	123
9	Flesh in the Age of Mechanical Reproduction	133
	Skin deep: interpreting the aesthetics of dead flesh	134
	Imagining the unimaginable	140
	Just merely asleep	142
	Emulsional damage: fading in albumen and gelatin silver dissection photographs	145
	Flesh under wraps	147
10	Location, Location, Location	149
	As above so below	152
	'Chris' Baker: the one who literally walked with death	154
	Gone in a flash	157

CONTENTS

11	Anatomical Deuteranopia	160
	Blood culture: red is dead	161
	Meat is murder	163
	The problem with color: determining the race of the dead	166
	Hueman beings	168
12	To Begin without Fear	171
	A dead anything	176
	A modern Golgotha	178
	Cadaverse: poetry in the dissecting room	181
	The word made flesh: dissecting table epigraphs	182
	Religious affiliations	185
	Not all dead	188
	Fear of rebirth	190
13	The Cadaver as (Self-)Portrait	198
	Everyone's a critic	201
	More than mortal	204
	The doctor and the devils	207
	Who dissects the dissectors?	211
	Conclusion: "Learning to Fight Death Next to Death Itself"	212
	Acknowledgments	219
	Notes	220
	References	243
	Index	255

Series Editors' Preface

Erica Borgstrom, Ruth Penfold-Mounce, and Kate Woodthorpe

Studying death can tell us an incredible amount about life. More specifically, it can illuminate a seemingly endless evolving relationship between humans and mortality. From sense-making and rituals around dying to how deceased persons are disposed of and even interwoven within human/non-human grief as ecologies shift, studying death not only deepens our understanding about loss and endings, but also of societies and culture. By attending to these matters, this book series seeks to shine a light on the cultural and social dimensions of death, exploring the wider contexts in which it is experienced, (re)presented, and understood.

At a time when recognizing the differences inherent in these broader sociocultural contexts has never been more important, the series adopts a broad use of the term 'culture' to enable us to bring together a rich multidisciplinary set of monographs and edited collections. We appreciate that the concept of culture has long been debated in several disciplines, most notably within anthropology, as well as contested in terms of how to optimally study 'culture.' While this series will acknowledge this, we do not seek to replicate some of these wider theoretical and epistemological debates. Rather, we want to open out 'culture' to include anthropological, sociological, historical, and philosophical perspectives as well as drawing on media and culture studies, art, and literature. By adopting such an open position to what culture is and how it can be known, we welcome both the sharing of new empirical work within the series as well as theorizing about how engagements with death (re)shape understandings of what culture is, how it operates, and what the future of culture(s) may be.

As social scientists spanning anthropology, sociology, criminology, and cultural studies, and supported by an international editorial board that includes experts in death, dying, and the dead, our default position when thinking about death is typically two-fold. Firstly, that death and dying are inherently social; that is, they are not only about biological or material processes and endings. Secondly, by attending to and foregrounding 'the social' when it comes to death, issues of culture and cultural practices necessarily organically come to the fore. Such is the importance of culture to death, that the topic does not 'fit' neatly into one discipline over another. It is a truly interdisciplinary issue that affects everyone who has lived, is living, or will live in the future; all life on the planet; and Earth itself.

This series launched in 2018 with Emerald Publishing, but relocated in 2021 to Bristol University Press. The series represents a commitment to empirically building our collective understandings about death and culture across time and places, in monographs and edited collections. As editors, we want to take this moment to thank existing and previous editors and authors, the presses we work with, and the wider academic and professional communities that facilitate the flourishing of studies of death and culture. It is only through this collective endeavor that books like this can be made, read, and built upon, and we are excited to see the series grow. We welcome enquiries about future volumes, and hope that you enjoy reading this book.

List of Figures

I.1   Class of 1882. Homeopathic Medical College, University of   5
Michigan (Ann Arbor, Michigan). Unidentified photographer.
Albumen stereograph, circa 1879–1880

1.1   Philadelphia School of Anatomy (Philadelphia, Pennsylvania).   18
Unidentified photographer. Albumen boudoir card, circa
1889–1890

2.1   Medical student with dissecting tools and anatomical   25
preparation of a dissected human arm. Unidentified
photographer. Albumen carte-de-visite, circa 1875

3.1   "Nightly Revels in STIFFDOM." Medical College of   46
Virginia (Richmond, Virginia). Unidentified photographer.
Gelatin silver print, circa 1912

5.1   Leeds School of Medicine (United Kingdom).   60
Unidentified photographer. Albumen print, March 1887

5.2   Dr. Richard Whitehead and the 3rd Dissecting Club.   66
University of Virginia (Charlottesville, Virginia).
Unidentified photographer. Gelatin silver print, 1909

5.3   "HE LIVED for others and Died for US." Unknown school   69
(likely Meharry or Howard University). Unidentified
photographer. Gelatin silver print, circa 1910

7.1   "Elizabeth at Medical College." Woman's Medical College   86
of Pennsylvania (Philadelphia, Pennsylvania). Unidentified
photographer. Gelatin POP, circa 1895

7.2   Joking around with dismembered cadaver. American   91
School of Osteopathy (Kirksville, Missouri). Unidentified
photographer. Gelatin POP mounted in scrapbook,
circa 1910

8.1   Unknown school (likely in Nebraska). Unidentified   97
photographer (possibly attributed to Stewart Elliott).
Gelatin silver postcard, 1909

8.2   Bellevue Hospital Medical College of New York City   114
(now New York University). Unidentified photographer.
Gelatin silver print, circa 1910

LIST OF FIGURES

8.3	The University of Pennsylvania School of Medicine (Philadelphia, Pennsylvania). Frederick Leibfreid, Jr. Albumen print, circa 1890	121
8.4	*Student Dream* variation. Skeleton as dissector. Unknown school. Unidentified photographer (likely attributed to "Jones"). Gelatin silver postcard, circa 1906	124
8.5	'Cadaver as self' with string tied around exposed penis. Unknown school. Unidentified photographer. Gelatin silver postcard, circa 1915	126
8.6	Students with 'gruesome instruments.' Unknown school. Unidentified photographer. Gelatin silver postcard, circa 1906	127
10.1	Jefferson Medical College (Philadelphia, Pennsylvania). Unidentified photographer. Gelatin silver print, circa 1910	150
10.2	Medical College of Virginia janitor and infamous resurrectionist 'Chris' Baker (bottom center, No. 25) posing with medical students. Medical College of Virginia (Richmond, Virginia). Unidentified photographer. Gelatin silver print, circa 1902–1903	156
10.3	Unknown school. Unidentified photographer. Gelatin silver print, circa 1910	158
11.1	Johns Hopkins School of Medicine (Baltimore, Maryland). Unidentified photographer. Gelatin silver print, circa 1912	167
12.1	Class of 1908, Kentucky School of Medicine (Louisville, Kentucky). Unidentified photographer. Gelatin silver print, circa 1904–1905	175
12.2	"Not All Dead." Unknown school. Unidentified photographer. Gelatin silver print, circa 1895	191
12.3	A cadaver 'wedding.' Unknown school. Unidentified photographer. Gelatin silver print, circa 1915	193
12.4	Master anatomist and demonstrator of anatomy, Dr. Rufus Benjamin Weaver (left), dissecting with medical students. Hahnemann Medical College (Philadelphia, Pennsylvania). Unidentified photographer. Gelatin POP, circa 1900	194
13.1	Anna Moon Randolph. Woman's Medical College of Pennsylvania (Philadelphia, Pennsylvania). Attributed to Alice Evans. Cyanotype mounted in scrapbook, Kodak No. 2, circa 1895	199
C.1	Students John David Miller and Paul Stenerson Epperson posing in their boardinghouse room with bones in front of large photographic display. Medical College of Virginia (Richmond, Virginia). Unidentified photographer. Gelatin silver print, circa 1906	217

xiii

Note from the Publisher

The images within this book do not reflect contemporary medical practice or ethics, nor do they represent the methods of modern-day medical education within the institutions discussed throughout.

Please be aware that various words which may be offensive or derogatory to some people have been included in this book in their original form within the context of the quotations from which they were sourced.

Introduction: My Companions in Misery

Do not pass judgment upon us by the appearance we make in a group picture, or individually. We are at the college for other purposes than to make nice impressions thru the medium of the photographer's skill and art. Ask about us singly or collectively from any of the student body. They know we are on the map. There is an individuality, a uniqueness, an intangible potentiality, which you cannot appreciate unless you could meet us, see us, hear us and listen to us when we are in action.

Atlanta Southern Dental College, Class of 1923[1]

When medical student H.H. Landes and the other members of the Class of 1907 first assembled in the dissecting room of the University of Maryland School of Medicine (Baltimore), they encountered something so shocking, so inconceivable, so completely unheard of, it could only be described as "a sight never to be forgotten." Among their cadavers stood class historian, J. William Harrower, dressed in a "stunning, snugly fitting white flannel lawn tennis suit," complete with "kid gloves," shoes shined to a mirror-like polish, and a "ten for a nickel brand of cigarette" dangling from his lips.[2]

Landes and the other lads were speechless. There was something different about Harrower that day. And no, it wasn't just his outfit. But, while on the topic of clothes, who dissected a cadaver dressed in their Sunday best? In 1905, a suit, let alone a white suit – not to be confused with a white *coat* – was unquestionably unconventional attire for performing an anatomical dissection. The cleanliness and otherworldliness of Harrower's formal civilian attire, worn inside the *sanctum sanctorum* of their dissecting room, sent feelings of unease and inadequacy creeping up the spines of his fellow dissectors; all of whom likely had clothed themselves in "faded" second-hand gowns and "misfit" rubber aprons.[3]

Indeed, it was the change in character more so than the change in clothes that made the Class of 1907 so anxious about Harrower. What was the man thinking? Why, on this day, on this occasion, *in this room*, was he acting, or at least appearing to act, so completely different? Described by the class as "sedate, estimable, and happy-go-lucky," now the 29-year-old medical student exuded an altered demeanor, directed toward his cadaver, that impressed upon the cohort his full determination to "take so mean an advantage of the helpless creature before him, as to skin him to a finish."[4]

Landes and his confused classmates had all but given up hope of understanding Harrower's behavior when, suddenly, the door to the dissecting room burst open and an unfamiliar man lumbered inside. The crowd likely gawked and then parted uncomfortably as the stranger made his way through the din; unfazed by his abject surroundings. He stopped in front of Harrower's dissecting table and began to assemble the tripod-mounted camera he had brought with him. Then it all became clear. The man was a professional photographer.

Cameras and cadavers. That was what this was about. J. William Harrower, of the University of Maryland School of Medicine, had adorned himself in a new suit, clad himself in a 'new' identity, all to have his portrait taken with his dissected cadaver.

At the close of the school year, Harrower found himself mentioned in the school's yearbook, the *Terra Mariae*. The collective reminiscences of the Class of 1907 reassured their class historian that, even if they had disapproved of certain wardrobe choices, the group still held him in high esteem. Their thoughts then turned to the day they had all taken a photograph together. "It will be a recollection far more pleasant (than the odor of the room was) to carry with me," wrote Landes of their opportunity.[5]

While the Class of 1907 may already have been exposed to similar photographs around campus, or perhaps had received one in the mail prior to matriculation, participating in the act firsthand, actually posing with their cadaver, was a singular, cherished experience. "[T]hanks to the photographer and the small sum of fifty cents, I shall always be able to glance upon a picture of my companions in misery," stated Landes, "with Harrower in his spotless suit of white, (specially pressed for the occasion) forming one of the group."[6]

Must be seen to be believed

Dissecting room portraits, also known as dissection photography, the act of students posing for or taking commemorative photographs with cadavers, was once one of the most pervasive, yet largely hidden, traditions in the history of the photographic medium. Although a global phenomenon of indefinite origin, in the United States, the genre began in earnest in the late 1880s and evolved, decade to decade, to include different tropes and conventions until roughly the early 1930s.

Dissection photography was a popular means for students of all ages, backgrounds, and disciplines to document and commemorate their participation in anatomical dissection, then the earliest defining experience of a medical education. In an age in which photography served to confirm occupation and establish identity, dissection photography became a ritualized tradition inextricably linked to a professional rite of passage.

For over 50 years, the combined enterprises of dissection and photography served as great equalizers within the field of medicine. In the United States alone, hundreds of thousands of students, from virtually every institution in the country that participated in anatomical dissection, joined in the creation of these images. They did so regardless of gender, race, ethnicity, country of origin, religious affiliation, or whether they matriculated at universities, colleges, or schools of medicine, dentistry, osteopathy, homeopathy, mortuary science, eclectic medicine, chiropractic medicine, or even veterinary medicine.[7]

Based on the considerable quantity of extant dissection photographs known today, modern scholars confirm that the vast majority of the nation's students and professional staff were, at the time, seemingly compelled to and complicit in the act.[8] In fact, as medical historian and dissection photography scholar, John Harley Warner posits, for the next half-century following the genre's inception in the 1880s, these images may well have been "the most common way that American medical students had themselves photographed together and at work."[9]

But dissecting room portraits were not just ubiquitous in quantity. Photographs came in all types of formats, sizes, and processes. By 1910, their abundance was matched only by their variability. From large-format prints and solar enlargements, taken, printed, and mounted by commercial photographers in cultural epicenters like Philadelphia, Chicago, and Baltimore, to student-made snapshots, faded, folded, and wedged in the back-pocket wallets of nostalgic physicians in California, Alabama, and Nebraska.

On a technical level, one would be hard-pressed to find a more diverse photographic genre than the dissection photograph. As a persistent tradition, the genre reached its prime at the turn of the 20th century and embraced almost every available paper-based photographic process of the times.[10] What's more, nearly every popular commercially available format was used, including cartes-de-visite, cabinet cards, and stereographs (Figure I.1).

By 1905, the genre's popularity expanded to include its own subgenre. Known as *Student Dream* photographs, this new subset focused on depictions of students' emotional responses to dissecting cadavers. The classic configuration involved literal role reversals between the living and the dead. The student took the place of the cadaver, and typically posed as if asleep upon the dissecting table. Meanwhile, surrounding them was stood a group of 'reanimated' cadavers; scalpels tied to their hands, each one seemingly eager to exact unholy revenge upon the living by dissecting their dissectors.

Renowned author, historian, and collector of medical photography, Dr. Stanley B. Burns, points out that posing with cadavers "was mainly an American practice of young medical students."[11] However, examples from England and France are confirmed to have been taken in the 1880s concurrent with those in the United States. This suggests (but cannot be confirmed at this time) that the genre's direct iconographic precedent may have originated in Europe. Although dissection photography was mainly a Western tradition, by 1910 the genre had blossomed into a prolific international phenomenon, with extant examples found in countries all around the world.[12]

Postmarked postmortems

In the early 1900s, dissection photographs began to be turned into dissection *postcards*, circulating the country in untold numbers through the United States Postal Service.[13] From the medical schools of New England to the dental colleges of California (and even Hawaii), intrepid students used the dissection postcard as a transgressive means of communicating to friends and family their professional experiential growth. "See if you can find me in the picture," teased Julia Taylor's brother on the back of a postcard sent in the winter of 1910. Taken by the Maurer Photo Company of the "Freshman Dessecting [*sic*] Room" of the University of Texas Medical Department (Galveston, Texas), the image shows an immense, factory-sized room, overcrowded with cadavers on tables, hanging skeletons, gross specimens under glass, and a corps of 30 students, both men and women, conducting their dissections. While it probably took her some time given the room's congestion, once Julia found her brother's likeness, she drew an arrow on the photo directly over his head to point him out to others.[14]

Furtive messages of this kind were not unique. Around this time the verso of the American postcard was divided in half, allowing for brief handwritten messages from sender to recipient. Students, like Julia's brother, used this space to comment upon a variety of topics, including tales of college life, questions about home life, or to provide lurid details about the dead bodies depicted on the postcard's front. A number of these messages included sarcastic taunts or missives about the student-sender's personal dissecting room experiences. As artifacts that reflected upon the times in which they were created, the verbal commentary associated with dissection portraiture, from dissection

Figure I.1: Class of 1882. Homeopathic Medical College, University of Michigan (Ann Arbor, Michigan). Unidentified photographer. Albumen stereograph, circa 1879–1880

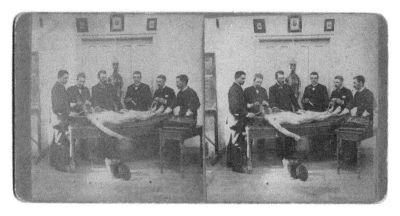

Source: Private collection. Originally owned by James W. Vidal (third from right)

table epigraphs to messages scrawled on the back of a postcard, or upon the border of a photo mat, commonly echoed the biases and bigotry of a nation still reeling from the sociopolitical changes shaped by the outcome of the Civil War.

In the 1880s, states began to codify anatomical legislation, called anatomy acts, which provided schools with a legal and steady supply of dead bodies from public institutions. By design, these laws were to forever change dissecting room culture by putting a (relative) end to the industry of grave robbing, and thus, the "traffic in human bodies."[15]

With the 'preciousness' and rarity of the cadaver mitigated through an overabundance of 'stock,' the dissecting room developed into a culture largely comfortable with the objectification of the dead. Indeed, many of the behaviors depicted through dissection photography extend far beyond normal levels of clinical detachment. As the genre evolved, an increasing frivolity toward the cadaver's subjectivity evolved with it; alongside a growing insensitivity to viewing the dead body as an essential object of knowledge production. For most students to reach either state of psychological detachment however, one had to first overcome immeasurable challenges on physical, spiritual, intellectual, and emotional levels.

The transformation from lay student to professional physician required a dedication to hegemonic equilibrium within two distinct spheres: the liminal spaces of professional identity, such as the lecture hall, laboratory, surgical amphitheater, and the dissecting room; and sites associated with lay identity, such as churches, boardinghouse dorms, public transportation, and family homes.

Successful cultural coexistence was dependent on a host of influential factors. For instance, the systemic prejudicial ideologies and biases, those associated with a student's non-medical identity, were often modified by whatever dominant cultural belief was upheld at their prospective schools. Principal among these customs were bigoted views and insolent behaviors extended toward women, the indigent, and, most especially, persons of color. Sadly, the prejudices marginalized communities experienced in life extended into death. As the Reverend Dr. Samuel Haughton confessed, "the dissecting-room degrades some characters and elevates others."[16] Despite students' oath to heal the wounds of humanity, the ingrained intolerances they expressed or were subjected to in the external world infiltrated the insular realm of the dissecting room. There they found ritual encouragement by like minds, and enhanced outlets of expression through novel traditions, like dissection photography and school yearbooks.

By custom, indifference, or shared viewpoints, schools did little to curb or prohibit the proliferation of immoral and unethical acts; except when 'sinful' student behavior, such as smoking, drinking, or gambling, threatened the 'moral standing' of professional practitioners within the surrounding lay community. To the institution of American medicine then, the indignities associated with students dehumanizing African American cadavers by hanging their dissected bodies in trees around campus to frighten the living, or later, using photographs to evidence the 'otherness' of their school's Black janitors by having them assume degrading positions, was a tolerated component of student experience and identity. Similarly, through the 1920s and beyond, racist and sexist cartoons, poems, and photographic reproductions proliferated the pages of school-sanctioned yearbooks. Unquestionably, the most overt and disturbing presentation is found in the 1926 edition of *The Howler*, the student-produced yearbook of Wake Forest College Medical School (Chapel Hill, North Carolina), now the Wake Forest University School of Medicine, which shows a montage of standard dissection portraits with the vile racial slur "Sliced N____R" printed underneath.[17] This vulgar display was reproduced directly across from images of the school's chapel, the chemistry lab, and a student rising in the morning from his dorm room bed, suggesting how truly ingrained structures of institutional racism were in educational systems in the American South.

The demise of cameras and cadavers

As I argue throughout this book, from around 1900 until the early 1930s, dissection photography *evolved*, as both object and act, to become a transformative modernist ritual all its own. Posing for and taking abject images with cadavers eventually overpowered the normative rituals associated with their dissection. These systems of normativity eventually came to include previous incarnations of 'classic' dissection photographs from the 1800s.

Ultimately, this evolved 'beast' of a genre went extinct. By the 1930s, the taking of dissection photographs, in any form, vanished from and was suppressed by an even more 'evolved' iteration of professional medical identity. Anatomical dissection itself was similarly affected; finding its significance to industry and popular culture likewise diminished. As a rite of passage, the act once served as a cultural lightning rod, inciting anything from civic outrage over the desecration of graves to religious condemnation over the supposed defilement of the human soul. But after the passing of nationwide anatomy acts, the need to rob graves or import bodies from other regions of the country became excessive and unnecessary. With controversies over grave robbing effectively dead and buried, newspapers stopped their sensationalized coverage of scandalous medical matters, such as dissecting room hijinks, or interviews with school janitors over the details of their ghoulish work. By the start of World War II, the influence of the "silent ones" of the dissecting room decreased so dramatically that they had become culturally inconsequential; silenced further by the thunderous applause emanating from the surgical amphitheater, or the riotous cries from the wards of newly built, and already overcrowded, state hospitals.[18]

A steady rise in the quantity of American training hospitals, including those for women and African Americans, expanded educational opportunities for a larger and more diverse student body. Coeducational schools were the wave of the future.[19] In this new era, a modern and moral medical education involved direct engagement with a host of different patients. The critical focus was about how one treated the living, *not* how one coped with the dead.

Meanwhile, photography's modernized application grew to include the documentation of effective surgical treatments, mostly by way of before-and-after snapshots. Witnessing the power of medicine in turn reified its curative potential. Thus, medical practitioners required updated identities to reflect their modernist roles and principles. The identity of the physician as healer needed to reign supreme. The image of the blood-soaked 'sawbones' would no longer be able to operate (literally) in this new world. Sanitized hands operating inside sanitized spaces; projections of a cleanly and ordered professional identity suggested by students and physicians literally swathing themselves in white coats; *this* was the identity of the future.

By the mid-20th century, dissection photography, as both a genre and tradition interwoven with the formation of an identity associated with inglorious death, began its steady decline into obsolescence. National participation plummeted. The quantifiable loss of vitality, dominance, and abundance was enough to render the dissection photograph culturally irrelevant; consigned to the same obscurities of professional representation as those popularized a century before – images of students and physicians posed in photographer's studios holding skulls and bones; the very emblems of death itself.

It should be noted that although the practice of dissection photography was reduced to the point of near extinction by the end of the 1930s, the commemorative potential of other facets of students' educational lives increased significantly. Photographs of dissecting rooms were replaced with images of humanity, such as students playing sports, pledging fraternities, studying together, engaging directly with patients, or raising their families.

For students at schools integrated into larger college systems, or relocated to university campuses, transitioning to a broader photographic representation of identity reflected a more truthful spectrum of personal and curricular experience. This 'truth,' in turn, proved relatable to both medical and non-medical audiences alike. However, the amalgamation of lay and medical communities, and the integration of medical humanities into their curriculum, guaranteed a dwindling audience for the dissection photograph. Although images of human remains were still provocative emblems of identity, they no longer encapsulated nor defined student experience in the same manner as when the genre first began. By the 1970s, students preferred to take transgressive photographs with the nude bodies found in the pages of a *Playboy* or *Penthouse* magazine over those in the dissecting room.[20]

For a time, students attempted the assimilation of the dissection photograph into the new visual economy of the all-inclusive American university. Starting in the 1910s, student-produced yearbooks featured elaborate photographic montages integrating transgressive imagery, like dissection photographs, alongside 'normative' social activities, such as fishing, playing the violin, skiing, playing with dogs, feeding cows, or relaxing around campus.[21] However, this plan ultimately failed. With their integration into the larger visual culture of American university 'life,' dissection photography had simultaneously become too normalized, and yet, remained too vile for broad public consumption; a venomous beast still, to be sure, but one defanged and clawless. When these photographs occasionally crossed a line, or were featured in campus-wide publications, non-stakeholders, like local churches, non-medical faculty, or students' families, publicly renounced their inclusion. But perhaps even worse than outrage, most mid-century audiences simply ignored them.

From the 1950s into the 1980s, the number of dissection photographs diminished exponentially until the genre found itself on the utter fringes of medicine's visual economy. Those who knew about the tradition mostly kept it to themselves. Fading from time as much as from memory, like snapshots stuffed into the recesses of an old wallet, the genre was demoted to the back pocket of medical history. Fractured by changing sensibilities toward bodily autonomy, it hobbled on for as long as it could. But ultimately, with each passing decade, it was driven further and further 'underground.'

By the end of the 20th century, as a time-honored tradition, the dissection photograph was only found in the high-contrast, halftone pages of school yearbooks. As an enterprise now thoroughly separated from its own historiography, these images were mostly uninspired reflections of the genre's earliest stage. Few presented any visual relation to the dominant tropes of the past. Instead, the vast majority were almost always poorly taken and appallingly printed. Many students skirted issues related to ethics and good taste by flipping their cadaver over onto its stomach, or by cropping out lewd elements, like genitals. Some cropped out the cadaver in its entirety, save for the student's scalpel-wielding hands.[22]

Although the dissection photograph still technically drew breath into the 1970s and 1980s, any chances of it being reborn for the 21st century – as it had been a century earlier – were dead on arrival. In an ironic twist of fate, the genre was now nothing more than a prop – just as the cadaver had once been. Pure illustration; a means for students to gaze back upon the outdated origins and missteps of medicine's past and reflect upon how far identity and industry had advanced for the betterment of all humanity.

Hiding in plain sight

The dissection photograph existed in numerous forms for over 100 years. And yet, over the course of the last half-century, the totality of dissection photography, from physical prints to recognition of its existence as a pervasive photographic tradition, has basically been 'hiding in plain sight.' In fact, its first real scholarly exploration only happened in the 1980s, right around the time that the genre went extinct. As a result, scholars theorized that the total number of extant dissection photographs numbered at around 30.[23] This stands in stark contrast to current projections, which estimate that by the end of the genre's prime in the 1930s, dissection photographs in America alone totaled in the tens of thousands.

So how did it come to pass that these numbers could be so divergent? After all, a miscalculation of this magnitude reflects a serious misconception of the genre's influence on national and international scales. One reason is the genre's obscurity in popular and scholarly circles. A sizable quantity of the medical and photographic historians whom I have interviewed over the past decade, as well as current physicians and medical students, all express equal levels of unawareness and confusion regarding the existence of dissection photography as an act or international tradition.[24] This is not totally without precedent. Despite its omnipresence and varied cultural significance to a global network of medical professionals, again, very little scholarship currently exists about the genre. As of the publication of this book, this will only be the second work published exclusively on dissection photography.

What's more, the dissection photograph is totally absent from all canonical histories of medicine and photography. It was not until 1983, about 50 years after the dissolution of the genre's 'golden age,' and right around the time that they ceased to be printed in student yearbooks, that photo historian, James S. Terry, published his groundbreaking article in the journal, *History of Photography*, titled "Dissecting Room Portraits: Decoding an Underground Genre."[25]

Terry's analysis of dissection photographs established the foundational concepts upon which we evaluate the genre today. Moreover, his article bears the distinction of being the first to identify dissection photography as an actual genre; a herculean task, in and of itself. But, when we consider the genre's abject subject matter, and its chaotic distribution across the nation's cultural and medical institutions (this was long before widespread access to archival collections via the internet and digitization initiatives), his evaluation is nothing short of miraculous.

To this latter point, as of 2024, the genre's surviving examples are scattered around the world in vastly different repositories. Although sizable caches can be found in the archives of medical schools, universities, museums, and historical societies across the United States, the majority currently reside in private collections and are not publicly accessible.[26]

Without looking

As sociologists of medical education determined decades ago, students regard anatomical dissection as an experience of initiation, "a rite of passage symbolic of their entry into the medical profession."[27] Although medicine has adopted more positive rituals to affirm professional identity these days, such as 'White Coat' ceremonies, generally speaking, dissection still maintains its position as a symbolic rite. Traditionally, dissection photographs served to validate this rite, representing and presenting "a professional coming-of-age narrative," in which "a new identity" was firmly established for student-dissectors.[28]

In the 19th century, the formation of student identity was contingent upon traversing the literal and psychological depths of dissection, an act largely reviled in public consciousness. As Terry suggests, photographic commemorations of dissected cadavers "flaunted the macabre and the taboo."[29] Notwithstanding their explicit content, these were deeply complex and personal images that featured layered, evidentiary meanings; as scientific as they were horrific.

Dissection photographs confirmed a professional scientific affiliation to an external audience (at least in the moment). As Terry points out, the genre also allowed students "to dramatize their experience to themselves" through transgressive experimentation and self-expression; their collective and individual identities validated by the material dissolution of the body of another.[30] Despite the significance of Terry's conclusions, it would take another 20 years before this grossly overlooked genre of gross anatomy would receive its first, and to date, only dedicated monograph: the lavishly illustrated, landmark 2009 publication, *Dissection: Photographs of A Rite of Passage in American Medicine 1880–1930*, by John Harley Warner and James M. Edmonson. Reproducing a sizable selection of dissection photographs from institutional and private collections across the United States, *Dissection* is a work in which image and text function in tandem to further dissection photographs as significant historic artifacts of the visual and material culture of a bygone era in American medicine. As Edmonson states: "Unsettling though they may be, they are a thread connecting us to the shared experiences among medical professionals over generations."[31] Perhaps most relevant to modern audiences, the authors position the genre as an inseparable part of American medical heritage, capable of conveying complex messages about the grim realities and shifting attitudes toward dissection, bodily autonomy, and the ethical use of mortal remains for medical education. Throughout his introductory essay, author John Harley Warner confronts the genre and profession's inglorious pasts – namely in relation to grave robbing – while simultaneously refusing to dismiss or make excuses for the images as a result of their often insensitive, unethical, and, at times, racist content. "Some of them are difficult to look at, and one is inclined to look away," writes Warner on the more unsettling tableaus. "But without looking we cannot see an uncomfortable past and begin to understand the legacies that American doctors and patients live with today."[32]

Dissection photography: an evolving genre

With the works of Terry and Warner and Edmonson as my primary guides, this book seeks to expand the interpretation of dissection photography as a legitimate and evolving photographic genre. Within these pages is a desultory exploration of the various cultures that created, defined, and initiated its evolution around the start of the 20th century. My analysis examines how the stimuli that triggered this evolution allowed for and in fact influenced the ability of student amateur photographers to claim their own representative agency, thereby forming an independent visual economy around the nexus of their fluctuating personal and professional identities.

As Warner states, dissection photographs served as "autobiographical narrative devices by which the students placed themselves into a larger, shared story of becoming a doctor."[33] But, as I aim to show, this story, this autobiography, evolved from a narrative situated solely within the confines of medical culture, to one that eventually straddled the liminal, untamed, and undocumented boundaries shared with the expanding enterprise of photography.

Just as we cannot examine the analogous imagery of a genre without dedicating attention to dominant iconography and its prevailing symbolism, the additional goal of this book is a theoretical exploration of the visual, material, and popular cultures surrounding the dissected cadaver; its power as an abject and ambiguous subject–object; and the ways in which culture influenced the initiative nature of dissection and dissection photography. For this analysis, I will discuss and utilize theories of abjection and the abjectified body as defined by the French theoretician Julia Kristeva, and as expanded upon in modern literature by author Rina Arya.

Obviously, in the limited space and even more limited photographic reproductions I am allowed here, this book cannot be exhaustive in scope, either as a historical narrative extending back to the advent of photography, or as a comprehensive 'visual history' of dissection photography's chronological evolution from the 1880s to the 1930s. However, despite the limitations at play, the following chapters cover many of the cultural and technological factors that prompted the most significant changes in the genre's aesthetics and primary posing conventions.

But before we get lost between the interstices of dissection photography, abjection, cadavers, and their relation to identity formation, I must reinforce the fact that the genre was a pervasive visual tradition aligned with *student* identity. Therefore, this book is an exploration of the behaviors of students; flawed, immature, prejudiced, frightened, and often woefully inexperienced students. I do not highlight this distinction to make excuses for the dehumanizing properties of dissection photography or attempt to justify the immoral and unethical behaviors of generations past. I merely seek to underpin the fact that, ordinarily, the identity and authority of a full-fledged physician was fixed within their community and within the larger medical industry. Student identity, meanwhile, was mutable, volatile, and hopelessly restless from one year to the next.

At the turn of the 20th century, the entrance requirements of most medical schools were quite undiscerning. Students needed only a high school diploma or a year or two of college to gain admission. The majority of those admitted lacked any form of medical background or preclinical training. Thus, with no prior experience in anatomy, biology, or dissection, when it came to cutting into cadaveric flesh, many students simply couldn't cut it. They either flunked out or just never returned after their semester break. Such was the case at Yale School of Medicine in 1908: "As we proceeded onward in our march to fame, the scourge of the cadaver drove others to seek another field of study."[34] Ironically, given the circumstances, sometimes the dissection photograph was the only proof that these students ever matriculated. Although most students stuck it out, those that remained often completed their freshman year (and their course in anatomy) unconvinced they were cut out to be doctors.

The nominal entrance requirements of the past stand in stark contrast to those of the modern era. Today, students go through rigorous pre-med and post-baccalaureate programs in preparation for the intense application cycle of medical school. They must take and pass Chemistry, Physics, and Biology, score high on standardized tests, such as the MCAT, and go through multiple interviews with interested schools – to say nothing of the stress of finding out where they will match for residency and fellowship once their initial education is completed. For many, the entire process across the continuum of the American medical education system is a whirlwind mixture of mental and physical exhaustion. The impact of these "systemic patterns and risk factors" have led to a steady rise in stress, depression, the likelihood of burnout, and even suicide among students, residents, and physicians. According to data presented at the 2019 Annual Meeting of the American Medical Association, medical students "are three times likelier to die of suicide than their counterparts in the general population."[35]

To combat a pessimistic view of the world and allow students to effectively govern themselves, during the era of the dissection photograph, most American schools nurtured a deep-seated fraternalist ethos. The freedom of this environment allowed students the ability to eke out a relevant (but ultimately conformist) identity, one that instilled purpose in both the individual and the collective during a time of great industrial, cultural, technological, and personal upheaval.[36] Many functioned with the normative borders of their lay and student identities. Others, simply put, took matters too far.

While student behavior and those of the larger medical profession make this book difficult to read in parts, I sincerely hope that upon reaching its conclusion you will join me in stating that regardless of its abject subject matter, as a virtually unexamined field of the visual culture of medicine and photography, not only is dissection photography a legitimate genre that evolved over time, but is a genre worthy of recognition, preservation, and continued scholarship.

1

The Stages of an Evolving Genre

As a rite of passage, dissection was essential to the formation of student identity at the turn of the 20th century. This differs greatly from concepts of identity formation today. Modern audiences do not usually cite occupation when discussing their identities – work is expressed as something you *do*, not a defining characteristic of who you *are*. But, as Richard Rudisill discusses in *Mirror Image: The Influence of the Daguerreotype on American Society*, throughout the decades leading up to and immediately following the invention of photography, "work" was considered a "national indulgence," it was the defining marker, the summation of the worth of the common American as put forth by enlightened opinion.[1]

With occupation being connected with a spiritualized means of dignity and enlightenment, a need arose for its concentration into a solid, tangible form, one which would allow for personalized spiritual reflection.[2] Out of this need for a symbolic and nationalistic totem of occupational identity was born a public interest in genre painting, and eventually, the introduction of photography. However, one occupation that seemed to initially struggle with the new visual syntaxes inherent to the photograph, and thus formulate a unified professional identity, was that of the medical profession.

At the same time as America as a country was becoming comfortable with its independence, seeking new methods of establishing its own identity, and its own culture and sciences, the medical profession had begun to adopt and replace the speculative, theoretical philosophies of the past with the empirical doctrines and fact-driven observation born out of the 18th century. Although the proliferation of quacks still threatened the purity of their profession, as did medical sectarianism, the first few decades of the 19th century saw an occupation becoming at relative peace with itself. Yet, in an age of increased representation, as photography grew its powers to commemorate and form identity, how best to visualize the identity of the medical profession to measure American professionalism?

Furthermore, with the increase in the country's medical and dental schools, and eventually hospitals, how did one differentiate the professional from the student? Plus, by the 1860s, what of the introduction of homeopathic physicians, Black physicians, or newly minted female physicians and students? Did these groups need to establish visual identities *separate* from the standard White male allopathic doctor? Or, due to the prejudices extended to their practices after graduation, was there no need for distinct separations?

The question of how to isolate and form student identity remained unanswered for decades. Complicating matters was that a student's purpose and identity existed in an ambiguous state in American society: no longer part of the lay community or workforce, but not yet a part of an ordained physician's world. Dissection photography effectively helped to solidify these ambiguities. Collectively, the genre featured two key discernible elements related to the formative aspects of medical identity. They showed tangible proof of a student's professional affiliation, and, confirmed (to varying degrees) the levels of psychological detachment necessary to participate in anatomical dissection.

As an object, the dissection photograph provided physical evidence of participation in a rite of passage, one irrevocably linked with the formation of a student's identity. As unflinching witness, it served as an irrefutable representation of physical and psychological contiguity to dissected cadavers – the embodiment of anatomical knowledge. A cursory review of extant dissection photographs shows students literally smiling in the face of death, scalpels at the ready, striking proud, transcendent poses over supine mounds of decomposing flesh and exposed bone. Within the borders of the photographic frame, student authority over the dead appears absolute.

However, more important than just mere proximity, was the embedded meaning of the dissection photograph, and how it confirmed, rather decisively, the levels of psychological detachment necessary for students to dissect a dead body. This concept is supported throughout the genre's evolution, taking a more passive role in the 'classic' staged group photographs of the 19th century, and a more assertive and literal position in the vernacular snapshots of the 1910s onward.

Confusing conventions of counterculture

When discussing the entirety of dissection photography, one cannot overlook the genre's glaring iconographic inconsistencies. If we consider these images squarely as agents of counterculture, as author James S. Terry suggests, as photos that "flaunted" the "macabre and the taboo" and "signified a breach of acceptable codes of behavior and prevailing social norms," then what do we make of prints that exist as paradigmatic models of the traditional standards of 19th century group portraiture?[3]

Contrariwise, if dissection photographs are in some way part of an increased formality in the visualization of the medical professional, one "intended to dramatize the new scientific basis of medicine as experienced by medical students," how then do we come to terms with their conceptual reversal, their dark reflection; images of abject enargia?[4] For on this 'side' of the identity spectrum, students chose to wield axes instead of scalpels. Skeletons dressed in Renaissance costumes smoked pipes. Lounging cadavers played cards and drank liquor. With direct ties and responsibilities to the communities they served, why would an increasingly discerning medical community – and if applicable, its associated hospital(s) – approve of the creation, display, and subsequent evolution of such objectively disturbing imagery? In truth, we will likely never know. But I assure you, while this paradoxical range of student identity formation appears infuriating at first to organize, the phenomenon of inconsistency is not as confusing as it seems.

I propose that the need of the American medical student to create divergently codified forms of dissection photographs did not originate nor proliferate purely from exploitative spectatorship. Rather, it *evolved* over time to not only confer identity by bearing witness to a rite of passage, but to become an initiation unto itself.

Let me explain. Trying to define the entirety of dissection photography as a single static entity is a structural module flawed from the onset, for it fails to consider that over the course of half a century, the intent behind the dissection photograph's dominant iconography changed significantly. So too did the *purpose* behind the radical changes in certain posing conventions. Change begets change; be it in the technology used to take a photograph, in the ability to control one's own representative identity, or changes in the physical and emotional relationship between a student and their cadaver.

Assuredly, if the earliest scholars of dissection photography had access to the same caches of extant collections we do today, they would not have defined the genre's incongruous visual economy as aesthetically incoherent, inert, or originating from a single iconographic precedent. Ultimately, in the case of Terry's assessment, the pioneering author is fundamentally correct. The genre of dissection photography *does* represent classic conventions as much as it *does* represent transgressive ones. For each photograph that demonstrated a student-dissector's reverence for their privileged position within the American medical educational system, opposing examples were taken that destabilized the performative tradition of dissection and abjectified both the identity and materiality of cadaveric bodies.

Thus, scholars were correct in their estimations that the genre exhibited both extreme similarities and contrasts. However, a limited knowledge of the genre's chronological, rather than typological boundaries – both in terms of quantities, cultural influence, and decades of operation – have heretofore prevented a comprehensive understanding that divergently themed images did not *originate* simultaneously or in a vacuum. Nor did they stem from a single source with singular intent. Instead, dramatic shifts in the iconography of and intent behind dissection photography occurred years or even decades apart, built upon the foundational conventions, aesthetics, behaviors, and technologies of the past.[5]

Dissection photography began at an historic but fractious time in photographic history. The genre benefitted greatly from a confluence of medical and photographic innovations, from advances in camera technologies, photographic processes, and printing papers, to increased sanitation and hygiene, and the passing of anatomical legislation providing legally acquired bodies for anatomical study.

Most notable in this complex equation, at least from an aesthetic standpoint, is that in the 1880s, commercial photographers shaped the genre's aesthetics according to the rules of classic portraiture. But by 1900, student agency over their own likenesses eventually overthrew standardized (and industry approved) representations of identity. New handheld cameras afforded students the freedom to accept or refute larger sociocultural, psychosocial, or political issues; to comment in their own 'words' upon their fluid relationship with the dead (depending on their visual fluency this was 'spoken' literally or symbolically) in the decades that followed. To fully understand how dissection photography maintained a relative consistency of conventions, despite the polarizing intent, imagery, and opposing backgrounds of the two primary users (professional/commercial photographers versus student amateur photographers), again, I must argue that we consider the genre as an evolving one.

The three stages of evolution

With the concept of evolution in mind, I propose that from 1880 to 1930, there were three distinct points, three catalysts, measured not by precise date, but by their resounding influence upon the aesthetic shifts in the genre's primary conventions and motivations. When overlaid upon each other, these stages constitute a distinct evolution, a photographic cladogram of the visual and material culture of dissection photography as we know it today. I use the analogy of the branching diagram here since the evolution of dissection photography is ultimately non-linear. For example, the static dissection portraiture of the 1880s did not go extinct upon the introduction of the more 'evolved' dynamic snapshots of the 20th century. Indeed, we might consider the amateur snapshot of the 1910s a different species altogether when compared to the trends of commercial dissection portraiture from its early years. The limitations of photographic technology, the cultural importance of photography, the introduction of amateur cameras, and so on, allowed for the cumulative but continuously advancing stages of representation. Let us then consider the three stages of dissection photography as such.

Stage I (circa 1880–1930)

Stage I includes 'classic' examples of dissection photographs, which largely set the genre's compositional standard for over 50 years. They almost always exhibit an identical composition: between four to six students standing behind a dissecting table parallel to the camera (Figure 1.1). The cadaver is prone, but it can be corporeally whole or partially dissected. Students either stare directly into the camera or adopt working positions. In the earliest years, images were made using the albumen process and were taken and printed by commercial photographers. Later examples were taken by student amateur photographers. However, their aesthetics did not stray from this convention. While posing conventions stayed the same throughout, this stage experienced the most variability in terms of photographic processes and formats.

Stage II (circa 1895–1930)

Stage II includes images taken by student amateur photographers, those who had access to both cameras and cadavers, yet operated without the aid or equipment of commercial photographers. Negatives and prints were developed either by returning film to commercial photo companies, like Eastman Kodak, or by purchasing relevant equipment directly from Kodak and processing materials themselves. As many early Stage II images were

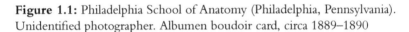

Figure 1.1: Philadelphia School of Anatomy (Philadelphia, Pennsylvania). Unidentified photographer. Albumen boudoir card, circa 1889–1890

Source: Private collection. Originally owned by William Charles Snider of New York (third from left)

experimental (such as cyanotype proofs), or taken by untrained students, they show a substantial decrease in quality. Many often lack the detail and focus of those made by commercial photographers using the wet plate or early dry plate processes. With the elimination of commercial outsiders is born a new intimacy of experience between an individual student and their cadaver. Students start to pose with their cadavers in opposition to dominant conventions. Typical Stage II posing conventions showed cadavers and skeletons simulating limited activities of the living, such as sitting upright on tables, embracing students, reading textbooks, or smoking cigarettes.

Stage III (circa 1905–1925)

Stage III includes the most thematically transgressive dissection photographs of the entire genre. Tableaus usually revolve around elicitations of dark humor, also known as gallows humor. They include skeletons dancing, cadavers playing cards together, or posed as if ready to dissect the living, also known as *Student Dream* photographs. Although cadavers are posed as if returned to life, visualizing the psychological and psychosocial aspects of dissection, such as shame, anger, or fear, overpowers a desire to simply 'reanimate' the cadaver by simulating mundane acts of the living. They are not about commemorating a rite of passage insomuch as they are about pushing preestablished boundaries and becoming a ritual unto themselves. Common tropes transgress the genre's conventional aesthetics, mock industry standards (such as the wearing of protective gloves) and transgress time-honored traditions or tools of the trade, such as substituting axes or hammers for scalpels and forceps. The bodily materiality of the cadaver is interrogated most in these images. Here the cadaver and its parts operate more as existential 'props' than as emblematic icons of professional identity. Students routinely attempt to convert dead flesh into objects, such as bones or limbs held like musical instruments, or cadaver heads turned into oil lamps. Cadaveric bodies are manipulated to reenact crude jokes, or staged as perverse precursors, harbingers of their own death (the motif of the 'cadaver as future self'). The majority of Stage III images are gelatin silver postcards, although neither process nor format are exclusive to this stage. Both commercial and student amateur photographers made images during Stage III.

It should be noted that conventions from each preceding stage overlapped those that followed. At this time, there is no quantifiable evidence to suggest the introduction of a new stage and its resulting conventions, typologies, and so on, had any effect on the longevity of earlier stages. For example, the year 1905 generated a plethora of different images capable of being situated within multiple stages of dissection photography. Commercial photographers created large, mounted prints of 'classic' dissection scenes (Stage I), as well as begot the *Student Dream* subgenre (Stage III). That same year, student amateur photographers produced real photo postcards of anything from 'classic' dissection scenes (Stages I and II), to images of students manipulating dead bodies in untraditional ways (Stages II and III).

This is not to say there were not distinct changes in how dissection photographs were taken. Eventually, student amateurs did become the primary stakeholders over commercial photographers. Likewise, the genre came to reflect the larger technological shifts of the era, such as the extinction of dominant photographic processes and formats. Those that had the biggest effect on dissection photography included images being shot on flexible film and taken with handheld cameras, rather than the cumbersome equipment associated with the wet plate process, gelatin silver prints replacing albumen prints, and real photo postcards largely replacing cabinet cards and oversized mounted prints.

2

Photography Is Dead

Understanding why medical and dental students of the late 19th and early 20th centuries were seemingly impelled to create dissection photographs requires one to step outside all conceivable comfort zones and embrace a type of photography that exists in flagrant opposition to the ethics of the modern world. To fully comprehend the importance and influence of photography and dissection upon American students in the 1880s and 1890s, we must spend some time in the 1860s and 1870s, the decades immediately preceding the genesis of dissection photography as a quantifiable genre.

The era that followed the American Civil War was marked by a significant increase in the nation's awareness of and proximity to "inhumanely objective" photographic records of mutilated bodies and decomposing corpses, such as the images of fallen soldiers from Antietam on display at Matthew Brady's New York exhibition.[1] Advanced technologically by innovations such as magnesium flash, gelatin dry plates, and handheld cameras, postbellum-era photography expanded the medium's reach until it penetrated even the dankest and rankest corners of the globe. Riding at the forefront of this expansion was photographic portraiture, since repositioned to exist *outside* the photographer's skylight studio in places as varied as the common American home, the scorched battlefield, and the filthy dissecting room.

By the 1860s, photography's popularity and cultural acceptance found dominant utility to enact a great equalization upon the various social classes of the world. Now anyone could sit and have their portrait taken. As the editors of the popular photographic journal, *The Philadelphia Photographer*, attested in 1864, when it came to the 'who' of photographic portraiture – which is to say, *who* had their portraits taken – anyone from the weary soldier to the local priest, to artists, politicians, and tradesmen, all were "compelled to submit to their faces being made articles of commerce," and sometimes "subjects of curiosity."[2]

In as little as 25 years following photography's 'invention' in 1839, photographic portraiture became an authoritative and patriotic pastime. Increasing its authority in the United States was linked to furthering

American industry. As the *Photographer* pointed out, even "[t]he pickpocket and the burglar" all had "their own part to perform in photography for the public good."[3] But what of the dead; surely, they took no part in this so-called performance? After all, what role could the portrait of the corpse play in the rise of photography's social and cultural dominance in the United States?

As it turns out, the dead played a pivotal role in establishing photography's social, cultural, and commercial value. Picture that in the years immediately following photography's invention, photographic portraiture had just burst onto the scene as a new and exploitable commodity. Within a few short years, the photographic object would become solidified in the collective minds of Americans as a tangible emblem of memory and identity. At this time, a photographer's ideal client was a dead one. No matter how long an exposure, or how young or old the decedent, a corpse did not move, blink, or speak (with few exceptions), nor did they require food, drink, or rest. They were plentiful in times of war and rampant diseases – specifically, high infant mortality rates associated with industrialization and impoverished living conditions in major cities like New York and Philadelphia – and thus, consequently, in high demand as photographic subjects. Best of all (for the industry), enterprising photographers discovered they could charge more to photograph the dead.[4]

In certain secreted "spheres of popular culture," photography moved the corpse, literally and symbolically, from out of the shadows and into the light.[5] Although never celebrated or acknowledged too robustly within mainstream society, memorial portraits of the dead, known as postmortem photographs, objectified human mortality to fulfil a culturally specific need. Historian James S. Terry writes, "in a century which sentimentalized death, portraits of human bodies were images of grim reality."[6] While a true enough statement, a grim reality fared better than a forgotten one.

Jay Ruby, author of *Secure the Shadow: Death and Photography in America*, asserts that throughout the 19th century in particular, photography was used "to mitigate the finality of death" by serving as an "unimpeachable and permanent" witness to life.[7] Images of the dead – the most common, again, being postmortem photographs – subsisted as a substitution of identity; an acceptable surrogate object that satisfied the collective longing for keepsakes of lost loved ones.

In the years leading up to the era of the dissection photograph, popular perceptions about death and photographs of the dead placed the camera and the cadaver along similar paths. Eventually, these symbiotic trajectories merged; commingling death and the photograph via a series of inseparable intellectual, literary, and aesthetic comparisons. The resultant cultural fusion spawned a new species of imagery, *photographs of the deceased*; a nebulously defined organism whose dual purpose was to memorialize mortality, while also bearing witness to death; true inglorious death.

Photographs of this kind confronted and overthrew the power, privilege, and hierarchies associated with 'the who.' Here the term 'who' is multifaceted, meaning who is shown in death, who sees death, who works with death, and who creates images (photographs) showing or glorifying death. In the minds of the masses, then, the anatomist and the photographer bore marked similarities. Both were magicians; holders of forbidden secrets, and governors of intellectual, aesthetic, and scientific authority. As explorers of veiled worlds others could not see, nor dared venture to, they were simultaneously loved and feared; and they knew it. After all, from their knowledge came power.

Whereas the power of the anatomist stemmed from centuries of secretive knowledge originating from the mysteries of the dead body, the photographer's authority derived itself from the mysteries of "dead machinery"; or rather, from a mix of popular opinion and superstition associated with the mechanical and alchemical inner workings of photographic apparatuses, such as the camera's earliest incarnation, the camera obscura.[8]

Although death comes for us all, photography ensured that it no longer separated the living from the dead in its totality. Nor did death factor into who could or could not have memorial portraiture taken. As such, with the increase in photographs of the deceased, so too increased the number of likenesses being captured without agency or consent.

No matter what century you lived in, not wanting your portrait taken is a universal that spans the ages. However, it is extremely important to note that photographic consent was *not sought* in the 19th century. That said, sitting for a portrait in a studio – the primary site of portrait-taking at the time – established a tacit understanding between photographer and photographic subject. With the introduction of snapshot photography in the late 1890s, however, this relationship would become increasingly strained. Hidden cameras took secret photos; often without the subject's knowledge – another element of equilibrium that placed the dead on par with the living.

By the time dissection photography solidified into a quantifiable genre in the 1880s, what had started as an increasing fascination with photographs of the deceased would later develop into a booming industry all its own. By 1900, 'photographs of the deceased' had grown so big, it could no longer sustain itself as an all-encompassing supergenre. It summarily exploded, churning out a plethora of genres and subgenres, many dedicated to taboo and abject imagery. The range in subject matter included anything from 'classic' funerary or memorial postmortems, victims of natural disasters, 'human oddities,' and beheaded pirates, to human zoos, desecrated Native American burial sites, and lynching photographs from the American South. Added to this grave genre, although not for public consumption to the same degree, was an equally wide range of anatomical and pathological photographs: images of students and physicians posing with skulls, spines, and skeletons; close-ups of malformed fetuses in jars; veterinary students riding flayed horse carcasses; and anatomists holding prized anatomical preparations (Figure 2.1).

Society's underground 'taste' for taboo subjects was furthered by the rise of an economically and socially diverse as well as visually attuned middle class. They were an audience who linked photography with knowledge production, who trusted the medium as a 'reliable' witness of the suffering of the human condition – *their* suffering. As normative portraiture had already run its proverbial course, transgressive images, such as photographs of the deceased, established unique identities at a time of radical changes in the methods of taking and preserving likenesses of the human body, as well as access to said likenesses. Hence, many of the images we deem shocking or unthinkable in our time, from postmortems to dissection photographs, were, at the time of their creation, more acceptable and desirable as souvenirs for their surrogacy of the variation of human experience.[9]

Dead machinery

Connections between death and photography are legion. In fact, many of the leading photo historians of the 20th century compared the camera, the photographic apparatus itself, to the deceased, or to the material culture surrounding it. Historian and author Alan Trachtenberg called the camera an instrument of "dead machinery."[10] John Tagg, in discussing Roland Barthes' meditations on death in the pioneering work *Camera Lucida*, likened the evidentiary aspects of photography to that of a death mask.[11] André Bazin, meanwhile, considered the camera a "nonliving agent," one that rescues time from its "proper corruption" by embalming it.[12]

Throughout the 19th century, the seemingly divergent roads of photography and anatomical dissection crossed paths in several unexpected ways. Once united, the industries of photography and anatomical dissection became conjoined in the popular imaginations of many Americans. Not surprisingly, the unification of these two branches of knowledge production, photographic and anatomic, ultimately brought forth hybridized offspring in the form of a worldwide phenomenon, such as dissection photography.

Illumination, be it on visual or metaphorical levels, was typically achieved through the systematic completion of both processes. Photography, which literally means "writing or drawing with light," and sometimes referred to as "the sunbeam art," does so explicitly: exposing sensitized plates to sunlight; or, by illuminating the information hidden within the darkness of night through magnesium flash bursts.[13]

Dissection, meanwhile, once Americans accepted cadavers as essential instruments of a proper anatomical education, became synonymized with the production of bodily knowledge and a new scientific modernity. At

Figure 2.1: Medical student with dissecting tools and anatomical preparation of a dissected human arm. Unidentified photographer. Albumen carte-de-visite, circa 1875

Source: Private collection

one point in time, wrote the 19th century anatomist, Velpeau, anatomy was "restrained within very narrow limits until the progress of civilization." Only through the banishment of prevailing prejudices, and by shedding light upon them – specifically, the light derived from other branches of the scientific profession – could new anatomical breakthroughs be made possible. Thereby, to paraphrase Velpeau, visual and cognitive illumination was achieved, and "discoveries multiplied with rapidity," whenever and wherever dissections were permitted.[14]

By the end of the 19th century, Velpeau's words seemed to border on understatement. Advances in the industries, pursuits, and empires of both dissection and photography were near incalculable. The successes and innovations associated with rapidly advancing anatomical, pathological, and surgical discoveries, and the methods and means used to uncover them – which included photography – measured themselves not in centuries, but in mere decades.

In less than 20 years, beginning in 1856, the photo world saw the daguerreotype relinquish dominion to the collodion process, which in turn disappeared by the turn of the century, replaced by the even more sensitive, and thus more useful, gelatin silver process.[15] At this rate, by 1890, the photographic world would be unrecognizable when compared to its former self.

Anatomical inquiry, meanwhile, showed vast improvements within incredibly short timespans, opening untold worlds to scientists and physicians in as little as almost a quarter of a century. "[T]he anatomy of 1843 may justly claim a well-marked and triumphant advance beyond that of 1826," wrote famed physician and anatomist William E. Horner, "organs before unknown, now discovered – arrangements of parts formerly in obscurity, now detected – textures not long ago of an uncertain and disputable character, now elucidated and settled."[16] Therefore, the continual advancement of anatomical knowledge required that didactic instruction be supplemented with actual human dissections. Often referred to as the Parisian Method, no other mode of anatomical instruction was considered as vital to the American medical student. "The Professor of Anatomy, it is true, may by animated and masterly demonstrations, do much to guide and assist the anatomical Student in the prosecution of his studies," declared the Trustees and Professors of Jefferson Medical College (Philadelphia) in 1832, "but it is in the Dissecting Room, with the dead body before him, by patient and assiduous dissection, that the Student can alone acquire a knowledge of Anatomy."[17] This knowledge, or rather the pursuit of this knowledge through the ritual of dissecting a cadaver, allowed medical students privileged access to unique transactions between interior and exterior, "health and disease, reason and unreason, light and darkness," living and dead.[18]

Convincing humanity

Photography's introduction to the New World in 1839 brought with it a new method of identity formation for the varying classes. Around the same time, the medical profession was in the midst of an identity crisis all its own, preoccupied as it was with relating basic anatomical knowledge to an educationally varied, non-medical audience. At first, their concentrated efforts seemed like an effective means of restoring bodily agency to the general populace, and to loosen the profession's authoritarian grip when it came to discrete knowledge of the human body. After all, knowledge was power. But in actuality, the design of this endeavor was to tighten said grip.

Disseminating general anatomical knowledge served as an effective means of purifying the profession by casting out the unlicensed and uneducated altogether, or by forcing them back into school to learn the 'industry's' way of practicing medicine. In his groundbreaking work, *A Traffic of Dead Bodies: Anatomy and Embodied Social Identity in Nineteenth-Century America*, author Michael Sappol defines the 1830s as "the decade when physicians began to vigorously promote the idea that patients and the public needed to be educated in anatomy and physiology, arguing that such knowledge would help them discern the differences between legitimate scientific healers over quacks."[19] To this end, a great expansion of basic anatomical knowledge would theoretically aid in the repairing of certain popular perceptions that dissection was an offensive and taboo act.

Catering to the general public through an increasing variety of generalized anatomical texts allowed lay communities to access published clinical discussions themselves, and to view illustrations based on actual human dissections.[20] Some of these works even targeted specific audiences, such as students, dentists, families, and women. If successful, meddlesome sentimentality would turn to tolerance, acclimation might yield to national acceptance, and the medical profession could continue, and indeed thrive, by way of relaxed views (and laws) toward anatomical dissection. The lay community, meanwhile, could reap the intellectual rewards generated from the deceased and begin to see the cadaver as the medical profession saw 'it' – as an object that facilitated the dissemination of knowledge.

The importance of changing public opinion toward the cadaver was paramount to the medical profession. "Whoever shall convince mankind of the necessity and importance of the study of Anatomy and Physiology," wrote self-trained water-cure physician Mary S. Gove in her anatomy book designed for women, "will do more toward promoting the general good and happiness of our species than he would if he gave us priceless gems and gold without measure."[21] In 1841, just two years after photography's introduction to the world, J.F.W. Lane defined in the preface to his translation of Edwards'

Outlines of Anatomy and Physiology the specific cultural changes to the medical profession brought about by this rather radical shift in audience:

> The subject of Anatomy and Physiology, until quite recently, was never presented to the scholar, or to the public in general. Previous to that period its study had been limited to medical men only, and a certain degree of opprobrium even was attached to those engaged in Anatomical pursuits. But such a change had been gradually wrought in public opinion upon this subject, that now no system of education is considered complete, without some acquaintance with the human form and structure be included. The prejudice is fast passing away, nay has already passed, which has so long kept back from many a knowledge of the healthy exercise of their organs and functions; and which no doubt in a great degree prevented more rapid advances from being made by physicians themselves in the intimate structure of the organs.[22]

Prompted by a great increase in the number of medical practitioners by the middle decades of the 19th century, many physicians became anxious and insecure over their position within their community. After all, their livelihood depended on public favor.[23] In order to distinguish themselves apart from their competitors, physicians and anatomists endeavored to gain "the respect of colleagues and patients through the quality and quantity of their training and researches in anatomy, physiology, and other subjects, and through a rhetorical commitment to scientific medicine."[24] Once again, as the act that produced knowledge, dissection was vital to this process – the inner workings of the human body being inseparably linked to professional identity.

These years saw a great increase in anatomical textbooks, particularly those designed for the education of the student-dissector. "As our medical institutions are now organized, the student must expect to obtain his knowledge of anatomy from *two distinct sources* – namely, the anatomical theatre, and the dissecting-room," wrote J.M. Allen in his 1856 work, *The Practical Anatomist: or, The Student's Guide in the Dissecting-Room.* "Impressed with the conviction that the dissecting-room affords the greatest facilities for acquiring that knowledge which the student, when he becomes a practitioner of medicine, will most need, I have endeavored to supply him with what might be regarded as his *text-book.*"[25]

Thus, in the years preceding dissection photography's introduction in the 1880s, we begin to see the purely didactic influence of the lecture hall overpowered by the tactile, visceral, and messy authority of the dissecting room. With its upward march to becoming the most important transformational space within the American medical school, it was only a matter of time before students found ways to effectively and permanently commemorate their individualized experiences within. Once photography found its way into the hands of student amateur photographers, this group went about fulfilling their material needs and commemorative desires by any means necessary.

A grim reality: "the heart is not satisfied"

And yet, notwithstanding the quantitative increase in the quality of American medical schools, nursing programs, hospitals, medical research, and anatomical works designed for lay audiences, the true, grim realities of medical education were still an exceedingly hard pill for the general public to swallow. "The idea that respect is due to the dead body is so deeply rooted in the human mind," stated Professor Thomas Dwight of Harvard Medical School, "as to be almost instinctive. ... We know, indeed, that no violence can harm the dead, but, though reason is convinced, the heart is not satisfied."[26]

Over time, the reality of this assertion became painfully clear to medical practitioners. Anatomical knowledge, regardless of the parties involved, demanded the sacrifice of the dead. Yet, due to continuous associations in the national press, popular culture synonymized dissection with the notorious act of grave robbing, and thus, routinely rejected its incorporation into the American fabric as medical culture appeared anathema to social progress. Was this a classic case of the lay community cutting off their nose to spite their face? Or was it simply the material byproduct of a modernist society's anxiety-riddled sprint toward its unknown, but rapidly advancing, future? In either event, the national suppression of anatomical knowledge derived from human cadavers seemed short-sighted. Perhaps it was just as the dystopian despot, Trevor Goodchild, opined in the opening lines of MTV's cult classic, *Aeon Flux*: "Light, in the absence of eyes, illuminates nothing."[27]

Indeed, as Michael Sappol outlines further, public perception over the use of the cadaver as a teaching tool was heavily influenced by widespread reports of desecrating bodies and graves. Fear of such defilement turned to civic outrage on grand scales, initiating, "an epic, centuries-long battle," one waged between "reason and superstition, of 'light' versus 'darkness,' in which 'the natural horror which attends meddling with human dead bodies' was gradually overcome through the heroic efforts of a line of anatomists stretching from the ancient Greeks to Vesalius to the moderns."[28] Here we must stop and ponder whether the origins of dissection photography had anything to do with creating an identity-infused refutation of public outcry. By providing tangible proof of the collective fears of the masses – even though these images were not published or distributed to lay audiences – did the genre's design, consciously or unconsciously, fan the flames of division? Did it seek to not just illustrate, but in fact expand, "the gulf between all those who never dissected and those few who had?"[29]

Life from lifelessness

> El sueño de la razón produce monstruos.
> [The sleep of reason produces monsters.]
> Francisco de Goya y Lucientes, Los Caprichos[30]

Simultaneous to what was going on in the world of anatomy, as some of the earliest published accounts on photography in America demonstrated, to the average viewer, photographs – and at this time we mean daguerreotypes – seemed "more like some ... delusion of necromancy than a practical reality."[31] While later photographic processes, such as wet collodion, and dry gelatin, allowed for the duplication and mass production of high-quality prints – including large-scale photographic narratives, viewed by throngs of people *en masse* – the daguerreotype, by contrast, was an intimate and powerfully personal experience; one best beheld by the individual and in private. Alan Trachtenberg writes that the power of the daguerreotype "lay in its physicality. Not only uniquely irreplicable, an image produced without a negative, yet embodying the negative-positive nexus on its face, it is also uniquely physical, a solid, palpable object ... it has weight, and yet behaves like a ghost."[32]

Trachtenberg's ghost analogy is appropriate here for this analysis, not only for its connection to concepts of incomplete, disembodied souls, and their relation to fears surrounding human dissection – as Sappol points out, the cadaver "could incite desire (necrophilia), inspire contempt for humanity, or lead students to reject Christianity ... and so jeopardize their immortal soul" – but also for its relation to a cultural view governing many early American perceptions of what *exactly* a photograph was: namely, an artifice of the devil.[33]

In the 1840s and 1850s, through its subsequent displacement by paper prints in the 1860s, the daguerreotype portrait was *the* dominant force in the American photographic industry. "If our children and children's children ... are not in possession of portraits of their ancestors," wrote T.S. Arthur in 1849, "it will be no fault of the Daguerreotypists ... for, verily, they are limning faces at a rate that promises soon to make every man's house a Daguerrean Gallery."[34]

Before enlightened reason prevailed, and "the daguerreotype [became] a significant and popular enterprise in the United States, with studios in virtually every city," many Americans saw these images as something inhuman, "something preternatural, magical, perhaps demonic"; a harbinger of death itself.[35] "There is something about the daguerreotype that bespeaks a hand not of this world," read a New York periodical essay in 1853. "Surely, to punish us for penetrating her mysteries. Nature touches us with the shadowy hand of death in revealing them!"[36] Fears concerning nature (nature in service to God) punishing humans for penetrating 'her' mysteries could easily be applied to the concurrent fears surrounding anatomical dissection, an act that literally penetrates the flesh and physically reveals the mysterious inner workings of nature, or perhaps more appropriately, reveals God's divine design.

Though it's a stretch, it is something to be considered that the superstitions and fears instilled in the youth of this era (1840s–1860s), once grown, might have become part of the tall tales passed on to their own children – the multitudes of medical students who grew up in the 1870s to 1890s. For in the minds of many Americans of the mid-19th century, the photographic arts were as synonymous with the mysterious, the unholy, and the unclean, as the events transpiring behind the closed doors of medical schools, or in the dark of night in unattended graveyards. Both acts were fraught with physical dangers. Anatomical dissection occurred in rooms overcome with corruptive effluvia and "noxious exhalations" of such putrescence, they threatened to poison any medical student who dared enter.[37] So too did photography emerge from comparably enigmatic crypts of darkness, from wooden boxes of untold depths, brimming with elemental mists.

The daguerreotypist was considered an alchemist, a necromancer, bringing forth life from the seemingly lifeless. At their command were pale apparitional likenesses – identities – which appeared upon cold, dead substrates, trapped behind occult looking-glasses, after being stacked in potions of transformative fluids, like bodies, preserved, floating in vats of alcohol and formaldehyde, "suspended in an ambiguously monochromatic float."[38] The latent image upon the daguerreotype's polished surface, and later the colloidal haze on the glass and iron of the ambrotype and tintype, was an image lying in wait, one that revealed itself only at a preordained moment, entangled, as it were, in the living, moving, reflection of the beholder. As if by its own choosing. Misconceptions over the chemistry involved in the latent image implied that these images, these identities, had consciousness.

Further complicating public perception was the daguerreotype's miraculous ability to exist simultaneously upon two visual planes, most especially its "capacity to negate itself when viewed in another light at another angle, to cancel itself into shadow, and rematerialize, as it were, from within itself."[39] This it did regardless of subject matter; be it a hand-tinted portrait of a loving spouse, or a somber postmortem of a deceased child. This temporal frisson of dissolving grey-silver flesh, appearing to disintegrate into an unknown underneath, absorbed by a shadow from within, was a frightening experience to some, and a symbolic one at that.

Indeed, it must have seemed as if the face of a lost loved one was decomposing in the viewers' own hand; only to be resurrected anew in the blink of an eye and the swirl of the wrist. Especially, as Trachtenberg states, when viewing a portrait in which "the eyes go black and the eye cavity appears a blank socket, how startling it is to find in your hands the visage of a skull — as if ... the image 'contains its own death's head'."[40]

Given the unparalleled and unprecedented realism indicative of the daguerreotype process, it is a rather simple conceit when it comes to understanding how superstitions flourished concerning such imagery as artifices capable of conjuring up and capturing the souls of the departed. It becomes increasingly probable when we consider how the technical limitations of early photography affected the outcome of the final corporeal object. Likewise, once additional processes such as tintypes and albumen prints emerged on the market, it is equally easy to see how those views rapidly changed, resulting in a total perceptual reversal of photography's 'devilish' behaviors.

With national perceptions now reformed, to be purposefully abject was to rely solely on one's subject matter. But there was one complication. Due to the mechanical objectivity of early photography – long exposure times requiring sitters to remain absolutely motionless, or to sit facing the sun with their eyes closed as if deceased – the visual similarities between photographs of dead bodies and those of living bodies became aesthetically indistinguishable. In fact, even to this day, many images of the living are confused with those of the dead.

Unless stricken by a disease that manifests on the skin (such as smallpox) or viewing a corpse showing signs of decomposition too severe to be effectively hidden, we often cannot differentiate 19th-century images of dead children from those merely asleep. To some photographers, such as Boston's most prestigious studio, Southworth and Hawes, questioning whether an image depicted a deceased or merely sleeping child stood as testament to their photographic prowess, as quantifiable confirmation of their ultimate authority over the identities, and bodies, of middle-class Americans.[41]

As photography spread as a dominant form of visual representation it became quite obvious that "views produced by these means will only be pictures of still-life, inanimate objects, buildings, mountains, rocks, and tracts of country, under settled aspects of the atmosphere."[42] In other words, in the earliest years of photography, as long as the object, or more specifically, the person, remained as motionless as a corpse, it would "be pictured with an accuracy of form and a perspective, a minuteness of detail, and a force and breadth of light and shade, that artists may imitate but cannot equal."[43] Thereby, as Marcy Dinius profoundly states, early photography, by proxy of its functional limitations, was "true to life only if what it represents is effectively lifeless."[44]

And yet, once the oeuvre of images of the deceased came to include dissection photographs – roughly 50 years after photography's invention – the historiography of initial posing conventions turned ironic to the point of becoming abject. Consider that photography's earliest aesthetic and technical principles required living sitters to pose as if they were dead. But, by 1900, the evolution of dissection photography allowed for and in fact required that the dead be posed as if they were still alive.

3

Defining Disgust: Abjection, Photography, and the Cadaver

The mummified and grotesquely mutilated fragments of unidentified humanity found in the dissecting-room have little personality. The individual who shrinks from the presence of a corpse often experiences merely a pleasurable thrill at seeing a skeleton or a mummy. The idea of horror recedes … until finally the human body is thought of simply as material for interesting and valuable study.

A.L. Benedict, "The Life of a Medical Student," 1896[1]

Modern audiences generally consider antiquarian photographs of the dead, decomposing, and dissected as offensive relics; mementos of a bygone era that are as disgusting as they are disturbing. Over the last two centuries, cultural perceptions about death and dead bodies have fluctuated repeatedly, shaping new and complex ways in which societies, accept, discuss, and deny the realities surrounding human mortality, *their* mortality. This denial, which usually entails some form of suppression, in turn establishes pervasive socially resistant attitudes toward death's consideration as a universal and natural phenomenon. Therefore, by proxy, those who demonstrate an affinity for the subject of death must exist on the antithetical outskirts of societal normativity.

Relatively recent cultural trends in the United States often identify a particular interest in or acceptance of death as something unnatural or morbid – this is especially true when it comes to collecting or collections of its cultural relics, such as photographs. Public discourse over such imagery often employs equivalent tropes (disgusting, disturbing) in order to satiate the demands of a dominant conservative culture. In the curatorial sense, mitigating public sensitivities over 'disturbing' content involves describing and defining said imagery in the safest yet basest ways possible. Safest, to not offend the beliefs, ethics, morals, or aesthetic sensibilities of sensitive stakeholders; basest, to connote a tacit understanding (again to this type of viewer) that images classified 'as disgusting as they are disturbing' are neither personally condoned nor culturally sanctioned.

When disapproval of socially transgressive visual materials, like dissection photographs, is perpetrated by an expert – such as a curator, professor, auctioneer, archivist, or historian – implications abound that these images are in fact abnormal outliers; unrecognized and unaccepted as essential components of a larger medium's established historiography.

For example, in 2015, while in graduate school, at the conclusion of my thesis presentation on dissection photography, a curator of 19th-century photography at the George Eastman Museum (Rochester, New York) announced that they felt the entire genre (and thus my presentation) amounted to "nothing more" than images of "essentially a bunch of mutilated bodies."[2] Their evaluation concluded with an astounding recommendation of censorship. Their 'solution' to my perceived 'problem' was simple: limit the number of dissection photographs in my presentation to only one or two; or, if I must show more, place black boxes over all the cadavers. This way, I would neither offend nor trigger certain viewers with an onslaught of abject imagery.

Despite the perception of credentials – again, this was a curator of 19th-century photography advocating for the expurgation of 19th-century photography – that lay audiences respond to dissection photographs, and their kin, with extreme negativity, irrespective of any form of historical context, and choose instead to use a litany of cognate terminology, like 'disgust,' to typify them as mere grotesqueries, is not only a global phenomenon, but, as some scholars attest, it's an entirely expected one.

In her book, *Body Criticism: Imagine the Unseen in Enlightenment Art and Medicine*, author Barbara Maria Stafford discusses how negative behavioral responses to images of the body (like disgust) are based on dominant, but experientially limited, personal biases and egos, specifically, private discomfort and fear over a sense of "vulnerability, shame, and powerlessness."[3] Author Colin McGinn likewise asserts that disgust is a distinctly human emotion, "an *aversive* emotion, belonging together with fear and hatred."[4] But, as he outlines in his work, *The Meaning of Disgust*, it is also a complicated phenomenon. Negative attitudes toward the visual economy of the dead, which includes the dissected body and the naturally decayed body, "coexist with positive ones in unresolved confusion and profusion."[5]

The confusing coexistences inherent to our complex bodily design, our mortal manifestations as amalgamates of the sacred and the profane – sinful flesh *and* holy spirit – creates a conceptual morass that is, undeniably, as disgusting as it is disturbing. Humanity was, after all, created in the image of God – or so many of us are told from a very early age. And yet, how unjust it is that we find ourselves fiendishly flawed by fleshy imperfections and gurgling excretions, filled to bursting with a "disgusting assemblage of grisly organs, damp tissues, and noisome fluids."[6]

To reduce the resultant emotions that flow from our dichotomous existence, our spiritual prison as "nothing more than meat puppets dancing to the whim of our creator," we become "self-critical, self-loathing, ashamed, and beset by anxiety about the betrayals the body may visit on us."[7] Society, in turn, adopts paranoid tendencies. It implements conservative aesthetic rulings and assigns gatekeepers of 'good taste,' all for the sake of self-preservation.

Instances of disgust, in all its various physical and visual permutations, are validated until they become the pinnacle of cultural normativity. Trailing swiftly thereafter, are efforts to limit access to 'disturbing' content, and following that, the birth of a new societal mandate; its common directive, "to conceal, to minimize, and to protect" ourselves from exposing ourselves to images that expose ourselves.[8]

Regarding the specifics associated with dissection and dissection photography, psychiatrists, sociologists, and historians have long established how personalized feelings of disgust intensify when engaging with images of exposed human entrails. Author Rina Arya connects the visceral response provoked by viewing our own viscera with "the mounting threat of abjection"; specifically, a primal, animalistic fear of being turned inside-out.[9] She asserts that "[t]he mere sight of these substances makes us [the viewers] contemplate the insides of our bodies, a journey which starts with the specific fluid, continues with disease and illness and ends with death."[10]

In the era of the dissection photograph, routine confrontation with visual evidence of the corrupt or dissected body threatened one's personal sense of self. As Kate Cregan discusses, it is downright "dangerous to the self-constituting self," since typically, a person "must abject (expel) the waste and enter the clean and ordered symbolic state to function effectively as a social being."[11] Coincidentally, that this confrontation is enabled mostly through the "incorruptible" technology of photography, a medium typically in service to society's greater needs of industry/art, surveillance, and identity-formation/self-expression, in turn, threatens society.[12]

The key to uncovering the discursive elements that populate many (but not all) audiences' hasty categorizations of certain imagery as 'disgusting' and 'disturbing,' as well as their analogous intransigence over the historic, artistic, vernacular, or scholarly values of such photographs, lies with their innate adverse reactions to the affective qualities of the ambiguously defined photographic supergenre of 'the dead.'

Connecting personal emotions with what society deems – at the moment – as an appropriate sense of self requires 'normalizing' responses to 'disturbing' stimuli. Cregan argues that an appropriate sense of self is formed through physical and mental detachment, "through the acceptance of what is considered 'good' into, and the rejection of what is considered 'bad' from, the self."[13]

With dissection photography, this includes the emotions evoked through their viewing, the method(s) in which said emotions are expressed or are allowed to be expressed, and the extent to which individual viewers visually, cognitively, and emotionally consume, interpret, and relate to or reject such imagery. Essentially, 'normal' social beings existing within the strict parameters of 'normative' social views.

While all of this is an obvious enough statement, for the purposes of this and future chapters, they require an expanded explanation, one which speaks to a particular theoretical concept, a "pervasive cultural code" that governs society's increasing aversion to all things dead and decomposing.[14] It is a process famed French theoretician Julia Kristeva defines as abjection.

Originally expressed in French literature by writers like Antonin Artaud, Georges Bataille, and the poet Charles Baudelaire, the abject was reintroduced into the modern lexicon in 1982 through Julia Kristeva's highly influential work, *Powers of Horror: An Essay on Abjection*. The abject, writes Kristeva, is that which "disturbs identity, system, order. What does not respect borders, positions, rules. The in-between, the ambiguous, the composite."[15] The abject represents that which "human life and culture exclude in order to sustain themselves." And yet, by virtue of its sense of uncanniness, it survives, and indeed thrives, in the interstices between temptation and revulsion.[16]

Within Kristeva's classification, the ontological boundaries of the dead body are fluid; its physical and metaphysical existence situated equally between two states: ambiguity and impurity. This chapter explores conceptual and theoretical applications of abjection toward the dissected cadaver, dissection photography's most abject and prominently abjectified element of its 50-year evolution. Also examined is the cycle associated with the cadaver's ambiguity as dual subject/object, as "non-object" simulacra that "*show me* what I permanently thrust aside in order to live."[17] Particular attention is shown to the direct correlation between its abject otherness and the transformative processes essential for its utilization by medical students for both anatomical dissection and, later, photographic commemoration.

To the lay reader who has never dissected nor witnessed a dissection before, the concept of the abject, and the abjectified body, assists with coming to terms with the myriad attitudes and questionable behaviors students adopted during the era of the dissection photograph. Of note are the substantial shifts in student–cadaver posing conventions. These shifts rendered the dissected cadaver mostly ambiguous; not only through the destruction of its structural unity and form, but the dissolution and derision of its personhood.

The theoretical concept of the abject provides clarity and context to the underlying signifiers associated with dissection photography. It is an ontological lens through which we may objectively interpret, re-examine, and hopefully reckon with the genre's more transgressive traditions. My hope is that abjection theory establishes a solid theoretical framework upon which you, the reader, will construct a better understanding of dissection photography as a significant and evolving genre.

Given the theory's reliance on specific, and sometimes conflicting, psychoanalytical principles – those which seek to challenge and investigate established categories of social taboos – my use here of the term 'abject' does not signify an artistic movement insomuch as it describes "a body of work which incorporates or suggests abject materials, such as dirt, hair, excrement, dead animals, menstrual blood, and rotting food in order to confront taboo issues."[18] For our purposes, the dually abject subject matter is the dead, dissected, and decomposing body, and the manner with which the living interacted with and visually represented it through their photography.

Exposing the cadaver: on becoming ambiguous and abject

As pioneering philosopher, Julia Kristeva, discusses in her work, *Powers of Horror*, the cadaver is "the utmost of abjection. It is death infecting life."[19] As neither pure subject, nor pure object, it is, by all accounts, something indefinable, that resists assimilation, a simultaneous and amorphous 'thing' that "lies there, quite close. ... It beseeches, worries, and fascinates desire, which, nevertheless, does not let itself be seduced."[20] Taking this concept further, we must understand that the cadaver is a sub-class of the standard human corpse, renamed through a new functionality and rechristened through its baptism in preservative fluids. The conceptual separation of the cadaver as bearing an identity distinct from that of the everyday *corpse* – an entity Kristeva calls "the most sickening of wastes" – is a tedious but powerful division.[21]

When viewed outside of proper medical context, or when placed external to the boundaries of its educational purpose – or, as Kristeva warns, "seen without God and outside of science" – the outwardly paradoxical task of transforming dead bodies into usable cadaveric objects could be seen as an abomination.[22] A loss of epistemological function in turn rejects the cadaver's normative associations with the identity formation of medical students. Within dissection photographs, this forfeiture likewise sterilizes the cadaver's transgressive potency as an abject hybridized subject-object. A loss of this magnitude reduces the cadaver to its prior designated status as a simple corpse, as "cesspool"; its materiality and utility (or lack thereof) once again governed by the rules, strictures, and consequences of a normative, anxious society.[23]

As an ambiguous entity, the cadaver is afforded countless names and forms according to the living actors who choose to interact with it. By its natural unnaturalness, a cadaver can be anything from a dead body to a "living image," a human referent but a natural horror, a treasured object, but also, a former subject.[24]

Through the processes of death, combined with an immediate halting of those same processes via chemical preservation (embalming), the cadaver opposes life *visually*. But, as a body whose earthly purpose is now governed solely by its objective functionality to medical education, it also opposes death *physically*; resisting (at least until said function is complete) its material place within the natural order of all organic beings: to die, to subsequently decompose, and to return to elemental form.

The cadaver's ambiguity is *essential* for functionality. When we consider that the expansion of anatomical knowledge is derived from its accelerated corporeal disfigurement, it becomes the embodiment of the abject; an entropic tool of knowledge production, but also, an abstruse source of emotional, psychological, physiological, moral, and intellectual conflict. Knowledge synchronous with fear.

The cadaver's affective powers derive from its dichotomous position as a morphological anomaly that is "neither human nor non-human," through its ambiguous existence as both indispensable primer and inexorable problem.[25] Dichotomies of this nature are routinely shown throughout the evolution of dissection photography. The corpse–cadaver division manifests itself rather starkly through the manner in which the ambiguous properties of the human body are photographically captured; which is to say, the various methods of visually transforming a dead subject into an ambiguous 'living' object.

The medium of photography is particularly well-suited for such transformations. As the great author and philosopher, Susan Sontag, once wrote: "One of the perennial successes of photography has been its strategy of turning living beings into things, things into living beings."[26] With the public's increased access to photography at the turn of the 20th century through handheld cameras, students were quick to learn how to use innovative technologies to visually exploit the physical boundaries of cadaveric flesh, as well as distort the boundaries between the living and the dead. By aligning themselves with this new visual economy, an equally novel epoch of student self-representation was born. Indeed, emerging from this time was an altered, some might say, progressive, identity-infused portrait of the American medical student. Thousands of intimate snapshots and real photo postcards show that this nascent 'type' of initiate reveled in the abject nature of their profession, outwardly driven to document the physical as well as metaphysical hazards of their work.

Handheld cameras allowed student amateur photographers to gain representative agency over themselves and to assert said control over the agency of their cadavers. Whether to adhere to preestablished aesthetics or go down the unknown road of abjection was now their challenge or choice; no longer required to be, or perceived as, a fixed conclusion because of their ignorance of photographic technology. When faced with a divergent plethora of options, a majority chose transgression over tradition.

Flamboyant poses usurped those of a more austere nature. Students literally smiled in the face of death; their once trembling hands, now slung confidently over the skinless shoulders of an upright cadaver, or extended downward, as a gesture of brotherhood, to execute a firm (but cold) handshake with the deceased. Before long, cadaveric participation became a critical component of student portraiture. The dead were no longer allowed to lay passively upon the slab. Photography 'proved' that they 'walked' the earth at night, drank whiskey, played cards, or conspired with smirking skeletons to take revenge upon their dissectors, those who had mutilated them with such reckless abandon. Flesh and bone, young and old, Black or White; physically maimed and morally mutated in unspeakable ways. And all for the honor and glory of the dissection photograph.

With the introduction of new aesthetics came a further abjection of the cadaver's proper function. Epistemological utility (at least in the time it took to take a photograph) became pathological, tumorous, and was summarily lanced from the cadaver; a benign byproduct of a defiant, abject desire to corrupt preestablished traditions. Indeed, with the didactic, epistemological, and relational utility between living and dead equally abjectified, standardized portraiture gave way to farcical subversions and defiant transgressions of traditional aesthetics and behaviors. All this, seemingly done without fear, or at least without consequence, of the opinions or demands of a dominant conservative culture.

Transcending the rot: turning ritual transgressions into transgressive rituals

In her influential work, *Abjection and Representation: An Exploration of Abjection in the Visual Arts, Film and Literature,* author Rina Arya asserts that the corpse "epitomizes the horror that abjection gives rise to. Its ambiguous status combined with its guaranteed putrefaction means that we, as living subjects, need to escape from its treachery, which we do in the form of appropriate funerary rituals, either by burial or cremation."[27] Funerary rituals establish a boundary that rigidly and rigorously protects the frontier of societal normativity, and by proxy, the self. As Arya discusses further, this boundary fluctuates in order to keep the subject (the living) away from the source of threat. Here the menace could be impurity, through various forms of decomposition and disease, or psychological peril from fixating on the body's infectious potential.[28] Kate Cregan similarly points out in her evaluation of the work of pioneering British anthropologist, Mary Douglas, that "the body is symbolic of social systems through rites and rituals, and it is the crossing of boundaries that bestows or determines impurity."[29]

As an aside, all things considered, the purity of the dead body cannot exist in a state of absolute. In the modern world, various acts and ministrations are routinely performed upon it, such as organ replacements, artificial joints and implants, embalming procedures, and autopsies. The latter act does not provide bodily purity so much as it does societal clarity over a cause of death. The body is sliced open, organs and tissues are investigated and removed as needed, then the incision is sewn shut – too often without returning the extracted flesh. Finally, it is delivered to a funeral home for embalming and either burial or cremation. But for these bodies, it is not always just about the deductions to their corporeal form that affect purity, but the addition of materials used to hold a freshly autopsied body together. In most cases, this exists as simple string or even monofilament. But occasionally, they can be something similar in structure but quite different in purpose. For instance, years ago a retired embalmer told me that once, while moonlighting at an unfamiliar morgue, he was in the middle of sewing up a corpse when he ran out of string. As the body was scheduled to be transported to a funeral home at any minute, and with no other options available, the embalmer opted to use the thick cotton–synthetic strands of a nearby mop.

★★★

While the corpse (the infectious threat to social order) is generally distanced and thus cleansed from society through rituals (physically, socially, and psychologically), escape from the cadaver is not possible; at least not for medical students, and not until the cadaver's function is fulfilled. In an ironic twist of fate, this fulfillment is achieved through the performance of another ritual: anatomical dissection; which guarantees the reduction of the cadaver's physical form until it is no longer recognizably human, and therefore, no longer an immediate threat to society and the self.

However, regardless of the successful ritualized enactment of dissection, if purity in all its forms is bestowed upon those who reject the dead, then what are we to make of students and physicians? Are they forever tainted, physically, psychologically, or socially, by their acceptance of the cadaver's impurities?

Throughout most of the 19th and early 20th centuries, the transgression of customary funerary rituals, via dissection and autopsy, established new boundaries concerning life, death, and life after death. Medical historian, Michael Sappol, states that during this time the enactment of any or all aspects of dissection resulted in students and physicians claiming "exemption from funerary customs and social strictures," at least among themselves.[30] Dissection then, to them, was a ritual of trespass.

This immunity of sorts included the act of dissection itself, as well as other forms of complicity in cadaver procurement, such as grave robbing. Most significant was the relocation of the deceased from traditional areas of mourning, such as the home, funeral parlor, graveyard, or hospital, to the liminal space of the dissecting room, a zone of initiation in which there was "no rest for the dead."[31] Exemption was further validated via additional professionally essential intrusions, such as the collection and preservation of gross specimens for biomedical displays in museums of anatomy and pathology. By the 1890s, these designated stakeholders, comprised of students, physicians, *and* both professional and student amateur photographers, began to trespass further; this time, upon the preestablished visual economies of lay society and professional medical identity.

Although dissection photography solidified as a quantifiable practice in the 1880s by way of commercial photography, by the early 1910s, student amateur photographers absolutely dominated the genre's image production. Fueled by an onslaught of innovation in the realm of camera technologies, their success involved drawing, transgressing, and then redrawing the boundaries of their own rituals and culture on a routine basis.

It should again be pointed out that as the industry of photography had yet to universalize its user base, only professional photographers, the proclaimed authoritarian makers of these images, could go beyond these boundaries and usurp time-honored rituals. Students had no choice; nor any skills or access to essential photographic equipment – including darkrooms. As such, they were forced to hire professional outsiders and to invite these non-medical technicians into their sacred spaces, regardless of whether their aesthetic and moral principles aligned.

To a commercial photographer, satisfying a client was key, even if that meant working inside a dissecting room filled with a stinking mélange of rotting meat and pipe smoke, or setting up camera and tripod amid students launching 'missiles' of cadaveric flesh at one another. Commercial motivations were, obviously, ruled by capitalist principles, such as industry, reputation, and money. To become the official photographer of an entire school – or in cities like New York and Philadelphia, multiple schools – meant big and repeat business. Not only in terms of taking dissection photographs, but in supplying students and staff with multiple sets of cabinet card portraits, which were later distributed among the student body and hung on their boardinghouse walls. Students needed graduation photos for use in yearbooks (mostly consisting of group shots of sports teams and fraternities) and administrators routinely requested updated interior and exterior shots of remodeled schools and hospitals for marketing and fundraising. To commercial photographers, taking pictures of dead bodies was just a means to an end.

Plus, exactly how discerning could this audience be? They were poor students after all, most of them in their early twenties, living away from their families, generally too young to remember or know about the photographic exactitude of their professional forebears. How good did a dissection photograph need to be to satisfy the abject component of their professional identities?

In truth, the majority of large format, professionally taken dissection photographs are nothing short of breathtaking. The clarity they achieved; the posing, the lighting, the balance; all carefully staged and masterfully executed. Overcoming obstacles, not just in terms of subject matter, but shooting indoors in dimly or overly lit rooms, stands as testament to the ineffable technical skill of the professional photographer of the era.

That said, the photographs professionals created in the 1880s and 1890s were typical, albeit treacherously slippery objects that successfully conferred and commemorated a baseline identity for their clients, all the while allowing for moderate modulations in non-photographic conventions, such as the introduction of dissection table epigraphs. With few exceptions, most images made during this period (Stage I) adhered to the preestablished aesthetics of standard portraiture, those crafted and endorsed by commercial industry.

Ultimately, however, these standardized portraits would be supplanted by those seeking to purposefully breach, what Terry outlines as "acceptable codes of behavior and prevailing social norms."[32] As previously discussed, by the start of the 20th century, this transgressive spirit would become the genre's dominant trademark until its demise in the 1930s.

An anus by any other name would still excrete: abjection and the limitations of cadaveric objectification

Obtaining knowledge through the basic rituals of anatomical dissection required that students establish a psychological disconnect from their cadavers, to begin to view them less as the corpses of (someone else's) loved ones and more as essential biological specimens. However, specimenhood did not always mean the elimination of personhood. Nor did the essentialities of a cadaver's being always encode themselves properly upon the average student's perceptive reality. For example, to those White students who regarded African Americans as intellectually and physically inferior, their cadavers were not viewed as temples but playgrounds. Violating or denigrating these remains in death functioned as an extension of similar social practices deemed acceptable in life, such as segregation, the desecration of pauper cemeteries, and lynching.

To this point, an extreme variant form of this type of detachment facilitated the cadaver's objectification to where students subverted its organic position as a once-living being. Here, objectification situated the dead body as a completely expendable thing; as non-human from cradle to grave; conceptually analogous to the carcass of a vivisected animal or a clastic model. Both degrees of ritualized objectification prevailed throughout the late 19th and early 20th centuries, be it in the form of specimen acquisition for dissecting rooms or medical museums, or initiatives involving medical testing and surgical experimentation. What's more, both found form and expression throughout the half-century reign of dissection photography.

Irrespective of the extent to which students objectified cadavers physically or visually, including instances of extreme, deviant forms of objectification, one endeavor that never fully succeeded involved the transformation of cadavers into *pure* objects. According to Arya, ultimately, as a formerly living being, a dissected human and its component parts "cannot be wholly separated from us," for they are "reminders of our inability to extricate ourselves from our organic being."[33]

As Arya's theories of abjection specify further, psychologically, the transformative processes inherent to the objectification of dead bodies can only advance so far before the mind forms a defensive barrier, a protective skin to shield the self; similar to how our bodies form the walls of an abscess to fortify against the spread of infection.

As is suggested, human remains cannot completely become objects, and thus be fully considered as such, for they are too explicit a reminder of our species' mortality; too recognizable as precisely what they are: *the remains of humans*. Even in instances where human remains are objectified to the point of abuse, the acts committed upon, with, or within them are done so with material awareness. Cavalier as students may be toward acquiring tokens of mortality in the form of actual cadaveric souvenirs, or once-removed commemorative photographs, it is their residual identifiable connection to humankind that makes them so coveted as objects.

Indeed, it could be said that material knowledge is often precisely what spawns particular forms of mistreatment or material indifference toward human remains, such as using the overturned calvarium of a skull as an ashtray or candy bowl. The 19th-century physician who uses the skin of deceased patients to create anthropodermic bibliopegy (books bound in human skin) often does so as an homage to them. In closed social media groups, literally as I write these words, money is exchanging hands between oddities dealers and collectors looking to acquire candles made from 'human tallow' and pocket watches or jewelry made from human skull fragments. Perhaps one of the most unusual examples I've encountered over the years concerns a tanned piece of a cadaver's peritoneum (the large membrane of the human abdominal cavity), preserved because of its reminiscent qualities, by the Class of 1926 at the American School of Osteopathy (Kirksville, Missouri). Inscribed directly onto the bit of flesh, students wrote out the names of those who partook in the cadaver's dissection, along with a class logo of sorts and the following inscription: "Piece of Peritoneum dissected from Thomas Butterfield. Age 63, White Race, Died of Valvular Insufficiency. Disection [*sic*] by Hiram T. Campbell during Upper Sophomore Year at The AMERICAN SCHOOL of OSTEOPATHY at Kirksville, Mo. Nov. 6, 1923."[34]

Additional insight into the objective meaning of cadaveric objects is provided through much of the correspondence between students and their friends and family. Writing to a relative in March 1918 from his medical school in Augusta, Georgia, a student, identified only as 'Paul,' writes:

> We have been getting the study of anatomy first hand by visiting the University Hospital. Tho not an exceptionally pleasant subject, but an interesting one let me assure you, was the dissecting room where the bodies of dead negroes are cut up for purposes of study. At least I found it interesting tho some one filled with a lot of foolish ideas about bodies after death might have rebelled a little at the idea.[35]

In a further demonstration of his emotional detachment to the cadaver as a formerly living subject, but again, speaking to the significance of human remains as objects instilled with a lingering connection to personhood, Paul lamented: "I was rather disappointed, that I could find no opportunity of obtaining a skull or some bone at least as a souvenir of the hospital."[36]

As demonstrated, material awareness existed regardless of whether the final artifact in question sought to honor or denigrate the dead. When material possession was neither wanted nor possible, photography served as viable means of preserving this form of material consciousness by adding the additional component of abjectified utility. In these instances, the cadaver's limbs and organs were depicted as abject props, visually transmogrified into other matter, such as disembodied limbs twisted and fashioned together to form letters and numbers, cadavers' heads converted into oil lamps, or leg bones held to students' lips to be 'played' like flutes and trumpets; a mockery of the anatomical landmark of the iliotibial band.

Regardless of the levels of abjection or putrefaction enacted upon it, the cadaver cannot be utterly disconnected from life.[37] Elizabeth Grosz explains further that "[n]o part of the body is divested of all psychical interest without severe psychical repercussions, [as] [t]here is still something of the subject bound up with them."[38] Arya similarly discusses in her essay in *Abject Visions: Powers of Horror in Art and Visual Culture* that the cadaver cannot be fully objectified due to the disgust and desire they instill in the living; emotions that are directly linked with the visual economy of the dead. Thus, the dissected cadaver and its corresponding body parts – disembodied limbs, tissues, organs, bones, and even expelled substances and fluids, such as pus, semen, urine, or feces – *all* maintain a facet of subjectivity in the eyes of the user/viewer through the mimesis of the body's previously living state.[39]

As Arya discusses further, the embedded link between vision, death, dissection, and the emotions they churn up threatens the stability of the subject – for our purposes, the subject could simultaneously include dissectors, photographers, and/or the viewers of dead bodies and dissection photographs:

> Ordinarily that which is other to the subject can be objectified and distanced from the subject, thereby not posing a threat to its subjectivity. In the cases of abjection, however, the source cannot be objectified and it threatens the subject with engulfment and dissolution. This is one of the unrelenting features of the abject as defined by Kristeva: it is not a subject nor is it an object but it displays features of both. It exists in between these two states, where it cannot be discretely separated from the subject (as an object would be) and where it lurks objectlike but without becoming an object. The non-object impresses on the subject's stability and hovers "at the boundary of what is itself assimilable, thinkable ..." but is itself unassimilable, which means that we have to contemplate its otherness in its proximity to us but without it being able to be incorporated.[40]

Arya and Kristeva's theories of the unassimilable and the abject find various degrees of corporeality throughout the evolution of dissection photography, particularly those that rejected convention in favor of forming new abject signifiers, such as perverting the normal utility of the scalpel, or cadavers reveling in their "stiffdom," sitting around the dissecting table at night engaging in socially transgressive activities, such as drinking and gambling (Figure 3.1).

As Arya pinpoints, images of a taboo nature are polarizing, establishing a "cycle of repulsion and attraction, fear and intrigue."[41] As tangible objects closely aligned with the abject, dissection photographs commonly participated in the classic abjection cycle of repulsion–desire with the viewer. They tug and pull at our emotional senses, showing us someone that appears living, but is in fact dead; a body that appears to be whole, but is in fact fragmented. This visual interplay drives many of us away. But some return, coerced to take another look and, in doing so, must confront both their own mortality and the fate of mortal remains.

A proper sense of disgust

As touched upon at the beginning of this chapter, such strong considerations engender equally robust emotions toward 'disturbing' imagery. These sentiments can either be accepted or rejected depending upon their applicability to one's sense of self or societal viewpoint. Maintaining a proper sense of disgust is seemingly imperative, lest we turn said emotions upon ourselves, and become "averse to ourselves."[42] But who are the gatekeepers

Figure 3.1: "Nightly Revels in STIFFDOM." Medical College of Virginia (Richmond, Virginia). Unidentified photographer. Gelatin silver print, circa 1912

Source: Private collection

of disgust? Who curates the collection of "psychological maneuvers" we reportedly need in order to protect ourselves from intense self-deprecation?[43]

To this point, the oracular conditions of the dissection photograph, as object, can only go so far before they too, like the cadaver, become socially and culturally unassimilable; abject expressions of a self-loathing society, one seemingly intent upon self-destruction. As discussed at length, the cadaver's resistance to visual and societal assimilation is inherent to the genre's larger iconography. We may attribute this to a strobic fluctuation within the photographic frame between contextualization and juxtaposition, one which highlights the conflicting interplay between the living and the living, the living and the dead, and the fragmented and the whole.

As McGinn discusses, the abject nature of these concepts becomes particularly telling from the viewpoint of the layperson, who prefers the human body "depicted in its more attractive aspect, as pure form, not as a vile sack of internal organs."[44] Photography served as a means for students to deal with the abject nature of their professional educations – particularly their role in the dissolution of a human body. As a multi-tiered palindromic ritual – the ritual of dissection documenting the ritual of photography and vice versa – the combination of experiences developed into a distinct culture; an insular and insulating society whereby certain cultural themes found expression through parallel acts of abjection. Rituals affect social relations. Thus, as Mary Douglas stated, "in giving these relations visible expression they enable people to know their own society."[45]

As non-physicians, as viewers positioned outside this insular, but outwardly self-sustaining 'society,' we especially reject the cadaver's abject status as mere object/non-object, because its transformative utility is utterly foreign to us and to the society we function within. We exist externally, far from the embrace of the visual economy of medical culture. Therefore, regardless of the level(s) to which cadaveric objectification is achieved, we cannot outwardly benefit from its enactment; be it to achieve epistemological knowledge, or to transgress previous systems of identity or knowledge production.

Disconnected from the cadaver's functionality, non-dissectors become equally hardened; concomitant with the very dissectors they claim to be 'disgusted' by. An impermeable crust, a rusty aura, is formed; resistant to the assimilation of such imagery into the collective fold of 'pure' histories, be they of photography, medicine, or aesthetics. But why do we/they do this? Why resist? Is it truly out of fear, disgust, and necessity? Or all three?

Dissection photographs expose dead flesh with an immediacy that rivals the scalpel. Like the very cadavers they depict, they are byproducts of human transformation, of transitional stages in human life. The abject elements they evidence 'disturb' us on unprecedented levels because they are us, they are an embodiment of *us*; reflected skin reflected back to ourselves in ways never thought possible, ways 'we' cannot come to terms with. For 'us,' there is no need for such literal retroflection.

However, is it not the divergent aesthetics and the moral, ethical, and societal dilemmas evoked through dissection photography's existence that defines its significance? Imagine for a moment, if, as Cregan discusses, "psychological universals held," and "all cultures" found "the same bodily products abominable or divine in the same way."[46] What would happen? And to what end? Experiences of abjection are the hallmarks of dissection as an act: to provide the methods, means, and utility that widens the great divide between medical initiates and the lay community they will one day serve; between those few who have dissected and those many who have not.

Curiously, if we were to seal over that great chasm that separates authoritarian systems of anatomical knowledge production from the reach of the layperson – thus, everyone could dissect and everyone, in turn, could be dissected – would the normalization of the act bring about the return of the dissection photograph? Only this time, as an indelible part of America's visual economy?

For unlike comparable images of the dead and decomposing, such as postmortem photographs, stereographs of slain Civil War soldiers heaped upon the battlefield, or even lynching photographs, dissection photographs never found a public consumer. Indeed, it seems far easier to define them as 'disturbing,' unworthy of study 'by us,' and censor them, rather than come to terms with their abject nature; to accept them as unacceptable and consent to a reality that these images are simply *not made for us*.

And yet, their assigned insignificance by virtue of their abject significance breeds countless inquiries. By defining the genre as abject and outside of the dominant cultural codes of normative society, as images of a counterculture, again, 'not for us,' this of course then begs the question, if dissection photographs were not made to be seen by the general public, then what is their relevant connection, what is their purpose to modern society or, even, to the modern medical student?

4

Is Dissection Photography *Really* a Genre?

> All camera work can or cannot be candid. Few recent pictures
> are more candid than those of Civil War corpses.
>
> Beaumont Newhall, "Photography:
> A Short Critical History," 1938[1]

At its basest level, what act is more abject than dissection? What action signifies the concept of challenging established social taboos, of blurring the boundaries between the self and the other more than the flaying and dismemberment of the body of another human being? And therefore, what photographic genre deserves a more prominent place in the historical canon of abjectified art than dissection photography? What photograph carries more abject significance than an image that coexists in the interstices between social repugnance and a hallowed expression of the cooperative social experiences of legions of students? Should it not be collected and stored in the vaults of the world's preeminent photographic archives? Should it not be hung on the walls of museums and studied as intensely as the portraits of photographic luminaries like Yousuf Karsh, Diane Arbus, or James Van Der Zee?

I can already guess your answer: No, they should not. For dissection photographs should never have been taken; and they most certainly should never be taken again. But you should know that genres like documentary photography and journalistic photography often portray the same subject matter as medical and anthropological photography. And yet, the genre of medical photography, in all its varying forms, has subsisted almost exclusively outside the scope of photographic history's authoritative canonical texts. Scholars view this lack of situation within the larger photographic realm as a marginalizing act, stripping medical photographs of their significance and aesthetic qualities. Even in the age in which informed consent was conceptually nonexistent, this mode of thinking was nothing new.

49

In 1859, the prestigious medical journal *The Lancet* wrote:

> We were, therefore, surprised, in passing through the rooms of the Photographic Society lately, to find so few photographs which had any bearing of what kind so ever upon surgery, medicine, and the allied sciences. It is much regretted that the great resources of the photographic art – seen here in a hundred beautiful forms – have not yet been fully applied to the purposes of our art.[2]

Historian Erin O'Connor believes this oversight is the result of a collective forgetting, within which the close link between medicine and photography was lost to the annals of time. At least, until the mid-20th century, when historians and collectors such as Alison Gernsheim, Stanley Burns, and Sander L. Gilman resurrected and connected it to larger concepts of aesthetics and art history.[3]

Dissection photography has indeed been written out of standardized histories of photography in much the same way as other forms of medically themed images, even when connected to pioneering (and canonized) photographers, like Eadweard Muybridge, who photographed a student-filled dissecting room in California in the 1870s. The genre's rather paltry mention or complete omission, even within histories of medical photography, or Muybridge's own oeuvre, forces one to again ask the question of *why*? Why is this photographic genre so undefined in its placement in photography's history, and so unacknowledged by scholars, medical historians, or even current medical students and doctors?

As discussed earlier, photo historian James S. Terry classified dissection photography as a "subspecies" of group portraiture.[4] But what exactly did Terry mean by this categorization? Given its prevailing subject matter, would it not have been more appropriate to consider dissection photography as a subgenre of medical photography, rather than a subgenre of portrait photography? Could its ambiguous categorization have in some way led to its modern obscurity or suppression?

With medical photography's long-standing underrepresentation within photographic canon, one could argue it was Terry's intent to make dissection photography more palatable, accessible, and socially normative, by removing it from the microcosm of medicine, and linking it to the supergenre of portraiture. As Daniel Chandler discusses, many audiences see genre "as an instrument of social control which reproduces the dominant ideology. Within this perspective, the genre 'positions' the audience in order to naturalize the ideologies which are embedded throughout."[5] If we subscribe to this social positioning, then much the way 19th-century postmortem photography was successfully adopted into the larger corpus of portraiture, and thereby managed expressions and elicitations of mourning and memory, could dissection photography, as an accepted, albeit underground, extension of commercial portraiture, in turn normalize and control abject experiences on historical, social, and commercial levels?

Sadly, it appears we will never know for certain. Unlike postmortem photographs, which carried industrial favor and commercial value throughout the medium's first 100 years, and are still prevalent today due to their cultural significance as an 'accurate' method of memorialization, dissection photographs never found widespread acceptance in either the 19th or 20th centuries. Everyone dies. But not everyone dissects. The paradox, of course, being that this was partially the point of their abject existence. They served no greater cultural or societal function outside the medical industry.

Yet, given the fact this was, after all, a *global* phenomenon, we must still question why these photographs were omitted from nearly all of photography's popular histories until the 2009 publication of *Dissection*? The reason can't just be their subject matter in tandem with modern sensibilities toward bodily autonomy and exploitation, can it? Did the secrecy of their creation, or their limited functionality, play a role? Perhaps it resulted from the genre's limited representation – either by accident or design – within the photo collections of major American cultural institutions, like the George Eastman Museum? I can personally attest to the fact that dissection photography leaves a bad taste in the mouths of many of the so-called modern 'tastemakers' of medical and photographic history. Could a century and a half of personal preference, disguised as curatorial gatekeeping, really be behind it all?[6]

In figuring out which images are or are not to be included in photography's accepted 'histories,' art critic, A.D. Coleman, says it best:

> To begin with, a truism: The history of photography encompasses all photographs ever made. This might seem self-evident. Yet much of what is generally defined as "the history of photography" has been restricted quite narrowly (and often politically) to certain branches of what is variously called "serious", "creative", or "art" photography.[7]

Failure to assimilate into one or more of these predetermined categories warrants ejection from the mainstream. Included in this category of categorically repositioned photographs are those of the medical, anthropological, and forensic fields: images of cadavers, corpses, murders, war atrocities, lynchings, the dead or still living bodies of the maimed and mutilated, medical and pathological oddities, and 'human zoos.' As a result of their cultural erasure, at least photographically speaking, antiquarian examples of subject matter classified 'as disgusting as they are disturbing,' such as dissection photographs, are instead forced to inhabit a position of counterculture. Today, this cultish and fetishistic realm, this clonal 'underground' peripheral and parasitic to the mainstream, is largely populated by contemporary photographers and collectors of photography who are actively engaged in shocking viewers through conscious elicitations of extreme emotions. The original intent or audience for vintage photographs becomes lost to the annals of time – or worse yet, misrepresented – as the intentionally and the unintentionally repellent become homogenized into one outlying 'supergenre' of image-making, once called candid photography, but in the modern era, more commonly referred to as grotesque photography.

While being accepted into the ranks of portraiture may have legitimized the genre of dissection photography as precisely that, a genre, we must consider that due to their abject nature, their lack of homogeneous techniques, attention to photographic trends, or canonical photographers, dissection photographs (and other abject imagery) poison the larger genre of photographic portraiture by perverting the medium's larger standards and shifting ideologies – particularly those designed to show the 'beauty' of life rather than the glory of death. After all, what would it say about society as a whole, medical culture as industry, or photography as a legitimate art-science, to accept freely and unequivocally a genre in which a proximity to death – not a glorious sleeping death, but an inglorious stinking death – was not only praised, but flaunted in every home and hospital in America?

This, again, rings especially true when faced with the realities and consequences stemming from cultural shifts toward bioethics, agency, and bodily autonomy, especially those bodies donated to or confiscated for science. As to dissection photography's modern acceptance and application, we must also factor the eventual outlawing of photography in most American dissecting rooms by the turn of the 21st century.

Lest we become too bogged down in the semantics of definitions, or what 'types' or genres of images are or are not included in photographic canon, let us conclude our discussion about genre by taking note of what Daniel Chandler says. While genres have traditionally been "regarded as fixed forms … contemporary theory emphasizes that both their forms and functions are dynamic."[8] Thus, for dissection photography to exist and survive as a genre, its conventions and utility could not be assigned indefinitely. Rather, they needed to be, as David Buckingham argues, in "a constant process of negotiation and change."[9] By 1910, dissection photography was indeed forever changed.

Adapting to life in a moral world

As a tradition, dissection photography was neither created nor expanded to coalesce its collective imagery into the shape of a legitimate, albeit ambiguously classified, genre. The initial goal was a simple one: to commemorate student participation in a rite of passage. Nevertheless, by the mid-1890s, the outright need for commemorative imagery, and the need for the subsequent growth and evolution of these pictures into a quantifiable genre, seem to have run parallel to each other.

The era of the dissection photograph was marked by near constant changes in the American social fabric, such as an increasing reliance on machines, women leaving the home to join the medical profession, as well as technological innovations, such as the introduction of new cameras and printing papers (to name but a few). Thus, dissection photography required modern alternatives to evidence a student's mutable identity within an ever-changing profession and national culture.[10]

Once the act of posing with the dead became a firmly established cultural tradition within the profession (originally at the hands of professional photographers), additional conventions were required to reflect consistent changes in student identities on sociocultural, professional, and technological levels, such as those situated in what I refer to as Stage II of dissection photography's evolution.

Like the ancient symbol of the ouroboros, student identity continually reaffirmed and renewed itself (dare I say resurrected itself) with each new generation. Display in dorm rooms, dissecting theaters, scrapbooks, and eventually, school yearbooks, also served to codify dissection photography and expand its legitimacy as both an evolving genre and a ritualized tradition.

Photographs of the past became part of an isolated cumulative sequence and showed new students what was or was not considered acceptable or popular; be they images of upperclassmen posing classically (Stage I), engaging in dark gallows humor (Stage III), or some other incarnate typology that had yet to take tangible form. An extreme example of this latter type is the infamous panoramic dissection photograph of the Class of 1920 of Queen's University (Ontario, Canada), in which students spelled the words 'Med 20' out of the lashed-together limbs of their fragmented cadavers.

As John Fiske asserts, a genre's conventions "embody the crucial ideological concerns of the time in which they are popular."[11] This concept could explain why some of the more transgressive poses of dissection photography were created circa 1906 to 1916, around the height of the postcard "mania" in America.[12] The creation of the dissection postcard not only contributed to a national preoccupation, but could also be considered doubly transgressive, occupying space in the layperson's mailbox alongside 'normative' views of national landmarks, cityscapes, or children at play. As stated previously, dissection photographs hid in plain sight. Just like those who dissected 'hid' among the lay community – that is, when they didn't reek of the cadaver lab. This also points to why the majority of racially insensitive dissection photos, those designed to dehumanize the bodies and identities of both living and deceased African Americans, were produced in Southern states during the first half of the Jim Crow era.

According to Steve Neale, "genres are instances of repetition and difference … difference is absolutely essential to the economy of genre: mere repetition would not attract an audience."[13] Neale's definition assists with answering a key question concerning who exactly dissection photographs were made for. Not surprisingly, they were made for the students. But just because they were made *for* them, did not mean that they were always intended to be kept *by* them. In other words, I made this for me, but so I could give it to you. "Here is a picture of me in the dissecting room," wrote medical student, "Elsie," on the back of her dissection postcard. "For the family."[14] As she attended a coeducational school and was the only woman in her photograph, 'Elsie's' identity was firmly established without any further need of identifiers.

What dreams may come?

> Don't suppose you ever have such horrid dreams do you?
> Message on back of *Student Dream* dissection
> postcard, 1908[15]

While the constant fluidity of the genre's dominant imagery seemed to confuse early photo historians in terms of defining the genre's origin, as Chandler again points out, such acts are in fact essential to the formation of a genre as we know it: "Each new work within a genre has the potential to influence changes within the genre or perhaps the emergence of a new sub-genre (which may later blossom into fully-fledged genres)."[16] A perfect example of an influential subgenre within dissection photography is the aforementioned *Student Dream* photographs, which began circa 1905 by commercial photographers, and was expanded upon well into the 1920s at the hands of student amateur photographers.

As previously discussed, *Student Dream* images are included in what I classify as Stage III of the evolution of dissection photography. Emergent during this stage were new 'types' of dissection portraits, those focused on staging and manipulating cadavers to create humor-driven, psychologically affective tableaus; defiant of all previous photographic conventions or industry standards. The precise motivation behind the creation of Stage III images, including variants on the *Student Dream* subgenre, varies considerably. Inspiration was often prompted either by changes in student need and experience, or, in the case of involvement by professional photographers, commercial appeal.

In most dissection photographs, the relationship between the living and the dead are graphically and often painfully clear. *Student Dream* images, like the one featured on this book's cover, dichotomize this relationship in inconceivably intolerable ways. As outsiders, we neither empathize nor embrace such fundamental role reversals. The toll upon a student's physical and mental state are the price that they and they alone must pay for such an unmitigated connection to disgraceful death. After all, it was as much a student's doing as it was their undoing. But it should be noted that *Student Dream* images were born from the actual experiences and dreams of real-life students. Worse still were the nightmares: vivid hallucinations of hordes of reanimated, partially dissected cadavers and skeletons, returned from the dead to exact revenge upon those who had dismembered them. For death may only be a dream, but *dissected* death, that was a nightmare; a nightmare of their own creation. In 1898, after facing their cadavers for the first time, first-year students at Yale University admitted to having difficulty sleeping: "That night it seemed as if all the people we had left in that room came round to see us, and in consequence our sleep was not of the pleasantest."[17] In the mid-1890s, medical student Edith Flower Wheeler recalled the following related to the dissected in her dreams:

In this dream [I] was alone in the room with about twenty bodies, each lying on its table covered by a sheet. Suddenly they all arose, throw aside their sheets and stood in their various states of ragged separations and dissolutions. They seemed threatening and about to do something but, what their intentions were, the dream did not say for [I] departed from that room quickly and returned to the land of reality without regret.[18]

Once student amateur photographers had access to handheld cameras, the psychological turmoil of this initial encounter with the cadaver found tangible expression in the form of a distinct subgenre. In 1909, one student jokingly attributed his bad dreams to a stomach disorder, akin to Ebenezer Scrooge's disbelieving tirade upon his confrontation with the ghost of Jacob Marley. "You may be an undigested bit of beef, a blot of mustard, a crumb of cheese, a fragment of an underdone potato," Scrooge famously remarked. "There's more of gravy than of grave about you, whatever you are!"[19] Indeed, taking a page out of Dickensian logic, the student, whose postcard of a commercially available *Student Dream* postcard featured a student sleeping upon a dissection table while surrounded by eight cadavers, wrote on the back: "This medic ate too much Welsh rare bit and then dreamed he was being dissected by the people that he had dissected. Don't you think this a pleasant dream? How would you like to be me?"[20]

Indeed, as an artifact born from the dissecting room, these photographs were imbued with the same disruptive potential of the cadaver itself. "This will give you some idea of what the notorious dissecting room looks like," began a message from "Will" to "Grace" on the back of a dissection postcard. "You can see the feet of one cadaver and the head of another. [Don't] let this picture interfere with your sleeping. Chuck it to the bottom of the trunk."[21] Others took solace in knowing that while these images were the literal stuff of nightmares, love conquered all. Writing to his sweetheart, Miss Lulu Clevenger, of Parker City, Indiana, medical student Charles, wrote: "Roy C. says he dreamed worse than this his first night after dissection but I never did. I have someone else to dream of."[22]

5

Iconographic Ambiguities

When a dissection photograph is considered as an isolated image, its various components – student, scalpel, book, dissecting table, and cadaver – might all seem arbitrary; no more than accessible props, included solely for the execution of a singular grotesque tableau, a "macabre expression of students' ghoulish perversity."[1] But when opportunity presents itself for examples to be viewed *en masse*, and considered as an evolving genre, it becomes readily apparent that each of dissection photography's distinct stages contain their own aesthetic and cultural conventions; remarkably, even in instances of performative hybridity, when components or tropes are purposefully deviated from or transgressed in order to form new ones.

To comprehend dissection photography as an evolving genre, we must first and foremost stop looking at the genre's raw elements, its repetitive subject matter (skulls, skeletons, and 'stiffs'), the typology of the dissecting room, as the *sole means* of grouping and thus defining dissection photography in total. Evaluating a genre in this manner, argues Robert Stam, "fails to take into account *how* the subject is treated."[2] While this structure is decidedly more palatable to a broad, non-medically inclined audience, it fails to position or contextualize these subjects and their influences from a technical or sociocultural standpoint. In other words, we need to comprehend that not all photographs of dissected bodies were created equal.

In John Harley Warner and James M. Edmonson's *Dissection*, the latter co-author emphasizes the importance of acknowledging dissection photography as a certifiable genre. Confirming this assertion may once again seem rather arbitrary. But I assure you, it is not. Accepting dissection photography as a legitimate photographic genre validates these images as important social documents. Validation also necessitates that both the photographic and medical communities acknowledge and reckon with the offenses represented throughout the genre's half-century evolution; specifically, how the culture of the American dissecting room, and thus, the institute of American medicine itself, participated in the systemic marginalization and targeted dehumanization of the bodies of African Americans. And yet, even if we accept Edmonson's declarations about the cultural significance of dissection photography (and indeed we should), questions remain regarding the genre's unspecified origins, its abject subject matter, and the conflicting meanings and intent behind a nexus of student posing conventions.

For almost 40 years, one of the genre's greatest hallmarks was the proverbial cloud of confusion surrounding its widespread adoption. As previously mentioned, in the first scholarly publication on dissection photography, author James S. Terry confidently classifies dissection photography as a "subspecies" of the standard group portrait, a "conventional (albeit underground) genre in its own right."[3] However, during his attempts to establish the originating purposes behind the genre, Terry found himself struggling to effectively explain dissection photography's divergent ideologies and aesthetic principles. For a genre that sourced its tropes from such an isolated iconographic oeuvre, how was it that dissection photography showed students engaging in such polarizing behaviors: both the reverential handling of the dead *as well as* grotesque tableaus that transgressed the boundaries of flesh, identity, photographic aesthetics, and societal good taste?

Furthermore, questions Terry, what potential sources served as archetypal standards or primary influences from which the genre derived its inspiration? Since no photographic precursor seemed to exist, Terry turned his sights to the anatomical portraiture of centuries past, attempting to establish a quantifiable visual tradition, a pre-photographic precursor, which might illuminate some aspect of dissection photography's seemingly chimeric, self-contradictory imagery.

Positioning the entire genre of dissection photography within a larger anatomical framework, and thus connecting it with the visual heritage of medicine, seems like a natural course of action, and, by all accounts, it is a likely and correct one. Indeed, a borderline overwhelming case can be made for a direct influence upon dissection photography by prominent anatomical paintings, such as Rembrandt's *The Anatomy Lesson of Dr. Nicolaes Tulp* (1632), Feyen-Perrin's *Anatomy Lesson of Doctor Velpeau* (1864), or even famous anatomical illustrations, like those found in Andreas Vesalius' immeasurably revolutionary work, *De Humani corporis fabrica* (1543). But Terry was not entirely convinced. And to be honest, neither am I.

In Terry's case, he decided that while probable that medical students "photographed themselves to establish some sort of kinship with the heritage of anatomy from Vesalius onward," a direct correlation was "not self-evident."[4] The ambiguity of Terry's argument left ample opportunity for other scholars to craft conflicting or similarly situated connections between early anatomical portraiture and dissection photography. In the book *Dissection*, author James Edmonson directs a sizable portion of his analysis to confirming this very relationship. His conclusion draws significant attention to the divergent aesthetics of Vesalius' *Fabrica*, specifically, its famous title page.[5]

Prior to Vesalius' text, anatomical works featured near identical frontispieces. Each mirrored the "stylized scene of dissection" depicted in the first illustrated medical text, the *Fasciculus medicinae* (1491). The illustration in question featured "a *lector* [lecturer] … seated on a *cathedra*, or bishop's throne, reading from an anatomical text while a *sector*, or surgeon, performs the dissection in accordance with the reading."[6] The image in Vesalius' *Fabrica*, by comparison, differed greatly from the tradition spawned by the *Fasciculus medicinae*. Rather than a group of men, Vesalius is shown alone, "arrestingly" turned to "engage the viewer's gaze," singularly occupying the distinct roles essential to anatomical dissection.[7] By repositioning himself as lecturer, demonstrator, and dissector (surgeon), Vesalius effectively eschewed classic anatomical tradition, and by doing so, ushered in a new empirical (rather than purely theoretical) and progressive attitude toward human anatomy.[8]

Vesalius' *Fabrica* is traditionally celebrated as the turning point, the inauguration of modern medicine because of its establishment of anatomy as a discipline dependent on purely visual systems of identification.[9] While there is no denying commonalities exist between illustrations of dissected bodies and *photographs* of dissected bodies, one still questions whether the mimicry of certain poses – such as a cadaver standing upright without supports (or skin), or the 'father of modern human anatomy' making direct eye contact with the reader while dissecting an arm – is sufficient enough evidence to provide irrefutable proof of a direct visual lineage between the pages of Vesalius' work and the dissection photographs of the 19th century.

All things considered; I am inclined to agree with Terry's original assessment. That the relationship between dissection photography and anatomical paintings and illustrations is not entirely explicit, at least not to the degree in which we can attribute the latter as being the direct "iconographic precedent" from which dissection photography was born.[10] While anatomical traditions, specifically, those surrounding the visualization of the anatomized human body remain firmly established, an aesthetic similarity between like subjects does not automatically indicate traceable connectivity, or direct influence. Again, as Robert Stam argues, "subject matter is the weakest criterion for generic grouping because it fails to take into account *how* the subject is treated."[11]

With dissection photography and medical portraiture, commonalities seem to constitute an indexical visual heritage, an inescapable overlap resulting from the use of two-dimensional mediums in concert with common posing conventions utilizing the same base materials, in this case, dissected cadavers. But, if we overlook this factor, we find the purpose of dissection photography and medical portraiture – and if not their genesis, then at least their evolution and perpetuation – were for entirely different reasons. One reveled in the iconography of the body as an expression of the glory of God's design and

Figure 5.1: Leeds School of Medicine (United Kingdom). Unidentified photographer. Albumen print, March 1887

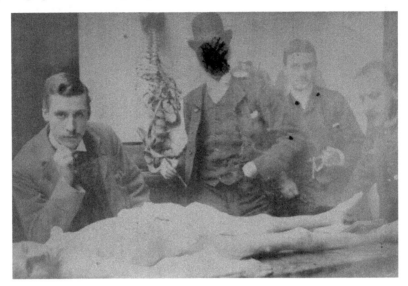

Source: Author's collection

the medical profession as equally Divine. The other frequently debased the materiality of dead flesh and the dissolution of identity to reflect upon personal achievement, technical acumen, or to express dominant beliefs and fears through gallows humor.

If anything, the stereotypical universality of posing conventions within dissection photography speaks more to the particularly limited aesthetic conventions inherent to the visual economy of anatomy. The repeated utility of these conventions in turn answer why, as Terry stated back in the 1980s, back when he believed the genre contained fewer than 50 extant examples, that "photographs taken of students in Iowa or Oklahoma closely resemble images found in Massachusetts or Maryland."[12] Indeed, even when armed with a greater knowledge of the breadth and depth of dissection photography, the near-identical similarities of posing conventions from image to image is staggering. Regardless of who, where, or how they were created, *profound similarities exist.*

That said, the marked parallels between conventions make identifying the image's location or its photographer near impossible without contextual clues – usually in the form of period notations written on the photograph's border or verso. Likewise, there exists no applicable geographically specific posing conventions (for cadavers or students) that identify one state over another, or one school over another. For example, note the similarities and differences between each of the figures in this book. If all traces of handwritten notations and photographers' stamps were removed, none of these images provide sufficient visual clues to establish location, such as that Figure I.1 was taken in a Midwestern homeopathic college in Michigan, or that Figure 5.1 was taken at the Leeds School of Medicine in the United Kingdom.

Indeed, even foreign dissection photographs can usually only be confirmed as such from non-English notations inscribed on the image's verso; or, through individual image-specific contextual clues, such as wardrobe, photographer's stamp, or collective ethnicity. However, without an awareness of these elements, images from other countries are easily mistaken as originating from the United States, or vice versa. Thus, in this case, our lack of visual fluency, in concert with period details, results in the blurring of the cultural customs and photographic traditions of various countries, regions, and schools.

Digging up the past: grave robbing and its relation to the origins of dissection photography

> My gentle reader, – start not at learning that I have been, in my time, a RESURRECTIONIST. Let not this appalling word, this humiliating confession conjure up in your fancy a throng of vampire-like images and associations, or earn your "physician's" dismissal from your hearts and hearths. It is your own groundless fears, my fair trembler! – your own superstitious prejudices that have driven me, and will drive many others of my brethren to such dreadful doings. ... You expect us to cure you of disease, and yet deny us the only means of learning how! You would have us bring you the ore of skill and experience, yet forbid us to break the soil, or sink a shaft! Is this fair, fair reader? Is this reasonable?
>
> Samuel Warren, *Affecting Scenes; Being Passages from the Diary of a Physician*, 1837[13]

Faced with an incongruous pairing of the phenomenon of dissection photography with that of ancient anatomical atlases, genre paintings, or even occupational photographs from the 1840s or 1860s, author James S. Terry turned to "a more complicated explanatory framework" that united the genre with "notions of the taboo."[14] He posited that dissection photography must have originated as some form of abject expression, some extension of, or reaction to the odious act of grave robbing – a deed as synonymous with 18th- and 19th-century medicine as dissection itself. However, by the time dissection photography solidified as a popular and quantifiable tradition in the late 1880s, many (but not all) medical schools considered grave robbing to be an obsolete and unnecessary practice – be it at the hands of paid 'resurrectionists,' or done directly by students, janitors, or professors.

Anatomical acts banning grave robbing were instituted state-by-state at varying times in American history. As argued, they effectively "put a finish to grave robbery and commerce in bodies," removed "the taint of association between ghoulish body snatchers and respectable anatomists," and provided "the state's medical colleges with a regular and cheap supply of bodies."[15] As Terry notes, "by 1881 15 of the 31 States had authorized the use of unclaimed bodies from State institutions for anatomical purposes," thus signaling the beginning of the end for grave robbing.[16] As for the other half of the country, a refusal to pass anatomical legislation necessitated the continued desecration of graves well into the 20th century. Some states, such as Louisiana and Tennessee, did not pass their anatomy acts until the 1940s.[17]

The demise of grave robbing signified a momentous change in the ways in which medical schools interacted with and were perceived by their communities. It also marked a substantial shift in the curricular activities, psychological conditioning, and affective bonds between American medical students. For those initially drawn to the study of medicine for its transgressive potential, or to obtain an exclusive authority resulting from the overriding of societal taboos, the erasure of grave robbing from popular culture must have caused quite a stir. Newly matriculated freshmen likely faced an internal struggle of epic proportions at the loss of such an abject facet of their occupational heritage. After all, grave robbing made the newspapers.

Indeed, it is hard to imagine that the elimination of an act so intrinsically linked with the greater ritual of dissection, coupled with the normalization of body acquisition through legislative acts, failed to resonate one way or the other with students of the late 19th century. A resurrectionist's work was certifiably traceable to the 'honorable' traditions of students' anatomical forefathers. For students at medical schools that no longer used illegal means to stock their dissecting rooms, did losing the opportunity to participate in the ritualized experience of grave robbing have repercussive consequences upon their educational experience? As a transgressive ritual and as a physical act, dissection, and the related act of grave robbing, distanced members of the medical profession from the general populace. Did this loss impede their psychosocial growth or obstruct identity formation by diminishing the social bonds or homosocial bonding between students and teachers? As author Michael Sappol discusses, participating in dissection and grave robbing were "not just a matter of social marking," these rituals "had cognitive and behavioral effects."[18] To learn how to be effective healers, students needed to insulate themselves from the restrictive normativity of their customary, non-medical surroundings. Thus, by failing to achieve this culturally specific form of cognitive dissonance, could the 'modern' student's perception of the cadaver as an abject construct have been altered?

As A.L. Benedict, writing of his time in medical school in the 1890s, declared: "Except to a person of obstinately refined taste, dissection may become one of the most fascinating parts of college work."[19] If the loss of grave robbing did affect cadaveric perception, how did students come to terms with such losses? Were they racked with conflicting feelings of relief and regret, jealousy and joy over their inability to not only participate in the dissection of their cadaver, but in the dangerous and abject method of its procurement?

A collective homogeneity of experience within the dissecting room bred distinctiveness outside the school. Failing to gain an equality of distinction *inside* the school, through acts like grave robbing, could have been perceived as a weakness; a professional shortfall likely heightened by criticisms, crude jokes, tall-tales, and heckling by upperclassmen or teachers. Did this in turn create a great internal divide between students who had robbed graves and those who had not? What's more, did anatomy professors view their students differently? After all, anatomists frequently engaged in the fond retelling of their own ghoulish exploits during their college years. Some even published such adventures in autobiographies.

In *I Swear by Apollo: A Life of Medical Adventure*, Dr. William E. Aughinbaugh recalled several of the times he robbed graves to make ends meet while attending medical school in Washington, D.C. in the late 1890s:

> To speak precisely, we became nocturnal grave robbers – primarily to provide ourselves with funds for an education, secondarily to insure a steady supply of stiffs. There was nothing original about our venture. Thousands of doctors of the old school had done the same things in the interests of science. … Our grave-robbing activities may seem heartless, but the lack of dissecting material was a problem that confronted every medical student of my day, and most of them solved it as we did. Few, of course conducted operations on so large a scale as we were obliged to do through financial necessity. I had no qualms of conscience. Neither had any of my associates, for it aided us in acquiring the medical knowledge needed in order to fight disease.[20]

A case could be made that with the transgressive thrill of this aspect of dissecting culture now dead, buried, and with little chance (or need) of resurrection, students were forced to restructure their relationship with their cadavers. With the existential energies resulting from their intrapsychic conflicts over grave robbing now heaped upon the dead, their attempts to fill a void of transgression, so to speak, required an equally abject, potentially dangerous, and taboo act. The old, purely verbal stories of grave robbing needed to be supplanted by a more modernized, tangible, and pervasive emblem. But all the while, one that continued to speak to their experiences on a ritualized and abject level.

In lieu of such a significant curricular and experiential divergence, it is entirely possible that dissection photography's widespread introduction in the late 1880s reaffirmed student standing within the larger visual economy and material culture of American systems of anatomical education. Reassertions of authority within these structures, seem especially pertinent in the liminal arena of the dissecting room; functioning on both practical, but mostly psychosocial and psychological grounds. This also speaks to how and why said authority was abused in certain geographic regions, like the American South, whereby postmortem violence, like grave robbing, was systematically used to terrorize African American communities. Although no proof has yet to be found that dissection photographs were reproduced or circulated through African American communities, akin to lynching photographs (which began to be barred from circulation through the United States Postal Service starting in 1908), these images still commemorated a form of postmortem defilement.[21]

Of shutters and shuddering horror

> Plain every-day and unscientific people will find it hard to overcome a feeling of shuddering horror at the idea of the bodies of human beings being shipped out two in a cask and doubled up together in such revolting manner. A human body packed up in this style and billed as "cold meat" will naturally give any sympathetic nature the creeps, and call for a protest.
>
> *The Commercial Appeal*, 1900[22]

As Terry discusses, "the psychological association between dissection and grave robbing may well have persisted long after the actual practice of the latter had ceased."[23] I would concur with this in terms of both internal and external audiences. As such, was the genre of dissection photography, born, or at least raised from this loss at this particular time in medical history, instituted to bridge the psychosocial and experiential gap left behind by grave robbing? If so, this connection provides more context – outside of sheer commemoration or technical limitations – as to why the practice of dissection photography began in earnest nearly 50 years after photography's invention in 1839, and with very little to no intermediary imagery in the preceding years, outside of students and physicians posing with skeletons and skulls in commercial photo studios.

It also points solidly to dissection photographs being conceived, as Terry says, as records "of the violation of law and taboo, portraying students with stolen goods or, at any rate, permitting that connotation" by outsiders – specifically, the same communities who formerly protested and rioted against the desecration of graves by medical students and resurrectionists.[24]

With these concepts in mind, it is quite fascinating to consider that once bodies were legally obtained, and the fear of legal consequences from being caught with a stolen body lessened exponentially, anatomy acts may have inadvertently facilitated the camera's full-scale introduction into the American dissecting room. Like Terry before me, however, I cannot give definitive answers to these questions or statements due to the lack of extant primary sources. Nor can I draw a direct link at this time between the end of grave robbing and the institution of dissection photography. Despite the consideration of grave robbing as being essential to the formation of student identity in the 19th century, and despite it helping, as Michael Sappol affirms, "to cement one's status within the band of student dissectors," this connection seems to have been rarely evidenced upon the photographic plate; be it out of fear, societal constraints, medical school mandates, or the limitations of camera technologies.[25] For what it is worth, I have no knowledge of, nor have I ever seen, photographs of students engaged in, or recreating the act of, grave robbing. This does not mean these photographs do not exist. However, to document this aspect of 'student life,' the camera would literally need to be positioned graveside. Given that body snatchers were in the midst of an illegal operation, this seems an ill-advised and technologically impractical endeavor. Moreover, magnesium flash would have been essential, thus defeating the purpose of a covert venture into a graveyard. That said, carte-de-visite portraits of infamous grave robbers, posed with their shovels, spades, and stolen skulls are extant, as are photographs of students with their school's janitors, most of whom achieved national infamy by desecrating the graves of African American cemeteries.[26]

Although the myriad fears associated with grave robbing may have contributed to the lack of dissection photographs prior to the introduction of many anatomy acts, the institution of one does not appear to have negated the practice of the other in its entirety. Fear of discovery did not stop the students in the medical department of the University of Texas, or for that matter the university's first professor of anatomy, William Keiller, from posing together for an elaborate tableau-style dissection photograph, complete with preparations of fetal skeletons, dried disembodied legs, and anatomical manikins. Students (or the photographer) positioned one of the cadavers with its face tilted directly toward the camera. If need be, identification, using the photo as proof, would have been possible. The image in question was made circa 1891. Yet, Texas did not pass its Anatomical Law, creating "a board to direct the procurement of anatomical material," until 1907, over 15 years after the dissection photograph was taken.[27]

Dissecting Black identity

On January 18, 1899, Dr. Richard Henry Whitehead (Figure 5.2), then Dean of the School of Medicine of the University of North Carolina at Chapel Hill (UNC) sat before members of the North Carolina House Judiciary Committee and offered his support of a new bill under consideration. If passed, this new "Stiff Law," as local newspapers referred to it, would provide the state's medical schools with something they desperately needed: a steady and legal supply of bodies for anatomical dissection.[28]

For almost a decade, the esteemed anatomist had been purchasing bodies "by open contract," at the rate of "$40 apiece." But recent changes in state legislation had left Whitehead with few options. "I have been buying bodies in Northern States, but I can no longer," he testified. "All the States now have laws forbidding the exportation of bodies, and no one can be found bold

Figure 5.2: Dr. Richard Whitehead and the 3rd Dissecting Club. University of Virginia (Charlottesville, Virginia). Unidentified photographer. Gelatin silver print, 1909

Note: In 1905, Whitehead left UNC to become the dean of the medical school of the University of Virginia. He is pictured here in the middle of the group (the man with the mustache). Note that the students refer to the janitor "Frank," who was responsible for the embalming and care of the school's cadaver supply, as the "Stiff Doctor."

Source: Private collection

enough to undertake it. Now I can't get them at any price, and personally I'm not going into the grave robbing business."[29]

Accompanied in the room by Dr. R.H. Lewis, of Raleigh, North Carolina, the two medical men spoke of the new law's economics. Where Whitehead had previously paid 40 dollars per body out of state, if they cut out the middleman, and acquired bodies locally and legally, the cost could be reduced to roughly ten dollars each. But regardless of financial costs, Whitehead wanted to make it clear that the "Stiff Law" would take no toll on normative society. Only the bodies of "outcasts," such as executed criminals and the unclaimed dead found in state prisons, would be used for his dissections. When his words failed to sway the committee, Whitehead attempted to allay their true concerns over cadaveric demographics, declaring that in the nine years he had been dean, only "one white person had ever been dissected in his school."[30]

★★★

While some other states had enacted anatomical legislation over 15 years before, the politics of North Carolina's Anatomy Act, and indeed, much of the American South's laws regarding the disposition of dead bodies from public institutions for anatomical dissection, had everything to do with race. For instance, at the turn of the 20th century, as African Americans increased in number and influence throughout the medical profession, laws were put into place to protect the bodies of White criminals from dissection by Black medical students. The ramifications of these regulations effectively safeguarded criminal enterprises, those who trafficked specifically in the desecration of African American cemeteries, and ensured that Black bodies, not those of poor Whites, would maintain their indispensable majority as the disposable fodder of the Southern dissecting room.

What's more, racist dogma by medical school administrations, coupled with the laws enforcing segregation, meant students of color had few choices on where they could matriculate. They either enrolled at Black schools – many of which had insufficient resources to train at the same level as White schools – or had to move North, leaving their homes and communities, to attend racially integrated schools. But even then, the presence of the African American student in the dissecting room and amphitheater was more tolerated than accepted.

During the era of the dissection photograph, nearly 50 medical schools permitted African Americans to matriculate. By 1906, there existed five schools specifically for the education of Black physicians – again mostly men. They were: Meharry Medical College of Walden University (Nashville, Tennessee), founded in 1876 and, by 1912, responsible for "at least half" of the total number of Black physicians in the South;[31] Leonard Medical School of Shaw University (Raleigh, North Carolina), organized in

1882; Flint Medical College of New Orleans University (New Orleans), founded in 1889 and considered by the infamous Flexner Report as "a hopeless affair, on which money and energy alike are wasted";[32] Louisville National Medicine College (Louisville), founded in 1887; and Howard University College (Washington, D.C.), founded as a medical department in 1868 and associated with the Freedman's Hospital, then the nation's largest hospital open to African Americans. The latter school also bears distinction for having generated a sizable quantity of dissection photographs over the years. However, this fact is tempered by the reality that fewer schools allowing Black students to attend meant fewer representations in commemorative portraiture.

Around the time dissection photography began in the 1880s, only 900 African American physicians worked in the United States (780 men and 120 women). By 1900, furthered mainly by the previously mentioned schools, this number increased over 90 percent, with "1252 living physicians" from Black schools and "213 from white [Northern] schools."[33] In 1906, the approximate midpoint of dissection photography's 50-year evolution, Southern schools, except the five founded especially for educating African Americans, still refused to admit non-White students.

Despite racial segregation and race-based injustices, the healing effect of the steadily increasing numbers of African American physicians upon their communities was felt almost immediately. "These physicians, by their skill and God's help, are doing the states, counties and cities in which they live more good than a careless observer would ever think," reported the newspapers of the times. "They are reducing the death rate of their people in all of the cities in the south in which they are located."[34]

And yet, despite such progress, plenty of schools still refused to allow Black students to matriculate. When Atlanta University sent out a flyer in the early 1900s, asking medical schools if they had any Black students or graduates, several Southern Whites-only schools answered the query through hateful tirades filled with racial slurs, which left little doubt as to their stance on the formation of Black student identity. These were not the responses of immature students, speaking out of turn based on their narrow worldviews or limited educations. Rather, replies came directly from school deans, the governors and gatekeepers of medical education and institutional heritage. Communicating on behalf of his school, Lucien Claude McElwee, Dean of the Homeopathic Medical College of Missouri, and President of the Missouri State Board of Health, proclaimed: "If you are looking for 'n____rs' go to Boston or other 'n____r' loving communities. *None*, thank God!! *None*, by God, sir!! And what's more, there never will be any *here*."[35] Meanwhile, the administration of the Medical Department of the University of Georgia (Augusta), known for purchasing enslaved men and then paying them modest fees to rob graves in African American cemeteries to supply their dissecting tables, likewise declared: "There are no n____rs in this school and there never have been and there never will be as long as one stone of its building remains upon another."[36]

With such stringent discriminatory rulings in effect, dissection photographs of African American students could only have been taken at one of two places: A racially inclusive school in the North, or, more likely, at one of the five Southern schools designed solely for the training of Black physicians. In the case of Southern schools, students appear to have had the same levels of agency over how they wished to be portrayed in the dissecting room as Whites. Indeed, African American medical students posed with the dead according to standard preestablished photographic conventions. As proof that professional medical identity superseded even racial identity, they likewise wrote cheeky and transgressive epigraphs upon their dissecting tables the same as White students (Figure 5.3). Though none of their messages or posing conventions sought to degrade the race of the dead, they did occasionally joke around with the bodies, placing scalpels in their hands or engaging in the 'cadaver as future self' trope.

However, while representative agency encompassed *how* Black students were photographed in the dissecting room, it did not extend to *who* they could be photographed dissecting. According to some state laws, Black students were legally only allowed to dissect Black cadavers.

Figure 5.3: "HE LIVED for others and Died for US." Unknown school (likely Meharry or Howard University). Unidentified photographer. Gelatin silver print, circa 1910

Note: The students dissect inside what appears to be a wooden shack. This structure was no doubt separate from the school and built in a secluded section of the campus.

Source: Private collection

In the South, African American communities had to maintain separate funeral homes, separate cemeteries, and even separate dissecting rooms. In 1903, North Carolina adopted its first iteration of an anatomy act, numbered (rather ridiculously) Chapter 666. Described as "an act to regulate the procuring and distribution of dead bodies for the promotion of medical science," this new law made three major points. The first, that only the dead bodies of incarcerated criminals who had no family were to be turned over for dissection – specifically, those "under the penalty of death, imprisonment or hard labor for the violation of the criminal laws of the State." Second, that the dead body of a former Confederate soldier – even if imprisoned or a patient at a state hospital – was to be exempt from the provisions of the act and given a proper burial. And third, "that the body of no white person shall be delivered to any school for colored race."[37] Therefore, White students could dissect White or Black cadavers, while Black students could only dissect their own kind. This not only established a racial hierarchy but ensured that White schools were sufficiently stocked with cadavers before those that admitted Black students.

We will likely never know the full impact this law had upon the formation of the identities of North Carolina's Black medical students, or its effect upon the state's African American population. Presumably, if there was a steady supply of cadavers, and they could continue their educations without interruption, Black students were at least partially satisfied in their work. And yet, being legally *forced* to dissect your own kind bespoke of an entirely different rite of passage than dissecting those same bodies by chance or circumstance. How does one not look upon the race of the cadaver as an extension of oneself when one's surrounding community uses racial laws to prohibit economic and educational growth; and then draws distinct color lines to ensure the continued dehumanizing treatment of both the living and the dead? After all, under the public laws of North Carolina, so long as they were White, the bodies of convicted murders and rapists on death row, shunned by society, unloved by family, and unwanted by friends, now had more agency over the disposition of their mortal remains, and more legal protections against their unwanted dissection, than the bodies of free African Americans.

6

A Necessary Inhumanity

On Halloween night in the year 1900, a "crowd of medical students" from the University of Michigan Department of Medicine and Surgery raced back to their dorms under the cover of darkness.[1] With their devious plan implemented, and their filthy clothes – soiled from the dissecting room and their nocturnal adventure – now changed, each one dove straight into bed, eager for the coming of the dawn.

The following morning began just like any other. The medical department's janitor arrived early and proceeded to make his usual rounds, unlocking doors and tidying up as he went. But on entering the dissecting room, he noticed something was not right, something was missing. No, make that some*one*. During the night, "the crowd of medical students" had "spirited away" one of his cadavers.[2]

Meanwhile, across campus, a college attendant made his way toward the university's main hall. As he approached the entrance, he spied something propped against the building's folding doors. It had an unnatural anthropomorphic silhouette and emitted a pungent odor that stung his eyes and nostrils. Drawing nearer, the attendant soon realized that there, 'facing' him, stood a "headless corpse of a woman" – the stolen cadaver – her body "still swathed in the antiseptic bandages" of the dissecting room.[3]

Exactly how many students or staff witnessed the beheaded cadaver before it was 'spirited' back to the spirits of the embalming tank is lost to history. However, the incident caused enough of a stir that it made both local and national news. Reports called it "a grewsome joke" by area medical students, one that set a new record for "Hallowe'en Pranks" – implying cadaveric hijinks of this nature were an annual occurrence at the University of Michigan. But it wasn't just the act itself that had everyone so upset this time. Tales circulated of a further transgression. For unlike previous medical mischiefs, rumor had it there was tangible proof of this year's macabre scene in the form of a photograph, "taken at sunrise" by one of the medical students.[4]

★★★

As Horace Montgomery once wrote: "At the growing edge of human knowledge moral dilemmas multiply."[5] For a society to move forward, it must leave something of itself behind. Famed author and historian Ruth Richardson discusses in her pioneering work, *Death, Dissection and the Destitute*, that anatomical knowledge by dissection required in its student practitioners "the effective suspension or suppression of many normal physical and emotional responses," in order to conduct "the willful mutilation of the body of another human being."[6] In the modern era, the suppression of emotional response is commonly referred to as clinical detachment. In the 18th century, legendary physician and anatomist, William Hunter described it as "a kind of necessary inhumanity."[7]

As a "harrowing ritual of initiation," one that "left the participant forever changed," dissection set students apart from the conservative ideological matrices of normative society.[8] Within their own ranks, it served as the principal authoritative procedure for medical professionals to measure, on physical and psychosocial levels, the affective bonds and formative boundaries of their identities, specifically, those of recent inductees.[9] Therefore, as objects that visualized bodily objectification allied with a ritual of transformative, transgressive, and even transcendent power, the dissection photograph stood as silent witness to a "moral, and professional boundary crossing."[10]

This boundary was traversed by students both male and female, Black and White. That said, during the era of the dissection photograph, American medical and dental schools were the domain of White Christian men. In keeping with their significant majority, this same demographic were the dominant consumers and benefactors of dissection photography's use in the formation of identity.

As a collective group, the White male majority were an undisciplined, "irresponsible and unsophisticated" lot, emotionally trapped somewhere between the immaturity of adolescence and the God-complex of a sociopathic surgeon: "Constantly on the alert for something to laugh at."[11] Unruly hordes were known to race through the halls of their schools, scampering away from the scene of a terrible prank, or rushing to join a brawl, usually involving freshmen and upperclassmen. Indeed, when the need arose to preserve their authority or restore a sense of self-imposed order, upperclassmen frequently instigated group fights with first-year students. The majority of these conflicts were rambunctious jests, amounting to little more than bruised egos and, on occasion, a few bruised lips and elbows. In 1910, a student was "knocked through" a glass door at Jefferson Medical College, but he sustained no real injuries.[12] When these 'playful' bouts escalated to the point of drawing blood, faculty wasted no time in providing a medical dressing to those involved, followed by a very public dressing-down of the culprits. However, their reprimands usually stopped there. In rare and extreme cases, local police were called to the school to intervene.[13]

Despite infighting among the classes, incoming students were considered the lifeblood of a school. They restored its culture with an essential infusion of enthusiasm, humor, and seemingly indefatigable energy. When they were not studying for exams, they engaged in team-building activities, rushed fraternities, played organized sports against other schools, or socialized in the dissecting room. In major cities, equal time was spent 'educating' oneself to the more socially unacceptable behaviors of gambling (aka 'rolling bones'), chasing after women, and smoking. As a means to cope with the offensive smells of the dissecting room, many a student took up the 'taboo' of smoking, chewing, and "the use of the weed."[14] The Sigma Theta Chi fraternity of the University of California Dental Department even founded a "Star" brand tobacco club, which met the first Saturday of the month in the school's dissecting room – where the smell would not offend anyone's senses.[15]

But once the winter weather set in and the doors to the even colder dissecting room were thrown open, everything and everyone changed. Make that, they changed for the worst. As the students at Wake Forest College Medical School attested: "When the work of dissection began, the morals of the whole were slightly lowered."[16] The environs of the dissecting room were now 'in bounds' as part of the students' proverbial playground. Professional and transgressive behaviors pivoted focus from coping with the tribulations caused by upperclassmen, to surviving interactions with the cadaver, the proverbial bane of their academic and social lives.

Many handled these situations in the only way they knew how, by engaging in dark humor. "I am very much afraid that some of the 'Medics' now here are unruly," confessed student Franklin Wilson, about the medical students at Bowdoin College (Brunswick, Maine). Upon waking in the spring of 1852, locals discovered the cadaver of a 16-year-old boy, "sitting naked in the crotch of a tree," in the green space of Brunswick's principal street. Some believed the "dirty trick" must have been perpetrated by a master thief, a wraith-like entity, who stole the dead body in the dead of night from the nearby medical school. But student Wilson, like many of the learned townsfolk, knew the truth: "no one but a Medic would do it."[17]

From year to year, and semester to semester, students were known to change their clothes, political affiliations, hairstyles, and facial hair. But during the era of the dissection photograph, one thing remained constant: their behavior toward the cadaver. In the fall of 1910, nearly ten years after the aforementioned headless body was stolen on Halloween night, medical students from the same school, the University of Michigan Department of Medicine and Surgery, pushed the remains of a cadaver out of a second-story window onto a group of co-eds who were studying below. Apparently, the group sought revenge upon the innocent "girls" because they refused to flirt with them. According to area newspapers: "The young women fled screaming."[18]

Stealing headless cadavers made headlines. However, in truth, socially transgressive behavior of this magnitude was only one component of a male student's burgeoning professional identity. Beneath a calm façade of boyish exuberance, many were academically and socially "demoralized" by the great and terrible demands heaped upon them. As mentioned previously, many left during the semester break, never to return. Those that did come back often lived day-to-day with "quaking hearts" over an unshakable fear of failure; be it, failing themselves, their families, or the dominant fraternalist culture of the American medical school.[19]

Extreme failure resulted in ridicule by teachers and ostracization by classmates. During this era, many students joined the medical profession under protest of church and family, and thus, underwent and completed their training without an external support system, or the ability to seek absolution or reassurances about their chosen profession and its existential trials – like the formidable stressors of anatomical dissection. To survive, students formed quick bonds with one another or turned to more forgiving family members, like an aunt, sister, or younger brother – often the intended recipient of a mischievous messaged dissection postcard. Although married couples were in the minority, some did have the rare opportunity to gain experiential support from their student spouses.

Despite strong opposition from his family, Augustus Edwin Smith entered Jefferson Medical College in fall 1906. His older brother, Melvin, vehemently "disapproved" of him studying medicine. What's more, he "more than frowned upon" the fact that Edwin's wife, Elizabeth Cisney-Smith, would not only journey with him to the bustling city of Philadelphia, but was determined to become a doctor as well, ultimately joining the ranks of the nearby Woman's Medical College of Pennsylvania, the nation's first degree-granting medical school for women.[20] Upon learning of the couple's combined plans, Edwin's father became "so righteously mad" that "he took to his bed for a few days."[21] At risk of being effectively ostracized from the family unit, Edwin and Elizabeth were forced to make the final plans to attend their medical colleges in secret.

Many of the students at this time were neither wealthy, nor came from families of means. This stands counter to the conceptions of class and privilege we commonly associate with members of the medical profession today. In the case of Edwin and Elizabeth Smith, the couple could only afford to move to Philadelphia, and pay for their schooling, after selling their home, described as a quaint "little farm," along with all its furnishings, including "every last pot and tub."[22] Interestingly enough, Edwin, an amateur photographer, kept his collection of cameras.

Cruel winter: hazing rituals and the American dissecting room

Fear, apathy, confusion. At the onset of their educations, many students showed a complete lack of discipline when it came to committing themselves fully to the difficult road ahead. Reflecting upon their "unpropitious beginning," the Class of 1918 of Wake Forest considered themselves near pestilential in character, decreeing, "we inflicted Wake Forest with ourselves."[23]

Collectively, incoming students were a "non-homogeneous body," comprised of "individual members of which presented many different phases of humanity in their varied teachings, ambitions, deportments, and addresses."[24] While privileged in their own ways and impassioned to create a future for themselves for the betterment of humankind, medical tradition dictated first-year students be "absorbed and mastered" before being purified, reshaped, and born anew.[25]

This was not a religious rebirth of the soul but a reincarnation of professional identity. During their final days of matriculation, many a graduating class reflected upon and paid homage to their personal growth at the hands of their educators. "It has been nearly four years now since we were born," remarked the University of Virginia's Medical Class of 1911.[26] The language here – while easily construed as slightly cultish in its application – suggests an experiential transformation that existed utterly adjacent to their former lives. The external lay world played no part in such processes. In fact, transformation not only signaled the birth of a new identity but heralded the death of the old. Were such transformations present at the turn of the 21st century, a potential class yell might have been: "Long live the new flesh!"[27]

The first signs of new life began on the first days of school. Incoming students at Tulane Medical College (New Orleans) were knighted with the title of "embryonic 'les docteurs' of the order of Aesculapius."[28] Looking back on their former selves, the sophomores of the Philadelphia College of Osteopathic Medicine were but eager "neophytes" ready to start life anew by stepping through the transformative "portals" of their school.[29] Indeed the notion of the school as a transformative womb was embedded into the medical culture of the times. "As you gaze at us today, ladies and gentlemen, you will find difficulty in recognizing us," announced senior Henry Linn Bassett to the crowd of the 1901 graduation ceremony at Jefferson Medical College. "With our portly airs and proud appearances, the verdant lambs of but four short-long, bitter-sweet twelve months ago. Then we were indeed lambs, gathered from all quarters of the globe under the one shepherd, – our *Alma Mater*, – forsaking other cherishing mothers, both literally and figuratively."[30]

To this point, dissection photographs became an integral part of this process of forsaking. They served as a memento of an intensely formative time in students' lives. But more specifically, they evidenced in an exacting manner a singular recallable moment of student rebirth: the precise transitional instant of separation from and abandonment of their birthmothers (those who brought them into the world as laymen); immediately followed by the smothering embrace of the bosom of science herself, their new mothers (their new lives as professionals).

Indeed, motifs of transformation and rebirth were not confined to the bodies of the dead. At the forefront of these processes was the "embryonic" student whose pursuit of knowledge brought about a profound metamorphosis; transmuting humble beginnings and even lowlier identity into that of the learned ordained physician.[31] Although the rigors of medical school were life-changing, none more so than anatomical dissection. The transformative potential of the act operated on large and small scales, being both public and private, collective and individual, emotional and cognitive, subtle and explicit. Changes of this kind, on any level, required the rejection of the former self. With the introduction of photography, these transformations became literal embodiments of identity, giving students reason and purpose to evoke the ancient Delphic aphorism, *nosce te ipsum*, to 'know thyself'; to know their *new* identities.

Some students chose to reflect upon the symbolic meaning of this maxim by devoting themselves fully to ensuring the prosperity of the human race. Others took it literally, inscribing the very words on the side of their dissecting table; a direct reference to "the shared corporeality of dissector and dissected," or most assuredly, to "knowing the new sense of self" acquired through the transformative ritual of dissection.[32] But before they could avail themselves of this new identity, first things first, students had to learn their rightful place within the confines of their new world.

To assimilate properly into the cultural hegemony of their school, a student's first step was to learn the rules and traditions of the new regime, both academically and socially. This was, again, a lesson customarily taught by an eager, albeit pitiless corps of upperclassmen. Ritual hazing by the upper classes was not only common but considered normative behavior at medical and dental schools across the United States. Under the lens of the modern moral microscope, these rituals are nothing less than physical and emotional torture. As an accepted rite of *their* passage to becoming upperclassmen, hazing – mainly by sophomores and juniors – needed to jumpstart acculturation to the world (and underworld) of anatomy. From day one, Yale's "sneering" upperclassmen took delight in grinding down "ambitious, half-frightened, worry-worn Freshmen."[33] Subjecting them to the literal filth of the dissecting room – and in as abject a way as possible – was considered a time-honored tradition, designed to further identity formation and build character by separating 'the men from the boys.'

Hazing rituals crossed various social and cultural boundaries and functioned more like punitive pranks than modes of relevant experiential conditioning. Like the dissection photograph that evolved to be more than just pure commemoration, hazing rituals increased in their severity until they became something 'other.' In these instances, the point was not about intimidation or culture shock. Upperclassmen sought revenge. As one student recalled of his first year at the University of Maryland in 1897:

> Under the guise of being very accommodating, a Soph, would kindly take one of us and initiate him into the "sacred room of skull and bones." We were told to carry something to eat, such as peanuts, as everybody had to eat in the dissecting room to overcome the effects of the sights, etc. How he would have the creepy feeling, which can be better understood when felt, and his horror can only be imagined when in diving down into his pockets his hand would suddenly come in contact with something cold and clammy, and he would fish out a few fingers, or an ear of a departed fellow-being, placed there by a generous Soph. How the latter delighted to see that look, and know that the Freshman's cardio-inhibitory center in the pneumogastric nerve had been excited, causing a slowing or stoppage of the heart's action. Oh! His revenge was sweet, and he could look back on the day when he was made to feel the same way.[34]

It is here that the dissecting room descended further into the realm of the abject. In these contexts, it became a transgressive arena of cyclical knowledge production paired with cyclical methods of psychological torture; dissection itself, rendered both conditioning and punitive in nature. Only this time, punishment for the living, not the dead.

As previously mentioned, violence factored heavily in these initiative customs and appears to have been an accepted component of sophomore identity. In 1930, the "untamed" sophomore class of Tulane University was depicted in the school yearbook as a raving band of "wild Indians," issuing bloodthirsty cries while brandishing knives and tomahawks.[35] The violence upperclassmen instigated varied in severity from throwing impudent freshmen down staircases, pitching eggs at whomever went against the student majority on new school rules, to using dissecting instruments to forcibly alter the facial hair of non-seniors who refused to shave.[36] When it came time to exploit the abject significance of the dead as a means to torture or denigrate the living, a common sophomore tactic involved locking newly arrived 'Freshies' inside dissecting rooms piled high with disembodied limbs and headless cadavers.

As misguided as these rituals were, the perception of the times was that their design reinforced the importance of proper student etiquette, be it in the dissecting room or the lecture hall. Know thyself; know thy place. In 1896, first-year students at Hahnemann Medical College, tossed one of their own into a vat of embalming fluid. The offending classmate had a penchant for interrupting their professor during clinic. This intolerable behavior set his fellow students' blood to boil. To put him in his proper place after class – literally – a mob of students grabbed the 'fresh' freshman, rushed him upstairs to the dissecting room, and "soused him into the pickling vat" where cadavers were being prepared for dissection. The hazing concluded with both freshmen and sophomores lecturing the obdurate student about his lack of "professional ethics" during clinic.[37]

Instilled with an innate sense of authority over and responsibility for the social behaviors of incoming students, upperclassmen often gave first years outlandish or degrading tasks to complete. Once, to obey the orders of their "august" senior class, freshmen in the Medical Department of Yale University had to "carefully" save "all the fat" carved from their collective cadavers. At the semester's end, to demonstrate their submission to the dominant transformative culture of the school, they were told to present the saved fat to their anatomy instructor, who, to no one's surprise, was neither amused by the act, nor in a position to do anything about it.[38]

Again, be it by situation or choice, school administrators held little sway over the student body with regards to the pranks they pulled on each other, or upon the dead. One therefore wonders what degree of influence upperclassmen exerted over the types of dissection photographs first years could or could not take? Were some of the more grotesque and disrespectful poses taken against their will, and thus, at the command of and design by their elders? Or, as a time-honored tradition associated with identity formation – not to be confused with a rite of passage; we know students did not hold these as sacred as they said – was dissection photography on par with the tradition of hazing; perceived as an inviolable right, a communal ritual of brotherhood, and therefore, too sacred to profane?

Let all men be brothers

Despite the generational obstacles between first years and upperclassmen, generally speaking, *actual* anatomical dissection did in fact bring about an innate sense of brotherhood between the classes. As the students of the Chicago College of Dental Surgery stated: "The dissecting room gave us a chance to get acquainted."[39] At the University of Maryland, students learned more about each other during dissections then they did the study of anatomy: "It was while working here that the bond of friendship was more securely welded. It was here that we came to know one another better and to feel the ties that bound us together."[40]

Although it manifested in different ways, expressing camaraderie through dissection photography was of the utmost importance to students. Friendship was articulated through a variety of conventional poses, including, but not limited to, standing shoulder-to-shoulder, embracing one another, smiling together, or outright laughing (usually because of something done to the cadaver).

In many cases, this collegiality was extended toward the cadaver itself. Once dissected, the dead body was no longer an outsider deserving of ridicule. For instance, at Wake Forest College Medical School, a group of six white coat-clad students gathered for a dissection postcard around a cadaver propped against a classroom wall. Behind its fragmented skull, the students hung a handmade sign, which read: "The Brotherhood of Man." Naturally, this 'brotherhood' extended itself to the living. But in this 'family' tableau, membership also incorporated cadavers and anatomical preparations, including a flayed cadaver, its lungs pulled out of the torso and inverted toward its shoulders, making it look as if it had angel wings; an articulated skeleton, shown draped over a student's lap in a suggestive pose (implying it might be female); a severed head; what appeared to be a South American shrunken head; and the cadaver of an eyeless child sat upon a student's knee.[41] A poem, written by one of the 'Brotherhood,' accompanies the image, a solemn reflection upon the collective relationships of this unconventional convention of symbolic unity: "Here we toil while man weeps / 'Tis not for us but others / Then may all animosities sleep / And let all men be brothers."[42]

Seeing the dissected as essential dynamic players in this prospective 'brotherhood' became an increasingly popular posing convention throughout dissection photography's evolution. However, it should be noted that it is rare to see the remains of identifiably Black cadavers integrated in a respectful way into the 'iconography' of White human-cadaveric brotherhood. After all, during the reign of the dissection photograph, racial segregation was the law in the American South. Confusingly, while these images suggest an opportunity for students to create a greater sense of equality, or at bare minimum, to show a modicum of respect toward the dead, most displayed themes of 'brotherhood' ironically, creating humor-driven tableaus using fragmented cadavers as a literal way to undercut all forms of corporeal and societal 'togetherness.'

★★★

Many students travelled considerable distances to study medicine, be it to new towns, cities, or states. Often, they were "strangers in a strange land," acclimating to a transitional life all their own while on their own; "jostled and snubbed by everyone."[43] Upperclassmen gave first years little time to acclimate to their new surroundings. Compliance to the rules was immediate and unceremonious, no matter whether these systems were an endemic part of the American medical education system, or exclusive to an individual school's cultural practices.

For example, a number of schools forbade incoming students from growing or maintaining facial hair until their senior year. Beards were symbols associated with the identity of seniors and ordained physicians only. "Some of us ... tried to raise a beard," confessed freshmen at the University of Maryland in 1897, "and one of our member succeeded very well, and took a kind of sub-rosa enjoyment in being taken for a doctor by the patients in the dispensary. He was, of course, the pride of the Class."[44] But as we shall see, by 1901, that pride would turn to shame.

Within the microcosm of medical professionalism, specific traits, like beards or top hats, denoted one's occupational standing. Incoming first years, those who had yet to cut their professional teeth by way of cutting cold flesh, were told to cut their hair and adopt "a hirsute adornment" in order to properly reflect their nascent position within medical culture.[45]

A first year growing a beard or mustache stood in open defiance of cultural tradition. If they subsequently refused to shear off their facial hair and conform to custom, they were labelled troublemakers. As the status quo needed to be maintained, eventually, these student agitators would be assaulted by upperclassmen, taken up into the dissecting room – the locus of abject behavior and student identity – held down, and forcibly shaven with dissecting instruments. In 1901 this very thing happened at the previously mentioned University of Maryland. Ironically, right under the nose of a group of students who were in the middle of taking their dissection photograph. As *The Sun* (New York) reported:

BALTIMORE, Md, Feb. 17. — The sophomores at the University of Maryland in this city have a rule prohibiting members of the class from wearing mustaches. Henry Schurman, a student, disregarded the edict. He was accordingly inveigled into the dissecting room, where the class was being photographed behind a cadaver. Schurman's entrance was the signal for a general rush in his direction. He was seized and tightly held while Guy P. Asper, one of the sophomores, snatched up a pair of clippers and in a twinkling, Schurman's luxuriant mustache was off. Schurman swore out a warrant for Asper's arrest and the case was heard before Justice Poe at the Western station this morning. The squire said he was not up on the value of mustaches, but judged one to be worth $25. He imposed this fine, which was paid.[46]

Waste not want not

In the dissecting room of the 1890s, wasting time was a favored pastime. An uncommon, but nevertheless fatal mistake for any student of anatomy, was to reject proper training on how to dissect, or to dismiss the importance of dissection altogether. Some argued over the particulars of the act. "It has sometimes been urged that the student should not dissect until he has learned something of anatomy," debated the Buffalo-based physician–dentist, W.C. Barrett.[47] "This argument would be cogent if the object were to learn how to dissect. But we dissect to learn anatomy, and do not learn anatomy to discover how best to dissect."[48]

Many prominent physicians strenuously disagreed with Barrett's sentiment, positioning that the technical aspects of learning *how* to cut needed to be concurrent with the *where* and *what* they were cutting. Competent dissecting guaranteed professional success. The acquisition of anatomical knowledge or technical proficiency (such as proper blade handling) had real-life applications. After all, skills learned among the dead transferred over to the living.

As the eminent surgeons, Heath and Keen, reminded their readers: "The student will do well to bear in mind that [they] will probably be called upon … to operate on the living body, the only true preparation for which is careful dissection."[49] Notable country doctor, Arthur Hertzler, emphatically concurred, stating that the bulk of the nation's timid "poky" surgeons resulted from their "lack of anatomical knowledge"; essential skills that should have been gained in medical school. "A couple of years spent in the dissecting room will save time in later years by increasing operating speed. Also – it is better for the patient."[50] Hertzler's words touch upon an important aspect of dissection and its photographic commemoration that cannot be undervalued: students gained technical competency, such as specialized operative techniques, to save the living by perfecting them *first* on the dead. To many, the cadaver was their first patient. To others, it was nothing more than their first "Stiff."[51]

Regardless of how one viewed their cadaver, the sentiment of the dead in service to the living is just as relevant today as it was in the era of the dissection photograph. For example, a few years ago, while observing a laminectomy demonstration on a cadaver, I witnessed a medical student dig too deeply into its back to remove a portion of a lumbar vertebra – a necessary procedure in order to reveal the spinal canal. "You've pushed too deep," informed the visiting neurosurgeon in a matter-of-fact tone, softened at the end with a knowing smile. "That's why we practice. But, if this man was still alive, he'd likely be paralyzed now." The student who improperly excavated the vertebra furrowed his brow, apologized needlessly, and handed his instrument to the student standing next to him. As he backed away from the body, he said aloud to the group: "I'm so happy this guy's dead."

Traversing the land of the dead

To the students of the late 19th century, within the scientifically sanctioned environment of the dissecting room, the cadaver existed not only as a formerly living person, but as an uncanny 'thing'; that which functions through the revelation of its abject nature. Such thinking required one to mentally overcome metaphysical ideas of death through a physical proximity to the deceased. The objectification or dehumanization of the dead body (within reason) was essential for the cadaver's utilization in the obtainment of medical knowledge. But, as Ruth Richardson notes, be it on physical or metaphysical levels, "the ability to regard the human corpse as an object of close physical study represents a cultural detachment of no small dimension."[52]

Therefore, for students to formulate their new professional identity and adapt to their surroundings, a litany of defensive techniques and conditioning through medical socialization were necessary. Humor, specifically dark humor, was (generally) considered a mature response. Not only for its effectiveness, but it was cheap and easy to come by. As dental students from the University of California declared in the late 1890s: "The relaxation of a moment of humor is medicine."[53]

Involvement in the rite of dissection signaled a singular moment in the formation of a medical student's identity. Regardless of race, sex, or religious affiliation, it proclaimed their induction into the collective fold of medical professionalism. "When we were admitted to the dissecting room we felt like doctors for sure," remarked the Class of 1905 at the University of Maryland School of Medicine. "We used to swell with pride when we boarded a street car and saw the ladies turn up their noses while they whispered to one another, 'I'll bet he is a medical student'."[54] As a profoundly transformative act, dissection stimulated the reconfiguration and rebirth of identity. At the onset of training, most students walked into their dissecting rooms feeling as though they had entered "the land of the dead never to return."[55] But, once acclimated to the sights and smells of the cadaver, once they understood the significance of their participation, their views routinely changed "from one of dread to one of enthusiasm."[56] Such revelations – commonly a mixture of awe and fear – were confessed by students across the nation. For instance, the Class of 1915 of Tulane University recalled entering their freshmen year with "all the enthusiasm of youth." Yet after being "confronted by the difficulties of the dissecting room," the gravity of their situation made them realize, "we had branched out upon an entirely new path of life."[57]

Dissection bound a student to their fellow initiates and to legions of anatomists from centuries past. The longer they toiled in human flesh, the quicker their transformation. "For who can describe the changes which take place in a man while he is being transformed from a Freshman into a Sophomore?" asked the Class of 1905 at the University of Maryland.[58]

Who indeed? For the identity that entered the dissecting room and was tempered in that crucible of flesh and death was not the same as what came out. Students knew this. They felt this. Photography captured this.

While the dissection photograph confirmed a new stage of professional affiliation for students, by literally fixing their identities to a tangible substrate, identity itself was not permanent. Keep in mind that by their own admission, a student's time in the dissecting room was transient; the first stop on a "road to maturity."[59]

What's more, during this era, medical training was not standardized. Ranging from the wretched to the sublime, dissecting facilities varied state-to-state and city-to-city. Until the late 1890s, many schools forbid men and women from dissecting together. Some barred men from attending female patients altogether. For instance, as late as 1909, male students at the College of Physicians and Surgeons (Los Angeles), were not permitted into the obstetrical ward of their school's adjoining hospital. By 1930, coeducational schools had become the vast majority, but they were still not universal. The last two single-sex schools in the country would not go co-ed until the 1970s.

★★★

Humorous hijinks, be they with each other, or with the dead, guided students through the (then) necessary processes of suppressing the horror of the cadaver's new objectivity. For many this was a critical step. Societal norms deemed such transgressions morally and ethically reprehensible. Only after joking about death could they muster the courage to overcome the cadaver's former subjectivity.

Photography was merely one of several transgressive tools at students' disposal. The Class of 1905 at Tulane Medical College routinely bellowed ritualized excitations around campus, commonly called 'Class Yells,' which reinforced the guiding principles of their cultural detachment toward both layman and cadaver alike:

> Sick man, well man, dead man, stiff,
> Dig 'em up, cut 'em up, what's the diff;
> Humerus, tumorous, dead or alive,
> Tulane Medical College – 1905.[60]

Countless variables contributed to the degree to which a student objectified their cadaver. These included individual or familial morals and principles as well as the overall social climate of a school's dissecting room. Customarily, the anatomy professor or demonstrator set the tone of this liminal space in terms of the reinforcement of or resistance to the cadaver's status as a formerly living being.

During the last quarter of the 19th century, compassion toward the dissected dead was considered anathema to the process of effective anatomical investigation. Such thinking could hinder a student's own psychological progression and thereby inhibit their complete indoctrination into the medical profession. Thus, dehumanization, to the point of seeing past personhood, was deemed acceptable. Commemorating and commenting upon this process through a novel visual technology, such as the amateur camera, was equally tolerated, with no known enforced restrictions.

Processes of indoctrination and 'coping' have changed drastically since the era of the dissection photograph. In the 1890s, students selected their cadavers methodically, but dispassionately. Dissecting teams or 'clubs' were formed, made up of between four to six students each. Team members preemptively selected the body part they wanted to dissect first; the most common denominator being, "which to [their] mind seemed the easiest to begin with." When the day finally came for students to enter the dissecting room for the first time, they received no introduction, guidance, or fanfare. As students at Yale University School of Medicine recalled in 1898: The doors swung open, "we rushed in."[61] The whole encounter played out with such apathy, it could almost border on farce.

In those days, students chose their own cadavers. Upon entering the room, they were instructed to stroll around to the different tables and inspect the virtues and flaws of the dead, like how one might select livestock, or a piece of ripe fruit. "Some kept their hands carefully in their pockets, others pinched and handled the arms and legs, discussing their merits with a great show of coolness."[62] Once the selection process was over, the students left the room in silence.

The culture(s) surrounding the selection of cadavers in turn established yet another layer of student ownership over the dead. Once a cadaver was chosen, a perceived power relation was conferred; an incontrovertible 'right.' To those who embraced this exploitative aspect of the power relations in American dissecting culture, feeling guilt or shame over their scholastic exploits probably never crossed their minds. Regardless of its use as an educational tool or a quasi-photographic prop, the cadaver was theirs, plain and simple.

7

No One Ever Did: Dissection Photography and Female Identity

Some things I find not so trying as I expected or at any rate you become used to them soon – dissection for instance. I confess I dreaded that, yet thought thus far I have only watched it, I find that when the spirit of scientific research and inquiry is roused, you soon lose sight of all the rest. But then, from what I hear of it in other colleges I have no doubt that a dissection as managed by women is a very different matter from one under the charge of male attendants. Every possible precaution is taken to spare the senses and feelings of those engaged in it.

Harriet "Hallie" Gilliland Belcher, Woman's Medical College of Pennsylvania student, 1879[1]

Contrary to popular belief, by the time dissection photography became a ubiquitous tradition by 1900, it was not uncommon for women to study medicine, nor to see women populating dissection photographs; be they intermixed in crowds at coeducational schools or comprising the totality of dissectors within single-sex dissecting rooms. The nation's first degree-granting medical school for women, the Woman's Medical College of Pennsylvania (WMCP), was founded in Philadelphia in 1850, roughly 30 years before dissection photography effectively 'began.' Fortunately, sizable collections of dissection photographs are extant from this school and include some of the genre's earliest examples showing female dissectors. The largest single collection, the scrapbook of WMCP medical student, Alice Evans, dates from the 1890s, and is, what I consider to be, one of the most historically significant caches of dissection photographs known today.

Since the 1890s, student amateur photographers at WMCP used photography to construct more personal iterations of their identities using conventions that were near-identical to their male counterparts (Figure 7.1). Countless examples exist showing women posed according

Figure 7.1: "Elizabeth at Medical College." Woman's Medical College of Pennsylvania (Philadelphia, Pennsylvania). Unidentified photographer. Gelatin POP, circa 1895

Source: Author's collection

to the preestablished male-dominant conventions of Stage I and Stage II: standing in rows behind their tables, holding scalpels, or adopting working attitudes.

In rare instances, WMCP students engaged in initiative hazing rituals – minus the inherent physical violence native to the schools of men – and, in similar fashion, used the abject nature of the dissecting room to test the dedication and emotional maturity of incoming students. In fall 1906, first-year Elizabeth Cisney-Smith and her classmates were, as she wrote in her diary, "initiated" to the WMCP dissecting room. Per tradition, on the first day of dissection, a crowd of older students assembled in the third-floor hall, just outside the door to the gross lab, to see which of the "squeamish" freshmen might faint at the sight of a cadaver. Much to their dismay, when the draped dead were dramatically uncovered with a flourish of fresh white sheets, not a single new student collapsed. Stated Smith proudly, "no one ever did in my class."[2]

★★★

A cursory review of coeducational dissection photographs shows a host of similarities existed between the posing conventions of men and women.

However, there are a few significant differences; intent being one of them. Conceptually, women posed with cadavers, and each other, in part to free themselves from the limiting conventions of centuries of anatomical imagery, a visual heritage (constructed by men) that "desired to place them in the eternal role of the dissected, never the dissector."[3] Indeed, since the time of Vesalius, up through the end of the 19th century, male students and physicians believed that when it came to participation in anatomical dissection, a woman's role was twofold: to be absent from the dissecting room, or to be dead upon its tables.[4]

Much has been written on the prejudices women faced in joining the medical profession in the 1850s and 1860s. Generally, dissecting rooms of the late 19th and early 20th centuries were grotesque, filthy spaces. With no long-term means of preserving human remains or administrative oversight to police morally questionable behaviors (usually involving the cadaver), these rooms were filled with "the rotting bodies of the dead and the equally rotten behaviors of the living."[5] According to public opinion, such an environment was no place for a woman. Thus, within the confines of the American medical school, many "wise men and honorable women" feared for the purity of the female form and psyche.[6]

Always the dissected, never the dissector

> One day a man, his wife and a small baby called to see her, and of course, well full of curiosity about what she did and studied in a medical college. In course of the conversation she brought out her small case of dissecting instruments, containing forceps and two or three scalpels. She sat in front of them describing the use of the instruments calmly, but in her mind she was busily dissecting the little white throat of that baby. To counteract these thoughts, she got up and put those tools away.
>
> Autobiography of Edith Flower Wheeler,
> WMCP student, circa 1897[7]

While the external world disapproved of a woman's choice to join such an unwomanly profession, perhaps the staunchest objections came from within medicine's own ranks. To male students at the Long Island College of Medicine (New York), the presence of a single female classmate meant "a limitation of our freedom. We wished to mouth masculine oaths, to be free and unfettered in our actions."[8] Prominent male physicians went so far as to lecture against women becoming doctors. They were convinced such a path could only result in "scenes of maternal neglect, domestic discord, and annihilated social distinctions"; a corruption of both social identity and social responsibility.[9]

In 1870, famed surgeon, David Hayes Agnew, spoke against women in medicine during a lecture at the University of Pennsylvania (Philadelphia), stating: "let her remember there are laws controlling the social structure of society, the operation of which will disrobe her of all those qualities now the glory of the sex, and will cast her down in the dust of the earth."[10] Similarly, skeptical Massachusetts physician, Dan King, condemned female dissectors in the pages of his popular book, *Quackery Unmasked*, warning readers that if a woman gained anatomical knowledge, it threatened to transform her from the "pride and ornament of the race — the sacred repository of all that is virtuous and lovely," into a sexless

> monster in the garb of a female, a nondescript, a being *sui generis* ... when she enters the fetid laboratory of the anatomist, and plunges her hands into the gore of dead men, she loses all her feminine loveliness, and appears like a fallen angel, an object of universal horror and disgust.[11]

Although professional prejudices of this magnitude had lessened by the time dissection photography became popularized, the objectification of female bodies now found expression through national newspapers and yellow journalism; articles that compared and contrasted the abject nature of medical professionalism with explicit descriptions of female students' physical appearances. While these reports made no decrees that the American social fabric would be cut to shreds by way of women cutting up cadavers, misogynistic commentary posited a student's "feminine instincts" only remained intact through sheer willpower and an unwomanly eye toward business.[12]

"Miss Agnes Eichelberger is not a ghoul," declared an article on the Chicago Woman's College in the 1880s, punningly titled, "Beauty with Brains." While the editorial sought to demystify and celebrate the female physician by confirming their comfort in participating in abject acts – such as removing the head of "a pretty babe with yellowish red hair" out of a four-gallon jar in front of the reporter – this commitment was undone by a fixation on how "pretty" the students were, and how the majority's "tall and slender physique" found contrast with the inclusion of "a few stout young ladies." As to this latter category, stated the article of Eichelberger's appearance:

> In fact, she is a rather pretty young woman with pleasant, girlish manners and a vigorous enthusiasm common to the plump, healthy country girl she is. Nothing hard or cruel in her features indicates that she would delight in sawing off the top of a pretty child's head and in making preserves of feet and brains.[13]

★★★

Women physicians (and students) of the 19th century overcame many of the era's prejudices by facing the sociocultural and industry-based challenges of the times head on. While societal constraints greatly limited who female physicians could attend – men commonly refused to be seen by woman doctors – students at WMCP dissected both sexes without issue.[14] However, there was still a considerable price to pay regarding their representative agency.

By the end of the 19th century, women physicians – as physicians but especially as women – had learned to protect themselves from unnecessary attention or scrutiny. "You will avoid, by all suitable means, the unenviable distinction of being peculiar," decreed WMCP Professor of Obstetrics, Emeline H. Cleveland, during the school's Annual Commencement in 1868.[15] Although she instructed her students not to "sacrifice in any measure your independence of thought," Cleveland warned that certain concessions had to be made to keep up appearances in a male-dominated profession – make that, a 'man's world' – actively working against their professional growth and development.[16] As physicians, declared Cleveland, "you will be subjected to the common doubt regarding the inexperienced"; while as women, "neither the profession nor the community will judge lightly of your errors."[17]

Becoming a female physician or student in the 19th century then meant being exposed to "public observation ... severer criticism, if not to harsher judgement."[18] Lest detractors debase and dismiss the entirety of women's efforts and accomplishments in the field of medicine, a professional "ethical code" needed to be established; one consistent, above reproach, and strenuously governed "by the rules of common morality and of Christian charity."[19] The vast majority of these rules governed public behavior as practicing physicians. However, there appears to have been at least one tacitly expressed rule regarding female students and their interactions with the dead while in the dissecting room: *never joke around with the cadaver.*

To this point, *every woman in medicine* across the nation – not just those at WMCP – needed to be mindful of the professional and vernacular imagery they projected of themselves, both publicly and in private. In the case of photographs, representative agency could not jeopardize the moral, ethical, or social standard of the status quo. Transgressive images, such as dissection photographs, needed to walk along a scalpel's edge of appropriateness, never fully committing to extreme elicitations of the abject. Thus, throughout the era of the dissection photograph, from 1880 to 1930, it was virtually unheard of for a woman in medicine – regardless of discipline or specialty – to pose for a photograph in which she is shown joking around with or dehumanizing a cadaver.

It's no joke

> The faculty will expect the most rigid adherence on the part of the ladies of the class to all the rules of propriety and deportment which characterizes a lady and distinguishes a physician.
>
> The Woman's Medical College of
> Georgia and Training School for Nurses[20]

Across the country, the convention of women refraining from debasing their cadavers through abject photography was upheld to a startling degree of consistency. In over a decade of research, the closest I have come to finding an image of an *actual* female student – as opposed to a hired model – joking around with a cadaver in a 'disrespectful' way is Figure 7.2, part of a photo album from the American School of Osteopathy in which two women, and one man, embrace and taunt a cadaver as if it was still alive.[21]

This unofficial, yet omnipresent mandate even extended to dissection photographs of coeducational settings. For example, in a large group shot of 16 students (13 men and three women), taken in the Medical Department of Northwestern University (Evanston, Illinois), the male majority pose with the severed limbs of their cadavers held as if transformed into musical instruments: fleshless arms strummed like a banjo; a humerus (long bone in the arm) mimics a flute; a radius and ulna (the two bones of the forearm), wielded like drumsticks and beaten upon an overturned bucket 'drum.' But, while men revel in their 'bad' behavior, at the center of this macabre musical recital, a trio of women stare directly at the camera, their faces a combination of stoicism and disgust. Each one stands empty-handed.

Joking with cadaveric remains created a threshold of abjection that women refused to cross. But it did not stop them from taking up their cameras, asserting control over their representative agency, and resorting to more visually progressive means of expressing their suitability to a career in medicine. This meant creating more standard forms of commemorative dissection portraiture, images of them working diligently and confidently within the confines of the dissecting room. Others chose to pose alone inside college medical museums, surrounded by biomedical displays of jarred organs and fetuses; a museum *for* women, *of* women, *by* women.

Starting in the 1890s, students at WMCP routinely engaged in a diluted form of gallows humor. Although never shown interacting with cadavers in 'inappropriate' ways, they made no bones about posing for transgressive photographs with articulated skeletons. Indeed, once the camera-savvy students of WMCP began taking their own photographs, a darker form of humor reigned supreme.

Figure 7.2: Joking around with dismembered cadaver. American School of Osteopathy (Kirksville, Missouri). Unidentified photographer. Gelatin POP mounted in scrapbook, circa 1910

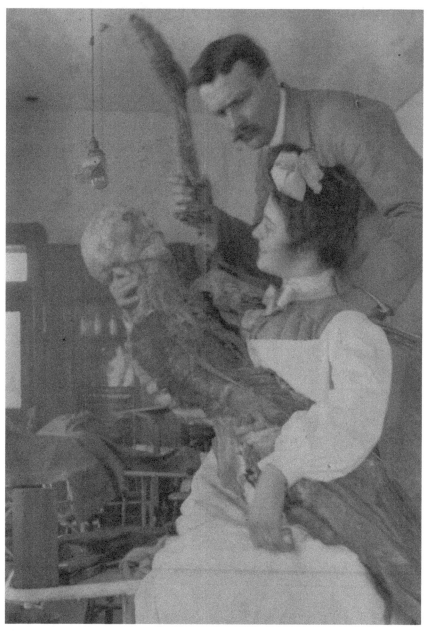

Source: Author's collection

Typically, these images flaunted societal conventions by demonstrating a macabre comfort with the transgressive emblems and acts of their chosen profession. They included a limited range of explicitness, such as dressing articulated skeletons in male street clothes, or pretending their bony companions were reanimated and engaged in everyday activities, such as getting a pedicure, or having a bath (most would be categorized as Stage II images). In extreme cases, students wore portions of their skeleton's skulls atop their own heads while in their boardinghouse room.[22]

Posing with dry bones posed less of a hygienic challenge than that of the cadaver. Perhaps because of the articulated skeleton's relative sterility and omnipresence in popular culture and medical establishments, from doctor's offices to dissecting rooms, this is also how it became an acceptable photographic prop for use by nursing students. Plus, when it came to dark humor, the "ever grinning skull invited jocularity."[23]

What's in a name?

> A little nonsense now and then is relished by the best of men – and women too.
>
> Agnes Eichelberger, first woman physician,
> Sioux City, Iowa[24]

While visual mockery of the dead body was out of bounds for women, giving their cadaver lewd or amusing nicknames was fair game. Many students based these nicknames on pop culture figures, or to ridicule the physical characteristics of their cadaver before or sometimes during its mutilation. It is not uncommon to find cadavers' nicknames jotted down on the backs of dissection snapshots from the 1890s or noted in the margins of scrapbooks of the mid-1920s. For instance, a dissection photograph from the scrapbook of WMCP student, Ida Scudder, features the phrase, "Hal," "short for "Halytosis [sic]," written at the top of the image; the cadaver's name, likely a ribald reference to its foul smell.[25] In another photograph, the same group poses with their study skeleton, so named "Billy Lightning."[26]

Before their graduation from the WMCP in the 1890s, student amateur photographer, Laura Heath Hills, took an unconventional group photo of four of her classmates in their caps and gowns, along with portions of "Ichabod," their study skeleton. Hills' photo shows the students posed at varying heights, one behind the other, with the topmost student balancing "Ichabod's" skull on her graduation cap, and the bottommost student sat with the skeleton's disembodied arms draped over her shoulders. In March 1896, now a fully ordained physician, Hills herself reminisced about the abject and commemorative power of her photograph, remarking to one of her former classmates: "I am sure to think of you at least once a week – on Saturdays when I do my dusting, and carefully wipe off the picture of you four girls and Ichabod. This photograph stands on the parlor mantel and has caused many a curious comment."[27]

The practice of naming cadavers and skeletons continued for well over a century. In the 1980s, at an unidentified medical school, a letter was found upon a cadaver's chest, addressed to its dissectors. Written by one of the students, but signed by the cadaver, nicknamed "ORCA," – due to its immense size – the letter's contents speak much to the ambiguities of the abject:

Dear Dr. Eisenstein,

I am an unmarrable monster, but I long for your gifted hands to turn me into a raving beauty. True, in life, I was called ORCA, but already you have removed much of the unsightly fat. Continue to improve my looks — I love the feel of you running your fingers over my viscera. Then when I look good enough for your high standards, put me back together and kiss me on the lips and I will magically come to life and we can live happily ever after on my father's money.

Love,

ORCA[28]

Assigning a name (human or otherwise) to a skeleton or cadaver does not necessarily mean that the labeler viewed it as human. Conversely, giving an object a name does not mean the labeler perceives it as human, or is attempting to anthropomorphize it (such as the near universal trend of giving ships or first cars human names). The particulars of why students in the era of the dissection photograph did or did not name their cadavers remains to be seen.

Incidentally, among the modern medical students I have observed over the years, there seems to be a divide as to whether naming cadavers is a sign of respect or disrespect. Many felt that calling the cadaver an 'it' didn't seem appropriate. Instead, they used the pronouns, 'he' and 'she'. Students established which to use based on the cadaver's biological sex, not on the deceased's preferred pronouns. As one third-year medical student told me in 2021, his dissecting group did not assign their cadaver a new name out of respect for its identity. Since they did not know the person's true name in life, it seemed rude to give their remains a different one in death. Others I spoke to felt giving the cadaver a name humanized the experience. Yet they fully acknowledged that naming the dead was solely for the comfort of the living.

Coincidentally, the anatomy lab staff I shadowed proudly gave the cadavers under their care loving nicknames. They did so both as a sign of respect – staff frequently talked to the dead while conducting their daily rounds, which included wrapping and unwrapping them – and to restore personhood; now able to refer to the cadaver as something other than a table number. For instance, a large cadaver whose height and girth had him spilling over the edge of the table was called "Bubba." The cadaver of a former physician was called "Doc." A small African American cadaver was called, "Miss 10"; named so because she laid upon table ten, but, as the staff member who named her told me: "She also needed a 'Miss' because she's small and delicate." For what it's worth, these same staff members also kept a human brain in a jar labelled, "Abby Normal," named so after the famous scene from the Mel Brooks masterpiece, *Young Frankenstein*.

When legs and arms won

> I have commenced my fourth part in dissecting. It is Dr. Parish's arsenic subject – the arteries are beautiful – we can trace them out to the finest hair like branches. The anastomosing about the shoulder and elbow is very interesting. To be sure the subject is rather odiferous! But la me! what difference does that make to a med.? The only trouble is we can only work a few hours at a time. If we overstay the proper time the effect is rather marked!
>
> Mary McGavran, WMCP student, 1893[29]

Before the institution of Pennsylvania's anatomy acts, the WMCP acquired its cadavers through the same surreptitious channels as those utilized by all-male schools. Like their male counterparts in cities across the nation, the WMCP spoke of potentially stolen cadavers in account books using ambiguous terminology, like 'subject' and 'material.' On February 25, 1853, almost 30 years before the Pennsylvania Anatomy Act of 1883, the faculty resolved that the WMCP dean, David J. Johnson, direct their janitor, Henry F. Birnbaum, to procure a "subject," with no specification as to how.[30] During the war years, in 1862, accounts state that the clandestine acquisition of a "subject for preparation," cost the college ten dollars, while the preparation of said subject, completed by its Professor of Anatomy, Mary J. Scarlett, cost 20 dollars.[31] Although the WMCP kept meticulous notes of its finances and faculty, the identity of "the person who brings dissecting material to the College Building" was kept strictly confidential. Coincidentally, until the WMCP's facilities provided for the incineration or burial of anatomical waste, the person(s) in charge of acquiring bodies was also responsible for their removal from the premises. In 1875, dean Charles Hermon Thomas reported to faculty that he had instructed his "person" to secret away "the refuse" of the dissecting room, which the WMCP routinely kept "packed as it accumulates in fish barrels in the cellar."[32]

It should be noted that while the WMCP mandated that its Demonstrator of Anatomy be a woman, the acquisition of cadaveric material was still routinely assigned to male staff, usually in the form of the janitor. Unlike male schools, like Jefferson Medical College, whose robbing of Philadelphia's poor and African American cemeteries by students was the stuff of legend, leading to great conflict between the races, there is currently no known evidence that the students of WMCP directly engaged in grave robbing. Thus, the abject qualities associated with female medical identity were never as explicit as those of males. But this is not to say that a woman's behavior in the gross lab was somehow above reproach.

Within the material economy of single-sex dissecting rooms, cadavers were commodities, just like at any other school. First-year students mapped their personal territories upon the cadaver's body like explorers laying claim to newly discovered lands. To declare dominion within these corporeal anatomical atlases implied an assumed level of ownership. Practically, though, it ensured that the cadaver – and the delicate work done within – was safeguarded from the potentially careless behaviors of the living. To this end, warned WMCP student Elizabeth Cisney-Smith, if "a head dissector ever edged in on an arm dissector or an abdomen person came around when the leg lady was working, there was a real war." That war she would soon witness firsthand:

One Mary Parker from Boston was a typical researcher — overzealous — domineering, etc. etc., and not content with doing regular scheduled work. [She] came in one day during my freshman period "on arm" and started extracting teeth from her "head" subject — a very big fine set of teeth in what was left of our colored subject — students were not required to extract teeth but Mary Parker of Boston wanted to do everything. Any way teeth began to fly and also the arms and legs were being disturbed — that was the first time I ever saw women in a real fight and it was not very dignified but did settle Mary Parker. Of course legs and arms won.[33]

Irrespective of the similarities or differences between the posing conventions of men and women, it still does not fully explain why either chose to pose with dissected cadavers in the first place, over say, anatomical preparations, or skulls and books. Certainly, student identities were bolstered through participation in a socially transgressive act. And certainly, photography was an effective means of commemorating professional experiences, such as dissection, in a tangible, repeatable, and distributable manner. But again, why take pictures with the dead in the first place? And, to this point, why did the overriding majority pose holding scalpels?

8

Of Sharp Minds and Sharpened Tools: Dissection Photography and the Ambiguity of the Scalpel

The Scalpel is the highest power to which you can appeal ... its revelations are beyond the reach of the cavils and the various opinions of man.

Valentine Mott, famed American surgeon[1]

In the spring of 1909, medical student, Stewart Elliott, mailed a dissection postcard addressed to his sister Ada, a schoolteacher living in Denton, Texas. "Dear Sister. This is a pleasant spectacle isn't it?" he inquired. "But this is what we do a day and a half out of five. I like it too. Isn't half as bad as it seems." Stewart's message concluded with an inquiry into Ada's own work. "How's school teaching [?] Coming along first rate I hope. With love from Stewart."[2] Ada no doubt smiled at this heart-warming note. That is, until she flipped the postcard over.

Upon seeing the 'pleasant spectacle' her brother had sent her from afar, Ada Elliott's smile likely didn't last long. For although the image was undeniably spectacular – in the sense of being visually striking enough to elicit emotional impact – *pleasant* was probably not the word a schoolteacher would have used to describe it.

The photograph showed Stewart; posed behind a draped dissecting table along with three of his classmates (Figure 8.1). Each member of the quartet stood dressed in their white coat and each clenched a scalpel. Their dissected cadaver sat upright and squat upon the table in front of them. The top edge of the photographic frame severed its head at the jawline. Its chest cavity, now empty, was all but a shadowy window to nowhere, framed by the rectangular remnants of a sawed-off breastplate. The students had bent and then crossed the cadaver's bandaged fleshy legs at odd angles.

Figure 8.1: Unknown school (likely in Nebraska). Unidentified photographer (possibly attributed to Stewart Elliott). Gelatin silver postcard, 1909

Source: Private collection

A mass of tangled fabric lay between them, obscuring its groin. From out of this makeshift womb of swaddling emerged an anatomical preparation of a human skull.

But why would Stewart and his medical brethren take a photograph like this? Why would they pose with a cadaver seemingly in the midst of rebirth/birthing its own skeleton? Once reborn, unburdened by skin, muscle, and membrane – all since mangled and mutilated by Stewart's clumsy hands – was the idea to have the reanimated bones walk around campus; to ponder fleshless existence amidst a swarm of scalpel-wielding students? Indeed, what a spectacle that would be.

Ada was an educated woman; a teacher. Her brother was a man of science. Surely, she had no delusions over the resurrection of the flesh. And yet, she probably could not make heads nor tails of this. Who could? And speaking of scalpels, to complete his tableau, Stewart had placed large dissecting kits on either side of the crowning skull. Both kits were densely packed with dozens of intricate instruments, the very implements the cadaver's flesh had been reduced by, and by which 'its' skeleton was now reborn.

Each tool had a different name and purpose: forceps, scissors, clamps, picks, saws, chisels, scalpels, and knives. Of this last grouping, there were blunt-pointed knives, sharp-pointed knives, simple bellied, resection, and amputation knives, as well as long-bladed bistouries, and tenotomes with both concave and convex cutting edges.

Although these kits were given prime placement within the photograph – front and center, eclipsing even that of the skull – Ada likely took little notice. Like most viewers, she probably considered them trivial by comparison. Instead, all eyes were on the eyeless cadaver and the abject tableau her brother and his friends had painstakingly staged and photographed.

But what Ada Elliott did not realize was the prominent position of the dissecting kits carried great significance to Stewart and to the visual economy of his chosen profession. The seemingly routine pose of the men – each holding scalpels – tapped into a long-standing tradition, a time-honored 'spectacle,' extending back centuries; long before the genesis of dissection photography, or even, the invention of the photographic medium.

★★★

This chapter examines the historiography of the scalpel within dissection photography. Its omnipresence throughout the genre's evolution raises a multitude of questions about its significance to students as a tool of dissection, and, as an iconic emblem of personal, collective, and professional identity.

Despite its ubiquity, I argue the scalpel's inclusion in dissection photographs is not for it to exist *solely* as a prop connecting student experience with the tools of a professional rite of passage. With the inherent ambiguity of its functionality – an implement used to cut into both living and dead bodies – the scalpel was an equal agent of violence and healing. This bifurcated utility often worked in tandem with and against its own historiography.

Ultimately, as this chapters suggests, strict industry-driven rules and progressive trends governing its inseparability with medical professionalism and identity caused the scalpel to become a prime target for farcical photographic subversion, with students using dissection photography as a variable, but highly controllable means to visually and viscerally transgress the blade's proper historical, theoretical, moral, and technical function.

★★★

Dissection photographs, like the one taken by Stewart Elliott, united camera, cadaver, and scalpel in ways rarely seen by American audiences. To say this stage of the genre's evolution (Stage III) transcended the entirety of the visual culture of medical and surgical photography may at first seem hyperbolic. But, at the time of their creation, in the early years of the 20th century, tableaus that showed the actual utility and aftermath of the scalpel had few iconographic predecessors.

Scalpels and surgical knives are a common feature of the iconography of Andreas Vesalius. However, in over 500 years of oil paintings, woodcuts, and lithographs, few featured the 'Father of Modern Anatomy,' blade in his hand, *actually dissecting the dead*.[3] Similarly, despite being the most recognized representation of anatomical education on the planet, Rembrandt's iconic painting, *Anatomy Lesson of Dr. Nicolaes Tulp*, curiously features no cutting instruments. Instead (likely because of his elevated status) the esteemed anatomist examines the flesh of a partially dissected cadaver using only a pair of forceps.

By the mid–19th century, it became more popular for physicians and surgeons to sit for portraits holding scalpels, knives, and operating kits.[4] Only now, it was their *subjects* that were missing. Indeed, no early occupational photographs feature medical professionals posing along with their patients. As Stanley Burns discusses, the reason behind this omission was the popular belief that surgical treatments "often brought about death."[5]

To point out the obvious, once surgical portraiture relocated to locales other than the photographer's studio, and surgeons were united with their patients within the photographic frame, their chosen arena was *not* the dissecting room, but the operating room or surgical amphitheater.[6] Patients were not just living, but conscious – a visual abrogation of years spent perfecting techniques on the bodies of the dead. Within the context and confines of their professional environs then, the cutting blade of the surgeon had to be depicted as an extension of unquestionable medical power, exhaustive training, and exceptional technical skill. After all, these were photographic systems of identity formation for professionals, not students.

Surgical portraiture deified the professional within the context of a larger system of authority by glorifying their specific pursuit to reveal and heal the living. And yet, despite the portrayal of the absolute power of the scalpel, it is rare to encounter a professional photograph of a surgeon actively cutting into their patient's flesh in which blood or exposed interior anatomy is visible to the viewer.[7]

Around the time of dissection photography's introduction in the 1880s, the visual culture of the knife was in the midst of a cultural upheaval. The most significant modification involved hands–on training becoming an essential component of an American medical education. Once universally adopted, students across the country had more opportunities to participate in various surgical exercises upon the cadaver, and to actually *use* scalpels instead of just watching them skip across dead flesh from afar.

A steady supply of dead bodies meant students were provided with both full and partial cadavers to dissect. Not just in standard courses on topical or regional anatomy, but in 'newer' classes, like surgical anatomy, gynecology, and obstetrics and diseases of women. These latter courses commonly utilized obstetrical manikins as birth simulators. Students practiced delivering 'babies' out of a "counterfeit birth canal" made from real female pelvic bones covered in rubber and wrapped in leather. Inside this "distensible womb" could be placed a doll or fetal manikin. In the case of the Medical Department of the University of Vermont (Burlington), their obstetrical manikin, a high-end model imported from Paris, was used in tandem with an actual "recent foetal cadaver" obtained from their dissecting room.[8]

By the early 1900s, the increased specificity of medicine demanded coursework that included more elaborate and specific dissections. For instance, when students dissected the male perineum, the intricacy of the procedure required that they spread and then hold the cadaver's legs up in the air, often, through the use of an elaborate system of ropes and pulleys extending down from the ceiling. The popularity of the procedure, no doubt incited by the bizarre pose of the cadaver and its visual similarities to giving birth, as well as its focus on the societal taboo of exposed male genitalia, made it too irresistible to be excluded from the visual lexicon of the dissection photograph.

With surgical aptitude fast becoming an important professional skill, and the historical and professional weight of an industry increasingly defined by 'the cut,' students felt the defining moment of their professional journey was the successful manipulation of the blade upon the cadaver. "The first incisions were made ... and we felt that we were really surgeons," declared students at Yale University School of Medicine in the 1890s; a sentiment that is still shared by many medical students today.[9]

To this point, scalpels carved out identity as much as they did flesh. Once student-made commemorative portraiture became a national tradition, the surgical tools of 'the cut' literally changed hands, becoming inextricably linked to the student–cadaver dyad, rather than an exclusive component of professional surgical identity.

Throughout the totality of its existence, no matter who, what, when, where, or how bloody, the scalpel became an omnipresent icon of the dissection photograph. With few exceptions, images from the early years (Stage I) show students in uniform fashion: blades in hand, standing proud and tall by their cadaver, their resolute faces upturned to meet the lens of the camera and the gaze of the photographer/viewer.

In those days, scalpels routinely hovered over dead flesh or gently rested upon its skin. Dissecting kits often lay nearby, positioned either alongside or on top of the cadaver itself, their intricate interiority a visual mimic of the exposed or soon-to-be-exposed innards of the dissected body. But in just a few short years, dissection photography evolved to showcase more instinctive "working attitudes" and postures.[10] Discarding the confining, static posing conventions of classic portraiture, students now looked down and stared *into* the cadaver. They literally stared death in the face.

In time, scalpels too became equally dynamic. No longer set upon or glided over the unbroken surface of a corporeally intact cadaver. Now they penetrated deep into cadaveric tissue. Flesh was cut. Fluids were released. Organs were removed. In this way, the trope of the student working among the dead expressed a more truthful dissecting experience. Aesthetically, however, these changes were not a huge departure from the genre's earliest incarnations. But, as documents imbued with identity and social power, this shift in posing conventions meant the dissection photograph was not just a commemorative object. It had become more.

It is worth noting here that while the 1890s saw the widespread adoption of the working pose, this 'trope' has existed since the 1870s. Perhaps the most famous example is a stereograph of college life at the State University Medical Department (San Francisco) taken circa 1875 by pioneering English photographer, Eadweard Muybridge – who had yet to achieve world fame with his experiments with chronophotography (humans and animals in motion).[11] Although not a 'traditional' example of the genre, Muybridge's dissection photograph bears significance as the only known image of a dissecting room taken by a photographer recognized within the historical canon of photography.

In a fascinating twist, by the early 1900s, the working trope became the simplest way for students to transgress the restrictive, preexistent cultures associated with the scalpel's proper function. The variability and capricious nature of this 'next stage' of student-made snapshots increased opportunities for more candid, vulnerable, and abstract imagery. As we shall see, within *these* photographs, scalpels, like cadavers, became literal and psychological agents of the abject.

The scalpel's pervasiveness as a standard and eventually transgressive posing convention within dissection photographs demonstrated its importance to American medical students of the late 19th and early 20th centuries. Throughout the genre's existence, no other artifact or agent of dissection, save for the cadaver itself, was given more prominence, nor was as abject, as the scalpel. Its conspicuous placement and arrangement in photographs in turn elevated the blade's status within the larger visual and material economies of medicine. However, despite its iconography being linked with professional standing, the scalpel was also an extremely dangerous instrument. It needed to be learned; had to be tamed. The consequences of its misuse could mean death to both students and professionals.

The purity of the knife

> The simple incision, consisting of a straight line, is the one in most common use ... to effect this incision, the point of the scalpel ... should be thrust into the skin at a right angle with the surface; the wrist should then be depressed, and the edge inclined upon the skin; when, after a requisite length of division has been made, the wrist should be elevated, and the instrument,

ere it is withdrawn, should again be held nearly at the same angle as when introduced.

William Fergusson, *A System of Practical Surgery*, 1852[12]

Before students could fully grasp, digest, and eventually photographically commemorate the complex intellectual results of their toils within the dead body, they had to first, or at the very least, concurrently acquire technical proficiency with the scalpel. As the indisputable method and means to anatomize and, by proxy, systematize the process of learning human anatomy, its skilled use and proper handling generated knowledge through a relationship admittedly reliant on violent force. Thus, rendering its utility safe in surgeries, autopsies, and dissections, required equally novel systems of management to ensure that within the human body, the scalpel continued to be orderly, predictable, and controllable.

In his monumental work, *A System of Surgery*, renowned American surgeon, Samuel David Gross, promised readers that adherence to his doctrines of the knife would eventually "enable any man of sense to execute, with facility, neatness, and celerity, any operation he may be called upon to undertake."[13] For surgical titans like Gross – men whose careers were built on wielding the authoritative power of the scalpel with style and confidence – learning professional discipline through the use of one's dissecting kit was the hallmark of a proper medical education.

A successful surgeon followed strict professional codes of conduct, those allied with the "moral purity" of the scalpel.[14] Straying from them was as hazardous to one's reputation as it was to their health. "Anything like a flourish for the sake of display or the hope of attracting the applause of the vulgar is as repugnant to good taste as it is out of place upon such an occasion," cautioned Gross.[15]

While such warnings expressed the dangers of corrupting one's moral standing within medical and lay communities, students and surgeons alike were told not to underestimate the physical perils of the blade. After all, the dissecting room of the 19th century was a dangerous place. In the wrong hands, a cut to the hands could be downright lethal.

As Gross and his surgical compatriots emphasized, to effectively survive the myriad dangers associated with cutting into both living and dead tissues required one to use "an accurate scalpel not destitute of grace."[16] In the pre-antiseptic era, achieving a level of technical proficiency was challenging to say the least. As early dissection photographs confirm, students routinely dissected the decomposing dead *without* the protection of gloves. The cadavers students worked within could be acquired from a number of sources, including being robbed from graves, packed in barrels of salt and shipped across state lines, or taken from prison gallows.[17] Not all were properly embalmed.

On account of their generally poor preservation, these bodies emitted toxic effluvia. Inside small, poorly ventilated dissecting rooms, the noxious vapors radiating from decomposing bodies could build up to near toxic levels. To combat these fumes, and because their dissecting rooms were literally nothing more than wooden shacks, schools like the American School of Osteopathy, and the University of North Carolina, held dissections outdoors. Coincidentally, the schools' dissection photographs confirm this change in venue.

In the 1870s, concerns over cadaveric emanations were so strong, that the annual announcements of the Medical Department of the University of California (San Francisco) boasted of the protective advantages of the Western climate upon them, stating: "[O]ur salubrious breezes not only preserve the *cadaver* for an indefinite length of time, but secure the health of the student from injury in consequence of the effluvium, so constant an attendant upon dissections elsewhere."[18]

Conducting autopsies or engaging with live patients with communicable diseases also came with risks of infection. In 1882, over 40 students at the Keokuk Medical College (Iowa) contracted smallpox after handling a cadaver brought over from Chicago. The outbreak resulted in the entire school being quarantined by the Board of Health.[19] Similarly, students at the University of Pennsylvania and the Woman's Medical College of Pennsylvania (WMCP) were required to sign documents absolving school administrators and the city's Bureau of Health of "all risks of contracting contagious diseases" before they could receive certain forms of onsite clinical instruction.[20]

In addition to the various anxieties associated with the cadaver's physicality, students also struggled with cadaver shortages. A lack of dead bodies caused many to fall behind in their required work, or, in some cases, to move onto graduation without acquiring the proper training. In February 1874, 18 students at the WMCP dissected only "two parts of the cadavre [*sic*], against three parts as directed in the printed Requirements for Graduation."[21] Although they failed to meet the minimal requirements, owing to a scarcity of dissecting material the previous winter, they were still admitted as candidates for final examination.

For those who fell behind and needed to catch up, dissections were completed in a hurried manner. This frequently resulted in treacherous conditions in the gross lab. One need only look to the floor of a dissection photograph for proof of the haste and waste that students literally waded through to fulfill their academic requirements.

At some schools, dissecting tables became so crowded during the day that students were forced to cut up the dead "by feeble gaslight at night."[22] Fewer cadavers meant fewer opportunities for students to dissect. In 1893, medical students Rose M. Dunn and Mary T. McGavran arrived at the WMCP dissecting room, only to find the latter student's name was not on "the list" of approved dissectors. With limited 'material' on hand, the frustrated McGavran was swiftly turned away. Per her diary, her re-entry to the lab remained uncertain. "I may get in in a few days," she later wrote.[23]

Rushing to finish a dissection was extremely dangerous. Sustaining a self-inflicted scalpel wound to the palm or a cut to the finger, no matter how superficial, was often compounded by the contamination of the "terrible poison of the putrefying human body."[24] While instructing at the Philadelphia Anatomical Rooms, physician and naturalist, John Godman, received numerous accidental cuts to his arms and hands. He documented his wounds, and the ravages of their subsequent infections (many of which worsened through poor or incorrect treatments), in the pages of his work, *Contributions to Physiological and Pathological Anatomy*, writing:

> Last season several of my class suffered very severely; the attendant of the rooms, from a slight scratch on his thumb, nearly lost his life, and was only saved by the suppuration of his axillary glands. In my own person, I three times suffered dreadfully; in one instance, the whole arm swelled, with immense irritation, accompanied by the most sickening sense of prostration, and several weeks elapsed before I could use my hand. In every instance the injury was slight. ... During this winter I have myself been wounded very frequently with a variety of instruments, even having my hand lacerated by a long used and thickly coated saw. I have been punctured slightly and deeply in the sides and extremities of the fingers, while dissecting bodies in various stages of putrefaction ... and which, without the treatment mentioned, must have produced most serious if not fatal results.[25]

As Godman's trials confirmed, when plunging their hands into the infective gore of the dead, no one, be they student or professional, was immune to the dangers of the scalpel.

After cutting his finger on his own blade during an autopsy of a suicide victim who had been "taken from the grave," Constantine Hering, legendary 'Father of American Homeopathy' and the founder of Hahnemann Medical College (Philadelphia), confessed he came extremely close to death. As he had been working "too long among the poisoned entrails" of the deceased, the wound went septic almost immediately. Since amputation was out of the question – at the time, any physician with missing fingers was considered an embarrassment to the profession – Hering was out of options; initially choosing death over disgrace. As a last resort, he heeded the advice of a student of Samuel Hahnemann, who persuaded Hering to take a homeopathic drug rather than consign himself to an agonizing death. Miraculously, not long after ingesting the drug, the infection vanished.

OF SHARP MINDS AND SHARPENED TOOLS

Happily, wrote Hering of the ordeal, "the finger is still my own."[26] But not everyone was as lucky as Drs. Godman and Hering.

In March 1890, *The Daily Republican* thrilled its readers with the retelling of the death of Dr. Bird of Jersey City, a young, promising surgeon, who had cut himself one night during a standard autopsy. Blood poisoning quickly set in, and within 24 hours, Bird was "himself a corpse, the victim of the most revolting death that can overtake a human being."[27]

In 1903, when two students at the North Carolina Medical College (Davidson and Charlotte) were "poisoned by a corpse," it made national news. One of the students contracted septicemia after accidentally pricking his finger "with one of the sharp instruments used in the dissection."[28] The other dissected with a preexistent abrasion on his hand that also went septic. Both had been dissecting the intestines of the same cadaver. Despite having cauterized their wounds at the onset of symptoms, neither had done it properly.[29] The first student recovered and returned home after two months in the hospital.[30] The other died within two weeks.

These accounts show that it took no more than a mere prick of the finger before the scalpel's journey began a gradual slippage from an indispensable tool of dissection to an abject instrument of ambiguous design. As the implement by which toxic "decomposed elements" filled with "a concentration of malignant death-dealing energy" could be introduced into the healthy tissues of students and professors, the scalpel no longer respected normative, delineated boundaries of either independent body.[31] With both the living and the dead now polluted through septic, biological cross-contamination, the blade's utility became relatedly abject through its misuse and the merciless betrayal of its operator.

Be it for a legitimate educational purpose, or as part of a dissection photograph, brandishing a used scalpel in such proximity to oneself, or one's classmates, was indeed risky business. A cadaver robbed from a grave would pose an additional risk. As would taking a photograph at a later stage of its dissection, when decomposition effectively overrode all efforts of chemical preservation. These conditions affected dissections, and thus dissection photographs, from schools in states like North and South Carolina. Until the early 1900, fresh bodies were procured in the Carolinas only "by stealth."[32] If a student refused or was unable to resort to illegal means, they were consigned to cut open "old and putrefied" bodies, most of which had been "dead a year or more."[33] Under such perilous conditions, noted newspapers at the time, the question was not, why were there so many dissecting room accidents, but so few.

★★★

During the era of the dissection photograph, scalpels were held in several different ways. Regardless of the consequences, for the first 20 years of the genre's established chronology, it was customary for students to pose without protective gloves. In part, this convention was shaped by limited scientific knowledge of proper hygienic precautions and germ theory.

Ultimately, the hygienic hazards associated with a student's medical training were mitigated through enhanced embalming procedures, by thoroughly disinfecting dissecting rooms, incinerating cadaveric remains, and the donning of protective rubber gloves. In terms of precautionary measures, some schools were more equipped than others.

When the Class of 1899 began dissecting at Yale University School of Medicine, they arrived prepared to "disinfect any cut a careless slip might make" with personal bottles of carbolic acid.[34] The class also brought along protective fingertips, made of rubber and collodion (the same material used to make ambrotypes and tintypes), to "prevent the infection of abrasions" on their hands.[35]

Eventually, commemorative portraiture reflected the progressive hygienic trends of the industry, with prophylactic precautions, like the wearing of gloves, established as a new posing convention. However, within the first decade of the 20th century, once the photographic medium was adopted as the primary means of transgressing normative aspects of dissection culture (Stage III), the students' subsequent photographs sought to corrupt the authority, utility, and perceived safety of the scalpel by focusing on its abject qualities; specifically, the innate risks of becoming morally and physically impure through its improper usage.

Students mocked what they feared most: fear of infection, fear of death; fear of bumbling through the entrails of the cadaver without gaining technical proficiency or sufficient anatomical knowledge. One of the most prolific methods of demonstrating a defiance of traditional standards and preestablished conventions, involved students once again posing without the safety of gloves. To emphasize the abject nature of this endeavor, many took up positions alongside cadavers that were not simply dissected, but rather, had been reduced to murky piles of fetid incoherent matter – a visual reference to careless dissection and a macabre commentary on the way of all flesh.

The hand of nature

> The truth is, that the labours of the dissecting room are the most essential to the surgeon. But something more is required for the accomplished surgeon. He is no longer a mere artist, a worker with his hands alone.
>
> Charles Bell, *Institutes of Surgery*, 1840[36]

For nearly 500 years, countless anatomists, artists, authors, philosophers, poets, and theoreticians have classified and objectified the human body for anatomical purposes using comparative, descriptive, and visual terminologies that betray the materiality of living or once living flesh. Traditionally, these long-standing practices involved transmuting the body into other materials, matter, or objects of natural or man-made construction, including musical instruments, flowers, architectural elements, machines, and books.

But by the end of the 19th century, photographic exactitude helped the referential terminology of the cadaver face the truth of its own putrid existence. The dead body was an undeniable site of abjection, a "meaty, decomposing, even dangerous mess."[37] Textbooks of the era referenced the cadaver using more elemental terms, such as it being a "recalcitrant substance," a pitiable material requiring systematic "excavation" before its hidden mysteries could be properly revealed.[38] As medical specialization increased, and formal education became mandatory in order to legally maintain or set up a medical practice, so too did the human body become more resistant to exploration by those without proper training (and a diploma) from a recognized (and usually allopathic) medical school.

Dissection required specific tools, along with the knowledge of how to "transform a dead body into the creation of a living body."[39] Such alchemies, such excavations, describes author, Barbara Maria Stafford, "stood for an investigative intellectual *method* that uncovered the duplicity of the world."[40] This new method featured both literal and figurative senses. "The literal, corporeal sense" derived significance from "tactile cuts inflicted by actual instruments." The figurative sense, meanwhile, "played upon the allusion to violent and adversarial jabbing."[41] Both senses shared "the connotation of a searching operation. … One involved manual probing, the other cerebral grasping."[42]

Unlike previous educational systems, which mostly relied on didactic methods of anatomical education, the foundations of this new analytic method were grounded in practical, tactile experiences. The new mandate of an American medical education was for students to get their hands dirty. However, for some, clean gloves hid dirty hands.

Anatomists soon realized that if a student failed to develop a sufficient routine at the onset of their anatomical education, "according to a definite method," it risked the creation of "inaccurate and dirty habits."[43] In the early 1900s, anatomist Franklin P. Mall, the first professor of anatomy at Johns Hopkins University, argued bad behaviors doomed a student to produce a cadaver that was "indistinct, bad-smelling, and repulsive-looking."[44]

To Mall, and those who shared his ideologies about modern anatomical education, the aesthetics of the dissected directly related to the dedication and proficiency of its dissector. Imagine then the anxiety. Regardless of what was or was not learned, or the physical state of your cadaver at the commencement of its dissection, scholastic expectations decreed that an aesthetically pleasing cadaver was equivalent to a skilled dissector.

With Mall's system finding influence around the same time as the introduction of amateur handheld cameras, it is entirely conceivable that in and around Baltimore, dissection photographs not only commemorated a rite of passage, but evidenced a student's technical adherence to the dominant analytic systems of the era. But, in doing so, these images would not necessarily commemorate true anatomical acumen so much as technical proficiency for the sake of literally keeping up appearances.

★★★

Many American schools endeavored to enhance the coordination between the senses of sight, touch, "and of the hand in the use of instruments" by banishing entirely passive forms of learning from the dissecting room.[45] Some were successful in their efforts at modernizing techniques of anatomical instruction; the majority, however, were not.

At the turn of the 20th century, medical innovation, or a lack thereof, appeared to be regionally encoded. According to the infamous Flexner Report of 1910, when it came to substandard medical education, some cities, like Chicago, were described as the nation's "plague spot."[46] To properly meet student demand, institutions needed to provide sufficient anatomical material, not just in terms of quantity, but quality. With new schools popping up around the country, as well as the proliferation of private dissecting rooms in major hubs like Philadelphia and Syracuse – all bragging of a seemingly inexhaustible supply of *fresh* cadavers – students expected the best. Stolen, stinking corpses (partial or whole), already in the throes of decomposition, would no longer be tolerated.

Dissection photographs could confirm or counter a school's published account of its resources and physical facilities. To this end, modernized methods of preservation were needed to mirror innovative teaching techniques. Those schools that looked to the future implemented these procedures in accordance with their new analytic systems. New laboratory and clinical facilities were built and maintained to the best of their abilities. Those "wretched" schools without "a single redeemable feature," that could not or would not evolve, were summarily closed.[47]

The most common practice of chemical preservation at the turn of the 20th century involved embalming cadavers with fluid injections and then wrapping them in cheesecloth soaked in water, glycerin, and carbolic acid. This method kept the dead body perfectly preserved for months, even years. Effective preservation begot a whole new level of student experience. It allowed them to cut into bodies untouched by the grave or the gallows, to witness firsthand the relationships of the body's inner workings "as it is left by the hand of nature."[48] With opportunities of this magnitude now at their literal fingertips, it is no wonder dissection photography became a worldwide phenomenon in just a few short years.

The pen is mightier than the scalpel

> You must dissect the body of your fellow man; you must examine the dead for the sake of the living; you must take the knife in your own hand, and with it turn over again and again every leaf, and read and re-read every section and chapter of this volume of nature's works; and not only see and hear, but handle and feel for yourselves. There is no other royal road than this.
>
> William R. Grant, *An Introductory Lecture to the Course Anatomy and Physiology in the Department of Pennsylvania College*, 1845[49]

Obviously, participating in dissection wasn't *just* about commemorating a rite of passage. First and foremost, students were there to learn from the dead, to "develop a third-dimensional anatomy, to be able to actually see in the mind's eye the structural relations of the various parts to each other without effort of memory."[50] Training their sensorium to the level of an accomplished physician meant students had to acquire what renowned English surgeon, Sir Charles Bell, called "an accordance between the eye and the hand."[51]

To achieve this harmony, Bell advocated for his students to apprentice with non-medical artisans, like carpenters, or spend time witnessing the "marvelous [*sic*] handicraft of a great violinist, or engraver, the maker of scientific instruments, or even those artists – many of them ladies – who with such wonderful dexterity and rapidity paint flowers and other designs on china."[52] Championing the momentary replacement of the scalpel with that of the paintbrush or drafting pen may seem like radical advice. However, mollifying the boundaries between the arenas of the pen and scalpel held increasing significance to the medical student of the 19th century. Eventually, this relationship directly influenced the scalpel's inclusion as a standardized posing convention throughout dissection photography's evolution.

★★★

During the first half of the 19th century, the strict rules governing the scalpel found enhanced expression throughout the pages of internationally popular student manuals called a *dissector*. As true 'instruction manuals,' rather than theoretical atlases, these densely packed guides earned their names separate from other texts through focused attention on practical anatomical techniques.

A *dissector's* practicality led to its robust usage within dissecting rooms; as opposed to lecture halls, the prevailing locus of didactic learning. Given their popularity, students frequently posed with *dissectors* tucked under an arm, or held in an outstretched hand.

The technical rules espoused throughout a *dissector's* pages outlined the most ordered way to cut into the cadaver's flesh. As anatomical compendiums of no small dimension, they advised students on everything from where to start cutting, the most efficacious order in which to dissect the body, and the proper handling of the scalpel during various dissection procedures. As one *dissector* stated,

> the position of the hand in dissecting should be the same, as in writing or drawing; and the knife, held, like the pen or pencil, by the thumb and the first two fingers, should be moved by means of them only; while the hand rests firmly on the two other fingers bent inwards as in writing, and on the wrist.[53]

This seemingly outlandish holding position may appear as a hyperbolic fusion of Bell's advice for students to learn drawing simultaneous to anatomical dissection. But the recommendation to hold the scalpel as if it were a pen or pencil was endorsed by the greatest surgical minds of their day, such as Sir William Fergusson, John Syng Dorsey, Joseph Pancoast, and Samuel D. Gross.[54] Coincidentally, the position is still recommended in medical schools to this day.

The handling of the scalpel to that of the pen holds particular significance to the genre of dissection photography. For over half a century, thousands of medical students posed for portraits holding their scalpels in this manner. It is by far the genre's most prevalent posing convention. Additionally, the scalpel could also be "grasped within the fist," or positioned, "like a violin-bow," between the thumb and the tips of four fingers.[55] If a single slice into thick fatty tissue was required, dissectors held their blades "like a table-knife," as if "paring fruit."[56]

Like many aspects of dissection photography, the motivations behind adopting one holding position over another differed image to image, student to student, and school to school. It is not unusual to see students adopting a variety of holding positions within a single image. Presumably, this was no accident. Rather, it suggests an individual preference to either conform to the conventions of classic photographic portraiture, or to be portrayed naturalistically, as a professional, thoroughly engaged in one's work and seemingly unaware of the presence of both camera and photographer.

Each holding position was likely dependent on personal skill and preference. Also of consequence would be the culture of the dissecting room, the social relations between dissecting groups, and the students' comfort level with whomever took the photograph, be they a fellow student or a commercial photographer.

There is the possibility that variations in posture, such as those of students facing down and away from the camera with scalpel in hand, reflected elements of shyness, shame, embarrassment, and even discomfort over having their portrait taken in such socially unaccepted environs. Given the abject subject matter, perhaps some found direct eye contact with the eye of the camera (not to mention the eye of a commercial photographer) to be an ultimate transgression; a personalized abjection of morality that simply took matters too far.

But even if unaccustomed to their new surroundings or uncomfortable in their new identities, would medical students of the era purposefully shy away from the camera? After all, wouldn't such averseness potentially risk the stability of the homosocial bonds of a dissecting group (group player versus non-conformist)? In all likelihood, variations in this convention reflect nothing more than the varying degrees of importance, indifference, or insignificance some assigned to the act of dissection *and* its commemoration through dissection photography.

★★★

On literal levels, the camera is by no means analogous to the scalpel. However, if we consider them as pseudo-analogous tools of their trades, as instruments with a functional kinship when it comes to abstracting and fragmenting the human body – living or dead – the camera and the scalpel occupy similar spheres of influence in that their technical mastery conveyed professional superiority over the bodies before them. Historically, in instances where the scalpel and the camera combined energies, the two artifacts shaped and altered the professional standing of those who wielded them.

Photo historians Daniel M. Fox and Christopher Lawrence discuss that in the late 1800s, surgeons utilized photography's evidentiary power to capture the significant advances and techniques of their discipline in order to modify the cognitive positioning of their medical subspecialty. The continuous change in surgical photography "was integral to the revolution during which surgeons made themselves the most vigorous of the medical specialists."[57]

Students, meanwhile, represented a distinct, but lowered sub-category of medical professionals all their own. While their station within the microcosm of medicine was firmly situated, the representational characteristics that accurately defined their status and place – both to outsiders and to each other – were ambiguous at best. Generic cabinet card portraits of students sitting in photo salons, or group shots of them dressed in their white coats and Sunday best – even if they included the occasional skull, book, or bone – simply did not cut it.

The growing need for students to accurately capture experiential advancements within the systems of their medical education undoubtedly contributed to the genesis and continuous evolution of American dissection photography. Student identities needed to be separate from that of medical *professionals*, but still vastly superior to the professional development of the layperson or tradesman.

Absorbing the bifurcated culture of the blade into their own subversive portraiture occurred at a time of drastic alterations to the experiential requirements of medical students. As previously discussed, chief among these revolutionary changes was eliminating the need to rob graves, the widespread admission of women and minorities to the medical profession, and advances in techniques and procedures regarding proper sanitation and hygiene. With surgeons pushing for a more sanitized and austere public image – rarely depicted in portraits with visible, blood-covered instruments – it can be no coincidence that by the end of the 19th century, the scalpel would become a totem of a student's professional standing. If nothing else, as a co-opted token of affiliation, it reflected the duality of their educational experiences, both light and dark, good and bad, life and death.

Adapting to the cut

> Dissecting is not merely cutting. The parts must be exposed in
> a dissection clearly and without mutilation.
> J.M. Allen, *The Practical Anatomist*, 1856[58]

Medical students often mailed dissection photographs home to their families to demonstrate their anatomical, and thus experiential superiority (regardless of whether this was true or not). In the 20th century, this mainly took the form of real photo postcards. Often, the intended recipient of these images were younger siblings, cousins, and close friends, several of whom planned to attend medical school themselves. The majority, however, were addressed to mothers, sisters, and other female 'acquaintances', suggesting the dissection postcard might have served a different purpose, such as to impress or entice members of the opposite sex.

Ordinarily, dissection postcards were the work of student amateur photographers. The standard three-by-five format included a full-length photograph on the recto, and a brief handwritten message on its verso, along with the recipient's address, and a postage stamp in the upper right corner. Shockingly, many student communications made no reference whatsoever to the abject imagery on the other side. "Best wishes for a happy Easter," wrote students from Wake Forest College Medical School on the back of a particularly grisly dissection postcard. "We lost every ball game so far. Have game this PM."[59] Messages that did allude to the photograph included anything from advice to humor-laden warnings, grotesque premonitions to boastful exaggerations. Typically, the favored subject of conversation was the student's requisite acculturation (both real and imaginary) to cutting apart dead flesh. In 1906, the sender of a real photo postcard from an unidentified Baltimore school offered the recipient (his relative and a prospective medical student) some friendly, but likely unsolicited advice on how to prepare for the mental and physical strains of dissecting cadavers. "How do [you] think you will like this kind of work," inquired the sender of his relative's scientific proficiency, before continuing candidly: "I would advise you to cut up all the dead horses, cats, and dogs you find so you will get used to it."[60] Ultimately, the importance of the purely verbal advice could be undermined or misinterpreted. But as commemorative proof of the sender's lived (albeit transgressive) experiences while away at medical school, the dissection postcard imparted experiential equivalency by analogizing the student–cadaver experience – in this case, of two separate men at two separate times; sender and recipient; past and future – as well as the preemptive measures necessary to adapt and overcome its subsequent trials.

★★★

Tempering the plethora of mental, moral, and technical challenges associated with the scalpel's ability to carve living flesh – or for that matter, a student's *inability* to cut into dead flesh – required typifying governance by way of moral codes, practical authoritative systems of handling instructions, and methodically outlined surgical techniques. The particulars of these governing systems were commonly passed down from generation to generation through anatomical texts, homosocial relations between upper classmen and lower classmen, didactic lectures and demonstrations by revered professors and prosectors, and, to a lesser degree, time spent in surgical clinics.

Many systems focused on technical proficiency, reinforcing the need for students to dissect "as methodically and with as much care as if operating on the living body."[61] The design of these systems also defined appropriate levels of conduct for initiate medical professionals. The implementation of preestablished norms and rituals sought to manage error, and in so doing, control unproductive emotions – specifically, those associated with incorrectly or ineptly cutting into the (eventually living) human body.

Photography's introduction to the dissecting room allowed for yet another system of governance. Posing for photographs helped students demonstrate their technical and mental mettle by way of haptic simulation. The evidentiary 'proof' of the photographic object substantiated proficiency and purpose not only to themselves, but to others. The 'others' in this case

Figure 8.2: Bellevue Hospital Medical College of New York City (now New York University). Unidentified photographer. Gelatin silver print, circa 1910

Source: Private collection

could be an external lay community, such as a disapproving family, or, an internal community, such as future generations of medical students.

For example, in Figure 8.2, students at the Bellevue Hospital Medical College of New York City (now New York University) reconfigured their dissecting room each year in order to take their dissecting class portraits against a wall covered ceiling to floor in framed dissection photographs. Displaying these identity-affirming images in this manner, framed *en masse* upon the wall – a dissection photograph within a dissection photograph – and contiguous to current anatomical efforts, established visual traditions through the discrete visibility of a direct lineage of student experience.

Like most aspects associated with the genre, the traditions, experiences, and results varied from school to school and student to student. Some chose to honor tradition, others sought to mock it. That being said, it is easy to concede that students who took little pride in their work, and who dissected in rooms classified as "foul," "wretchedly dirty," and filled with "dried-up filthy fragments" of cadavers probably failed to adhere to modern systems of anatomical instruction.[62] Assuming they even bothered to take dissection photographs, it's a safe assumption their images similarly failed to reflect an equally modernist view toward the remains of the dead or their own professional identities.

The authority of the knife

If the materiality of flesh embodies unbridled chaos, the scalpel then, as the literal agent used to systematically expose the body's interior regions, brought order to said chaos; accomplished via slicing, dividing, separating, and fragmenting the body with linear exactitude. Regardless of a student's timidity or boldness with a blade, a strict adherence to the accumulated theoretical expertise of past anatomists, surgeons, and prosectors, alongside the synchronized method(s) of cutting cold flesh, established structural order, reliable outcomes, and the promise of knowledge-based authority. Within the context of a medical education and the confines of both lecture hall and dissecting room, the scalpel's ability to cut became paradigmatic of knowledge production; or, as Eugénie Lemoine-Luccioni succinctly states: "Couper, c'est penser [To cut is to think]."[63]

Nineteenth-century anatomists furthered the long-standing ideologies associated with 'the cut' during introductory lectures at their prospective medical schools. By 1845, anatomists, such as William Grant, lecturing at the medical school of the University of Pennsylvania, decreed: "It is dissection alone that teaches you where you can cut the living body with freedom and dispatch, [sic] where you *may* venture with great caution and delicacy; and where you must not, on any account, *attempt* it."[64] Within Grant's schema, mastery of the scalpel's abilities equated a mastery of anatomical dissection, and/or surgical anatomy. When used in accordance with standardized medical practices, the blade of a student-dissector orchestrated a methodical system of calculated movements upon the unruly flesh of the body; choreographed, as it were, to bring about ordered and predictable outcomes.

Anatomical knowledge became directly influenced by and contingent upon technical proficiency, a thorough mastery of the utility of one's scalpel. To this point, medical students sharpened their minds by way of sharpened tools. By successfully cutting the body asunder with intelligence, purpose, and skill – but ideally, without fear – they too could become "knights of the scalpel."[65] However, wielding a blade, or in the case of dissection photography, commemorating the various physical and psychological experiences stemming from 'the cut,' required prerequisite and concurrent knowledge bases.

Initially, the 'system' of the scalpel was a difficult one to master. Those who achieved such coveted control were hailed as heroes, their competency worth recording in school yearbooks. As the Class of 1911 stated of one of their own: "You will notice that he was Laboratory Assistant two years, an honor which only the most worthy holds beyond one year. ... Bacteria know to scatter whenever he begins to search, and he wields the dissecting instruments with remarkable ease and aptitude."[66]

Photographically, however, establishing proficiency, or the illusion of proficiency, could be done with little difficulty. Simply holding their scalpels according to dominant custom guaranteed proper photographic representation. If in doubt, one could instead stand beside the cadaver holding a book.

In the limited social arena of the dissecting room, being memorialized in framed group photos or in yearbook snapshots holding a scalpel incorrectly or dissecting inappropriately – unless doing so to purposefully lampoon tradition – could prove injurious to a student's reputation, or unwittingly craft the potential for never-ending ridicule by peers or upperclassmen. The majority of freshmen from the University of California Dental Department agreed that "while not especially agreeable," anatomical dissection was "exceptionally interesting." True to their word, the class took anatomical work quite seriously. Improper dissecting room etiquette, therefore, was simply not tolerated. In 1909, these students used their yearbook to single out the undignified behavior of a reportedly rather dimwitted and garrulous classmate – a man once overheard saying he thought bacteriology "was the study of the back."[67] The published account went on to assert that if the offender simply sat down, remained "perfectly quiet," and stopped 'talking out of his ass,' or as the class eloquently put it, "could prevent the 'Gluteus Maximus' from crawling up onto his 'scapula'," his substandard knowledge of anatomy could exponentially improve.[68]

Jokes and insults aside, most students appeared to accept the technical and mental prerequisites decreed by the likes of surgeons and anatomists such as Gross, Grant, and popular dissection manuals like *Gray's Anatomy*. Photography's introduction immortalized the symbiotic relationship between the blade and the mind, or the blade as an allegorical extension of the mind, by providing empirical proof of technical proficiency – not to be confused with technical mastery. Admittedly, this method, and indeed the primary corpus of extant photographs, showcased the scalpel's inherent power to produce knowledge in ambiguous and passive ways. But remember, this genre was not about literal systematic documentation.

While a motion picture may evidence dissection in a more complete and aggressive manner, photography's strength lay in the simplicity of its provision of explicit evidence, its proof of the scalpel's physical and symbolic power as an instrument with which to cut and carve dead flesh. By association, those who wielded the blade with purpose held dominion over the human body, its flesh, integrity and interiority, and the intellectual method(s) used to organize and classify its varying parts. For better or worse, dissection photography confirmed that this authority extended throughout life and into death.

Learning the limitations of flesh required students to journey beyond its normative cultural, social, psychological, and physical boundaries. But with the introduction of dissection photography, the standard voyage routinely veered off course, resulting in a host of inexplicable moral and material outcomes for the cadaver which served no anatomical or even didactic purpose. These images, such as the 'pleasant spectacle' tableau made by Stewart Elliott and his cohort, celebrated the abject and, depending upon the stage in which they were created, either commemorated or mocked themes associated with the rebirth, repurpose, or ruination of flesh.

★★★

Dissection photographs were visual records of physical engagement with the dead. In this way, their existence served as a symbolic extension of the dominant educational traditions of the era.

Anatomical proficiency necessitated a delicate, but essential balance between theoretical knowledge of the body's inner workings through seeing, and the navigation of the ambiguous and variable materiality of flesh through haptic contact. In 1899, surgeon Howard Marsh spoke of a similar sensorial balance during his introductory address to his students. Throughout his lecture, Marsh advised them to seek equilibrium within their medical educations by devoting uniform attention to the apparatuses of sight and touch, and to use the act of dissection as a conduit for simultaneous knowledge production.

"Let me advise you," decreed Marsh,

> in order to cultivate both observation and handicraft devote a great deal of time to dissection, working with your head as well as with your hands, keeping your mind active and inquisitive, and paying critical attention to the structures you meet with; not merely searching out their form and relations to surrounding parts.[69]

To Marsh and the other anatomists of his time, the cadaver's lifeless body was an empty stage upon which they could perfect their skills and senses through the spectacle of dissection. By encouraging close visual observation, the development of the faculties of reasoning, and training "the mind in those two main divisions of logic – analysis and synthesis," dissection increased a student's "powers" through "long and careful practice."[70]

It can be no coincidence, then, that concurrent to the anatomist's plea for a synergistic balance between the visual and physical, their students began to commemorate ideologies associated with dissection's 'power,' the power of 'the cut,' or the power derived from touching dead bodies, through a medium designed to make tangible what was previously purely theoretical. Though many students started out afraid, they conquered their fears; the dangers of the dead overpowered by the power of knowledge.

When dissection photographs were used to communicate such victories, these images operated on more literal levels. Some featured the popular phrase, "Knowledge is Power," inscribed directly onto a dissecting table. Other non-dissection images showed students smiling along with grinning skulls – the symbol of anatomical knowledge – perched upon their shoulders or arms, like trained birds. When the aunt of San Francisco nursing student, "Oscar," wanted to boast of her nephew's professional accomplishments, she sent friends a postcard of him in his brand-new white uniform. "Thought you would like a picture," she wrote on the back of the real photo postcard. "So here [he] is in his nurse uniform ... Love and Kisses."[71] Interestingly, Oscar's aunt focused on the typifying emblem she (and society) commonly associated with professional identity – in this case, the uniform. Yet, she made no mention of the fact the nursing student chose to pose outdoors on the college quad, balancing a human skull on his outstretched hand.

By the late 1890s, those immersed in photography's technological advances embraced a host of new aesthetics, many of which highlighted the potent personal and personalized nature of modern experiences between students, cadavers, and skeletons. On the eve of a new century, intimate, identity-infused snapshots of single-dissectors – some no doubt self-portraits – illuminated a new power relation between the cadaver and the individual instead of the collective. And yet, despite all these educational and photographic advancements, despite the emergent genre of dissection portraiture gaining a global reputation as an undisputed method of confirming identity and bestowing 'power,' anatomists still warned their students that the advanced development of skills of observation and cognition, without an equal rise in technical proficiency (or vice versa), risked transmuting the cadaver's knowledge-infused flesh into everyday meat. And with it, the corresponding identity of the medical student, now reduced to nothing more than an informed butcher.

Impassioned anatomists, such as Marsh, railed against such a fate. He cautioned that without balance, the act of dissection would be threatened with obsolescence, becoming nothing more than

> a mere clumsy mutilation, the work, as it were, of a bull in a china shop, in which the "cleaning of a muscle" means the cutting away of all its fascial connections and expansions till it is completely isolated and nothing but its fleshy substance remains. But what a senseless act is this, what ignorance![72]

We should take a moment here to ponder the degree to which Marsh's characterization of 'ignorance' extend to the continuum of abuses rendered upon the bodies of the dead. Would the esteemed anatomist have considered it ignorant for students to hang dissected cadavers out of windows, or pose for photographs with scalpels embedded in their cadaver's eyes and mouths? Or was he only concerned with the abuses that affected *systems* of knowledge production? The opportunities of the mind being a terrible thing to waste.

At any rate, Marsh was not alone in his condemnations of the intellectual abuses of the flesh. School administrations across the country published similar denouncements in the pages of their annual announcements. "Dissection is not *merely* cutting – each part must be exposed clearly and without mutilation," declared the New York Homeopathic Medical College (New York City). "Poor or careless dissecting will not be tolerated, even though the parts have been well learned from a book."[73] Although the public face of the American medical school presented an institution cracking down on dissecting room 'waste,' photography showed this was mostly just a false front.

Dissection simply was not accepted by all who participated in it. Be it from an inadequate cadaver supply, ineffective faculty, or just personal disinterest, many students failed to realize the privileges associated with the power of 'the cut.' Instead, they chose to repudiate the cadaver and the potential knowledge that stemmed from it. This 'class' of student wasted the opportunities of the flesh in a flourish of abject objectification, needlessly reducing the cadaver to the corporeal equivalent of a defaced statue or a gutted animal. If they did pose for photographs, either alone or in a group, the poor physical state of their cadaver (as Johns Hopkins' Mall emphasized) no doubt reflected their equally poor views toward dissection. Here the dissection photograph would be a token of resentment instead of commemoration.

Cutting up while cutting up the cadaver

"You have appendicitis," said the doctor man to Jim,
"And I must operate at once, or else your chance is slim."
"You shall not touch a knife to me," was Jim's firm reply;
"I'll have no operation, and I ain't a-going to die."
"Unless I cut," the doctor said, "you'll surely pass away";
"You will be dead, believe me, sir, by two o'clock today."
So Jim was scared and yielded. The carving was a shock;
But Jim was very thankful that he lived at two o'clock,
For doctors know their business, and it's very plain to see
That this one saved Jim's life, because he didn't die till three.
                    Anonymous, "Poor Jim," 1891[74]

As assuredly as any photographer required quality lenses, a state-of-the-art darkroom, and photographic equipment to create superior, innovative photographs (again, at least until the introduction of the Kodak), so too did the medical and dental student, professor or demonstrator, need high-quality instruments to perform surgeries, dissections, and prosections. Eventually, as the medical profession bore unto itself a host of sub-industries, including anatomical purveyors and instrument makers, a physician or student could not just cut into human flesh – or perhaps equally important, be photographed cutting into human flesh – using just any old knife. Could they?

Before dissection began, students of both general and surgical anatomy received rigid specifications about the handling and composition of their scalpels, knives, and dissecting kits. When detailing the specific components of the blade itself, the founder of conservative surgery, Sir William Fergusson, instructed: "In all instances, dissections and operations on the subject should, if possible, be performed with instruments similar in every respect to those intended to be used on the living body."[75]

When constructing intricate photographic tableaus, students across the nation furthered their reverence for the authority of the blade by carefully arranging their dissection kits in prominent positions on the same table as the dissected, or soon-to-be-dissected cadaver. An extreme example was already discussed in the form of the dissection postcard sent to Ada Elliott by her brother Stewart in 1909. Kits of this era were commonly filled with a host of indispensable tools, such as "six or eight scalpels, two pairs of scissors, a pair of dissecting forceps, a set of chain-hooks, a blowpipe [surgical pins, thread and needles], and a probe."[76]

During the 19th century, tableaus featuring blades and kits in prominent positions were a standard convention. No matter where the image originated – be it a dental school in South Carolina or a homeopathic school in Chicago – dissecting kits were displayed in near-identical fashion: each faced forward, tilted upwards, their elaborate interiors, like those of the dissected dead, opened and exposed for the gaze of both camera and viewer.

Figure 8.3, an albumen photograph of the Class of 1892 at the medical school of the University of Pennsylvania, taken by the commercial photographer, Frederick Leibfreid, Jr., contains at least three separate dissection kits of varying construction, each displayed on the dissecting table alongside the cadaver. Two rectangular wood and velvet-lined cases – one placed near the head, the other at the feet – sit in stark contrast to the exposed sections of tattered flesh and glistening bone. The third kit, made from soft leather, hangs off the table's edge parallel to a similarly shaped flap of human skin. The unfurled kit reveals a regimented lineup of delicate instruments, their mechanical intricacies blending seamlessly with the organic textures of the cadaver's opened torso. Above the table-based tableau stands a sextet of dissectors. Each is dressed in oil-smocks and protective arm wear, a scalpel (or saw) in their hands. As was common at the time, the blades rest gently on the surface of the cadaver's anatomy.

Equally common was to prop up a dissecting kit against the dead body; or, to lay the kit on top of the cadaver itself. In the latter case, students placed

Figure 8.3: The University of Pennsylvania School of Medicine (Philadelphia, Pennsylvania). Frederick Leibfreid, Jr. Albumen print, circa 1890

Source: Private collection

their equipment near the sternum, high atop the hollowed-out body cavity. For modesty's sake, soft cases, made from cloth or leather, were unfurled over the cadaver's stomach or groin; the tools here now repurposed to obscure exposed, undissected genitalia.[77]

★★★

By the time dissection photography emerged in the late 1880s, a robust material culture was building up around American dissection kits. In major cities like Boston, Chicago, New York, and Philadelphia, the impact of antisepsis and asepsis necessitated lasting changes in medicine and included the tools commonly used in anatomy labs and surgical amphitheaters. The resultant desire, by both students and faculty, to adhere to the rise in antiseptic operations propagated fierce demands for instrumentation of a more hygienic nature. The 1923 yearbook of the Chicago College of Dental Surgery even went so far as to devote an entire page to asepsis, creating a photographic montage of nurses performing various sterilizing procedures in the school's Extracting Department.[78]

With the introduction of modern embalming techniques – eliminating many of the foul smells and disreputable opinions about dissection – the physical space of the cadaver lab became more hygienic, eventually divesting itself of "all of its danger and half of its horror."[79] It stands to reason then, that in addition to simply being props of "the stuff of dissecting practice," scalpels, saws, dissection kits, and other surgical instrumentation found prominent display within a majority of photographic endeavors – such as dissection photographs and yearbooks – in direct response to a growing industry linked with medical innovation.[80]

As early as the 1830s, editors of the *Boston Medical and Surgical Journal* began touting the craftsmanship of American instrument makers. Some editorials went so far as to deem the continued purchasing of wares from European competitors as unpatriotic. "The Philadelphia and Boston made dissecting cases are equal in every respect to any foreign make," stated the *Journal* in 1835.[81] "If our cutlers, who are complete masters of their business, will agree to supply the profession at a little lower rate, they would most effectually put a stop to the importation of English cases of surgical instruments."[82]

By the late 1860s, the Philadelphia firm, Charles Lentz and Sons, purveyors of instruments, microscopes, anatomical models, and human remains, mostly skeletal, began running advertisements on the inside covers of student notebooks and in medical school yearbooks, publicizing their abilities as "manufacturers of strictly high grade," American-made, surgical instruments.[83] Typically, the heavily illustrated ads of Lentz and Sons utilized a visual language that spoke to the quality of their wares, the merits of precision, and the advances in mechanical exactitude as wrought by American industrialization: "Our Scalpels, Bistouries, etc., etc., made from the finest steel that can be obtained, and properly hand-forged, hardened and tempered in our own workshops, are unexcelled by those of any other manufacturer."[84] Such declarations effectively united a student's patriotism with the prevailing trends of anatomical progressivism. By 1906, the firm had defined themselves as "THE FIRST CLASS Surgical Instrument House OF PHILADELPHIA."[85]

To this end, medical students of the late 19th century used the photographic medium to recognize a then booming American industry; accentuating the visual impact of recognizable American-made saws that students and professors would routinely see in the pages of lavishly illustrated trade catalogues or advertised in the back of school yearbooks.

Photography also showcased a student's taste in instrumentation in a fashion similar to their technical proficiency. This in turn illuminated various sociocultural determinants about their lay identity, usually based around class. For no matter what the ads said in terms of affordability, dissecting tools were expensive. "We have painfully parted with the price of dissecting tools," grumbled Yale's medical students in 1910.[86] The choice of one instrument brand over another, or if a student carried worn, rusted, or hand-me-down kits, could result in them being ridiculed by their peers. Moreover, by the start of the 20th century, the image of the mercurial doctor, the "genius of the shambles," ignorant to antiseptic measures, sporting gloves and gauntlets "bespattered with blood and brains ... wielding a rusty scalpel in one hand, and a bloody forceps in the other," had become an offensive outdated embodiment of professional identity and industry standards.[87] To gain control of this publicly perceived status, students used photography, and the pages of their yearbooks, to correct, control, lampoon, or completely reject such portrayals.

But how exactly did students know how to choose the best equipment? Instrument makers and purveyors certainly did not make things easy for them. During the era of the dissection photograph, incoming freshmen faced countless options, undoubtedly breeding further anxiety, shame, or envy over the 'correct' decision when it came to brand recognition. In 1898, the senior class of the New York Homeopathic Medical College queried 50 of their alumni in active practice to determine their preference for obstetrical forceps. No less than 13 different makes were returned as favorites.[88] Likewise, in 1917, the variability of instruments was so great, and student jealousy so strong, that the Southern Dental College (Atlanta, Georgia) instituted a series of "Ten Commandments" to address the issue of instrument envy in a light-hearted way: "Thou shalt not covet thy brother's instruments, either operative or laboratory ... for thereupon thou dost effect his progress, and so greatly irritate his feelings as to cause expressions of unthankfulness."[89]

By taking photographs featuring prominently displayed scalpels, saws, or other identifiable instruments, students demonstrated a collective form of nationalism by showing viewers that they were on the 'cutting edge' of American surgical innovation. For some, this meant using the medium to provide literal commentary on the act of dissection as being emblematic of national pride. In 1893, students at the University of Maryland School of Medicine (Baltimore) posed with the epigraph "Not for ourselves but for our country" written on the side of their dissecting table.[90] Per tradition, they also wrote the name of their home state on their aprons as a further confirmation of their national/regional identities. That same year, multiple photographs were taken to commemorate the first class of the American School of Osteopathy. Although no scalpels are visible in these cabinet cards, a group of men and women, comprised of the school's faculty and inaugural class, huddled closely around a mounted human skeleton – the primary 'instrument' of their osteopathic knowledge – shown with its bony hand reaching out and resting upon a large American flag placed in front of it.[91]

Over the top, under the knife: photography's use to "appear wicked"

As discussed throughout this chapter, the visual traditions associated with honoring the scalpel as a recognizable professional totem, inseparable from medical professionalism and progressive trends like sanitation and hygiene, were an essential component of the earliest, purely commemorative dissection photographs of the 19th century. But, by the first decade of the 20th century, students sought not only commemoration, but an expression of the normative and transgressive aspects of their changing modernist identities.

Rejecting the aesthetic conventions of the past became the crux of transgressive dissection photographs. Standard posing conventions, those that glorified the scalpel's practical utility, were purposefully destabilized, supplanted by tropes associated with the physical trials, psychological fears, and emotional obstacles of dissecting room culture. "Our pictures are fine," remarked Illinois student, "Jones," on the back of his dissection postcard. "Am making some finer ones this week." His 'fine' photo (Figure 8.4) shows an unidentified student lying upon a dissecting table covered in a white sheet, his head turned to stare directly at the camera and presumably "Jones" the photographer. Arranged upon his shrouded body lay a variety of instruments of medical and non-medical use, including screwdrivers and several types of pliers. An articulated skeleton looms over the table; an immense wood saw dangling precariously from its left hand. Tied to the bones of its right, "Jones" had placed a hatchet.

The utilization of new camera technologies in the context of a new century allowed students like "Jones" the freedom to form equally novel photographic tropes. In his case, that freedom led to the creation of a variation on the classic

Figure 8.4: *Student Dream* variation. Skeleton as dissector. Unknown school. Unidentified photographer (likely attributed to "Jones"). Gelatin silver postcard, circa 1906

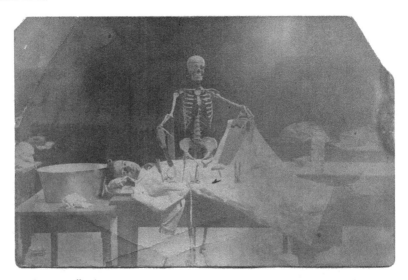

Source: Private collection

Student Dream subgenre. Now freed from the limitations of the tripod and the critical (and potentially criticizing) eye of a commercial photographer, students with handheld cameras staged photographic tableaus that drew upon farce, hyperbole, and dark humor. A reliance on outside props was often essential to this autonomy, and to subvert expectations.

The transgressive acts exposed to and by the camera included a host of elements that functioned on historical, theoretical, moral, and technical levels. These tropes effectively altered the visual landscape of the dissecting room and the physical way dissection commenced. Soon, the disciplined methods of anatomy, the time-honored rules of blade handling, and the material composition of dissecting instruments themselves were transformed into the unexpected, the unprecedented, and the unimaginable.

Chief among these new tropes was the subversion of the scalpel's proper iconographic function as a fundamental tool of dissection. Deviating from standard tropes associated with dissecting instruments applied equally to long-standing cultural traditions – those associated with the strict industry-driven rules governing the scalpel's proper, moral use – and photographic customs born after the genre's 'founding' in the 1880s.

To visually communicate the transgressive potential of their scalpels American students utilized three primary techniques. The first reversed the distinct roles of the dissector (the living) and the dissected (the dead) by placing dissecting tools into the hands of anatomized cadavers or skeletons. The "Jones" postcard showing a skeleton dissecting a student with a hatchet and wood saw is a classic example of this technique. Elaborate tableaus of this kind are often considered the more macabre and ethically dubious of the genre and coincidentally include the dark subgenre known as *Student Dream* photographs.

The second technique focused on the more socially transgressive moments of dissection. These photographs captured the use of instruments on or near bodily sites imbued with special meaning or identity, such as the removal of a cadaver's eyes, head, and heart (sites of vision, identity, and emotion), or the mutilation or mockery of its genitals (site of shame, lust, power, and so on). Figure 8.5, a dissection postcard from the 1910s, shows multiple forms of transgressive behavior in a single image. Students mock their headless cadaver by tugging on a string tied to its exposed shriveled penis, while also visualizing themselves as cadavers (the cadaver as future self – discussed in Chapter 14).

The explicit nature of these photographs, be it nudity or violence, guaranteed a visceral reaction from both lay and medical audiences. The need to create this type of imagery was as long-standing as it was irresistible. In November 1961, almost 60 years after Figure 8.5 was taken, a student smiles for the camera while inserting a long-handled scalpel directly into their cadaver's eye. The nearby dissecting group – also smiling – surrounds

Figure 8.5: 'Cadaver as self' with string tied around exposed penis. Unknown school. Unidentified photographer. Gelatin silver postcard, circa 1915

Note: Here the central student's head replaces the severed head of the dead; the cadaver's calvarium, its source of knowledge, transferred over and placed upon the student's own. Note also the group's adoption of the classic *memento mori* iconography.

Source: Private collection

the pair. Several hold the cadaver's hands as if to offer emotional support during an invasive, painful procedure.[92]

Theoretically, once amateur cameras became the primary method by which dissection photographs were taken, it stands to reason that representative agency fell to the students themselves and that all aesthetic choices were their own. Therefore, when students photographed each other inserting instruments into a cadaver's eyes or inflating a disemboweled body's intestines with a fireplace bellows, we assume this is the way they elected to be portrayed.[93] It is not that there is anything 'wrong' with these images, per se. A cadaver's genitals, eyes, and viscera are all dissected as part of a normal gross lab experience, as is the use of a bellows or other form of pump to inflate cadaveric intestines. However, certain aesthetic choices, such as a focus on a cadaver's genitals, or evidencing elicitations of melodramatic joy while performing overly violent or unusual acts of dissection, undermines the ultimate intent of the imagery, and brings student professionalism into question.

The third, and most elaborate, method of subverting the scalpel's authority involved students replacing the standard tools of the trade with theatrical exaggerations. These 'prop' implements were usually of a cumbersome or inappropriate purpose, such as a wood saw substituted for an amputation saw, or a railroad spike supplanting a chisel (once used in gross labs to open skulls). Again, we may turn to the "Jones" postcard as an example of this trope.

Replacement instruments were usually nothing special; common items found in every American home. Their normativity accentuated the transgressive 'fact' that the cadaver's body was both dispensable and reducible, its materiality nothing more than dirt, "raw clay or pigment."[94] The key component to this specific imagery was that the tools functioned properly in normative spaces *outside* the cultures and confines of the dissecting room. However, once recontextualized within the liminal space of the gross lab, and repurposed to appear to cut apart human flesh, the tool's normative function became something perverse and abject.

Perhaps one of the most significant student testimonies I've ever encountered regarding the subversive intent behind a staged dissection photograph was written on the back of the dissection postcard shown in Figure 8.6. "This is the bunch I dissected with. This picture was taken as a joke," confessed the student. "Can you imagine any more gruesome instruments?"[95] The tools in question include a massive wrench, common household wood saw, pickaxe, sledgehammer with accompanying railroad spike (placed directly on top of the cadaver's skull), and a garden hoe/spade (possibly used as ironic commentary on the tools students once used to rob graves). While these tools are more outlandish than gruesome, not one student mimics the cadaver's dissection with an instrument of normative surgical or anatomical use.

Figure 8.6: Students with 'gruesome instruments.' Unknown school. Unidentified photographer. Gelatin silver postcard, circa 1906

Source: Private collection

Photographic tropes destabilizing the instruments of dissection thrived for over 70 years, well after the demise of the standard dissection photograph. For example, in the 1982 yearbook of Tulane University School of Medicine, an interracial and co-ed group of smiling students pose beside a body in their anatomy lab while brandishing hammers and wood saws. Only, this time, the body to be 'dissected' was not that of a cadaver, but one of their own: a living medical student who lies shirtless (and smiling) on a gurney, enthusiastically awaiting dismemberment by his cohort.[96]

Again, it is important to note that in either era, the tools in question do not consist of dissecting kits of Cronenbergian origin, designed for operating on mutant anatomy. All were common household tools. Abjection lies in their repurposing, not their construction.

Similarly, in an early 20th century dissection photograph, taken at the Northwestern University Dental School (NUDS), a student holds a large fire axe while posed next to an upright cadaver. Student proximity and posture intimates the use of the axe, or rather, its desired use, to quickly hack the cadaver to pieces. Staged scenes such as this do not readily suggest true aggression, hate, or a desire for overt violence toward the dead. Nor do they reflect even the blade's intended use to 'kill' or mutilate a cadaver's already lifeless remains. Instead, the axe's inclusion hyperbolizes the material culture of dissection by speaking to the students' desire of accelerating – in an undeniably primitive and callous way – the tedious, frustrating, and mentally exhausting processes involved with human dissection.

This facet of dissecting room culture – a need to accelerate the literal act of anatomical dissection – was frequently commented upon via the dissection photography of student amateurs. A handwritten caption on the back of a 1915 snapshot, featuring a dissector holding an ornate butcher's saw in one hand and the headless remains of a cadaver in the other, lends further insight into this trope: "Firmly grasping the cervical vertebrae with my left hand and wielding a butcher's saw in my right, I proceeded to make a saggital [sic] section of the cervix when someone cried, 'Quick Nero the axe, the saw is too slow'."[97] It should be pointed out that the dissectors in the NUDS axe image are dental students. In their professional capacity, this cohort only concerned themselves with the anatomy of the head, mouth, and throat. Commenting upon the tedium associated with dissecting the *entire* body, rather than just the relevant parts encountered in their professional sphere, was likely at the core of their decision to subvert classic instrument-specific posing conventions. That said, during the era of the dissection photograph, dental students were expected to be familiar with "every part of the anatomy from the Galea Aponeurotica to the Flexor and Extensor Hallucis Longus" – basically, from head to toe.[98]

Ultimately, the darkly humorous intent behind the NUDS and "Nero" images are jovial in tone and do not suggest violence, but rather frustration over the tedium of anatomical dissection. The same cannot be said for a pen-and-ink illustration of an axe-wielding student, featured in the 1917 edition of *The Howler*, the yearbook of the Wake Forest College Medical School.[99] In this cartoon by student F.W. Speight, two White students dissect a clearly identifiable African American cadaver. Its body lies flat upon a dissection table and is mostly covered by a sheet. One of the students uses a wood saw to remove its left leg. He slices away with determined ferocity, a hammer sticking out of his back pocket, a cigar dangling from his mouth. On the floor next to the dissecting table sits a metal bucket. The cadaver's severed right arm juts out from along the rim alongside several discarded bones. Meanwhile, the second student adopts a truly unconventional posture for anatomical dissection: He stands directly on top of the dissecting table itself; literally straddling the cadaver. In his hands he holds a large axe, which is raised far behind him. Speight's inked motion lines suggest the student has already begun his downward blow; the trajectory of the axe head eventually splitting or completely severing the Black cadaver's head.

Unlike the photograph from Northwestern, the cartoonist's use of non-traditional instruments does little to lampoon or transgress the technical aspects associated with a legitimate anatomical dissection. Although just a cartoon, its imagery, and inclusion in an official organ of the school, reflects a visual and material culture content with the dehumanization of the 'other.' It is a culture seemingly at ease with explicit depictions of racial brutality toward the bodies of African Americans – a community that at the time, likely comprised the entirety of Wake Forest's cadaver supply, since the school's founding in 1902.

Why students chose a cartoon over a photograph is uncertain. Especially as the oeuvre of dissection photographs from Wake Forest is replete with callous dissecting table epigraphs, like: "Of more use while dead than living," and "SUCH THE VULTURES LOVE."[100] A cartoon softened the brutal nature of the scene, making it more palatable and perhaps humorous than a photograph. Given the yearbook's exclusive audience and that the desecration of Black bodies was considered 'normal' in the South at this time, one wonders if the choice had more to do with the defilement of the dissecting table than that of the dead.[101]

Here the borders of the abject begin to tip and collapse in upon themselves. Transgressive depictions of bodily mutilation, such as the Wake Forest illustration, consistently maintain their abject qualities and emotional impact. And yet, they also assist with delineating acceptable and unacceptable forms of transgressive behavior within the dissecting room; thereby establishing clearly defined borders. For example, dehumanizing a dead body for its material 'otherness,' essentially because its dead and can feel no pain, is one form of abjection. Dehumanizing it because it is a dead *Black* body, to do so solely because of its race, is a completely different form. Dissection photography evidenced both relationships. However, here is the paradox. To modern society, the latter case is the more repulsive of the two. Whereas, in the era of the dissection photograph, lynchings, mob justice, racial segregation, all of this was either legalized or tolerated. Thus, vivid depictions of racial brutality and juxtapositions of blackness and whiteness – the dark skin and blood of the dead contrasted with the white sheets, coats, and skin of (most) of the living – were not completely abject relics confined to the dissecting room, but were fast becoming part of the visual and material cultures of the United States.

The Wake Forest cartoon shows another important method of visual subversion. By hyperbolizing the instruments of dissection, students cast the materiality of the cadaver into question. Axes are used to chop up wood, not flesh – except perhaps when disassembling the carcasses of animals. That said, the axe and hatchet were popular methods of murder in the 19th and early 20th centuries. Lizzie Borden famously murdered her parents with an axe in 1892. And although largely forgotten today, Anton Probst, and his slaughter of the Deering family at their South Philadelphia farm on April 7, 1866, remains one of the most gruesome mass murders in American history. The eight victims – the youngest of whom was only two years old – were hacked to pieces in the Deerings' barn, brains bashed in with a hammer, throats slit with an axe, "felled to the ground like dumb cattle."[102] By using an axe instead of a scalpel, F.W. Speight used ink lines to blur the lines of acceptability, suggesting overt racial violence and indifference by drawing ambiguous parallels between the dissection of a cadaver, the slaughtering of an animal, and the murder of an unconscious Black man.

★★★

When a dissection photograph features an unconventional cutting instrument, such as an axe or hatchet, the repulsion–desire cycle of abjection spins again. Doubt is cast over the photographic 'truth' of the cadaver's body and questions whether these men pose and cut into a real dead body; or, whether it is merely an effigy, some kind of scarecrow or wicker-man, something that requires an axe to splinter it into manageable pieces, like so much firewood.

Hyperbolizing 'normative' dissecting experiences served to shock a lay, yet familial audience; one whose naiveté and inexperience left them to ponder the image and its aesthetics as photographic truth. Yet these viewers must have had sufficient understanding of the normative visual and material cultures of anatomical dissection. Otherwise, how could they recognize that what was being transgressed in the gross lab, and how it was being transgressed, was in fact ... gross!

In truth, this external audience was not entirely without some form of budding knowledge of the inner workings of the human body. Most known recipients were either a student's family, close friends, or perhaps even a fellow first-year student at another school. If the recipient of the photo or postcard was not at least partially in on the 'joke,' the transgressive and farcical implements of dissection would become lost in translation.

For example, around April 15, 1910, Joe Klein, of Grants Pass, Oregon, received a dissection postcard from his acquaintance, "Charley," a Midwestern medical student. "Hello Joe: What do you think of this bunch," inquired "Charley's" message. "This work is not very pleasant but it is very interesting." His note was brief, almost comically so, considering that the image on the front shows a student resting a butcher's saw against the side of an upright cadaver's head, its flesh reduced in mass to all but thin drippy sinews of dark flesh and dangling bits of teased-out vasculature. A cohort of eight stands around the void of its emptied chest. Large chunks of skin hang down from the incised hole. To the left of his image, "Charley" posed another question: "Just regular cut ups aren't we?" he asked.[103]

The butcher saw "Charley" and his classmates posed with is a less exaggerated instrument than the axes used by the students of NUDS or Wake Forest. As such, it does not subvert the materiality of the cadaver to the same degree. However, although intended to be humorous to those involved, posing in such ways would have found limited expression, and an equally limited audience, had they not been channeled through a visual medium.

While this is an obvious enough statement, it is important to note that in the case of dissection photographs, purposefully subversive images of this nature were staged solely for the benefit of the camera. Unlike predecessor imagery from the genre's earlier stages, they had little to do with commemorating the standard rituals associated with dissection. In fact, they almost seem like distant relatives of the early classic portraits, the kind of images that confused previous photo historians during their attempts to define the entirety of the genre's divergent breadth and purpose.

I should reiterate here that the 'othering' of classic instrumentation was not a byproduct of dealing with normative aspects of an abject subject matter. Rather, it was crafted by the students themselves and done so with singular intent. "The ordinary apparatuses used for dissection, usually consists of knifes and scissors," wrote an unidentified female medical student on the back of her dissection photograph. "On this unusuall [sic] occasion [event of taking pictures] hammers and 'saws' were substituted to make it appear wicked. Otherwise, it is quite natural, in its entire aspect."[104] Her caption here speaks volumes by itself.

First-person accounts such as this, which not only mention the act of dissection photography, but detail the methodology behind photographic staging, are exceedingly rare. What's more, the image–caption dyad furthers the argument that after decades of photographically commemorating the ritual of dissection via a conventional manner – one consistent with standardized commercial portraiture – eventually, the creative purpose of these images evolved to become something else.

Despite posing conventions being quite traditional in their execution, the intent behind the image's very creation was no longer about photographically commemorating a ritual event, or even to use tools of the trade to affirm orthodox aspects of student identity. Instead, it became about the newly ritualized event – however brief or "unusuall" – of creating an aberrant visual economy of the dissecting room, thereby challenging any or all preconceived notions about the identity of the American medical student and their use of the scalpel to dissect cadavers.

9

Flesh in the Age of Mechanical Reproduction

To take up a scalpel, to pierce through a cadaver's skin and reflect it back, is to expose the inner dead world of the body's ordered obscurities to the affective chaos, judgments, and misconceptions of an external living world. As a layered gateway between these interior and exterior worlds of transmissions and retentions, excretions and absorptions, human skin serves semiotic purposes extending far beyond its materiality.

Hans Gercke relates the function of skin to that of a mutable barrier, one that "shields what is innermost yet exposes what is most intimate; it opens a connection to the outer world; it is the most important organ of communication. ... Our identity is determined not least by the structure of our skins."[1] Author James Elkins positions skin as a communicative conduit between body and mind, with human identity and human skin inextricably linked to each other. "The skin," he writes, "communicates the self."[2]

But what of dead bodies; what of dissected bodies, bodies without skin? Do they still communicate? And if so, what do they communicate? *How* do they communicate? If personhood and self are communicated through skin, anatomical dissection mutes (but does not always silence) the body's communicative capabilities through a series of systematic penetrations and incisions. Typically, it starts with the skin's obligatory removal via flaying. The process, although destructive (and some may say violent), is applied universally, regardless of who or even *what* is being dissected.

The ultimate fate of identity once skin is cut, peeled, and discarded spawns countless debates over certain visual disparities inherent to photographic representations of cadaveric skin.[3] Equally important, but not entirely germane to our discussions here on the visual culture of dissection, is whether cadavers maintain an identity once they are broken down further into component parts and preserved as anatomical and pathological specimens in school medical museums.

One of the biggest communicative obstacles inherent to dissection photography is the photographic medium's ability or inability to effectively communicate dead flesh as being identifiably human. With no material understanding of the dimensions of the cadaveric body, all forms of identity, all forms of self for cadaver and student-dissector, lose relatability and are thus rendered suspect.

To expand upon this further, if we fail to consider a host of mitigating factors when viewing dissection photographs, inexperienced viewers run the risk of gaining an inaccurate assessment of the visual economy of the dissected body. For example, throughout the entirety of the genre's existence, one of the most prevalent misconceptions about dissecting room portraiture is that *all* dark-skinned bodies are the cadavers of African Americans. Our concept of skin, and skin color, is based on what we see day after day, in a living world, through our own eyes. Our perception dictates our reality.

Little time is spent challenging or reconsidering photographic 'truth.' The 'truth' of this matter is that the bodies we see in dissection photographs are not just dead. Skin and flesh has been changed through a host of different factors, including period embalming techniques to being reinterpreted through the lens of (now) antiquated camera and concurrent printing technologies (more on this phenomenon is found in Chapter 11).

As discussed previously, Julia Kristeva categorizes the cadaver's position within the abject as an ambiguous entity resistant to assimilation. I would argue that throughout the defining era of dissection photography (1880–1930) the cadaver's photographed skin – as well as its exposed interior topography, including blood, bones, muscle, and viscera – contributed cooperative proof of its abject, ambiguous, and inassimilable nature. This chapter examines this assertion in further detail, focusing on the uncertainties and inconsistencies of cadaveric skin, as shown throughout 20th century amateur-made dissection photographs.

Working independently of, or cooperatively with one another, a host of natural, photochemical, and technological agents demonstrate the collective capacity to disturb reliable visual translations of the natural textures, color translations, and tonal values of dead flesh. These disruptive agents include, but are not limited to, common types of photographic image deterioration, the limitations of early 20th century photographic technologies, poor lighting, as well as natural decomposition processes, and the eccentricities of period embalming techniques.

Skin deep: interpreting the aesthetics of dead flesh

Human bodies are sites of contradictions. Skin, the body's largest and most visible organ, is equally an organ of contrasts. It functions as both a softened wall and an interior shell, tasked with containing the unruly fluids of the body's inner workings, while simultaneously maintaining enough elasticity to adapt without tearing, chafing itself to shreds, or sloughing off the bone.

Be it of our own bodies, or those of others, we face and touch skin daily. And yet, for most of us, skin's innermost layers remain physically, visually, and conceptually ambiguous. Visually and conceptually, we lose track of it in the interstices of corporeal consciousness. Physically, we encounter it, but mostly take no notice, due to our preoccupation with mitigating pain during incidents of bodily trauma, those involving deep penetrating cuts, scrapes, or wounds. Other confrontations include surgery, childbirth, or anatomical dissection; the latter act, the only one performed exclusively on the bodies of the dead.

As a necessary component of anatomical dissection, cadaveric skin must relinquish its role as a barrier to an internal frontier and become thoroughly ambiguous in both form and function. The inner world no longer needs protection from the outer world; the outer world no longer affects the proper function of the inner world. With the theoretical and physical limits of inner and outer collapsed upon each other, the more skin is sliced into shreds, torn, or inverted, the more its functional ambiguity turns its aesthetical readability into an imponderable mess.

Dissection photography exacerbates this imponderability of cadaveric materiality. It forces viewers to make up their own decisions; to ponder either the true hierarchies of inner and outer anatomies, or to scrutinize the methods used in their visualization. Since lay viewers are traditionally unaccustomed to the true extent in which a cadaver can change visually before, during, and after dissection, our conceptual model typically focuses on questions pertaining to subject matter, with virtually no time spent interrogating processes of visualization.

Throughout the 19th century, renderings of the rent body were achieved either by the artist's hand or the photographer's camera. However, the final outcome of either medium operated under various restrictions. Paintings of dissected bodies were limited by the skill and imagination of the artist. For centuries, countless painters have attempted to confront and represent the thickened liquids, interconnected membranes, and coagulated jellies of the body's "invisible inside," using the "sticky media" that is paint. Indeed, painted flesh benefits greatly from the medium's dichotomous properties of viscosity and translucency. As author James Elkins attests, the analogous materiality of paint and flesh creates a natural affinity between the visual arts and representations of bodily interiority, between "the slurry of fluids in a surgical operation – the saline wash, blood, and cut tissues – and the mix of pigments and oils in a painting."[4] But remember, paint does this regardless of whether the depicted subject is living, dead, or is a completely fictional construct.

Photography, meanwhile – and here we mean analog photographs unaltered by any imaging software – has infinitely more limitations imposed upon it. Photography requires light. No light, no image. Moreover, the camera captures only what is placed in front of its lens. Unlike the idealized, abstracted, or imagined bodies of the dead in paintings, a photograph of a 'true' dead body must translate to a real-life encounter. Thus, with camera and photographer having occupied the same time and space as a cadaver, we must therefore 'trust' the accuracy of the resulting photograph as evidence of and witness to this encounter. And yet, truth be told, how often do we stop to consider photographic accuracy when viewing images of dissected bodies? The answer, obviously, is never, since how many of us spend significant time viewing such graphic images?

For those of us that do, admittedly, shock usually trumps logic in most cases. But, in our defense, how many of us have an appropriate indexical baseline for comparison or identification in these instances? Thus, considerable doubt is cast upon the inherent 'truth' of the medium when a dead body is photographed in such a state of advanced dissection that it exists as an aftermath, its flesh and bone reconfigured into shimmering drips and accumulations, staining ruptures, what Bataille called the *informe* [formless].[5] In these images, incredulity is generally tempered only through the recognition of visual cues relevant to the individual viewer. It should be noted, although confusion may be lessened, understanding, in this case, often leads to amplified emotive responses.

A fine example of this is found in black and white crime scene photographs of the 1930s and 1940s.[6] The fusion of two typically distinct visual economies, life and violent death – represented in these images in the form of a victim lying in a recognizable space, such as the interior of a house or on the sidewalk of a city; their belongings covered in blood, or entwined in exposed internal organs – is somehow considered more palatable, perhaps because it is situated with a more readily identifiable context. As a society, we are both victims and perpetrators. Thus, our capacity to murder or be murdered is infinitely higher than to dissect or be dissected (although autopsies to determine cause of death have become more normalized in modern times).

Unlike cadavers, who are shaved bald and devoid of any personal accessories except tattoos, and sometimes, nail polish, many murder victims are photographed clothed, have hair, or could be adorned with makeup or jewelry. If a murder victim is photographed at the crime scene nude, they are typically located inside relatable relational spaces of vulnerability, like bathrooms or bedrooms. Inside these spaces, the identifiable features of humanity encroach upon the incomprehensibility of the dead body and reconstruct it into something pliably human. Even when corporeal form is fragmented or obliterated, embodiment is maintained through environment.

An example here might be an image of a severed hand ornamented with a wedding ring on the carpeted floor of a hotel, or a headless suicide victim sitting atop a toilet seat in a nightgown.

To this point, and an answer to one of our earlier questions about the communicative capabilities of cadavers, much is deduced from a crime scene photograph of a man murdered in his kitchen that is not present in a dissection photograph. Socioeconomic status can be gathered from the state of his clothes or the condition of his home. A close-up might reveal his age, sex, and race before additional factors interfere with identification. If the viewer is particularly clever, even the cause of death is determinable by way of photographic evidence. Dissection photographs, meanwhile, include no artifacts of humanity to help identify or contextualize the cadaver's life. When relevant contexts or artifacts do appear, such as students and cadavers wearing street clothes and hats, smoking cigarettes, or gambling, they are not only resistant to societal norms, but are perceived as socially and culturally repugnant. Both corrupted and corruptible.

★★★

As previously mentioned, dissection photographs amplify the disparate nature of fragmented cadaveric flesh through transformative qualities inherent to the larger medium's own particular form of image creation; namely, bodily metamorphoses generated by numerous steps and conversions of photographic processing and printing, such as: living skin made dead skin; dead skin made photographic skin (which includes becoming a negative and then a positive of itself); photographic skin made paper skin; paper skin made faded, torn, scratched, distorted, curled, reticulated, glossy, or silver-mirrored skin – depending on environmental conditions and conservation efforts.[7]

Throughout the genre's evolution, cadavers have occupied an unprecedented position of visual apposition. Disparities native to their imaged flesh are challenging to quantify, even for those accustomed to viewing them. When compared to the skin of living students posing next to or crowded above it, or when likened to the skin of the dead found in other photographic genres, such as postmortem photographs, dissected cadavers seem to reject the organic elements of the body's original and ultimately final material stations. Aesthetically, lay viewers are unaccustomed to seeing a human body in such a paradoxical state: half-halted decomposition, half-artificially accelerated mutilation. But the lay community isn't alone.

Throughout the 19th and 20th centuries, even medical students confessed they felt their cadavers simply didn't look real. As a medical student once admitted to sociologist, Frederic Hafferty, the cadaver "just stops looking like a human being the more you take it apart."[8] Speaking further of his experiences in the dissecting room observing student behavior, Hafferty asserts the more students dissected, the more there were associations between "human and nonhuman."[9]

Occasionally, the ambiguous properties associated with dissection and photographic truth were compounded by other factors, like a school's anatomy curriculum. In the first decade of the 20th century, schools like the Medical Department of the University of Alabama (Mobile) blurred the lines between man and animal by mandating all students dissect the carcasses of goats before transitioning to the bodies of humans.[10]

But before the camera even entered the room, bodily extremes intensified by the embalming process, or by the conditions of death, often resulted in objective analogical comparisons to things other than flesh. If a cadaver was too dry, students described it as "emaciated and leathery-looking." Plump cadavers proved to be harder to work on because they were "much juicier."[11] Today, the diagnostic literature of the field of pathology is overrun with similar eponyms, only these compare pathological conditions with common food entities. The term 'anchovy sauce pus' is used when referring to a brown pus found in liver abscesses. The red papilliform appearance of a cervix infected with *Trichomonas vaginalis* is called a 'strawberry cervix.' Those stricken with salmonella routinely have 'pea soup' diarrhea, a condition that speaks for itself.[12]

At the University of Michigan in the early 1900s, swollen cadavers were very much the norm. Professor of anatomy, G.L. Streeter, insisted all dissection material be saturated "to the point of edema." His directive was not so much a personal preference as it was a practical one. As an experienced anatomist, Streeter knew the bulk of Michigan's cadaver supply were elderly individuals "with sclerotic arteries and frequent thromboses."[13] More often than not, normal channels of embalming, such as venous injections, proved unsuccessful. To Streeter's students then, aged flesh and oedemic tissue encompassed the totality of their anatomical experience. Thus, the logical conceit at the University of Michigan was that edema was inherent to the cadaveric condition. Likewise, if students only encountered and dissected the cadavers of African Americans whose bodies were stolen from potter's fields, it is not outlandish to consider they would make intellectual connections between poor Black identity and cadaverousness.

★★★

Aesthetically, if we consider all the naturally and artificially induced changes inherent to cadavers of the 19th and early 20th centuries, most embalmed bodies do not look like the living. Yet they also do not appear like 'standardized' depictions of the dead; or at least the dead body typically seen by the lay community, be it in photographs or real-life. Unsurprisingly, these same visual distractions manifest throughout dissection photography.

Most visually fluent viewers will spend little time pondering the original cohesive structure, or species of the dissected in such images. But there are those moments when our "inability to extricate ourselves" stops time and perception, and even the most discerning viewer cannot come to terms with the imaged cadaver's 'true' materiality.[14]

On these occasions, viewers are instead left to guess whether the photograph shows a human vessel, shattered like a marble statue into a pile of rubble, in this case a wreckage made of flesh and bone. Or, if it is a composite heap of indeterminate flesh, crudely sculpted into an incongruent form of human equivalence, like some sort of Golem. Only, not one built from dirt and clay, but rather heaps of wet meat, glistening viscera, and canvas-like swaths of flayed skin.

Under these circumstances, a photograph of a single cadaver can evidence a world of divergent textures. Skin can appear solid, yet cloudy; the cadaver seemingly coated with a translucent mucilaginous membrane with a viscosity that is almost wax-like. But skin can also appear hardened, marble-like, "shells of what once were men."[15] This is especially explicit in dissection photographs that show a cadaver mid-dissection, with flayed portions juxtaposed against undissected sections. Or, when organs and viscera are removed and placed on top of the body – the internal now made external.

Perhaps these polarized aesthetics are not the result of bodily decomposition and strange juxtapositions at all. Rather, they are caused by photographic deterioration, such as fading, cracking, silver mirroring, over-lighting, or overexposure. But when faced with such extreme levels of visual and chemical changes, how can one tell the difference?

In terms of changes in corpses, the 19th century anatomist, Béclard, sheds some light on the matter, in his discussion of the stages of the body's natural putrefaction – its complete and *true* putrefaction to the point of dissolution, not the idealized version found in paintings. The process of decomposition involves the disappearance of the body's textures in toto: "the soft parts, confounded with the fluids are reduced into a half fluid putrescence. ... Soon, nought remains but the bones, which in their turn, become friable and pulverulent, leaving nothing but a small earthly residuum."[16] Remember that the cadaver technically represents halted, or delayed, putrefaction. But even so, the realities of the initial stages of unrestrained decomposition (especially if the body was robbed from a grave) no doubt contributed to the partial erasure of the subtle values and varied textures of cadaveric flesh in dissection photographs.

Remember too, that we are looking at *images* of dead bodies, rather than dead bodies themselves. Therefore, Béclard's observations may not serve as the primary cause for the cadaver's ambiguous appearance in photographs. In fact, as previously mentioned, the cause might not be natural at all, but technological.

Due to the limitations of the photographic medium and subsequent photographic printing at the time (especially in the hands of novice student amateur photographers), answering questions about the realities of cadaveric skin involve countless variables on both sides of the anatomic and photographic spectrums. Anatomical variables include "the person's appearance before death, the cadaver's state of deterioration before it is infused with preservatives, the technique used in preservation, the care taken in storing the preserved body, and the length of time it has been held in storage."[17]

Photographically, we must consider what processes and cameras were used to make the final prints, the availability of light in the dissecting room, if they used flash, how much care went into printing and finishing the photographs, or where the prints were stored or displayed after development.

Imagining the unimaginable

> The sight that met our eyes was altogether different from what we had expected. The bodies stretched on the soapstone slabs were of various sorts – some were so thin that it seemed as if they had died of starvation, others had an amount of adipose tissue that was appalling. The jaws were artistically bound up with cotton cloths, while the beards and especially the long hair of the women were in a great state of confusion. ... The station in life of some of the men could be told by the tattoo marks plentifully inscribed on their arms. After selecting the body on which we were to work we left the room. Although it was time for supper we did not all go.
>
> Freshmen Class, Yale School of Medicine, 1898[18]

On a purely visual spectrum, the most aberrant organ of the photographed cadaver is its skin. If you look at a large collection of dissection photographs, you notice, almost immediately, how the cadaver's skin fails to adhere to its own photographic historiography. Visually disjointed from our conceptions of normative human flesh tones, the cadaver's appearance bears no more resemblance to previous photographs of dead bodies then it does to those of living bodies. It is a body dismantled by science rather than by nature.

In the United States, during the latter half of the 19th century, tangible recordings of human-induced bodily deconstructions were rarely encountered in public settings. To clarify that statement a little further, even in the photographic aftermath of the Civil War, the realities associated with images of an unnatural death at the hands of man were ultimately more implied than explicit.

Although shocking to audiences of their time, the famous stereographic prints of dead Civil War soldiers by Brady and Gardner rarely showed abject elements up close, such as bodies flayed, disemboweled, dismembered, or decomposed to the point of becoming the mucosal putrescence observed decades earlier by the likes of Béclard. Although these photographs boasted that they were taken 'directly from nature,' the explicit signs of death had little to do with rotting skin or exposed innards. The majority focused on the lifelessness and unnatural positioning of the dead, the death of humanity over the rotting of flesh.

Stereographs, like postmortem images, seemed to show the body more asleep than deceased. Even by the 1880s, photographs of anatomized cadavers had no real popularized, reliable precedent upon which a discerning photo-centric public could base the realities of its photographically recorded state; particularly in relation to the specificities of exposed internal anatomy.[19] This is not to say that due to the textural and tonal aberrations of the cadaver, its body was thereby rendered wholly unrecognizable to a lay audience — although the ambiguities and homogenization of sex, race, age, and social status must have caused quite the stir. Merely that aesthetically, its ugly and unknown viscera, exposed by the camera and previously unimagined outside of expensive, hand-colored anatomical atlases, did not find a popular audience via widespread distribution. As such, dissection photographs simply were not included within nor an integral part of the visual economy of the American populace.

Indeed, confronting a dissection photograph meant viewing a body without clothing or other markers of identity such as race, age, or even sex. Most confusing of all would be making sense of the body itself. Interpreting a dissection photograph, even in the era in which they were created, requires one to distinguish between bordering and sometimes competing layers of absent, intermingling, or inverted flesh; to identify organs (perhaps seen for the first time) or make sense of their removal and relocation. A common convention of the 20th century was for students to be photographed touching their cadaver. Later images saw them upgrade the convention to include posing alongside the dead body with its disembodied organs held in students' bare hands. These conventions not only showed total comfort with death — a stomach-punching modernization of the classic *memento mori* postures of the past — but demonstrated a borderline animalistic form of transgressive dominance over a body 'sacrificed' to science.

Other extreme examples of this type of posturing involved arranging the remains of fetuses or full-term babies around the dissecting table, the specimens presumably procured from a morgue or affiliated hospital. Although rare, dissection photographs featuring the remains of children or fetuses are unquestionably some of the most abject images of the entire genre. Even to seasoned scholars of dissection photography, like myself, these images are exceedingly difficult to look at, and even harder to comprehend and contextualize. Intensifying their abject significance are the ways in which students staged the dissected children amidst the elements of their larger cadaveric tableaus.

The tamest form of inclusion involved students placing fetal skulls upon stacks of books, or precariously propping a dried skinless anatomical preparation of a child (also known as an écorché) against the leg of a dissection table. More intense images included full-term infants sat upon the dissecting table, leaning against the dissected remains of adult cadavers, cradled in its arms, or placed inside an adult cadaver's hollowed-out stomach (but not necessarily one that was biologically female).

In particularly macabre examples, premature fetuses were hanged from their necks from dissecting table light fixtures, while impassive students adopted classic postures, seemingly indifferent to the remains suspended in front of them. Meanwhile, in rare variants of the classic *Student Dream* subgenre, the cadavers of newborn children served as the resurrected. Although scalpels were placed in their tiny infant hands, turning them into standard reanimated dissectors, students did not reimagine themselves as cadavers. Instead, their role was as 'puppet-master,' to stand and hold the dead child above a supine adult cadaver, as if its role in dissected death was to assist with or lead the student in the dissection of another.

Just merely asleep

Even in postmortem photographs, the first photographic portraits of the dead ever taken, an artificially created homology exists between the flesh of the living and the flesh of the dead that is wholly absent from dissection photographs. Postmortems exhibit a fascinating visual aberration that's worth noting here. The vast majority show the dead body (usually a child) posed and photographed as if it were alive, just merely asleep. Most, if not all, vestiges of the true material status of the body have been effectively erased via the photographer's craft, and hidden from the lens of the camera, and by proxy, the commemorative gaze of bereaved family members.

Testimonies of photographers discussing the use of ingenious lighting techniques and other industry tricks to assist in mitigating the visual signs of death and decay are surprisingly plentiful. Many of these self-proclaimed 'experts' in the field of postmortem photography boasted of their skills in local newspapers and trade journals. In the 1870s, the accomplished Philadelphia photographer, James Gihon, offered up his advice: "Make it your effort to produce the most *life-like* picture of which you are capable," he told *The Philadelphia Photographer*. "Avoid a full face view. Do not bring the body *alongside* of a window. The evils of such a course are almost irremediable, even in the hands of the most skillful colorist." Afterward, but only if a pose was convincingly natural, instructed Gihon, should a photographer hire an artist to color in the corpse's eyes to maximize its lifelike appearance.[20]

Gihon was not the only photographer who weighed in on photographing the dead. The inevitable decomposition of the skin and its resultant textural abnormalities presented a challenge to many 19th-century photographers. "Rather a grave subject," stated an article in *The Philadelphia Photographer* in 1873, "is in reference to the difficulty encountered from the discolorations about the neck of deceased persons." To this end, recommended the author, a Mr. Carlisle, "I have found the use of a mixture of equal parts of creosote and essence of peppermint will entirely change and remove the discoloration, then you can go on and get good results."[21] For professional photographers, like Carlisle and Gihon, the true aesthetics of death were a thorn in the flesh. In order to satisfy a client's need, and thereby perpetuate their standing within the photographic industry, the visual signs of decomposition needed to be obliterated; and done so immediately.

While it is hard to imagine a photographer painting a corpse white in order to take its picture, such endeavors are not wholly beyond the pale. As author Frederic W. Hafferty states, the general public's expectations regarding the appearance of the deceased were, and still very much are, highly influenced by the mortician's arts:

> Armed with rouge, eyebrow pencil, and cotton padding, the mortician is called upon to snatch the body temporarily from the world of the dead and return it to the world of the living. Mourners do not see the stiches that hold the jaw together, the cotton padding stuffed into the oral cavity to keep it from collapsing under the weight of tissue now unsupported by a blood pressure system, or the plastic cup that has been inserted under each eyelid to serve a similar supportive function. What they do see is a body in peaceful repose, as if asleep and thus alive – not a person now dead, undergoing a natural process of biological decomposition.[22]

Let us take a moment to seriously reflect upon this. Regarding aesthetics, it is rather interesting to consider that within the genre of postmortem photographs, the skin of the dead exists as an artificial construct. It is a conceit, bearing more in common with living flesh doused in makeup, or the imagined and idealized flesh found in paintings. For the image to be an effective memento of mortality, all visual signs of disease, injury, and natural decomposition must be effectively erased.

Given postmortem photography's larger cultural and industry-driven need, it is easy to see how and why the genre achieved a more socially accepted status over that of dissection photography; or, why postmortems are still taken to this day. These images preserve and commemorate a life, often through an intrinsic obscuring of the true material nature of death. Dissection photographs, meanwhile, commemorated a proximity to death in all its gruesome glory. Many students of the 20th century counted on the aberrative nature of the cadaver's 'natural' form – be that natural to life, or natural to an embalmed death – to separate their identities from that of the lay community. The more transgressive its appearance, the more 'transformed' the student who dissected it appeared, both to themselves and outsiders.

The transformation of both living and dead bodies required commemoration and commentary. When "Lewis," a student of the Dental Department of Midwestern University (Chicago), mailed out a dissection postcard in 1913, his accompanying message pointed out the abject qualities of the photographed cadaver's bandaged, blackened, and corrupted shape:

> Say Guy: You living? What do [you] think of the D.D.S. ... The picture was taken in our Anatomical Laboratory where we dissect the dead one (stiffs). Got the guy on [the] table just about skinned, looks pretty rotten doesn't it? The guy died last April sometime and ought to stink pretty bad, but they don't, they are all pretty well pickled when we get them.[23]

The note from "Lewis" to his recipient highlighted the abject nature of his cadaver's appearance. Yet it also served to manage his friend's limited, lay-interpretation of the flesh of the embalmed dead as being "rotten."

Although it is a completely 'unnatural' and untruthful construct, the reality of a sterile and peaceful death, one that leaves behind a body exhibiting no signs of leaking, abnormalities, or deformation, is the cultural norm in the modern-day United States. As Hafferty points out, the real 'truth' of the matter is that "most lay people in this culture see a dead body only after it has undergone cosmetic ministrations."[24] Therefore, our aesthetic expectations (and reality) are based on what we have become accustomed to.

Although they are a byproduct of an era long since passed, dissection photographs, again, aesthetically speaking, are considered more socially transgressive – 'as disgusting as they are disturbing' – since they expose and often exploit death in more 'truthful' ways. There is no denying their graphic nature in terms of subject matter. But they are also graphic in the portrayal of the realities and vulnerabilities of death. They exhibit no documented attempts to cosmetically hide or remove the true nature of the skin, tone, or texture of the cadaver for the benefit of any industry or familial recipient.[25]

While it is true, postmortem photography and dissection photography existed in two very different arenas, and appealed to two very distinct audiences, the analogies between their disparities of reality and half-truths, normative and subversive, explicit and implied, are defining hallmarks of the sociocultural landscape that birthed both genres. It is remarkable to consider, then, how aesthetics affected public consumption of the dissection photograph as a legitimate and time-honored genre. In the end, either as a determiner for the unreality in portraits of deceased loved ones, or the denigration of the truthfulness of dissection photography, perhaps it's exactly as the poet T.S. Eliot said in *The Four Quartets*: "human kind / Cannot bear very much reality."[26]

Emulsional damage: fading in albumen and gelatin silver dissection photographs

One of the most significant long-term limitations of 19th-century photography is that improper storage or display invariably leads to photographic fading. The photographic processes most susceptible to this form of chemical deterioration are salted-paper prints and albumen prints. In both cases, fading occurs from improper environmental conditions, namely excessive humidity and overexposure to light.

It is currently believed that the oldest surviving dissection photographs are albumen prints from the 1870s. Thus, the genre's originating imagery is susceptible to erasure from excessive fading. Obviously, a photo fades regardless of its subject matter. But in albumen dissection photographs, fading alters the material understanding of what is and is not part of the cadaver's natural anatomical features, textures, and topology.

Invariably, the overall "decrease in optical density" of an albumen dissection photograph causes the diverse textures of the cadaver's skin to become unintelligible.[27] Fading in albumen prints start in the lightest areas where there is little imaging material (silver particles). The subtle tonal variations found in highlight areas often shift to a homogeneous, yellow-white haze, giving the image an overall appearance of overexposure. Much like the appearance of a cadaver photographed with the aid of flash powder, bodily cohesion and bodily decomposition become as one; exogenous and endogenous features melt into each other, skin merging with viscera to create a whitened, meatloaf mixture of indistinguishable forms.

Although fading in albumen prints, or any photographic print, is not purposeful (or for that matter reversible), the process exhibits startling comparisons to the focused efforts of what James Elkins calls the "unimagined skin"; a Western tradition beginning in the Renaissance whereby painters depicted human skin *"as an absence,"* as immaculate, unblemished surfaces, devoid of "folds, dimples, softness and hardness, hairs and pores, translucent veins, white knuckles, and the entire catalogue of visual forms specific to skin."[28] Elkins posits that this artistic trend corresponded to religious beliefs, specifically, "Christian thoughts of the ideal bodies and skins that would be donned in heaven, so that marmoreal textures were natural candidates for expressing the new amalgam of Catholic doctrine and recovered antiquity."[29]

While flawless, featureless skin may have spoken to the body's incorruptibility in painted form, when these features disappear from the photographed cadaver, they effectively corrupt its relatability to a primary function, be that anatomical education or identity-formation. Technically, to those who took or posed for them, dissection photographs served no educational function. Effectively differentiating between interior and exterior bodily surfaces was therefore not a requirement of its commemorative outcome. However, as integral artifacts of the visual heritage of American medicine, confusion over the erasure of bodily integrity strips the cadaver of its transformative power. When faded to the point of unrecognizability, doubt is cast further on the authenticity of the commemorated scene. The cadaver's vaguely anthropomorphic shape overturns its inseparability to living beings, becoming nothing more than a hoax, a simulacrum of the basest sense, something "that had never lived ... a two-thousand-year-old creation that somebody had stolen from an old horror-movie set."[30]

Connections between the cadaver's ambiguous appearance and faded photographs persist with the albumen print's successor, the gelatin silver process. Though not as susceptible to unsuitable environmental conditions as the albumen process, many gelatin silver prints were displayed in the very dissecting rooms they were taken in. These rooms contained a host of volatile agents known to cause rapid physical deterioration in photographs, such as extreme temperature fluctuations, hazardous chemical vapor and particulates (both preservatives and those coming from the decaying body), and prolonged exposure to natural light.

From the early 1890s up to the early 1920s, one of the most frequent causes of fading in gelatin silver photographs was an excess of sodium thiosulfate fixer (aka 'hypo'), a chemical used to develop silver-based prints and negatives. If all traces of hypo were not thoroughly washed off a print's surface during photofinishing, the residual fixer could alter the photo's appearance, causing severe fading, or the development of a greenish-yellow stain.[31]

Many images affected by this form of fading were created by amateur photographers with little to no previous photographic experience. In the 1880s, with the introduction of a host of new gelatin silver printing-out papers (commonly called gelatin POPs) and the emergence of developing-out papers, dissection photos could be printed anywhere from a light-sealed darkroom to a student's poorly lit dorm room. The advantages of these images lay with the speed in which they were developed. Students no longer needed an eternally sunny day. Instead, "printing by development required only a brief exposure to light followed by immersion in a bath of 'hypo' that would reveal the latent image."[32]

Flesh under wraps

As mentioned previously, gelatin silver prints comprise the vast majority of extant dissection photographs. The photographic process reached its popularity at the end of the 19th century, coinciding with a time in medical history when cadavers began to be presented to students for dissection wrapped head-to-toe in preservative-soaked bandages. These wrappings were essential, keeping the body wet and supple both before and during its dissection. If tendon or tissue dried out, they became as hard and immovable as stone. Similarly, a lack of preservative encouraged damage by biological growth, insects, and even rats.

Bandages were commonly made from layers of tissue paper and cheesecloth. As a preventative measure against decomposition, the cadaver's face and hands were first smeared with Vaseline (petroleum jelly) then wrapped with tissue paper. After that layer set, a second coat of Vaseline was applied over the entire body. Anatomical preparators then wrapped it again, this time using foot wide bandages of cheesecloth. If time permitted, it was "well to wrap the legs and arms separately."[33] This way, limbs could be exposed individually, while the rest of the body remained protected.

Until modern forms of embalming were perfected, wrapping cadavers in this manner, and placing them in cold storage, was instrumental in the long-term preservation of the dead. Some bodies stayed in cold storage, or were submerged in tanks of alcohol, for months or even years. Although the freezing process helped preserve the body and was more sanitary (cold kills bugs and mold), it inadvertently accelerated the drying out of bodily extremities.[34]

Once a wrapped cadaver was photographed, and that photograph began to fade over time, the homogenized values of faded or toned gelatin silver prints (some using tinted gelatino-bromide papers), rendered exposed layers of inner-flesh, flayed skin, and ripped bandages as analogous matter. Depending on the extent or locality of photographic fading it is often impossible for modern viewers to determine where jagged layers of bandages stop, and flayed layers of human flesh begin.

Regardless of its originating source, fading in gelatin silver dissection photographs simultaneously reduce and expand the cadaver's conceptual and corporeal form. When visually indistinguishable, intermingled layers of peeled skin and loose bandages further the abject nature of its material cohesiveness. This is more than a simple denial of the natural textures of cadaveric skin – as shown in albumen prints. Rather, this fading inadvertently furnishes the dead body with a resurfaced epidermis of allografted *and* autografted flesh; its appearance much like that of a molting insect shedding a coagulated exuviae; making way for the emergence of a new embryonic flesh.

Adding to the already complex aesthetics of photographically rendered and environmentally or photochemically altered skins, there exists a certain form of irony in viewing gelatin silver dissection photographs. The irony here being that we gaze at these images of skin and bone through an emulsion made from bones – animal *gelatin* being the primary ingredient. As this is an emulsion that flexes and breathes as if it (still) had lungs, one must wonder whether the genre's few surviving dry plate negatives absorbed any of the noxious effluvia emanating from the decomposing body. Could tiny particles of airborne body fluids and preservatives bear any responsibility for the delamination of these plates? Did gelatin silver prints, exposed and subsequently displayed in humid, dank dissection rooms, attract microscopic particulates of dirt, dust, and dead skin cells, and in doing so cause oxidative deterioration, like silver mirroring? How ironic would that be? That finally, after all this time, the cadaver no longer exists as a morally corruptive agent of identity. And yet, while society now accepts its intrinsic value as an object of learning, its visual history could be forever polluted by the literal agents and environs used to legitimize its utility.

10

Location, Location, Location

> The dissecting room still continued to be a vantage ground for
> our mirth and reckless conduct.
>
> Freshmen Class, Yale University School
> of Medicine, 1904[1]

Poor lighting affects the outcome of any photograph. In the case of a
dissection photograph, it can also contribute to the ambiguous appearance
of a cadaver's skin and bones. The availability and quality of light within
a dissecting room was contingent upon where it was located, be it on the
school's topmost floor, a basement, or in a small windowless structure
built elsewhere on the property. In some cases, a private interior space was
abandoned altogether, and dissections were instead held outdoors, in the
open air.

Dissecting rooms varied considerably from state to state and school to
school. By the end of the 19th century, most (but not all) states had instituted
anatomy acts, which provided most schools (but again, not all) with a legal
and steady supply of cadavers. Flush with equal amounts of student bodies
and dead bodies, schools like Jefferson Medical College and Rush Medical
College (Chicago) expanded their laboratory facilities and spared no expense
in the process. No longer dingy, cramped spaces, these new, cathedral-sized
dissecting rooms accommodated hundreds of students, all dissecting at once,
and all underneath a luminous combination of electric and gas lighting, and
an immense skylight, which spanned nearly the entire length of the room.
With these physical changes so too changed the visual economy of various
dissecting rooms. In the case of Jefferson and Rush, classic group shots (four
to six students and one cadaver) became a relative thing of the past. Instead,
as Figure 10.1 shows, now the entire freshmen class could pose together
among a sea of the deceased.

But not all schools had this luxury. At the onset of incorporation, until
matriculation increased, and financial stability afforded the opportunity to

Figure 10.1: Jefferson Medical College (Philadelphia, Pennsylvania). Unidentified photographer. Gelatin silver print, circa 1910

Source: Private collection

build new structures according to their specifications, many schools located in major cities frequently rented their buildings or held classes in private homes. These schools had no choice but to improvise their dissecting facilities, adjusting the needs of the gross lab to the parameters of preexisting structures. For example, the "intolerably foul" dissecting room of the Philadelphia College and Infirmary of Osteopathy was formerly a horse stable.[2] The first class of the Texas College of Osteopathic Medicine (Fort Worth) dissected in a garage apartment adjacent to a four-room house that the Dean and the Director of Financial Aid used as office space. Until a proper dissecting room could be built at Wake Forest College Medical School, dissections were held in "the west half of the basement of the Gymnasium."[3] Once completed however, the latter school's new laboratories and dissecting rooms were exemplars of the industry. The famous Flexner Report of 1910 deemed them "clean and odorless" with "the bodies undergoing dissection being cared for in the most approved modern manner."[4]

Sometimes, dissections were held in specially constructed buildings, or makeshift shacks. These structures were erected on the property, usually as far away as possible from the street and the public's prying eyes. In the 1880s, the overcrowded "glum," "poorly lighted," and "badly ventilated" brick building of the medical school of Harvard University (Boston) had an "even worse wooden shed" attached, which served, in part, as the school's dissecting room.[5]

In 1864, the Female Medical College of Pennsylvania (Philadelphia) held their autopsies and anatomical course work next door, in the dissecting room of the Woman's Hospital of Philadelphia. Given the growing stigmas associated with the room, the managers were desirous of its removal. The functional hospital was, after all, overcrowded with living patients, mostly women and children, whom were all aware of what transpired within.

Eventually, management settled on erecting a "one storied brick building" against the east wall of the hospital for the dissection and storage of the dead. At "thirty-two feet long by sixteen feet broad," the building was quite substantial, complete with an entrance at its north end, and its interior "lighted by two skylights."[6] As it was still located on the hospital grounds, there were presumably no windows at ground level for those strolling by to peer into.

Students dissected there undisturbed for approximately a decade. In 1874, due to the needs of a rapidly expanding hospital, more space was needed for patient care. Equally important was quelling the fears of the hospital's Board of Trustees. Once again, the "too close proximity of the dissecting room" to the wards had "executed an unfavorable influence" upon patients and their subsequent recovery.[7] Thus, the college was required to immediately surrender the use of the dissecting room to the hospital and find other accommodations. As new facilities took time and money, the school, now named the Woman's Medical College of Pennsylvania, improvised its cadaveric storage and disposal practices. In 1877 it was decided to sink a well in the northwestern section of their property for the disposal of dissecting room debris.[8]

But even in rural areas, where land for expansion was more plentiful, dissecting rooms were still cramped, dirty rooms with little natural light. Extant dissection photographs from the late 1890s show that the anatomy lab of the American School of Osteopathy was so small that, together, a standard dissecting table and photographer (who needed to stand several feet away from their subject) could not fit comfortably inside. As a result, students had to improvise. Two slanted sawhorses, topped with a door or a long piece of plywood, replaced the dissecting table, upon which was placed the cadaver. It's unclear whether this makeshift table was used for actual dissecting purposes, or merely constructed for the occasion of taking photographs.

In either event, around 1905, the American School of Osteopathy began to hold its anatomical dissections outdoors. This drastic change in venue was quickly reflected in the school's dissection portraiture. Dim, front-lit group shots of students clumped awkwardly behind their cadaver were replaced with high-contrast photographs (usually in postcard format) of a hospital gurney, complete with a relatively untouched cadaver, positioned in the sun in front of a red brick wall (rendered dark grey). Gathered around, with room to spare, were large gatherings of students. On occasion, photographs of these open-air classes featured the school's founder, and the founder of osteopathic medicine, Andrew Taylor Still. The bearded and beloved osteopath, dressed in a dark suit and hat, usually stood at the head of the gurney, pointing at the cadaver with his hand, or the end of an exceedingly long walking stick.

Regardless of whether students posed in small groups or alone, this outdoor location, posed against a wall, became the school's visual tradition. But by the 1910s, likely encouraged by other examples of transgressive dissection portraiture, students decided to relocate themselves, the cadaver, and all applicable dissecting room furniture away from any conventional setting. Their chosen site of photography, the middle of the nearby woods.

As above so below

> A man would be very foolish to eat potatoes raw rather than to have them cooked. No photographer would take any flat light to work in.
>
> Albert Sands Southworth, daguerreotypist, 1873[9]

Regardless of whether they were located within old, retrofitted, or new structures, dissecting rooms typically occupied either attic spaces or basements. As such, the lighting within was either overabundant or nonexistent. Taking dissection photographs inside either environment took skill. Experienced commercial photographers were adept at working in difficult lighting conditions. The technical quality of their work usually spoke for itself. Student amateur photographers, meanwhile, had much to learn. Many of their blurry backlit snapshots rendered the landscape of the dissecting room as visually indistinct as the cadaver was conceptually ambiguous.

Generally, most American dissecting rooms were located on the topmost floor of schools. The ideal lab featured a surplus of windows, large skylights, and either electric or gas lighting. All were needed to maximize the availability and quantity of light during gloomy day-time dissections in the fall and winter. In 1890, the dissecting room of the Medical Department of the University of Vermont comprised the entire top floor of their school. Architectural drawings show the room accommodated 16 dissection tables (and thus upwards of 96 students), along with a private dissecting room for the professor of anatomy. It also featured a great skylight and eight circular windows.[10] In 1894, the newly constructed Birmingham Medical College (Alabama) boasted in its first annual announcement that "our territory [the dissecting room] is second to none," for it "had been specially designed" to include proper ventilation and superb lighting.[11]

The light that poured through dissecting room skylights was neither controllable nor changeable. Its color, intensity, and direction went undiffused and unrestrained; shining down through regular panes of glass, rather than the more desirable (and expensive) ground glass windows of high-end portrait studios. Although a dissecting room bathed in a sea of light on a cloudless autumn day would have been the preferred environment for conducting a dissection, such conditions were less than ideal for photographic portraiture. Intense light and its resultant deep shadows obliterated all detail from the photographed body, transforming it into a texture-less void. The same could be said of dissection photographs taken outdoors under similar conditions. The issues arising from excessive sunlight were not easily mitigated, even by the most accomplished of professional photographers. Albert Sands Southworth, the famed Boston daguerreotypist, considered extreme light and shadow too harsh for human portraiture. To him, the contrast resulted in images deemed "charcoaly," "inky," "muddy and dirty"; like "shadow pictures; the most hateful things that were ever met with."[12]

Likewise, the bodies of fresh cadavers, still wet with colored preservative, or with newly exposed organs swelled with fluid, reflected direct light with an intensity that further obliterated the subtle variances photographers normally hoped to capture in highlighted flesh tones. But too much light was preferred over too little.

In a symbolic reflection of popular opinion over dissection as either a sanctified or devilish act, those schools unable to house dissecting rooms on top floors instead relegated them to basements. By the nature of their subterranean location, basement dissecting rooms were gloomy cave-like spaces, not just physically, but emotionally. In 1909, the Flexner Report excoriated the lighting conditions of the "dark apartment" that was the basement dissecting room of the Pulte Medical College (Cincinnati), a homeopathic school, stating: "Anything more woe-begone than the laboratories of this institution would be difficult to imagine."[13]

With their dark mysteries impermeable to even the power of the sun, the basement dissecting room quickly developed a notorious reputation as an ambiguous and fearsome place, maligned more so than the attic dissecting room due to its proximity to other liminal spaces, namely, the janitor's living quarters, and the room in which they preserved cadavers, also known as "the dead cellar."[14] Being associated with either chamber blurred both spatial integrity and the integrity of student identity.

At schools in which racial intolerance was allowed to thrive, sharing physical space with non-doctors, specifically, African American janitors, was no mere blurring of identity, but an affront to it. What went on in these basement rooms was integral to a student's education. Yet these same students often expressed extreme reluctance to venture down into these spaces alone.

'Chris' Baker: the one who literally walked with death

In 1900, the Medical College of Virginia (MCV) was located in what was known as the Egyptian Building (named so for its exotic Egyptian Revival architecture). The basement of this imposing structure was the domain of its African American janitor and an infamous resurrectionist, 'Chris' Baker. Commonly referred to as "The Ghoul of Richmond," Baker not only embalmed cadavers and boiled bones in the basement to make articulated skeletons, but he reportedly lived down there as well.[15]

Student reminiscences about the physical layout of Baker's basement describe it as if it were a graveyard unto itself; a limitless necropolis or some kind of sentient labyrinth.[16] As eyewitness reports attested of Baker, "he glides about the awful, malodorous apartment without the least fear or veneration for the 'lifeless clay' that is used to advance the cause of science."[17] Interactions with Baker within these liminal spaces were often conveyed as clandestine contraband exchanges, rather than what they were: the necessary and completely routine occurrences of purchasing anatomical material for study. Nevertheless, students chronicled that they felt nauseous, anxious, or downright terrified from such encounters. For instance, in the fall of 1888, student John F. Woodward was instructed to see Baker to obtain a set of bones to begin his osteological studies. As he later confessed, he was unprepared for "the shivers" that passed through his body when he "entered the dark hall" at the rear of the Egyptian Building. "A dim light flickered some distance to my left, and I was met by the most peculiar nauseating odor I had ever known."[18] His narrative continues with the embellished drama and exoticism of a men's adventure magazine: Woodward, a wayward soldier or lost explorer, wandering the subterranean wasteland of a foreign unnatural clime in search of treasure, with darkness and danger lurking around every corner.

Now lost in the dark, Woodward eventually called into the misty gloom several times, but his words were met by silence. Suddenly, the sound of splashing water off in the distance, followed by "a black face with a greasy skull cap" darting out from some "sort of window in what looked like a black silo." It was Baker. He emerged from the darkness, dressed in a greasy jacket and pants, "redolent of the sickening odor" born from preparing cadavers and stripping skeletons of their flesh. In his hands he held a human skull. "This beauty – bones scarce – all I got," Baker told Woodward. The nervous student paid the porter five dollars, wrapped the skull in newspaper, then left hurriedly with the bony remnant under his arm.[19]

The hyperbole students and staff associated with meeting Baker in the indescribable confines of 'his own' basement rooms were obviously a product of their times. Southern, White, middle-class men in their late teens and early twenties likely never had pretext to rely upon, interact with, or be judged inferior by a Black man the way they did with Baker. Many students feared him more than they did the sternest of professors. His knowledge even gave him power over staff. William H. Taylor, MCV's Professor of Chemistry, Toxicology, and Medical Jurisprudence, considered Baker "the lord of the dissecting hall."[20] Yet, as the years went by and involvement in detestable acts, such as grave robbing, waned considerably, becoming the stuff of legend, students internalized Baker's position, knowledge, and former 'ghoulish' endeavors as something foreign and 'other' to themselves and their educations. Thus, to them, Baker, or as they called him, "Old 'Chris'," became a symbol of the most challenging and mysterious aspects of their medical educations. While he and his fellow janitors were referred to as "a class of celebrities well known in story and song," students simultaneously denigrated their contributions, past and present, by bestowing upon them the title of "boogas" and "Bogey Men."[21]

To the surrounding community of Richmond, Virginia, Baker was a literal paradox. The local newspaper, *The Times Dispatch*, probably said it best when they labeled him "one of the most beloved," and "most feared" characters in the city's history.[22] As a Black resurrectionist who raided Black cemeteries to appease the demand of White professors and students, Baker's identity and role(s) within the two opposing communities he served were extremely complicated. It causes one to question if the tales about him and the conditions of the rooms in which he lived and operated within were in fact truth; or, merely embellished reminiscences designed to accentuate the otherness of his race and taboo work.

One assumes similar attempts at othering were in place in 1908, when MVC sophomores of the class of 1910 took a dissection photograph that included Baker. Seven students pose above their cadaver in white shirts and ties, their sleeves rolled up in a combined gesture of informality, comfort, and practicality. But off to the side, separated from the group and literally bisected by the photographic frame, stands Baker, clothed in a frayed, knee-length oilskin jacket.[23]

Two years prior, the Class of 1906 had also posed with Baker (Figure 10.2). Only this time, the janitor was made to sit on the ground at the base of a dissecting table, flanked on both sides by seated students. Given the size of the group, this position is likely out of necessity, not collegiality. Due to the preestablished aesthetics born from the antebellum era of African Americans seated at the feet of White families and soldiers, it would be uncommon for a Black man to be photographed standing above a White man, unless he was their servant.[24]

Figure 10.2: Medical College of Virginia janitor and infamous resurrectionist 'Chris' Baker (bottom center, No. 25) posing with medical students. Medical College of Virginia (Richmond, Virginia). Unidentified photographer. Gelatin silver print, circa 1902–1903

Source: Author's collection

Racial tensions in the South, furthered by state and local Jim Crow laws, established a social hierarchy that greatly limited interactions between African Americans and Whites. However, due to his responsibilities for and knowledge of the school's cadaver supply, Baker exhibited an autonomy on the MVC campus that likely flourished nowhere else in the surrounding city of Richmond, or possibly even the state of Virginia. The dissection photographs he features in connote an element of that autonomy. Yet, they also reflect an anxious relationship between the student body and a man who, depending on whom you spoke to, was either considered a living legend, or a "man-eating demon."[25] Though we will never be certain of the degree to which Baker exhibited control over his representative agency, within the photographic frame, institutionalized and internalized structures demanded his subservience to Southern visual politics, often to the point of degrading his identity.

The trope of the Black janitor, usually seated upon a dissecting room bucket, dominated the first half of dissection photography's evolution (see Figures 5.2 and 12.2). It not only asserted student authority over the janitor by partially segregating him from the dissecting room group, where his dominion was normally absolute, but it also reinforced racial stereotypes, namely the trope of the 'lazy and shiftless' ex-slave. Photographs that tapped into these forms of racist dogma demonstrated what author Matthew

Fox-Amato discusses in his brilliant work, *Exposing Slavery: Photography, Human Bondage, and the Birth of Modern Visual Politics in America*, as "a quiet habit of domination."[26]

In the antebellum era, Black men were commonly pictured seated beneath either White slaveholders or Union soldiers. This pose denoted a combination of obedience, animality, and ownership by recalling "the supplicant depiction of prayer and liberation from abolitionist culture (the kneeling slave)" as well as "the conventions for picturing dogs in contemporary photographic culture."[27] As Fox-Amato points out, in the case of Union soldiers, sitting portraits allowed Whites to act out the "role of emancipator even as they subordinated African Americans to the status of pet-like inferior."[28]

In the case of 'Chris' Baker, MCV dissection photographs, in combination with urban legends, hyperbolized and fetishized his role and identity, especially when we compare images of him from the 1890s to 1900s with concurrent student–janitor encounters at other medical schools. For at the same time Baker was being shunted off to the side of his own dissection room, Katrina Friedenberger and Ellen 'Ellie' Patterson, two first years at the Woman's Medical College of Pennsylvania, posed informally, and intimately, alongside their dissecting room janitor (likely a White man named Israel Walton) in the shadows of the school's basement; or, as the students knew it as, the "cellar where bodies are prepared for dissection."[29] In addition to being a 'working shot' of students and janitors engaging cooperatively in a normally vilified space, the cyanotype print shows the realities of cadaveric preservation at the turn of the century in explicit detail. A preservative vat rests in the far-right corner of the circular frame. The two students stand behind a wooden table, upon which rests two cadavers (possibly African American) being prepped for embalming. Friedenberger and Patterson adopt working attitudes while gazing down with muted expressions as Walton works on finishing up the removal of the cadaver's brain. Per Victorian tradition, the cadaver's genitals have been covered with a sheet.[30]

Gone in a flash

Basement labs served as the ideal environment in which to preserve cadavers. They were cool, dark, and private. To perform a competent dissection in these conditions, however, was a different story. Even when windows were present, light was minimal. Significant supplementation via gas or artificial lighting was essential.

Photography, meanwhile, was made possible only through the aid of magnesium flash. Its technological benefits made it an essential component of any photographer's tool kit, be they amateur or professional. But when used at all –particularly in basement labs – its utility reaped bizarre results upon the appearance of the dead.

Indeed, the incoherency of photographic form and formlessness became particularly egregious with the additional use of magnesium flash. The firing and misfiring of the intense flash 'burst' greatly reduced the body's dissected forms and textures into contrasting biomasses of imponderable materiality; blackened and impermeable, a visual betrayal of the 'transparency' of its purpose to medical education. Many of the dissection photographs taken using flash suggest a cadaver that wasn't so much dissected as it was digested; cut open and left upon the slab to deliquesce into an inky, enzymatic jelly. When a human face did emerge from this oscillating conjunction of stark-white encrusted meat and glistening darkness, its features appeared as a shapeless erosion of structural integrity; both distinct yet incongruous, like bubbling tar (Figure 10.3).

As literal shadows of their former selves, many of these bodies do not even appear as photographic. Instead, the cadaver's innards – comprised of red and white muscle fibers (rendered black and white), iridescent membranes and multi-colored viscera (rendered shades of grey), and coagulated blood

Figure 10.3: Unknown school. Unidentified photographer. Gelatin silver print, circa 1910

Note: Note the coffins in the background.
Source: Private collection

and tinted preservative fluids (rendered black) – bear more in common with artistic representation than photographic exactitude; precursors to the violent figurative paintings of meat sculptors like Graham Sutherland and Francis Bacon, or the kind of abstract materiality Hermann Rorschach prophesied in the inky depths of his two-dimensional cards.

With the 'transparency' of its utility rendered conceptually opaque, and the abject physicality of its photographic appearance condensed to a waxy formlessness, some amateur photographers found the unrecognizability of their artificially lit cadavers a questionable disappointment. "What do you know about this?" asked a student of the outcome of his dissection postcard. "Not so bad for a flashlight [photo] is it?"[31] Another photograph shows students gazing down into the contour-less negation of their cadaver, its flesh transformed by a flash burst into a glowing void, as if its innards somehow contained an internal light source. Appearances aside, there is no denying that artificial flash made it possible for several postcards to be taken of students dissecting the bowels of men from within the bowels of the Kansas City Dental College (Missouri). With its red brick walls, low ceilings, dangling light fixtures, and blacked-out windows, the basement was more dungeon than dissecting room.[32] Although flash made flesh incomprehensible in these images, all around it were the school's industrial innards, lit up in perfect detail, such as iron girders, floor joists, water pipes, and massive heating ducts; the proverbial 'bones' of the building. Here the visceral conjunction of emotionless student and torn flesh, situated within a bleak industrial setting, reads as if ripped straight from the pages of a gothic short story by Edgar Allan Poe: The cadaver's body soon to be sealed inside the basement walls; or, dismembered further and its parts hidden underneath the floorboards.

And yet, despite the shadowy conditions of the Kansas City Dental College's dissecting room, students still lit up with pride over the photographs they took there. In 1921, student, Theo A. Walters, sent a dissection postcard home to his physician father, along with a message on the back that read: "Greetings: – to the dear doctor, from his only son who would become learned in the scientific lore of his profession!"[33]

11

Anatomical Deuteranopia

To give to this perception an intelligible shape, we must dissect
the mass of colors, and arrange them in thought.

Edward Neale, *The Analogy of Thought
and Nature,* 1863[1]

Poor lighting, poorer focusing, and other limitations associated with early
handheld cameras, such as the No. 2 Kodak (released in 1889), Brownie, or
3A cameras (used to make real photo postcards), all likely contributed to the
visual anomalies associated with the cadaver's photographed appearance. Yet,
while these cameras exhibited a marked decrease in detail compared to wet
plate photography, and flash bulbs produced notoriously unintelligible and
inconsistent results, their combined limitations still fail to explain why, for
over 50 years, the cadaver's red blood, embalmed skin, and colorful internal
organs were consistently portrayed as black.

Each dissection photograph is a unique visual record all its own.
Collectively, however, the genre demonstrates a pervasive attribute of
aberration that breeds frequent visual and cultural misunderstandings
over the color and tonal value of dead flesh, especially when attempting
to identify the race of the photographed cadaver. Confusion propagates
regardless of the governing variables of each image, such as posing
conventions, location, cameras, camera operators, printing techniques,
or photographic processes.

The high-contrast disparities of the interiors of cadaveric bodies, to say
nothing of the near always deep-grey or black appearance of blood-soaked
and preservative-infused skin, is, at least in part, a byproduct of the use of
orthochromatic and non-orthochromatic photographic plates. Both wet plate
and early dry plate and/or film bases were highly sensitive to blue light, and
almost completely insensitive to the colors of yellow and especially red – the
color of blood and exposed interior anatomies.

Blood culture: red is dead

> The true rendering of the relative values of colors – to say nothing of that philosopher's stone of the art, the rendering of color itself – has always been one of the stumbling blocks in the photographer's path, but it is fast being removed.
>
> *The Photographic Times and American Photographer*, 1889[2]

From the era of the daguerreotype up through the 20th century and the dominance of the gelatin silver process, the eye of the camera recorded red as near indistinguishable from that of black. During this time, both photographically and anatomically, red was the color of the dead. In the 1880s, dissection manuals, like Holden's *Manual of Dissection of the Human Body*, drew scrupulous attention to the reddish-gray, reddish-brown, or "pale rose color" of flesh, or the "livid red or violet color" of the lungs "produced in the act of dying."[3]

Skilled embalmers were known to add a few drops of red aniline to their injections to impart "a life-like hue" to the cadaver's skin.[4] In the mid-1800s, Dr. S. W. Wetmore implemented an antiseptic injection that included "melted tallow colored with Venetian red." This blood-colored booster shot not only maintained the body's solidity and natural (living) colors, but also rendered it "free from vermin."[5]

Photographic colorists, meanwhile, used red pigments to "kill the blackness" of their tinted images.[6] Generally though, the photographic industry agreed that red had no place in a proper portrait studio. Clients were told to avoid wearing any kind of warm-colored clothing, as the final product would appear as if the sitter were dressed in mourning. "Remember that positive red, orange, yellow or green, are the same as black, or nearly so," warned legendary portraitist Albert Southworth to the readers of *The Lady's Almanac* in 1854. "And violet, purple and blue are nearly the same as white."[7]

The eye of the camera was quite unforgiving when it came to the hues of human skin, especially fair or thin white skin. Overheating in the summer, becoming flustered, or merely having a few freckles or acne had potentially deleterious effects on the final photograph. Sitters with reddened cheeks looked stricken with contagion or bore a close resemblance to a corpse. "Don't go to the photographer in a hurry," warned experts in the *American Amateur Photographer* in 1895, "for even if your face does not appear to be flushed, the blood will not be far from the surface, and it will appear in the negative, making the shades appear darker and the lights whiter."[8]

Dr. Hermann Wilhelm Vogel and Frederic E. Ives pioneered advances in the color sensitization of dry plate emulsions as early as 1873. But it was not until the early 1900s that the Eastman Kodak Company, then the largest manufacturers of film and dry plates in the world, first released commercially available orthochromatic dry plates.[9] Orthochromatic plates, while 'truer' to the color spectrum than previous non-orthochromatic plates, were nevertheless, still insensitive to rays of yellow and red. Both gelatin emulsions rendered warm colors as if black. Given Eastman's dominance in the United States at the turn of the 20th century, there is no question that student amateur photographers used Kodak plates and/or films to make their dissection photographs.

In 1911, Eastman claimed to make one plate, called "the Panchromatic," which was sensitive to a full color spectrum, including the illusive color red. Their advertisement, titled "The Truth About Orthochromatism," which ran in several magazines that year, including *The Photographic Times, Saturday Evening Post,* and *Collier's,* boasted: "This plate is so sensitive to red that not even the usual ruby lamp can be used in the darkroom. It must be developed in absolute darkness." The ads went on to state in plain terms: "It is quite evident that such a plate would not be practical for ordinary use."[10]

Even once panchromatic film was produced on a larger scale in and around 1928 – which would have allowed for truer values of the reds and yellows of the cadaver's muscle tissue, viscera, and adipose tissue – it is highly unlikely that student amateur photographers would have used panchromatic film, or plates, to take their dissection photographs. Photo historian, Robert Taft, points out that this film was only a benefit to serious amateurs and professional photographers.[11] The added complexities of panchromatic development, and its additional cost, no doubt contributed to its sparse utility at the time.

Generally, there is no discernible difference in the tonality of the cadaver's flesh from the era of the wet plate to the era of the orthochromatic dry plate/flexible film bases. Again, this is not surprising. Both were still highly insensitive to red light. Any significant differences in the depiction of the cadaver's skin or muscle tissue during this era resulted from other variables, such as the quality of the camera and lens, intense direct lighting (skylights versus artificial lighting), the use of magnesium flash, and the variability of the cadaver's physical freshness. This could involve the period between death, dissection, and photography, as well as its physical condition (flesh still wet versus dried out and hardened).

By the 1930s, panchromatic emulsions saw near universal usage. But by then, as an omnipresent tradition in American medical schools, dissection photography was already in the throes of decline. A truer sense of the colors and tonal values of the cadaver's skin and interior flesh would find limited expression in the genre's waning years through rogue snapshots.

Meat is murder

> After we had completed Osteology, we started dissecting muscles.
> Thus we dealt in meat for weeks for Uncle Sam, while the balance
> of the country were observing meatless Tuesdays.
>
> Freshman dental class, Medical College
> of Virginia, 1918[12]

As photo historians Fox and Lawrence acutely argue, throughout the 19th century, blood "must have been part of the visual experience of all surgeons, and yet it rarely appeared in photographs."[13] The authors point to the scandalous reception of *The Gross Clinic*, the 1875 masterpiece of heroic surgery by Philadelphia portraitist, Thomas Eakins, as an exemplar of this phenomenon. For unlike the black and white medical photographs of the times, the painting depicted blood in all its gory glory: dripping from an open surgical incision and thoroughly coating the hands and raised scalpel of surgeon, Samuel Gross. Vibrant, visceral, red.

Tableaus this explicit were branded inappropriate for lay consumption. The painting was taken off public display and relocated to where only those in the medical profession were permitted to view it. Thus, the omission of blood from publicly accessible medical imagery, specifically those of hospitals and surgical demonstrations, was unquestionably purposeful. One reason, states Fox and Lawrence, was that its inclusion "would have contradicted the image of cleanliness and order which characterized photographs of hospitals."[14] Another was the harmful effects blood had on public confidence, emphasizing surgery's association with pain, suffering, and abject elements, such as cut flesh and exposed viscera.

Publishing photomechanical reproductions of blood in newspapers, or including it in medical school bulletins and annual announcements could have been disastrous for public image and the bottom line. But while surgeons may have resisted visualizing bodily fluids in order to solidify their positions as governors of public health and sanitation, medical students did not mind such associations. Blood was hardly the most abject or dominant element of a dissection photograph. Its presence merely amplified the transgressive nature of images taken in a dank, filthy dissecting room. After all, as Fox and Lawrence profoundly observe, "in a black and white picture," blood – now turned black by the camera – "is indistinguishable from dirt."[15]

With the body's life-giving fluid rendered analogous to that of literal filth, one questions whether conceptual clarity might be enhanced were dissection photographs in color. Vivid saturated pigment would almost certainly increase their abject nature, effectively showing the chromatic, tonal, and textural changes of dead skin as observed by the likes of Béclard.

But a full, or even partially applied color spectrum might also modulate the cadaver's taxonomic traits, consigning it to the same state of flayed ruination as carcasses of butchered animals, such as pigs, cows, or sheep. Would this zoomorphic transference in turn reinforce to lay audiences, or to the students themselves, the cadaver's indispensable nature; transforming the feared (but respected) dead house into nothing more than a slaughterhouse, a grotesque abattoir of carnivorous, carnivalesque culture?

And what of the medical students posed within? Would they, by proxy, be similarly converted into butchers or beasts? Could they find themselves subjected to the same transformative properties they relished in inflicting upon the dead? For if the cadaver was merely something to 'carve' up, and be treated as or compared to literal meat, then by extension, this means the students dissecting it were nothing more than a "gang of high-class butchers."[16] Or, as the students of the Chicago College of Dental Surgery called themselves, the "R.O.B;" the "Royal Order of Butchers."[17]

The Class of 1912 at the University of Maryland School of Medicine certainly believed themselves on par with roughnecks when they posed for their dissection room portraits with the epigraph, "Butchers! of 1912," inscribed along their dissecting table.[18] Meanwhile, on the back of his dissection postcard, Baltimore medical student, "Frank," asked viewers: "How does this look for *Dr's. to be?*" His query, directed at a militant row of four men plunging scalpels and tweezers into the skin of their cadaver, each student dressed in a butcher-style apron instead of a standard smock.[19]

If we base an answer to "Frank's" question on the self-reflective poetry of medical students, then indeed, a removal of human-like traits was endemic to dissection, making *doctors to be* into "beastly lions," satisfied only "after they have done their respective butcheries."[20]

Sometimes, leaning into the more bestial components of dissection lead to repercussions upon student daily life as much as it did the formation of identity. A dissection postcard sent from the Baltimore College of Dental Surgery, the first dental college in the world, taunted its recipient with the message: "Dear Bob, This is a cadaver. Will I send a slice. … Think of this when you eat."[21] With the visual similarities between cadavers and carcasses blurring the line between eating humans and consuming animals, students routinely abstained from eating meat of any kind, lest they become abject themselves in the process. "At this time we begin carving on the human cadaver (which means elimination of hash from the menu)," declared students at the Atlanta-Southern Dental College in 1918, their macabre commentary linking dissected human tissue to the meat of animals.[22]

Over a half-century later, projections of the 'student-butcher' or 'student-cannibal' were still common. "These meat prices are unreal," read a photo caption published in the 1974 yearbook of the Texas College of Osteopathic

Medicine.[23] The associated image shows a student standing at a dissecting table in his white coat, the disembodied heart of his cadaver grasped in one hand, while at his waist lay the dead body's completely dissected and collapsed head.

Visual misconceptions over medical students being nothing more than butchers were exacerbated by the fact that cadavers, whose value as a commodity was contingent on flaying, were commonly treated in a style similar to racks of beef. In big cities, like Chicago, freezers, such as those at the Rush Medical College, could reportedly keep upwards of 300 to 350 cadavers at a time. Extant photographs of cadaver storage facilities and embalming rooms in Philadelphia show bandaged bodies suspended from the ceiling via metal tongs affixed to their heads. As the medical literature of the times confirmed, the culture surrounding these stockpiles of cadavers was such that if a student or demonstrator required less than an entire body, they simply cut off what they wanted and returned "the rest to the freezing chamber."[24]

★★★

One of the awful truths of dissection is that clumsy 'butcheries' are a common occurrence no matter what century they are performed in. For those students armed with piercing scalpels and an equally penetrating disdain for dissection, the result is nothing short of a massacre. For instance, while enrolled at the University of Buffalo (New York), student Clarence E. Lauderdale routinely complained about the careless behavior and disgusting dissecting habits of his fellow students. "The dissecting of the Dental students amounts to nothing," wrote Lauderdale to a friend.

> [T]he boys go up and slash into the head a little, put down their time and then light out. There were four students on the head on which I was put on. You can imagine what four could do on one head. I started in to do something but the other fellows came up and spoiled it all by cutting [off] the muscles I had dissected out.[25]

Soon after, be it from disinterest, disrespect, or an inability to gain knowledge from 'the cut,' the dental students resorted to the senseless mutilation bemoaned by so many anatomists. Already melancholic over his lackluster dissecting experience, Lauderdale arrived at the dissecting room one night, only to discover that someone had needlessly decapitated his cadaver and stole its head. The dejected student lamented that his dissecting experience was an abject failure, amounting to nothing more than being "just a place to drop $10."[26]

Lauderdale's testimony points to a rarely discussed reality of the American medical education system, and one that is still true today: not all students enjoy or want to participate in anatomical dissection. The associated query here being, in the era of the dissection photograph, did those who hate dissection still pose for pictures with the dead?

The problem with color: determining the race of the dead

"Color remains other," declares David Batchelor in his book, *Chromophobia*.[27] In fact, continues the author, "it often becomes more other than before. More dangerous, more disruptive, more excessive. And perhaps this is the point." Indeed, to this point, we must consider that when it comes to dissection photography, colorized clarity could destabilize the abject through a disruption of the cadaver's corporeal ambiguities. In other words, the dissected dead would look more like the dissected dead.

Subverting the subversive could bring dissecting room aesthetics full circle. It could effectively lead to a normalization of our visual comprehension of dissected forms, skin colors, and bodily fluids. Though the lay community may be shocked at the true shades of embalmed cadavers, the use of color would certainly assist us in attempting to confirm the race of the dissected, a characteristic of cadaveric identity that, as stated before, has been misrepresented since the genre's inception.

Historians contend that most of the cadavers shown in dissection photographs are those of African Americans. As historian and author of *Dissection,* John Harley Warner, discusses: "Most (but not all) of the [photographed] dissectors are European American, while a very large proportion (but not all) of the dissected are African American."[28] This statement is supported visually throughout the entirety of dissection photography's evolution, as cadavers are routinely imaged as dark-skinned or near black in appearance. Support is validated further when the visual is coupled with historical statistics and textual narratives – such as physicians' autobiographies, letters, and diaries – which collectively confirm the frequent and unashamed targeting, overuse, and abuse of Black bodies for medical dissection.

The collective supposition then that all dark-skinned cadavers in dissection photographs are therefore the bodies of African Americans seems, at least initially, to be an accurate conclusion: The 'truth' of the camera confirming the 'truth' of the historical record. During this era, Black bodies *did* comprise a disproportionately large percentage of all cadavers supplied to American dissecting rooms. Supporting this claim, is the question, why else would a dissected cadaver and/or its skin appear black in a photograph (see Figures 10.3 and 11.1)? The answer, while surprising, is relatively simple: the camera lies.

Unfortunately, as discussed earlier in this chapter, throughout the entirety of dissection photography's evolution, the veracity of cadaveric skin color

Figure 11.1: Johns Hopkins School of Medicine (Baltimore, Maryland). Unidentified photographer. Gelatin silver print, circa 1912

Note: Here, even the cadaver's bones reproduce as black.
Source: Private collection

is simply not reliable. While scholars' commentary of the glorification and celebration of a dominant White culture exhibiting control over the bodies of the dead (of which African Americans comprised a majority) is respected and understood, we must temper these evaluations when it comes to using dissection photographs as empirical proof with the words of Warner, who emphatically states: "It is notoriously tricky to try and discern race in [dissection] photographs."[29]

Again, there is no denying the imbalance of power and control over the bodies of vulnerable populations in the American medical system, particularly, the bodies of impoverished and marginalized communities, such as those of African Americans. However, extrapolating or confirming this data using dissection photographs, specifically, cadavers' black skin as exemplars of this injustice, is an endeavor fractured by the limitations of photographic technologies (which we have previously discussed), as well as the processes of the body's natural decomposition, and the era's unstable embalming techniques. Adding to the mix is the cadaver's often-deformed facial features, such as squished lips and cheeks, flattened noses, and shaved heads. Indeed – assuming they still had heads – it was, and still is today, quite difficult to determine the race of a cadaver, even when standing next to it in a dissection room. As Hafferty points out, while a cadaver's biological sex "was always readily identifiable," the same "was not necessarily true of its age at death, its nationality, or even its race." The color of cut cadaveric skin was not always as clear cut as it may seem. Skin color ranged "from chalky white to the shade of a redwood coffee table, texture from somewhat pliable to the consistency of dried leather."[30]

Although admittedly difficult to envision, the truth of the matter is that within the dissecting room, there are such things as dark-skinned White cadavers and white-skinned Black cadavers. To say nothing of the changes in the skin of biracial bodies. I have personally seen the dead bodies of both Caucasians and African Americans with pink, grey, brown, and yellow skin. Once, an enormous cancerous organ turned the insides of a cadaver neon green, as if a Nickelodeon-themed, bilirubin-filled dye-packet had exploded inside its thorax. In the 1990s, an embalmer working for the Medical College of Pennsylvania (Philadelphia) routinely injected all his cadavers with such potently pigmented preservatives, their skins turned a vibrant bubblegum pink from head to toe. The psychedelic color change was reportedly an easy way to determine whether fluid injections successfully saturated the cadaver's entire body, or if the liquid had instead pooled in places due to the weakened vascular system of the dead.

Although confusion over skin color, and thus the race, of cadavers is quite ubiquitous, the chromatic perplexities of dead flesh are not exclusive to the dissection room or to dissection portraiture. For although we can attribute much of the misperceptions of 'black bodies' to the limitations of camera technology, we must also consider the color-changing effects of the embalming process, as well as various natural processes of decomposition.

Hueman beings

In the aftermath of the Battle of Gettysburg, White soldiers expressed disgust over the fluctuating colors of their fallen brethren's decomposing flesh as their bodies lay in the fields. As one soldier confessed, the natural elements turned the faces of the dead black, "not a purplish discoloration, such as I had imagined in reading of the 'blackened corpses' so often mentioned in descriptions of battlegrounds, but a deep bluish *black*, giving to a corpse with black hair the appearance of a negro."[31] As author Drew Gilpin Faust discusses, the visual transformations of bodies in death "must have borne considerable significance in a society and a war in which race and skin color were of definitive importance."[32]

Ensuring that bodies maintained their natural colors after death was imperative to many 19th century undertakers and embalmers. In 1863 they advertised that: "Bodies embalmed by us NEVER TURN BLACK! But retain their natural color and appearance."[33] When throngs of Americans flocked to Washington, D.C. in the fall of 1881 to see the embalmed body of assassinated President, James A. Garfield, early spectators were aghast at the condition of his mortal remains: Garfield's emaciated face had turned leathery and black, his eyes "sunken and hollow," complete with dark circles under them that "extended down to the cheek bones." As first-person accounts testified, the "dark skin" of the president was "drawn so tightly over the bones of the face that it would seem as if it would be cut by the pressure."[34]

By the afternoon, the guards stationed beside Garfield's open coffin noticed that "the face was changing." Black spots had begun to form all over the darkening skin. Some believed it the result of poor embalming; others believed it evidence "that the body was fast decaying." Soon after, the coffin was ordered closed; "the remains were not fit to be seen." Garfield's face had turned completely black. Those who saw the body earlier in the day confessed that the president's coffin should have never been opened to the public.[35] Noted the newspapers: "The people who see the face will remember it forever."[36]

Despite being embalmed, or perhaps *because* of it, Garfield's white skin turned black in a matter of hours. For centuries, anatomists, and later, embalmers, struggled with overcoming this issue. J.N. Gannal, the eminent Parisian embalmer, commonly referred to it as the "black putridity," an aspect of embalming that all too often rendered anatomical subjects "so disgusting and unhealthy," as to make it unusable for medical education.[37]

In 1913, after years of studying the various chromatic phenomena associated with corpses, Dr. Gustav H. Michel provided a scientific explanation as to why the body changed colors after death, specifically, the various causes of the skin turning black. "When the skin turns dark, black or coppery," stated Michel, "it indicates the presence in the skin of a certain bacterial toxin which, under the influence of light and temperature, becomes oxidized (chemically allied with oxygen taken from the air by absorption)."[38]

As to the reason behind why the face turned black, Michel pointed out that this was not just a result of the body's decomposition, but a consequence of improper embalming. The irony here being that in a rush to combat the body's drastic color changes, the use of intense chemicals inadvertently exacerbated the very process it sought to stall. "The next most common cause of the face turning black is a strong formaldehyde fluid used in the first injection." The more intense the formaldehyde, warned Michel, the more likely the body's muscles tightened too early, pressing upon fragile veins and causing them to contract. Once "narrowed and compressed by rigid muscles" the corpse's veins "cannot hold more than half of the amount of blood they contain otherwise, and consequently, part of it is forced back into the most accessible capillaries, such as those of the face, neck and ears."[39]

When these factors combine with additional variables, such as decomposition and the limitations of photography, the results can cause a frustrating and misleading visual representation of the skin color and tonal values of dissected cadavers. Why this matters is that as a genre, dissection photographs are an unreliable witness to the use and abuse of the remains of persons of color throughout medical history. This conclusion is not designed to diminish, counter, or refute the unquestionable facts associated with the (il)legal or (un)ethical treatment and predominate use and display of the remains of African Americans. Merely to identify technological, natural, and chemical biases that yield values of visual misrepresentation and confusion.

While it is verifiable truth that photographs of students dissecting and disrespecting the remains of *identifiably* African American cadavers are extant, they are not legion. In some Northern states, hiding the race of the dead was likely purposeful. In Southern schools, however, students frequently celebrated the race – and therefore the otherness – of their cadavers through their photography. Their imagery invariably highlighted racial difference for the purpose of dehumanization via the inclusion of slurs and other forms of denigration. As previously discussed, the images produced at the Baltimore College of Dental Surgery and Wake Forest College Medical School serve as grotesque exemplars of how far racism pervaded academic and social structures into the 20th century, and how essential the vilification of Black skin was to certain groups of American medical students in solidifying professional identity. Nevertheless, without additional contexts, such as epigraphs, letters, or other supporting archival documents, scholars should take caution when attempting to utilize the corpus of dissection photography as unflinching visual proof of racist acts toward communities of color.

12

To Begin without Fear

For I know that in me, that is, in my flesh, dwelleth no good thing.
Romans 7:18

Then God said, "Let us make mankind in our image, in our likeness ..." So God created mankind in his own image, in the image of God he created them; male and female he created them.
Genesis 1:26–27

Visualizing the Judeo-Christian notion of the *imago Dei*, of human beings created materially and morally in the image of God, presents a fascinating challenge for all manner of photographer, past or present, commercial or amateur. By virtue of its technical limitations, the photographic medium repudiates tropes of corporeal idealism and divine materiality; illuminating the truth of humankind's inglorious materiality, our earthly suffering, with a representational precision so sharp, it rivals the cutting edge of even the keenest scalpel.

The visual realities associated with photographic flesh stand in stark contrast to centuries of religious iconography. Archetypal depictions in painted or sculptural form show the human body in a state of quasi-divinity, basking in God's embrace, unblemished and corporeally whole, regardless of death or supposed level of decomposition. As an extreme departure point from these classic works, dissection photography haunts religious representations of an idealized earthly body, or the body as a sacred vessel of the soul, by inculcating viewers to the innumerable authenticities and unavoidable imperfections of mortal flesh. These images depict the body as a graveyard, not a temple; a charnel house of jaggedly cut muscle, broken spines, and buckets of fat. Gore by gaslight; such is the ferocity of the dissecting room.

Coming to terms with such stark visual dichotomies thrust many a medical student, and student amateur photographer looking to capture this arena on film, into the midst of an epic battle of beliefs. Faith pitted against science; the eschatological doctrines of a religious upbringing, struggling with the inglorious reality that a "young sawbones" must "mutilate the remains of their deceased fellow citizens" and live amidst the fragile and foul materials of human mortality.[1]

In most if not all instances, science won the battle, but not necessarily the war. Regardless of the intensity of a student's educational training or how indoctrinated they became to the 'truth' of humankind's existence through dissection, reflections over mortality were still common among first- and second-year medical students. Many used photography to contemplate corporeality.

"The beginning of the end. Don't take it too hard," declared students from the Chicago College of Dental Surgery, their brusque message scrawled on the back of a particularly explicit dissection postcard.[2] The accompanying tableau shows students clustered around the remains of their dissected cadaver. A wooden stake juts upward into the skull from underneath its jaw, securing its eyeless, brainless head to its heartless chest. To the viewer's eye, or by the photographer's design, the punctured skull is effectively crucified.

Student handiwork within the cadaver's torso is also on display. They have burrowed deep and removed its heart. A member of the group holds the missing muscle in an outstretched hand. He gestures toward the camera with it, as if it were a sacrificial offering intended for the viewer.[3]

As we discussed in early chapters, the cadaver stands, or more appropriately, rests, as an abject enigma. It is a lifeless body, wrought by the hands of a living God and dismembered by the hands of mortals. Since emptied of the gift of life, it remains to be seen whether a cadaver remains as a manifestation of God's image after dissection; or what we might call its 'second death.' As an act, dissection unquestionably interrogates God's 'incorruptible' design. And yet, given that the cadaver's form and function is "physically deformed and destroyed, mentally laughed at ... totally reduced from the human to the biological," the question remains, does dissection kill it?[4]

Similarly, does dissection photography, as a visual process aligned with a destructive process, sufficiently challenge the conceit of the *imago Dei*? Would confirming the dissolution of identity-instilled form thereby prove the theoretical, physical, anatomical, and visual separation or abandonment even of the proverbial soul?

If dissection photographs do indeed shatter eschatological conceptions of the *imago Dei*, then they must also call into question the resurrection of exacting flesh as depicted in centuries of Judeo-Christian iconography. And, if we follow this line of thinking and concede that form follows function, then questions abound as to whether the revocation of bodily divinity, be it in appearance or resulting from the purpose of its utility, forever marks the cadaver as an unholy site of unremitting (and usually reckless) violence. As

Woman's Medical College of Pennsylvania student, Edith Flower Wheeler, emphatically stated at the conclusion of her anatomical education in 1897: "The cadavers, called 'stiffs' by irreverent students, had served their purpose."[5] Indeed they had. However, the purpose of dissecting the dead was grounded in the noble pursuit of anatomical knowledge. As a continuously evolving genre, dissection photography developed to the point where it began to subvert said purpose. The nobility of dissection tainted; corrupted by the abject nature of its varied visualization, or perhaps we could say, by the devolution of its primary stakeholders (students). Thus, to question the philosophical purpose of the cadaver is to interrogate its relation to God; to question whether the cadaver's new visage, its corrupted *imago*, is one which allows for and in fact encourages the perpetration of aggressivity and ridicule.

Questioning the *imago* of the cadaver seems especially pertinent when considering the various forms of abjection shown toward the remains of marginalized communities, such as indigent populations and persons of color. In the 19th century in particular, medical students robbed the graves of Black and poor White individuals with impunity. In cities like Baltimore and Philadelphia, the targeting of African American cemeteries was directly linked to the ease of access. Upon visiting Baltimore in 1835, Harriet Martineau observed that only African American bodies were taken for dissection. As to the reason why: "the coloured people cannot resist," she stated.[6]

Allaying the emotional suffering of Black communities over the desecration of their cemeteries seemed of little importance to members of the medical profession at the time. All too often, the words of indifferent physicians did nothing more than fan the flames of speculation, anxiety, and fear. Systemic grave robbing, and its associations with the medical profession, are indeed rampant throughout history. Most, if not all, of the nation's earliest physicians engaged in these "great abuses" throughout their careers.[7] In 1805, pioneering American physician, Daniel Drake, acquired bones to form an articulated teaching skeleton by robbing the burial site of a vagrant in Mays Lick, Kentucky. Ironically, Drake resorted to this act as he himself was too poor to purchase a full human skeleton from an anatomical purveyor while studying at the University of Pennsylvania.[8]

Spurred by lack of proper nutrition and impoverished living conditions, the bodies of African Americans comprised the majority of cadavers in American dissecting rooms at the turn of the 20th century, particularly those located in Southern states. Almshouses and city hospitals were likewise overrun with the poor; whose bodies, if left unclaimed, were fair game for use by medical schools through State Anatomical Boards. In 1865, the *Annual Circular of the Trustees and Faculty of the Medical College of the State of South Carolina* commented upon this new development, stating: "The political changes brought about by the war, have very largely increased the clinical facilities of this institution, by throwing upon the city charities an immense colored pauper population, who, in former times, were never found in Southern Hospitals."[9]

Proclaiming the dissolution of slavery as the primary cause of Black communities' 'newfound' health inequalities was a common propaganda tactic in the 'new' South. However, those Southern medical schools that bemoaned such changes initially, stayed suspiciously quiet when a steady supply of African American cadavers, a byproduct of these same overrun hospitals, started showing up on their dissecting tables two years later. As the Medical College of the State of South Carolina boasted in 1867: "The material for dissection so generally scarce in most Medical Schools, will in this be found ample; so that students will have every facility for the practical study of Anatomy – the real foundation for future practice."[10]

During the era of the dissection photograph, lynch law, and racial segregation flourished in the American South, permeating the insular culture inherent to the region's dissecting rooms. Similar infusions of bigotry and hate affected the images produced within these institutions. Here, racial prejudice assured that the cadaver was not as ambiguous a construct as it was in the North. Students enrolled in Southern schools routinely spoke of their cadavers using racially distinct terminology. Systemic behavioral patterns geared toward disrespect and dehumanization painted clear pictures of racial hierarchies and power structures, even in death. Sometimes these displays were directed toward the living and focused on ensuring Black physicians or dissecting room janitors knew their place alongside that of the Black cadaver. In 1908, a dissection photograph from the Kentucky School of Medicine (Louisville) shows students and staff posed with their African American janitor at their feet, his shirt adorned with a placard with the word "NEXT" written upon it (Figure 12.1). This single word sent clear signals to all who viewed it. Despite school janitors being a locus of institutional power and secretive knowledge, in the end, no matter their station in life, successes, or the power maintained at their school, the institution of medicine viewed them as little more than a future cadaver.

Similarly, to students at Southern schools, like the Medical College of Virginia (MCV) – one of the largest producers of dissection photographs known today – Black bodies and cadaveric bodies were tantamount to each other. Reminiscences at the turn of the 20th century showed no restraint in criticizing the terrible conditions of their school's dissecting rooms. As soon as they opened the doors of the dissecting hall, dental students at MCV were assaulted with "a wave of air filled with perfume" – a flippant turn of phrase to describe the malodorous stench that rose from the dead.[11] This "peculiar odor," which wafted from "strange-looking figures," "piled in the corners of the room," was a pungent effluence of putrefying flesh and chemical preservatives.[12] Once tasked with staffing hospitals with at least half

Figure 12.1: Class of 1908, Kentucky School of Medicine (Louisville, Kentucky). Unidentified photographer. Gelatin silver print, circa 1904–1905

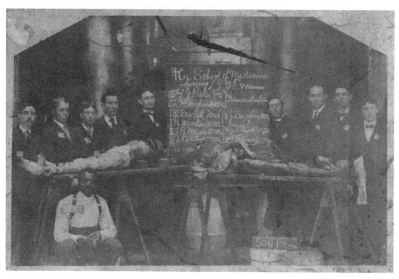

Note: The name "Little Willie," written on the dissecting table, is most likely a reference to the seated school janitor, who is probably William Mukes.
Source: Private collection

a patient-base of poor African Americans, a majority of whom ended up as cadavers, Southern students began to associate the distinctive smell of the dissecting room with Black identity. To be clear, they likened the smell of their living African American patients to the emanations rising from the dead.

Black cadavers, pulled from great bathtubs of preservatives, exhibited what school yearbooks jokingly referred to as the "Bouquet d' Afrique"; a fetid stink deemed so identifiable, so characteristic of their race, that the "Meds of '97–98" at the University of Virginia remarked, "now and forever afterward ... all c__ns are alike."[13] Similar sentiments were expressed through the dissection photography of the Baltimore College of Dental Surgery. Both the Class of 1900 and the Class of 1902 found it imperative to underline the racial 'characteristics' of their cadavers, and thus, their collective views toward poor Black bodies, by writing the grotesque epigraph "All c__ns Smell Alike to Us" upon their dissecting tables.[14]

Coincidentally, by the time these oversized prints were taken – in this case, both were presumably made by Baltimore-based commercial photographer, John Henfield, then considered the oldest living photographer in America – the college's cadavers were usually reduced to little more than scraps upon the slab. Normally, this would make confirming the race of the dissected near impossible. Notwithstanding the racially motivated epigraphs that drew attention to this biological fact, extant records of Baltimore medical schools confirm that around this time, the bodies of African Americans comprised around two-thirds of the city's entire cadaver supply.[15]

The racially insensitive 'humor' shown in several Southern-made dissection photographs, or 'joked' about in school yearbooks, were not just a series of harmless gags, on par with the same risqué remarks the Protestant majority often made about Catholic or Jewish classmates. For one thing, Southern schools refused admission to Black applicants, believing the entry of just one would "be a great injury" to the student body.[16] What's more, the abject hatred White Southern students directed toward African Americans was ratified by school faculty; establishing structures of racist behavior that, in some cases, left literal trails from the Dean's office to the dissecting room. In 1906, P. Richard Taylor, Dean of the Hospital College of Medicine, the Medical Department of Central University of Kentucky (Louisville), decreed that his school "never matriculated a 'c__n' in all its history and never will so long as I am Dean."[17]

Preventing the training of Black physicians yet mocking their collective health, as well as engendering bigoted sentiments over the biometric similarities of African Americans, living and dead, of them all looking or smelling alike, engendered a cultural norm, a hegemonic, visual system of indexicality, one that upheld the belief that African American communities were not only interchangeable, but *disposable*. The commercial taking of racist dissection photographs, and their continued allowance by (and perhaps at the encouragement of) school administrators, tapped into a visual codex of pain, suffering, and fear that had real-life consequences for Southern Black communities. For example, in 1900, during a riot between White and Black communities in New Orleans – then considered "the leading medical center of the entire South and Southwest for almost one hundred years," and "one of the fairest cities in Free America" – the on-the-scene editors of *The Colored American Magazine* watched in horror as an angry mob of enraged Whites raced up and down the city streets howling: "Kill a n____r and don't leave one. Kill any one you meet so long as he is a n____r, for they are all just alike."[18]

Thus, the microcosm of the Southern dissection room reflected the real-life perspectives of the region; sending clear signals to poor and vulnerable African American families, even those living in more progressive Southern cities, that when it came to discrimination, injustice, and brutality, there was no escape, not even in death.

A dead anything

At the apex of this rather nihilistic framework rests another question: whether dissection photographs prove the nonexistence of a God through the visual confirmation of spiritual absence in anatomical aftermath. Or, conversely, by some notion of the *anti*, do they substantiate that which they *do not show*: the otherworldly residence of earthbound spirit; the intangibility of the human soul.

Based on what dissection photographs do and do not show about human materiality, a more pointed theological question might be: can God, does God, exist, not just in death, but in *dissected* death? Is a higher power effectively 'dead' once the cadaver (an entity of unnatural preservation) is dissected (mutilated unnaturally) at the hands of man (not God)? If the body's corporeal form is no longer recognizably human, are we to therefore presume it is no longer (made in) God's image?

Were we to ask the 19th century preacher the same gut-punching question *TIME* Magazine asked readers on its April 1966 cover, "Is God Dead?" the answer would have been a resounding no. According to the religious figures of antebellum America, human beings cannot exist in a godless world. In the 1850s, popular lecturer, William Maccall, proclaimed that humankind "cannot satisfy our insatiate soul with a dead God, a dead humanity, a dead anything."[19] Death was (and is) an inescapable eventuality. As a natural process interwoven into the fabric of creation, without the existence of death, there would be no life. And yet, confusion over the *imago Dei* and God's involvement with(in) dead flesh abounds with the addition of his direct progeny, Jesus Christ; a dualistic demi-God, whose body exists "in the likeness of sinful flesh," yet sustains the inherited spiritual traits of his heavenly Father.[20]

Christ suffers and dies. But, according to Christian doctrine, he also resurrects anew. Incorruptible. Clothed in transcendent eternal flesh. It is said that absolution of the flesh and freedom of the flesh in the form of immortality are granted upon those who accept Jesus as their savior. His resurrection and conversion of temporal sinful flesh, specifically *dead* flesh, into everlasting holy spirit becomes inextricably linked to earthly suffering, *his* suffering, through sacrifice, through death as an act of love. With this dogma in mind, is it possible that the conceit of the *imago Dei* bears more in common with the form and function of the cadaver than that of living mortals?

Consequently, Christ's martyrdom and death for the 'ungodly' occupies a distinct position of abject singularity within the Christian religion. Here, the literal act of purposefully dying for our sins supersedes all previous earthly deeds; a single act of death to absolve the world, and the decedent, of all their sins.[21] This principle of absolution is shared by the cadaver. Death and standard acts of dissection make it both redeemer and redeemable through its associated sacrificial utility as a 'living' textbook.

Following the ideology of Christ's resurrection, and that rising from the dead equates a future life for the mortal body – or for medical students, the added distinction of dissection serving as a portal to a new 'life' as physicians – humans maintain an enigmatic relation aesthetically, morally, and materially to Christ and to God. This applies even in death. As one of the living, but also of the dead, of "being put to death in the flesh, but quickened by the Spirit," Christ's body then, like our mortal bodies, like the cadaver's body, is an embodiment of contradictions. Death is the antithesis of life. Yet, in death, Christ became alive.[22] The paradox of course here being that our bodies decompose and rot. The body of Christ, so the story goes, did not.

But how then can it be possible for such diametrically opposing characteristics – a living cadaver – to exist in a single earthly form? After all, as author Caroline Walker Bynum discusses, "specific adjectives, analogies, and examples," many used for centuries in Christian treatises on the resurrection, suggest "that the palpable, vulnerable, corruptible body Christ redeems and raises was quintessentially the mutilated cadaver of the martyr."[23]

Although dissection photography occasionally attempted to try and recreate these imponderable Christian doctrines, they were never executed convincingly, or with any fidelity to religious texts or iconography; never seeking to photographically 'prove' the existence of the human soul on literal levels. But this did not mean that students were not curious about the human soul. Nor did it stop them from looking for it every now and then.

In the early 1890s, soon after student, Edith Flower Wheeler, began dissecting at the Woman's Medical College of Pennsylvania, her father, an award-winning amateur photographer, asked her one day "if she had discovered where the soul is located."[24] As Wheeler's father had trained her in photography, "both at home and by mail," even loaning her "his little camera" to use while away at school, it comes as no surprise that a visually attuned person would seek visual confirmation of various aspects of human mortality.[25] And although Wheeler never recorded the answer to her father's pointed question, she no doubt spent some time looking for the human soul, as she wasted no time in photographically recording almost every other aspect of her time at medical school. "They all were time pictures, snap-shots being a thing of the future," she later wrote of her photographic exploits, "but they came out quite good and now are nice to have to recall years long since past."[26] As to any further eschatological questions posed by her curious father, Wheeler mentioned only a single humorous query in which he remarked that "he had heard of some people being full of Hell and asked: 'Do any of them smell of it?'"[27]

A modern Golgotha

When dissecting cadavers, students had infinitely more pressing issues to contend with than the location of the human soul. Nevertheless, the paradoxical convergence of transvalued flesh, and the sacrificial resolve inherent to the contradictive notion of the crucified Christ, of the Corpse Christ, were concepts not lost upon God-fearing Christian students of the late 19th and early 20th centuries; many of whom doubled as amateur photographers.

If "awe and apprehension" were present in the dissecting room, such feelings eventually dissipated with time and experience.[28] Likewise, if a fear of death lay ahead of them, lurking behind closed doors, lingering in the air, or hovering over cold slabs covered in blood and bits of torn flesh, it too had to be overcome. Academic necessity demanded it. Fear of the secrets of the dead had to be suppressed, reborn as a proclivity for "macabre horror."[29]

Even if students did not believe in the resurrection of flesh, dissection photography often made direct visual references to redemptive utility through dissecting table epigraphs, or the use of popular conventions from Stages II and III, such as posing the dead as if reanimated. With a customary flair that straddled the borderland between soulful reverence and a devilish sense of humor, students frequently integrated the allegorical and metaphorical mysteries of the resurrection into the visual and verbal culture of their prospective dissecting rooms; their own private sepulchers, their secret Golgothas.

Like the valley in Ezekiel, "which was full of bones," dissecting rooms were laden with the explicit iconography of mortal death.[30] Extant photographs show an abject landscape of greasy skulls and flesh-speckled bones hanging from hooks; racks of internal organs, injected and shellacked, left to dry and harden in the sun. From the shadowed obscurities beneath each dissecting table were placed lonely buckets, often appearing in photographs with the word "SOUP" written upon the side. Inside these tin pails sloshed a chunky potage of discarded skin, fat, and preservative-soaked bandages.

Bats clung to the beams of the ceilings and rats raced around the floorboards. Dissecting room janitors stacked freshly preserved cadavers in the corners as if they were hewn planks of wood. Often, the severed, bisected heads or severed legs of these bodies served as popular photographic 'props' for the students of the 20th century, who cradled them in their arms or slung them over their shoulders, like an ax or bindle. According to A.M. Perkins, class historian of the Medical College of Virginia's Dental Class of 1917, their dissecting room was nothing short of a "ghastly scene." Cadavers lay out in open coffins. When enough sunlight penetrated the din, one "beheld dark objects floating in bath tubs." If a student arrived early, or stayed too late, they often watched in horror as janitor 'Chris' Baker, ascended from the gloom of his basement laboratory with "a dead negro" strapped to his back.[31]

Photography confirmed this macabre environment as a dwelling place devoid of souls yet filled with the soulless. In December 1919, a student was photographed twirling around the dissecting room of a medical college in Toledo, Ohio, in the embrace of an articulated skeleton. While this man literally dances with death, another picks at the brain of a cadaver through a sawed-off section of its skull. Behind the dancing couple, the phrase: "If you love me," is visible upon a blackboard.[32]

While bones and brains served as effective props, at the center of it all was the intact cadaver; a customizable anatomical Christ. Its skull, ceremoniously ringed with a crown-like cut to access the interior; its body, adorned in a preservative-soaked shroud; all laid upon a slab-like table with modular arms, repositionable to make literal cruciform postures. Though this position was symbolic and graphic, photographs show its purpose was practical, not *iconographic*. To this point, despite the intensity of a religious affiliation, students did not appear to draw literal inspiration or seek to make too direct an association with biblical texts when referencing Christ in the dissecting room. We see no photographs of cadavers adorned with crowns of thorns; no sign of the cross, marked in ash, upon the foreheads of severed heads.[33] If photographs of cadaveric stigmata do exist (a miracle in and of itself since, generally, the dead don't bleed) they have yet to be uncovered. At most, a skull, or skull and crossbones, would be added to a dissecting room tableau. This could take the form of actual bones, or a drawing made upon an anatomy lab chalkboard or, more commonly, a student's smock. As the token symbol of death's inevitability, inclusion of any kind paid homage to traditional *memento mori* imagery.

When a skull was not balanced upon the shoulders of nursing students or accessorized with crossbones and held up during panoramic group shots taken on the front steps of a medical school's entranceway, the osseous sigil was usually positioned at the head or feet of the supine cadaver as it lay upon the dissecting table. Here, placement alluded to the iconography of the crucifix itself, a direct reference to the legend of Jesus' crucifixion originating at the burial place of Adam − "the place of a skull."[34]

*** ★★★

Despite its transgressive and abject nature, dissection was depicted as "a spiritual rite."[35] However, throughout the 50-year evolution of American dissection photography, references to spirituality through observable religious iconography, such as crosses, were largely absent. The inference here being that the only 'religion' allowable within the 'cathedral' of the dissecting room was what medical historians, like Michael Sappol, routinely refer to as a "death cult."[36] The creation of religious tableaus, outside of the general symbolism associated with themes of resurrection, could be seen by an audience (internal or external) as heretical or sacrilegious; something that even the most atheistic physicians might perceive as perverse idolatry. Mocking dead flesh, and even the resurrection of dead flesh was acceptable − evidenced by the existence of the *Student Dream* subgenre. Mocking the savior of dead flesh, however, was apparently a step too far.

One could argue that the need to represent a literal resurrected Christ was supplanted by the earthbound form of a student's anatomy professor or demonstrator: "Born of science and suffering, [the doctor] lives amid the sadness of death and the gladness of birth."[37] Impressionable initiates venerated their anatomy professors with such fervency, their adoration reads as a mixture of fierce loyalty and sycophantic idolatry.

For over 50 years, the faculty and alumni at Hahnemann Medical College (Philadelphia) considered master anatomist, Rufus Benjamin Weaver, one of "God's noblemen."[38] To the generations of students who dissected beside him, he was not just a man, but a father. Some, even referred to him by the nickname, 'Daddy' Weaver. Meanwhile, to the student body of the Medical Department of Tulane University, the corporeal body of their dean, Stanford E. Chaillé, was saintly; incorruptible in both knowledge and form. "To us he is a god – a *man*; not going to heaven – not afraid of hell. … To us his hoary locks are as a crown of thorns endured through years of constant upward toil; the penalty for being honest and faithful and bearing others' burden."[39]

Cadaverse: poetry in the dissecting room

Regardless of their individual beliefs, students continued to ask questions and express religious connections over the metaphysical aspects of dissection using the visual and verbal means available to them. Many still do. As photography is now (mostly) forbidden in American dissecting rooms, poetry has become the predominant form of student self-expression. Janessa Law, a 21st century medical student, pondered of her cadaver: "Had you no want of hallowed ground / Having never felt Him around?"[40] Law's verse here implies cadaveric agency. That the dead, while alive, chose this postmortem life due to a separation from God. Most (but not all) cadavers of the late 20th century were supplied to medical schools through donation programs. The same is true to this day. Modern reflections upon a cadaver's conscious choice then are neither naïve nor farfetched. They represent distinct changes in the industry supplying cadavers for American medical schools and thus, a perceptual reversal of the student–cadaver relationship. No longer a helpless victim, the cadaver is now a willing participant whose last wishes are fulfilled by an obliging student.

Poetry could also help students express their fears over dissection or make direct references to spiritual concepts, like the *imago Dei*. Alex Cuenca's poetry referred to cadavers as: "Ghosts sealed up tight in their skin suits / Drunk and toxic with preservatives / God's fixed image … for us." As author Johanna Shapiro points out, religious references such as this "unmistakably" suggest "the sacred nature of the human form." And yet, the inclusion of an ironic twist intimates that "even the image of God is not safe from the depredations of first-year medical students."[41]

The word made flesh: dissecting table epigraphs

SHE RESTS IN PIECES.

Dissecting table epigraph, Baltimore
Medical College, 1908[42]

In 1914, A.R. Brunsman and nine of his classmates from the Kirksville College of Osteopathic Medicine (Missouri), stood over the body of 'George,' their cadaver, and had their photograph taken together. Later that year, Brunsman mailed the photo, now in the form of a real photo postcard, home to his sister, Edna. Scribbled on the back, he left a little message that left Edna little doubt as to 'George's' contribution to her brother's medical education: "He is serving a good cause. 'Alas Poor Yorick.'"[43]

Dissection photography afforded students both means and opportunity to reference the symbolic and totemic power of the cadaver through various reflections upon its relation to the philosophical function of Christ's sacrifice – his death, his body, his *dead* body – in service to humanity. Before postcards allowed students to write messages on their backs, the most effective means of embedding explicit verbal commentary into an otherwise purely visual tradition, was for students to inscribe an epigraph directly upon their dissecting room table prior to photography. This rather ingenious technique also served as their primary method to comment upon "the rites of Christian mystery" through cadaveric utility.[44]

Epigraphs became a popular feature of dissection photography starting as early as the 1890s. Its prominence extended well into the 20th century, even after the rise of the real photo postcard. These chalked inscriptions were written on the side of dissecting tables, scrawled onto blackboards, or sometimes drawn directly upon a photographic negative.

Moments before their portrait was taken, the medical Class of 1915 at the University of Maryland wrote the phrase, "A martyr to Science," upon a large chalkboard, which they then placed in front of their dissected cadaver.[45] "Peace to his Ashes," reads another, this time from the university's dental school.[46] "Gone to Heaven"; "Meet me in the 'Sweet' bye and bye," wrote the 1908–1909 dissecting class of the University of Louisville (Kentucky) – the latter epigraph, likely a reference to lyrics from one of the most popular Christian hymns of the 19th century.[47]

As a multimodal tradition, epigraphs became almost as ubiquitous as the genre itself. Many inscriptions directly referenced death and dissection as a form of martyrdom; or, as a means of redemption. The inference here being that the cadaver required salvation by virtue of its postmortem position upon the dissecting room table. The two most popular epigraphs in the history of the genre, "Man's usefulness ends not in death," and "He lived for others but died for us," provided further, albeit ironic, commentary on the link between the utility of dissected cadavers and the crucified Christ: their death in service to life-saving medicine; his death, to absolve humanity of their sins.[48]

The redemptive power of sacrifice was bestowed upon the dissected by its living dissectors, most of whom knew nothing of the life of the deceased or their cause of death. Today, a cadaver's biographical details are kept highly confidential and administered by the medical schools and the donor programs that supply them. At baseline, students are provided with limited facts about their cadaver, such as its age, occupation, and cause of death.

★★★

Although many chalked epigraphs were honorific in nature, not all reflected a spiritual tone, or strove to respect the utilitarian aspect of the cadaver's posthumous life. "We have shuffled off his mortal coil," wrote students from the Medical College of Virginia (MCV) in the 1890s; their epigraph, written underneath a flayed, eyeless cadaver; the onus, the identity of student-as-destroyer here established with singular purpose.[49] "She May Have Seen Better Days," acknowledged the Class of 1899 of the Southern Homeopathic Medical College (Baltimore).[50] "THE LORD GIVETH, WE TAKETH AWAY," proclaimed students at the University of Louisville, circa 1908.[51] Here again, student inference demonstrates a fiendish delight, a moral ambivalence toward supposing a union between dissector and executioner; a throwback to the era in which the act of dissection served as a form of posthumous punishment, one that justified "anatomy's direct or symbolic involvement in the rites of judicial power."[52]

By rendering the nature of bodily acquisition as suspect, students satirized and envenomed dissection's complex heritage to abjectify the act's ultimate purpose. What's more, given the Southern geographic location of schools such as MCV and the University of Louisville, such blistering irreverence combined with the underlying retributory tone codified the then rampant practices of mob justice, lynching, and lynching photography.

★★★

Not all epigraphs were merely iconographic associations with symbolic representations of redemptive rituals. Students did occasionally dissect, and take photographs dissecting, the bodies of executed criminals, as well as other societal 'criminals,' such as suicides – then considered a moral sin. As part of the punishment they levied upon themselves, and to prevent family from having to pay for their funerals, many who died of suicide preemptively donated their bodies to area medical schools. Students in turn took dissection photographs with their cadavers, often writing applicable details on the dissecting table or a propped-up chalkboard.

On November 21, 1895, a dissection photograph was taken of ten students (or a mix of students and staff) at Starling Medical College (Columbus, Ohio), now Ohio State University College of Medicine, dissecting the hanged body of Charles Hart, convicted murderer of William Ashby Goode and his younger sister, Elsie. Hart was hanged at Ohio Penitentiary in April 1895, after which, his body was turned over to the students at Starling. Relatedly, in the early 1900s, ten students at the Hospital College of Medicine (Louisville, Kentucky) posed alongside a cadaver whose cause of death was written out on a chalkboard thusly: "Toney the Florist, committed suicide March 15th 190[4?] at the German's Protestant Orphan's home. Willed his body to the Hospital College of Medicine."[53]

For those who dissected a known criminal, the ability to participate in an act that served to both punish and redeem, instilled in them something other; something God-like. As famed historian, Ruth Richardson, discusses, "dissection represented a gross assault upon the integrity and identity of the body *and* upon the repose of the soul."[54] Clearly, those who posed for photographs with the dissected remains of executed criminals, featuring epigraphs that highlighted the punishing legacy of dissection, stood unapologetic about their role in the execution of a "severe yet just death penalty."[55]

Equally firm was their resolve over this aspect of dissection codifying their self-identities. Author, Peter Mitchell, suggests this stands as a marked shift from the concerns of the anatomist of ages past, whose "direct or symbolic implication in the exercise of judicial power" drew unavoidable connections to "the infamy of the executioner." This proximity "sat uncomfortably" with the anatomist, for they desired "cultural inclusion" and society's acceptance of their profession.[56] Here, then, photography serves to communicate a variant form of modernist student identity, one that was as abject as it was frightening.

By repositioning the student as a punisher or avenger, a culpable but mostly unrepentant agent whose actions stood in direct opposition to the sacrosanctity of their Hippocratic Oath, 'to do no harm,' the photographic medium facilitated the perversion of the standard role of the medical initiate as a trusted healer. Although we will never know the limits to a student's willingness to participate in this specific 'type' of dissection, their agency in posing for photographs of its enactment stands evident. After all, it was common knowledge that the role of a dissector, the official "function" of their "interest" in the cadaver of a murderer, "was not to revive, but rather to destroy it."[57] Richardson discusses further: "Dissection was a very *final* process. It denied hope of survival – even the survival of identity after death."[58] With this understanding behind them, a student's literal and symbolic stance within this type of dissection photograph was less about an association between the self and the pursuit of a pure form of anatomical knowledge. Involvement, anatomically and photographically, was an exploitative venture, to inflict a postmortem 'justice'; a form of defilement upon the body – and if a believer, a spiritual violation as well – that was not only morally justified and legally sanctioned, but visually compelling.

Religious affiliations

> As for theology, most medical students are quite content with what their mothers taught them at their knees.
>
> R. Temple Wright, *Medical Students of the Period*, 1862[59]

"An old fashioned expression," wrote Dr. James J. Walsh, in 1918, "is that, where there are three doctors, there are two atheists."[60] In truth, during the era of the dissection photograph, the vast majority of medical professionals, including students, were devoutly religious and attended church regularly. What's more, around the turn of the 20th century, most schools connected with or relocated to larger university campuses were blessed with their own chapels, allowing students (for a time) to worship external to the lay communities they served. As a hub of spiritual and social activity, the exteriors of these houses of worship served as the backdrop for countless amateur-made snapshots and graduation photos. In the era to follow, these images would become a staple of school yearbooks and personal scrapbooks.[61]

School commencement ceremonies customarily opened with prayers by local pastors.[62] In 1870, Howard University held its third commencement – which included students from its medical department – at its congregational church. It not only opened with a prayer, but closed with a benediction.[63] In the 1890s, in an effort to bring men "nearer to each other and promote Christian fellowship," schools like the University of Maryland School of Medicine formed organizations like the Young Men's Christian Association (Y.M.C.A.).[64] By 1902 the rapidly expanding Sioux City College of Medicine (Iowa) shared its building with the city branch of the Y.M.C.A.[65] In 1911, the Birmingham Medical College attempted to entice good God-fearing students by pointing out there were "131 churches and two missions" within the city limits alone. "Nearly all creeds and denominations are represented."[66] By the 1930s, there existed at least ten Catholic medical and dental programs. All part of Jesuit higher education. At the same time, the Baptist faith not only thrived on the campus of Wake Forest College, but its president, Charles E. Taylor, stood firm in his conviction "that the College was an instrument for the spread of the Kingdom of Christ in the world."[67]

For most of the 19th century, schools across the United States advertised that in order to matriculate at their institutions little to no prior study of medicine was necessary. Standard terms of admission required only that a prospective student possess a "good English education," be of a certain age, and exhibit good moral character.[68] Throughout a student's educational career, it was essential that this latter trait, *good moral character*, be vigorously maintained.

Students either obeyed the moral regulations of a school, or they faced the consequences. Penalties included anything from expulsion to being refused the final examination for the Degree of Doctor of Medicine. In his annual report for the year 1885, President Taylor of Wake Forest College informed the Board he had expelled two students for public intoxication. He went on to state that in order to "maintain the supremacy of law" the campus needed to be purged of "vicious habits" and those who failed to "restrain themselves from mischief."[69] The first step in his plan was to increase the moral regulations of the college tenfold. As to these new rules of morality, decreed Taylor: "The only pledge now required of a student at his matriculation is that he shall conform to them."[70]

As the moral hub of their communities, religion then, in the form of church, served as an essential component of a student's personal and professional lives. Regardless of whether they returned to their small hometowns or remained in residence in the cities they immigrated to for school, recent graduates were expected to properly reintegrate themselves into their prospective communities. This included attending regular church services. After all, maintaining a strong moral character, or the perception of one, was just as important for their moral standing within industry and community as it was for profit. "[A]s we mingle with our fellowmen may it be our highest ambition to become Christian gentlemen," declared the dental students of the University of Maryland, "not envious, plodding 'tooth-carpenters,' but skilled and courteous Doctors of Dental Surgery."[71]

By the end of the 19th century, medical schools had become legion, "springing up" with "an impromptu rapidity" equal to "the birth of Minerva from the head of Jupiter."[72] Determining the collective 'moral character' of an exponentially expanding constituency was not only so school administrators could maintain order. Rather, the nebulously defined character trait grew into an exclusionary edict. It enforced the profession's own doctrines and laws of morality through a school's authoritarian control over the exclusivity of its accepted members.

By using the shifting terms of one's 'moral character' to police and purge their ranks, schools could deny entry to, or if need be, prohibit the graduation of "any scoundrel" deemed mentally or morally unfit to bear the mark of a Doctor of Medicine.[73] With fringe schools of homeopathic, osteopathic, and eclectic medicine circling like buzzards, allopathic schools feared for the moral purity of the profession (as they saw it) and likewise, the sanctity of their identities. Inadvertently allowing admission to those who might seek to commit "publicly forbidden" acts held the potential to soil professional reputations, strain fragile relationships between racial or ethnic groups, or usurp the physician's authority within their own community.[74] Given the dominance of grave robbing and what dissection photography showed in terms of the unethical treatment of the dead, it is ironic that the profession's list of unlawful, publicly reprehensible acts extended mainly to deeds like gambling, drinking, fraternizing with prostitutes, or theft. For example, one chief concern of both medical and dental schools was ensuring new students did not rifle through "the mouths of the embalmed 'stiffs'" and steal the dental gold from out of their teeth.[75]

While school administrators went to great pains to guarantee the proper moral behavior of their classes, these same schools expressed no concern (at least publicly) over their students schlepping home boxes of greasy bones on public transportation or taking photographs of one another lounging on the campus green wearing necklaces made from human vertebrae. Clearly, the true 'laws' of the dissecting room existed external and above the morality of society and organized religion.

★★★

Students used photography to document their social interactions as much as they did their interactions with the dead. Photographs of dorm room parties and snapshots of students walking down bustling city streets together, to and from school or church, became increasingly plentiful with the introduction of amateur cameras and the institution of the American camera store.

Once photo albums became part of the visual and material cultures of the American medical student, vernacular photographs of daily life began to frequent the same black-paper pages as those containing dissection room portraits. Although religion and school generally occupied two distinct spheres of (opposing) function – one catered to the mind (and stomach), the other the soul – looking through these scrapbooks, one would be hard-pressed to determine which arena exerted more influence, the church, or the dissecting room.

Both were uniquely sanctified spaces. Both had their own value sets, secrets, rituals, confessions, and confessors. Although one was genuinely devoid of spirituality and emotion (except perhaps fear and disgust), both provided essential social opportunities to affirm identity by bonding with a like-minded constituency. Students of law and medicine at Wake Forest College, notorious for their cruel and dehumanizing antics toward African American cadavers during the era of the dissection photograph, simultaneously "found joy in religion and in the worship in chapel and church."[76]

In major metropolitan meccas of medicine, like Philadelphia, it was common for students from various schools to live together, join the same churches, or attend services together at multiple churches, sometimes over the course of a single week. When attending a medical college that was not part of a university, and thus, without its own chapel, the location of both church and school invariably influenced where students decided to live. In 1876, Rachel 'Jennie' Jane Nicol, a student at Woman's Medical College of Pennsylvania (WMCP), rejoiced in finding board that accommodated easy travel between church and school. What's more, by her moving in only three doors down from her college, Nicol could partake in the opportunity to bring home a box of bones with which to study osteology prior to dissection season.[77]

Church services provided a safe, communal, and coeducational setting that allowed men and women to meet and socialize on neutral ground. Despite her busy schedule dissecting, finishing clinical work, and attending demonstrations at the nearby German Hospital, Mary Theodora McGavran (also of WMCP), found time in the winter of 1893 to attend church services upwards of twice a week. There she met men from nearby medical schools. "I talked to two young men at church tonight from Jefferson Med," McGavran confessed in her diary. "I did not learn their names but they seem to be good young Christians."[78] Given the limited time they spent together, it is highly unlikely that McGavran and the 'boys' from Jefferson Medical College sat in pews trading putrid stories about dissection, or that they surreptitiously swapped snapshots of their cadavers like baseball cards. Nevertheless, opportunities for any kind of social engagement between the sexes outside of their prospective schools were highly prized, especially during the era of the dissection photograph.

In the 1890s, interactions between men and women in professional medical settings was fiercely restricted. In Philadelphia at the time, only men could attend Jefferson Medical College, and WMCP only accepted women. Interestingly, in McGavran's day, despite WMCP having several male professors and lecturers, the school's by-laws forbade men and women from dissecting together. Until the school went co-ed – almost 125 years after its founding in 1850 – the WMCP required that its Demonstrator of Anatomy always be a woman.

Not all dead

> We come from every class, clique, clan, and category existing in the memory of man.
>
> Atlanta-Southern Dental College, 1922[79]

"The origin of the horror concerning dissection arose undoubtedly from the superstition of the resurrection of the body," decreed an anonymous Chicago physician in the pages of the *St. Joseph Herald* in 1889.[80] When it came to the public voicing religious principles in opposition to anatomical dissection (especially unsavory methods of cadaver procurement such as grave robbing), student and doctor alike wasted no time in excoriating public opinion as either weaknesses of character or as some kind of delusory hokum.

When cornered by a reporter in Kansas City, Missouri, an anatomist, identified only as 'Dr. S.,' seemed to relish the opportunity to mock his local community's concerns over the supposed source of his dissecting material. "Dr. S, there is a good deal of talk about town at the present times, as to where you secure material for the dissecting room," inquired the reporter. "Can you give me any information on the subject?" Dr. S. swiftly evaded the question, responding curtly: "The angels bring them to us."

Dr. S.'s choice of words here sought to pervert the protective nature of spiritual beings, to rebuke both reporter and reader over what he considered to be an impertinent question about his professional activities, and thus, his professional identity. When the Kansas reporter pressed the stubborn physician further for an answer, asking how often his so-called "angels" called, Dr. S. replied again in kind: "As often as we are in need of subjects."[81]

Ordained physicians were not the only ones who felt the need to defend themselves from public shame. After a year away dissecting cadavers, WMCP student Rachel Nicol was told by close friends that they felt her theological views were no longer in proper spiritual alignment with the rest of the faith. Nicol responded that her morals and faith were in fact unchanged. "Morals and bringing up stand very much in the way of one's acceptance of the theories presented by some who claim to be investigators in the different departments of science," she declared. "You say who would be an M.D., looking at it from your standpoint but you see we are not obliged to look at it from *your* standpoint and that makes the greatest difference imaginable."[82]

★★★

The medical 'perspective' on spirituality is quite interesting considering that most medical students attending allopathic medical schools during the era of the dissection photograph were White, middle-class, Protestant men and women. By the end of the first decade of the 1900s, so-called 'fringe' schools, like Hahnemann Medical College (Philadelphia), a homeopathic school, were known to accept increasingly large numbers of non-Protestants. But, as historian Naomi Rogers writes, the increase in Italian, Jewish, and South American students reflected Hahnemann's "lowered status in the medical marketplace." Regardless of their qualifications, other more prestigious allopathic schools considered non-Protestant students "unacceptable," and typically used "quota systems" to restrict their numbers.[83]

To add insult to injury, bigoted commentary on the ethnicity and heritage of non-Protestants was a common occurrence in school yearbooks. Although these controversial jokes were mostly lighthearted, their design still set 'foreign' outliers apart from the principal student body. At Hahnemann Medical College, Morris Fiterman was called "Moish" by his classmates as he was both "a Hebrew and a Republican."[84] In the 1897 edition of the *Chaff*, the yearbook of the College of Dentistry of the University of California, dental student William Herrington's appearance and Jewish background found ridicule by way of a derogatory poem: "He sticks no fork in ham or pork, / Observe, my friends, his nose."[85]

Catholics, meanwhile, gradually pushed for the founding of schools of medicine that taught a specific blend of instruction more suited to their ideologies, one committed to teaching "ethical principles" designed to solve "a whole series of problems."[86] Accordingly, these issues required "the most careful application of Christian morality," and included topics such as "abortion, habit-forming drugs, and sex morality."[87] Although desecrating the resurrection of the flesh was also important to Catholics, it apparently failed to make the cut.

Stereotyping the physical characteristics or religious backgrounds of minority students were ripe for commentary and derision in school publications. And yet, these distinctions did not appear to stop most students of any religious denomination, state, or country, from building a sense of comradery or matriculating from afar. "We came from almost every section of the country, from the Atlantic to the Pacific, and from Canada to the Gulf," recorded dental student, K. Funderburk, of the Southern Dental College. Since most traveled great distances, alone, to study medicine, and had little time to engage in social activities outside of school, students' classmates were often the only friends they had during their first year.

Differences of country of origin or religious affiliation had little effect on student portraiture in the dissecting room – photography, again, being the great equalizer. For example, in Figure 12.2, when six students posed for an early 20th century dissection photograph, likely from a school in New York City, Baltimore, or Philadelphia, other than the standard practice of writing the two-letter abbreviations of their state or country of origin on their aprons, no signifiers indicate that two of the students were originally from Pennsylvania, or that the central figure, student Abdul Nur, was a native of Syria. Indeed, the only qualifier incorporated to separate one 'group' from the other, was the implicit dissecting table epigraph: "Not All Dead."

Fear of rebirth

> The human body, on the departure of the spirit from it, has never been regarded in the same light as other matter.
>
> Tayler Lewis, *Harper's*, 1854[88]

Figure 12.2: "Not All Dead." Unknown school. Unidentified photographer. Gelatin silver print, circa 1895

Source: Private collection

Throughout the centuries, religious doctrines opposing anatomical dissection were upheld not only by the devoutly religious, but by eminent thinkers, such as the 17th-century physician Thomas Sydenham, and philosopher and physician John Locke, who believed that "to anatomize the world beneath its superficies was an intellectual sin."[89] Such views were accepted well into the 19th century, with the gospel narrative of the resurrection supporting the argument for a literal revival of dead bodies and a restoration of rotten flesh: "Thus saith the Lord GOD unto these bones; Behold, I will cause breath to enter into you, and ye shall live: And I will lay sinews upon you, and will bring up flesh upon you, and cover you with skin, and put breath in you, and ye shall live."[90]

Regardless of whether one believed in a literal return of flesh, or a symbolic one involving the rise of an ethereal 'ghost,' hosts of students took photographs of their cadavers with a goal towards photographically preempting its resurrection. Hundreds of staged photographs exist showing the dead as if returned from the dead. These reimaginings included anything from cadavers sat upright upon dissecting tables, their arms wrapped around dissectors' shoulders, cigarettes dangling from their lipless maws, to taking part in unholy marriage ceremonies or performing dissections upon the living.

For centuries, human cadavers served as the catalysts for student reflection upon their own mortality. Photography brought these contemplations of death to life. But in the time spent performing *actual* dissections, conventional anatomists thoroughly rejected the romanticizing of any eschatological questions by students, especially those concerned with the human soul. In fact, in the late 1800s, emotional sensitivity of any kind toward the cadaver was thoroughly repudiated by professional staff. Fully embracing the scientific objectivity of the medical profession during the transitional period of medical school almost always guaranteed the successful conversion from layperson to medical professional. Therefore, as an anonymous anatomy professor at the Woman's College of Medicine (New York) told reporters in 1881:

> I discourage all sentiment in the dissecting room. Some of my students are inclined to speculate upon where the soul is of this or that person we cut up. The other day we had a very interesting subject – a young girl who had died at Bellevue – and the students were given to considering what her life had been and where her spirit was: but I discountenanced such surmises and went to work. I tell my class this is the time they can cut without hurting, therefore to begin without fear.[91]

Indeed, the majority of the era's physicians were cut from the same cloth, lambasting students for wasting precious time in the dissecting room contemplating the state (or location) of their cadaver's soul. There was a time, and most importantly, a place for these distracting thoughts: church or chapel. But, when such musings turned sardonic or dismissive, they were consigned to the pages of school yearbooks, or to the backs of dissection postcards in the form of humorous or self-deprecating poems.

Medical and dental school was complete with its own rituals, principles, trials of socialization, and time-honored traditions, of which anatomical dissection occupied a prominent position within, and which dissection photography eventually became part of. Personal biases – namely in the form of religious stigmas – and the influence of public opinion were supplanted by the promise of an elite form of epistemological authority, one that situated dissectors apart from, and to an extent intellectually superior to, the rest of society.[92] As G.W. Corner declared in 1930: "The day when the medical student enters the dissecting room is the time of dedication to his profession; for then he puts his hand to a task that other men dread, and joins the company of those who have laid aside the deepest fears and prejudices of mankind."[93]

And yet, despite laying down their own fears and prejudices by way of medical conditioning, students still needed to reflect upon and sometimes mock prominent religious doctrines, or religious ceremonies, through their dissection photography. For instance, most students of this era were proudly

Figure 12.3: A cadaver 'wedding.' Unknown school. Unidentified photographer. Gelatin silver print, circa 1915

Source: Author's collection

single. Marriage was as taboo an act to them as dissection was to the general populace. Thus, it is particularly fascinating to encounter a 20th-century cadaveric tableau featuring both sexual overtones and the added taboo of staging a marriage ceremony between cadavers (Figure 12.3).

This single photograph is filled with abject, and one could argue, profane imagery for the times. Student-priests reach out to bless the dissected 'couple,' while others pose holding their anatomy books like bibles. The arms of the upright cadavers are interlocked in a forced embrace, while upon their heads, and in their hands, are placed crude tokens of their corresponding gender: a hat and watering can; a bonnet and bucket.

Each cadaver has been rendered sexually ambiguous via the removal of their external genitals and breasts (assuming the cadaver on the right is biologically female). The inclusion of the sexual iconography of the watering can (masculine/phallic symbol) and bucket (feminine/yonic or womb-like symbol), further demonstrates the macabre, but juvenile sexual fantasies students manifested at the time; perverse fictions (although extremely tame by modern standards) that prove, yet again, just how far the genre evolved beyond being purely commemorative.

★★★

With extreme Stage III images on the rise, we must again ponder the extent to which school administrators banned or allowed photography to function in their dissecting rooms. Throughout the genre's earliest period (Stage I), anatomy department staff tolerated and indeed participated in the practice. Many popular anatomists, demonstrators, and school janitors can be found posing beside students in classic dissecting room portraits. Indeed, with the possible exception of 'Chris' Baker, the African American janitor and infamous resurrectionist of the MCV, master anatomist, Rufus Benjamin Weaver of Hahnemann Medical College, is likely the most-photographed staff member associated with dissecting room culture in the history of the genre. As both men were monumental personalities, literal legends within their schools' histories during their lifetimes, Baker and Weaver found inclusion in an overwhelming majority of their school's dissection photographs.

Considered the leading anatomist of his generation, and the creator of what many considered one of the most comprehensive medical museums in the country, Rufus Weaver was a celebrity within the culture of his school, and his likenesses, therefore, honorific souvenirs that every incoming class coveted (Figure 12.4). His legacy was further immortalized in 1888, upon the creation of the world's first complete dissection of a human nervous system;

Figure 12.4: Master anatomist and demonstrator of anatomy, Dr. Rufus Benjamin Weaver (left), dissecting with medical students. Hahnemann Medical College (Philadelphia, Pennsylvania). Unidentified photographer. Gelatin POP, circa 1900

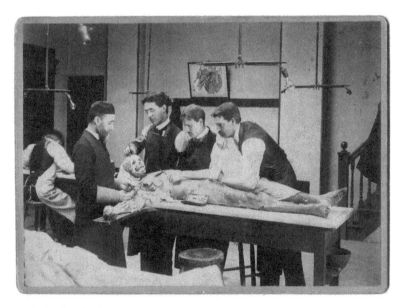

Source: Author's collection

commonly referred to as 'Harriet,' an honorific reference to the African American woman whose remains were reportedly used to create the dissection. But while Weaver's role as beloved professor and famous anatomist was clearly defined, 'Chris' Baker's contribution was complicated. As previously discussed, despite his omnipresence in early MCV dissection photographs, most of these images cast doubt on the janitor's willingness to participate in commemorative activities and the true nature of his relationship with students and staff.

Nevertheless, if faculty, like Weaver, and support staff, like Baker, viewed dissection photography as an adaptive process that inadvertently facilitated their end goal – for students to move forward in the profession *without fear* – did they view the genre as therapeutic, a necessary evil, or the future of identity formation? Or, was posing with cadavers merely a tolerated trend, spurred by the gimmick of technological innovation and student infatuation, destined to fall out of favor once the novelty of new cameras wore off? Remember that an awareness of photography and its results, even within impoverished or marginalized communities, would have been commonplace by the turn of the 20th century. By 1900, regardless of one's familiarity with the ever-changing species of Kodak's new handheld cameras, few were unfamiliar with the concept, process, and result of sitting for a photographic portrait. Case and point, it was said that 'Chris' Baker rarely travelled around the MVC campus without a photograph of his mother in his pocket.[94]

★★★

For some physicians, that students would even think to investigate the cadaver's decomposing innards for evidence of a soul, let alone try and take a photograph of it, was a futile venture that bordered on farce. To famed surgeon and President of the Royal College of Surgeons of London, Sir William Lawrence, the theological doctrine of the soul, specifically, proof of its separate existence from flesh, "could never have been brought to light by the labors of the anatomist and physiologist." Lawrence argued, rather bluntly, that the dissecting room was a foul cradle of knowledge, not an enlightened sphere of divine illumination. Had the esteemed surgeon lived to see the genesis of dissection photography, he likely would have concurred that even with the aid of the camera, an "immaterial and spiritual being could not have been discovered amid the blood and filth of the dissecting-room."[95]

And yet, while the general populace would agree with Lawrence on the sanctity of the human soul, they were not entirely convinced it did not reside within the body. To the readers of *The Wilmington Messenger* (North Carolina), a failure to locate the human soul inside a dead body was a matter of faith, not science. At the turn of the 20th century, devote North Carolinians wanted only Christian physicians at their bedsides, those "who could feel at the same time both the pulse of the body and the pulse of the soul." Under this statute, a Christian physician needed to be licensed on multiple planes of existence. "[A]nd when you take your diploma from the medical college to look after the perishable body be sure also to get a diploma from the skies to look after the imperishable soul." This way, if spiritual council was required, the Christian physician or student was properly trained; able and willing to dispense "an earthly and a divine prescription" and to "call on not only the apothecary of earth, but the pharmacy of heaven!" Extravagance, licentiousness, and atheism ran counter to the moral behaviors of proper healers or healers in training. "A doctor who has gone through medical college, and in [the] dissecting room has traversed the wonders of the human mechanism, and found no God in any of the labyrinths, is a fool, and cannot doctor me or mine," decreed devote North Carolinians.[96]

Clearly, the *Messenger's* readers were unaware of what the bulk of their 'Christian physicians' were up to at the time, particularly when it came to the production of dissection photographs. For example, from 1890 until it burned down in 1907 and was replaced by a more formal structure, the University of North Carolina School of Medicine (Raleigh), held its dissections in "a wooden shack which stood in a small grove," and took its dissection photographs outdoors.[97] The school's resultant imagery then, taken by commercial photographers, featured the classic dissection scene restaged outdoors in bucolic surroundings. This added a distinct primitiveness to their tableaus, as if the doctors had infiltrated Eden and begun dissecting Adam himself.

Whether photographers were conscious of it or not, such tableaus diminished the cadaver's abject significance – reduced to a dead body outside of a barn – and tapped into preexistent Transcendentalist thought of the body as nothing more than a soulless hunk of "cold clay."[98] Whether these questions, or the ways in which they were visualized through photography, reflected what Catholic schools decried as the decrease in "authoritative moral teaching," due to the espousing of "radical evolutionary doctrines" that made humans "only an animal and nothing more," remains to be seen.[99]

Meanwhile, those students who acquiesced to the existence of the human soul believed that it transcended mortal flesh upon death, and in doing so, became utterly impervious to any form of earthbound butcheries. "Sweet spirit rest in heaven where all is so fair. / You can rest contented for there'l be no students there," proclaimed a poetic dissecting table epigraph from Wake Forest.[100]

In his poem titled, "The Anatomist," published in the 1915 edition of the *X-Ray*, the yearbook of the MCV, Dr. John W. Brodnax, Associate Professor of Anatomy, sided with his students in the belief that a cadaver's soul sought sanctuary while in heaven, writing:

This comely maiden, once buoyant in life,
By the dread hand of disease, expires,
Is now the subject to the dissector's knife,
To carve and mutilate as he desires.

Perhaps she may have been a father's pride,
Nursed in a doting mother's fond embrace,
In manner modest, pure and dignified,
The proud idol of a courtier's grace.

Though ruthlessly this form he may despoil,
And will skillfully strive to gain his goal,
May in science be renown'd for his toil,
But cannot harm the sanctity of her soul.[101]

Assuredly, the ideology of spiritual transcendence as a genuinely held belief, versus it being just a conviction of convenience, varied from school to school and region to region. Regardless, extant dissection photographs confirmed the sum of students' sense of authoritarian immunity; a seemingly inviolable right to violate the dead. As a discarded vessel then, cadaveric remains 'belonged' to students, be it the coveted cadaver of a beautiful woman, or a horrific "stiff," "grinning at you with their big, pearly teeth," or "looking at you with their ghostly eyes in a tone which seems to say ... 'O, grave, thou hast been robbed of thy victory by the students'."[102]

As spiritless shells then, saved by self-proclaimed saviors of flesh and bone, defilers of even Death's grand design, cadavers were perceived as property. No matter their age, race, or sex, cadavers did not belong in our world. They belonged to students; to do with as they 'desired,' whenever and however they wanted. Even if, as Dr. Brodnax's poem affirms, those desires be considered *ruthless*.

13

The Cadaver as (Self-)Portrait

We are far apart, my soul and I,
As I hang along, under God's blue sky.
Can it be true, is it just as it seems?
Shall I build no more castles, nor dream no more dreams?

Some day we will be united, my soul and I
Never to be dissected, never to say goodbye,
In the forever in unknown space,
And suffer for the sin, which time can not efface.

Now I'm a gruesome object; if ought from me you gain,
It sometime or other caused sacrifice and pain.
My skeleton is all I have — last opportunity
To do some little good, and bless humanity.

Remember this O student, as you shall pass me by,
As you are strong and active now, so once was I,
As I am now O student, you are sure to be,
You pass this way but once, then comes eternity.
                    "Lines to a Skeleton," *The Howler*, 1911[1]

Sometime between the fall of 1895 and the spring of 1896, Anna Moon Randolph, a first-year medical student at the Woman's Medical College of Pennsylvania (WMCP), had her portrait taken seated beside the skinless arm and brainless head of a cadaver (Figure 13.1).

Before the shutter clicked, Randolph raised her scalpel, then her sights, and met the gaze of her photographer. This was no ordinary camera man, being neither a professional photographer nor, for that matter, a man. Instead, the tall, thin, dark-haired photographer standing eight feet from her, clothed in the shadows of the dissecting room and a floor-length dress, was none other than her classmate, WMCP second-year, and student amateur photographer, Alice Evans.

Figure 13.1: Anna Moon Randolph. Woman's Medical College of Pennsylvania (Philadelphia, Pennsylvania). Attributed to Alice Evans. Cyanotype mounted in scrapbook, Kodak No. 2, circa 1895.

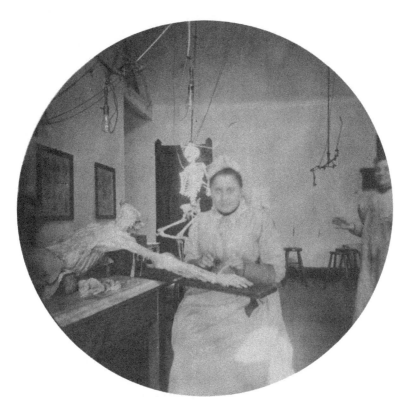

Source: Legacy Center, Drexel University College of Medicine

In her hands she held a camera unlike any Randolph had ever seen before: a brand-new No. 2 Kodak box camera. It required no tripod or plate holder. Not even a bellows. From where she sat, Randolph could not even see a lens. To the casual observer, Evans appeared to simply be standing there, holding a plain oblong black box.

Randolph watched as her classmate fiddled with a tiny reflecting finder on the camera's top. Evans then pulled a short cord to set the shutter, pointed the front of the box at Randolph and her cadaver, told her to stay still, then pushed a button.[2] That was it. Within milliseconds, the pair had made history: a WMCP dissection photograph, taken by a WMCP student, inside the WMCP dissecting room.[3]

The series of dissecting room portraits taken during Evans' time in Philadelphia in the 1890s would have been unthinkable a decade earlier. She was an amateur photographer, a woman no less, who needed no prior photographic training to take her photographs; no darkroom to develop her negatives or make her prints. Now self-reliant, Evans was guided, no doubt, by skilled friends and family, and a handy instruction manual produced by her camera manufacturer, Eastman Kodak. This comprehensive pamphlet steered her through a range of technical issues, including principal photography, how to develop her own negatives, and the manufacturing of prints using various types of patented printing papers, such as albumen, collodion, and cyanotype.

By the time they graduated medical school, Evans and her classmates would produce an unprecedented array of photographs of college life. A photo enthusiast who enjoyed experimentation, Evans used multiple processes to make her prints. But one she favored most was the cyanotype process. All in all, Alice Evans took approximately 75 photographs during her time at WMCP. Chief among this oeuvre are at least ten dissection photographs. The other Evans photos include portraits of staff, students studying in the school's medical museum, blurry working shots taken in the college's surgical amphitheater (neither patient nor physician held still long enough), as well as snapshots of students being vulnerable together in intimate settings, such as their boardinghouse rooms.

The significance of the Evans photographs is in their innovative approach of visualizing student life during a period of climactic upheaval in the photographic industry: the introduction of amateur handheld cameras. The Evans dissection photographs offer an unprecedented glimpse into the visual and material culture of the American dissecting room. I consider them to be the proverbial 'missing link' between dissection photography's first stages of evolution: the standard portraiture of commercial photographers (Stage I) and the innovative portraiture of student amateur photographers (Stage II).[4]

The Evans photographs show medical students posing by themselves, alone, confident with the dead. Distinctive, within a collection of the unique, are portraits like that of Anna Moon Randolph in the dissecting room, or 'Kid Jarrett' in the WMCP medical museum surrounded by cases of anatomical specimens. Until the 1890s, photographically commemorating a one-on-one relationship between student and cadaver was virtually unheard of. By the early 1910s, the commercial availability of camera technology, such as those manufactured by Eastman Kodak, influenced both ability and convention, leading to a steady rise in single-dissector portraiture. Many took the form of real photo postcards. Although the convention never reached the same level of production as group shots – dissection is, after all, a collaborative act – at the 'end' of the genre's popularity in the 1930s, single-dissector snapshots had become fully integrated into the larger iconography of dissection portraiture. Had the tradition survived into the early 21st century, dissection self-portraits ('selfies') taken with one's cellphone would most assuredly have become part of the next stage in the genre's evolution.

Everyone's a critic

> Unlearned infants we entered the halls
> Of our school, thirsting for knowledge—
> Hoping that we would weather the squall
> We would meet in our four years of college.
>
> "Out of the Maze," G.R. McLaughlin,
> Class of 1924, Chicago College of Dental Surgery[5]

Handheld cameras led to an increase in representative agency. With them came the next level of self-representation and self-awareness – *critical awareness* – which provided students with an opportunity to pass judgment on each other, in part, through the quality of their skills taking and developing photographs.

Prior to photography's increased popularity, those with limited knowledge of the medium's technical aspects relied on the expertise of others for the literal development of their identities. With handheld cameras, this amateur lot could eventually participate at or near the same level as trained professionals, or photo-savvy classmates. All one had to do was push a button. In this modern age, having never processed negatives before or even set foot inside a darkroom was irrelevant. Spent film was simply sent back to the camera manufacturer through the mail. A short time later, beautifully mounted prints and developed negatives would arrive, along with a freshly restocked camera. If a student needed additional prints, they simply took the negatives to their local camera shop and extras were made, or one bought the supplies to make them yourself, which is just what Evans did. Singular identity wrought by the convenience of mass production.

As proficient equals – labeled thusly by the burgeoning industry of camera companies and print shops – this new class of amateur photographer could level praise or throw shade on the imagery of others; not only for the content of their photographs, but on their aesthetic merits; evaluated based on whatever technology (such as the use of magnesium flash) or posing convention (dynamic versus static poses) was popular at the time.

Competitive judgmental behavior, bullying, and a resultant culture obsessed with aesthetics comes as no surprise to the modern world. During the era of the dissection photograph, much like the classrooms of today, students frequently ridiculed each other over their physical appearances, vices, intellect, or unconventional interests. "His mind is mathematical and logical," observed the Class of 1911 at Wake Forest College Medical School of one of their seniors. "His appearance would never suggest either, however."[6]

While not all commentary was negative – per se – the most common remarks had to do with appearance, such as whether a student was starting to go bald, or if they were overweight. Usually, these character traits became an inseparable part of student identity, manifested in the form of class nicknames.

Many nicknames were straightforward and pointed towards an obvious (but not always flattering or politically correct) origin. For instance, at the Atlanta College of Physicians and Surgeons, being the youngest member of the class automatically earned a student the nickname "Embryo." Another, received the more pejorative moniker of "Nuts," a comment upon his aptitude for caring for the terminally ill at the House of Incurables. Remarked the class of his situation: "He has one consolation, he needn't feel bad if he loses a patient."[7]

But an equal number of names originated from so inside a reference to a school or student, that their meaning is impossible to decipher. For instance, we will likely never learn the reason why dental students of the Medical College of Virginia called a classmate, "Ovary."[8] Or, why students at the Chicago College of Dental Surgery called each other: "Sauer Kraut Joe," "Peroxide," and "Grandma."[9]

Dissection was a popular social litmus test for establishing appropriately inappropriate nicknames, regardless of whether one was technically competent or behaviorally incompetent. Either extreme ended in a career-spanning sobriquet. In 1906, seniors at the University of Maryland School of Medicine called one of their cohort, "Butcher," after they saw how badly he mutilated his cadaver.[10] Meanwhile, due to the deliberate, unhurried manner in which he finished his dissections, the Class of 1930 at the Hahnemann Medical College, bestowed upon one of their ranks the nickname, "Slow Death."[11]

★★★

Beyond mere name-calling, the focus from the collective to the individual reinvented the culture of the dissecting room. In the case of this new 'type' of single-dissector portrait, the inherent intimacy left students in a state of intense vulnerability; separated from the collective and isolated via photographic framing and a heretofore unrealized 'close-up' proximity. With student identity no longer presented within the preestablished confines of a collective, an individual could no longer hide; neither protected by the safety of the group, nor from its derision, be it photographically, physically, or socially. For example, remember how, in this book's Introduction, the Class of 1907 singled out their class historian, Harrower, for dressing in a more formal white suit then the rest of his cohort.

Group photographs served as tangible proof of the collective's role in anatomical dissection. Although this evidentiary facet remained true to single-dissector photos, instead of finding attribution within a larger industry or homosocial arena of educational experience, now the whole of the cadaver's mutilated appearance was conferred upon the individual. Thus, with the consequence of student action upon the cadaver no longer distributed equally among a 'gang' or cohort, the single-dissector accepted all credit, as well as all blame, for what was wrought through cameras and cadavers; a direct corollary of choice and skill thusly heaped upon the identity of the individual. Like Atlas' burden, a solitary student might bend but must not break under the weight of this newfound scrutiny of their individual and individualized identity.

We assume portraits of this kind were consented to, and therefore students could elicit total agency over the way(s) they wished to be portrayed. But remember that technology and technological awareness, especially in the era of the dissection photograph, were in a constant state of flux. For instance, prior to the advent of the innovative Kodak camera (1888), WCMP Professor of Obstetrics, Dr. Anna Broomall, was notorious for refusing to allow any of her students to take her photograph. But, once Alice Evans had the convenient and surreptitious No. 2 Kodak at her disposal, photographic 'consent' was no longer under Broomall's control. As Evans' handwritten notations on the back of her covert portrait of the elderly obstetrician confirms, the undercover photograph was taken without incident or awareness: "A snap shot taken by Miss Evans. [Dr. Broomall] would never allow her picture to be taken but did not happen to know."[12]

★★★

By the 1920s, dissection photographs of single-dissectors were a staple of the photo-literate physician's college scrapbook or family photo album. Hundreds of these often tackily decorated scrapbooks are extant. Most exhibit little to no concern for the fraternization of abject medical imagery with the more normative snapshots of American family life. The jarring experience of flipping through an old family album, only to find captioned photographs of eviscerated cadavers juxtaposed next to images of smiling babies, family vacations, and tourist postcards from Atlantic City and Niagara Falls, is tempered only by the commonality of the occurrence. Clarence Waring, a student at Hahnemann Medical College, from 1919 to 1923, pasted his sole-dissector photographs into an album marked "Scraps" (amusing here given the subject matter within); its cover, adorned with an illustrated advert of a bonneted child playing with a bulldog, and the phrase, "Murphy, Do You Love Butter?" written underneath.[13]

By comparison, the college scrapbook of Ruby Inouye Shu, WMCP graduate, and the first Japanese physician in Seattle, Washington, shows off a wide range of commemorative vernacular photographs, including formal headshots of her and her classmates (likely used for a school publication), graduation photos, as well as Shu and her classmates (including Kazuko

Uno, the only other Japanese student) walking together along the Atlantic City boardwalk during the centennial celebration of the American Medical Association.

Yet, rather inexplicably, Shu's scrapbook, otherwise filled to the brim with images that exude camaraderie, positivity, and inclusion, opens upon a trio of photographs of a dissected African American cadaver. While Shu herself is not present, two of the three images are close-ups; inferring this cadaver, and its dissected state, are a direct result of her handiwork. Also attributed to Shu is the derogatory caption, "Poor Uncle Tom," written at the bottom of the page in white pen; a heading she (or perhaps a descendant) later tried to hide by scribbling over the letters with a black marker.[14]

Although this insensitive epithet is less offensive than those of all-male schools from the early 1900s, and even if the viewpoint was shared by others (which it undoubtedly was) Shu bears full and sole responsibility for its message. With the images and caption associated with individual rather than collective identity, we do not question the structural racism endemic to this dissecting room as much as we do the beliefs of the individual. In this case, these words are not just shocking and uncharacteristic of a woman who went on to be a pillar of her community but are also sadly hypocritical.

Shu herself experienced discrimination after the attack on Pearl Harbor in 1941. The following year she was forced to drop out of college due to the proclamations resulting from Executive Order 9066, which began the forced relocation and detention of over 120,000 Japanese Americans living on the West Coast. Before being allowed to leave to continue her education, she and her family had been forced to spend a year incarcerated in internment camps, including the Minidoka Relocation Camp, located in the deserts of Idaho.

After receiving her M.D. from WMCP in 1948, Shu found that no hospital would accept her as an intern based on her race. The overt discrimination caused her to break down in tears.[15] She eventually found placement at St. Francis Hospital in Pittsburgh, Pennsylvania. Thus, perhaps it was a crisis of identity, or a classic case of the abused becoming the abuser, that in a time of helplessness, the intolerance shown toward Shu was extended, in kind, by her, toward the identity of the helpless body of her African American cadaver.

More than mortal

> Does it ever occur to us that among the other divine acts, Christ was healing the sick, was restoring the health of those pronounced incurable, making the blind to see? Precisely the same divine work we are going to do. ... *We* are not just witnessing, but actually participating in the creation of a new world on earth.
>
> Graduating Class of 1918, Medical College of Virginia[16]

Although classic postures and tropes (such as holding scalpels) were still realized in single-dissector snapshots, the overriding symbolism bonded single bodies together: one living, one dead, one passed, one present. Be they mythologized, fetishized, or simply judged together through a host of sociocultural stimuli or self-induced fears, photography made tangible a long-standing psychosomatic relationship between the dissector and the dissected; what Hafferty describes as the phenomenon of the "cadaver as future self."[17]

Inversion from the collective to the individual placed a heavy burden on the student-dissector. Included in this encumbrance was the consequence of a direct correlation between a single living student and a single cadaver. Though a broad sense of identity may initially form through collective participation in dissection, its success or failure depended upon the agency and maturity of the individual.

Single-dissector images depict the individual as the sole antagonist toward the dissected body. Thus, it must be the individual who seeks absolution for their trespasses upon mortal flesh; the individual, who tosses and turns in their bed, terrified of what dreams may come. For in these dreams, when cadavers rose to seek vengeance upon the living, the dead returned for the individual.

In this context, professional identity abandoned the medical student to their own inner thoughts. It consigned them to the lonely depths of their own self-worth. From within this death-like darkness, from within this isolation – in tandem with their professional (in)experiences – emerges the question, do medical students ever see themselves as cadavers?

Blurring the boundaries between the living and the dead found widespread application throughout the visual economy of the 20th-century dissecting room. When referencing the degenerative effects of medical training upon their own health, students routinely adopted the language of the reanimated dead to describe themselves. While cramming for final exams, the Class of 1900 at the University of Maryland School of Medicine underwent a "peculiar metamorphosis" that left them zombified: "more dead than alive."[18] As they came closer to finals week, "symptoms of this peculiar malady increased" and they became beset with a "strange 'hollow eye' and 'leanness'" reminiscent of the cadaver.[19]

In 1914, as commentary on his 'wasting away' from studying anatomy, a student posed for a photograph in the embrace of an articulated skeleton, both dressed in identical white doctor's coats. The skeleton's attire included additional accessories, such as the student's hat, glasses, and a cigarette placed between its teeth. Written into the negative and printed underneath the 'identical' pair, the student posed the question to his viewers: "Who's who, and why?"[20]

Relatedly, when exposure to the cadaver's putrefied remains compromised their health, students could not resist making connections between the homogeneous appearance of the living and the dead – both colorless bodies; one sick, one sickening. For instance, when a student fell ill prior to being photographed with her cadaver, "Aphrodite," who had a literal "rotten brain," the two became as one. "I look sick, and I probably was," wrote the student of her pale appearance. "Question: which is the cadaver?"[21]

Student amateur photographers frequently took photos that highlighted a passive form of self-loathing. The image served as a confession of necrotizing identity, which resulted from the various rigors of anatomical education in tandem with prolonged exposure to the physical and moral hazards of the dissecting room. Despite the development of their 'necessary inhumanity,' many students of the late 19th century still struggled with their role in the dissolution of human materiality, as well as the concept of the human soul in relation to its physical location within decomposing matter. Photography, again, showed no visual confirmation of intangible spirit. Thus, complicating public perception over the sanctity of the human body, were the opinions and fears of the medical students themselves. Contrary to the mostly confident projections of identity captured through the photographic medium – some referred to students looking as "profound as a judge, or as lofty as a demigod" – many experienced internalized feelings of guilt, shame, and doubt.[22] As the continuum of emotions centered around participation in dissection was so polarized, we assume at least a portion of the American student population sought introspection, soul-searching (not that kind), and the contemplation of one's own self-worth, while the others thoroughly rejected such meditations.

Indeed, plenty of students posed for dissection photographs without blinking (metaphorically speaking). The act meant little to them; the photo, no more than a souvenir of their college days alongside embroidered pennants or their cap and gown. After graduation they tossed their scrapbook or mounted print in a box and chucked it in an attic; only for it to be found decades later by a spouse or adult child who considered it 'as disgusting as it was disturbing' and elected to destroy or sell it.

Plenty more students passed through the doors of the dead house without feeling what others felt. This did not mean that they were dead inside, merely that identity-affirming responses to dissection were secondary or inconsequential to the formation of their professional identity. Engaging with cadavers was simply a means to an end. Thus, the pressures and fears of the dissecting room were inconsequential to those placed upon them by the external world or those imposed upon the self. These were not identities formed by dissection, but in spite of it.

★★★

While participating in dissection is no less emotional for students of the 21st century, it is generally not as spiritual an act as it was for those during the era of the dissection photograph. To the freshman medical students of the 1890s at Yale University, the "gruesome mysteriousness" of the dissecting room "reflected on us and makes us seem more than mortal, certainly in our own eyes."[23] But what exactly is meant by this? Did their actions, especially those commemorated through their photography, make them more God-fearing or God-like by their estimations?

More than mortal could mean several things. But, according to religious doctrines, God only destroys the body, not the soul. Therefore, by superseding the will and power of God, were they demigods themselves, or rather, had they become devils?

The doctor and the devils

> But all these faults and frivolities of ours were not natural – some were acquired.
>
> Medical College of Virginia, Freshmen
Class, 1917[24]

As highlighted throughout this book, acclimating the living dissector to the sights, smells, and feel of the dissected dead was an arduous procedure of biblical proportions. "Can we ever forget the impressions the odor of the stiffs made on us on our first entry into the dissecting room?" asked the graduating medical Class of 1918 at Tulane University.[25] Indeed, coping with the abject sensorial experience of dissection stayed with students throughout the entirety of their academic careers, and even beyond. Many students, across a variety of backgrounds, religions, and universities, considered slicing into the cadaver's flesh a horrific and arduous ritual. Ordinarily, adaptive strategies were implemented in order to effectively navigate and overcome such obstacles. Evoking silent personal prayer was customary.

During a particularly explicit dissection in November 1847, Elizabeth Blackwell, America's first female physician, described how her male classmates at Geneva Medical College had "blushed," were "hysterical," and too often, "held down their faces and shook" at the "ludicrous" sights before them.[26] As to her own response, declared Blackwell: "My delicacy was certainly shocked ... I had to pinch my hand till the blood nearly came, and call on Christ to help me."[27]

Nearly one hundred years later, New York University student, Irma Gross Drooz, felt "very much nauseated and somewhat faint" following her first encounter with a cadaver. She too sought God's help.

> Fifty coffin-size tables with slate tops. Fifty cadavers wrapped in canvas sheets. Fifty people, who were born, loved, raised, and then died. Fifty unclaimed people. ... I found myself, perspiring, although I felt not

the least warm. "Please, God, let me *not* be sick," I prayed silently. "I want so much to be a doctor. I've got to spend several months in there. This is no good."[28]

The sight of the cadaver was liable to bring many a student to tears – a truth of experience that remains steadfast to this day. For those truly unprepared to stand in death's presence, there was "trembling, weakness in the limbs, goose bumps, loose bowels, even vomiting and fainting."[29] Such responses, although normal, were not universal. Many considered dissection a means to an end; a technical examination no different than any other professional test; and thus, the dissection photograph, just another commemorative image from their school days.

Although dissection had its affective qualities, for some, the corresponding stigmas and anxieties held little sway over their daily lives, behavior, or general senses (except perhaps smell). "I am on for dissecting again" wrote medical student Mary T. McGavran of her time at WMCP. "I have already done a head and upper, the head I did first befor [sic] vacation and had to hurry to get it done so it was not as well done as I would have liked." McGavran's dispassionate, matter-of-fact tone carried over into the following afternoon, when she and her friends made taffy. "It was no good," she confessed in her diary of the "stiff" consistency of her confectionery concoction. "Please don't blame me for mistakes."[30] But, for which "stiff" body was she truly apologizing for exactly?

★★★

Seeking spiritual guidance through prayer was a common enough act. By all accounts, it still is. But, if students at the turn of the 20th century required this help to commence and complete their dissections, that oversight was not reflected through the lens of the camera; unless we consider the taking of a dissection photograph a form of confession, or an act of attrition.

One way to interpret student behavior, particularly the prevalent posing conventions of the early 1900s involving cadavers staged as if reanimated, suggests that the closer students came to death, the more they sought a closer kinship with the organic elements comprising God's creation. Here it could be said that student altruism led to abjection, and vice versa. If they merely overcame their own sensorial difficulties, then familiarity with dissection and the inner workings of humankind's design should, by association, mean a keener connection to God. Elizabeth Blackwell all but confirmed such in her day, writing that eventually, the "wonderful arrangements of the human body excited an interest and admiration" in her that "simply obliterated the more superficial feelings of repugnance." In time, the dissecting room became her private chapel; just her and God's creation; toiling in the "intense stillness" of the night among the innards of man, while all around her "the rest of the little town" slept soundly.[31]

In the case of dissection photography, the accepted conceit is the more explicit the image, the more comfortable the student photographers were with dissecting their cadavers. The irony here being, if God's help was in fact needed, presumably, the architects of these images had asked for and received it already. Their faith and his Word provided the sustained ability to construct abject tableaus, which, in turn paradoxically glorified the utter *godlessness* of the visual and material cultures of the American dissecting room.

That said, as is usual with issues pertaining to the medical profession, massive contradictions exist regarding cultural views toward cadavers. One of the most prominent involved the previously mentioned self-reflective guilt students evidenced through diaries, letters, drawings and real photo postcards, all of which dramatized internal conflicts about their role in the dismemberment of the dead.

Although human beings have many killers – murder, accident, disease, drugs, animal attacks, old age – the mutilation and dissolution of corporeal form was still a process generally left to fate, aka God. Therefore, to the devotedly religious student, dissection photographs – especially those showing single-dissectors – did not memorialize a revered, sanctified act perpetrated by angelic entities who cast no shadows. Instead, photographic commemoration stood as a form of visual atonement. The print itself, proof positive of sinful flesh in the hands of sinners, confirmed devils, who dwelled not in heaven (where *some* cadavers went), but in the eternal darkness of Hell.

The classic trope of the 'doctors as devils' is found throughout countless school yearbooks across the United States. When dissection photography failed to provide adequate expression, students reimagined themselves in cartoon form. The most popular incarnation depicted them as literal cloven-hoofed pitchfork-wielding devils, romping through the night accompanied by multiple 'familiars,' such as black goats and fire-breathing serpents.[32] The medical students at the University of Virginia had multiple ghoulish iterations to choose from, including giant-headed, scalpel wielding skeletons in bow ties and aprons, to a surreal menagerie of predatory creatures, such as a human-vulture hybrid with a saw in its talons, perched atop a coffin beside a freshly robbed grave.[33]

An argument could be made that less literal interpretations of the 'devilish nature' of medical students is to be found in any dissection photograph that shows them acting disrespectfully with human remains. By their own confession, student behavior in dissecting rooms was at times "disgusting and sickening," even to medical school janitors, those, who by all accounts, had seen and done it all.[34] Under these circumstances, the inner sanctum of the dissecting room, that literal stinking tomb of mystery, became a symbolic den of medieval retribution. To descend to its depths of depravity, one had to customarily ascend to its heights physically; "to 'crawl' up four flights of steps alone in darkness"; hearts "beating 150 times a minute."[35] It was a place where cadaveric sinners were punished "not only by dismemberment" but also by "perverted nutrition and fertility – horrid consumptions, digestions, impregnations, excretions, vomitings, and birthings."[36]

Scalpels and saws did the deeds of pitchforks and claws. Instead of pools of burning oil, cadavers hung from giant hooks, suspended above tanks of pickling solution.[37] Genitals were shorn from the body and discarded into literal pits or ovens. The reanimated dead, complete with rotting zombie-like profiles and emptied of all vital organs, took up positions to affect revenge and judgment upon their living tormentors who, in true Demons Major form, cloaked themselves in dazzling white – usually a symbol of purity, but here corrupted; a destructive force of nature akin to Ahab's White Whale, or the name of Lucifer, which means 'bearer of light.'

Many a student embraced the abject, absent fear, absent morality, absent pain, absent guilt, absent repercussions from others – including God. Just as heaven was the sanctuary of (some) cadavers, so too was the dissecting room an unholy refuge for those who reveled in one's own moral decline. "This is the place where at nights we used to pull off our coats, put on the gowns and begin – rolling bones [dice], pitching pennies, and singing," recalled dental students at the Medical College of Virginia in 1917.[38] Sin begot sin.

However, absolution for their violations upon the cadaver – be it from a legitimate dissection or as part of some grotesque photographic tableau – was neither necessary nor achievable. Trespassing upon the mortal remains of others, violating their bodies as devils violate those in Hell, was sanctified through the greatness of their professional calling. As the Reverend C.J. Greenwood declared to rapt congregations in 1903: "To the ordinary mortal death is repulsive and life is pleasing. … No one but the grave robber or the medical student is supposed to be interested in corpses."[39] If we follow this line of thinking, then student absolution was either unnecessary or it was unachievable. Would priests even agree to hear such confessions? After all, how does one punish a devil? What must a demon do to atone for their sins?

And yet, if one was truly forgiven of the sins of dissecting human flesh, why feel shame, or fear retribution from those dissected? Perhaps in this case then, the transgressive dissection photograph truly was 'wicked'; an unforgivable representation of unholy behavior that students believed they should be punished for. A punishment that ultimately never came. With no need for absolution and no apparent fear of true retribution, was the student in essence goaded into aligning themselves with the dominant and basest forces of the universe? Their shame was not about needing to atone for what they had done, but for their utter lack of consequence. To them, was it truly as the great poet once wrote: "Better to reign in hell, than serve in heav'n?"[40]

Who dissects the dissectors?

Throughout the era of the dissection photograph, students and physicians alike recounted their fears over cadaveric rebirth through poems and photographs. It is rather ironic to consider that for a profession born from desecrating graves, comprised mainly by God-fearing Protestant men, that the resurrection of the dead would yield the most awkward and abhorrent imagery. For unlike Jesus or Lazarus, the revivified dead, as imagined by the student-dissector, was a vengeful and murderous entity. The particulars of their lives or the manner of their death, both seemingly of no consequence. All that mattered was the commonality of their dissection upon the slab. Thus, within the culture of the dissecting room, the reborn remains of a schoolteacher, priest, a child, or a mass murderer, all sought diabolical revenge equally.

That said, many of the tales associated with the resurrected dead involved the remains of executed criminals. Fitting, as dissection was originally a postmortem punishment for those who went against the laws of God and man. Stories involving the living dead are obviously pure fiction. But it is quite telling that these yarns occurred within dissecting rooms, and involved reanimating the bodies of the evil, to enact evil deeds upon dissectors; those society considered ceaselessly suspect, who operated in secret behind closed doors on the fringes of morality.

Acknowledgment of the cadaver's affective qualities, and student reflection upon their role, manifested through a combination of visual and verbal commentary. It is interesting to consider, however, that in group photos, students objectified cadavers to the point of subverting human materiality – using bones like musical instruments or bending limbs to spell out words. Many expressed a reluctance to consider the cadaver as a human. And yet, when posed *alone* with the dead, these objections, hesitations, and subjections were apparently rendered moot. For those students, both past and present, who viewed the cadaver as a future version of themselves then, the normative 'rules' of abject objectification – viewing the dead body solely as a learning tool, or as a piece of inanimate insensate meat – are either suspect, or the conceptual framework simply failed to take hold.

The photographic medium bonded student and cadaver visually, intellectually, and (presumably) emotionally. Such relationships made them coagents of abjection; the metaphorical blurring of singular identity commingling as typifying elements of human mortality: the cadaver the student's future self, the student the cadaver's former self. And yet, the eternal question persists: if they were so ashamed of their actions, why then did they take dissection photographs?

Heaven only knows.

Conclusion: "Learning to Fight Death Next to Death Itself"

Faces fade and people we once knew, some of them, are gone forever. Children grew up and go away. The house is torn down. Pets die or disappear. The time to take the picture is when you see it. The historic value of things, fixed in the form of a picture, is beyond price.

Elbert Hubbard, 1922[1]

As Drew Gilpin Faust pointedly asks in her influential publication, *This Republic of Suffering: Death and the American Civil War*: "Why do living humans pay attention to corpses?"[2] A similar question was asked in 1854, in *Harper's New Monthly Magazine*, by Professor Tayler Lewis in an article that pondered whether "the sacredness of the human body" was "a notion too outdated for a modern era of science and progress."[3] The question, unsurprisingly, was a rhetorical one.

The human body, continued the article, relying on the dominant Protestant doctrines of the time, should not be considered merely some disposable possession for the benefit of science, for it is "not like a picture," it is "something more than a belonging, a property, an association." Though "motionless" and "speechless," within remained "something of the former selfhood," that which would one day "be raised again – yea, the same body."[4] Thus, even in death, the human body demanded respect and care, lest its posthumous 'life' in the hereafter be one of pain and fragmented formlessness.

Sympathetic to the plight of the lay community of the times and their beliefs that anatomical dissection held the capacity to cut or somehow splinter the human soul along with its corporeal vessel, some 19th-century physicians expressed a more tolerant view. "The idea that respect is due to the dead body is so deeply rooted in the human mind as to be almost instinctive," stated Professor Thomas Dwight of Harvard Medical School. "We know, indeed, that no violence can harm the dead, but, though reason is convinced, the heart is not satisfied."[5] To lessen public perceptions over the abject nature of dissection, attempts were made to satisfy both the hearts and minds of the masses by championing the act as a legitimate and holy ritual; a profound ceremony essential to understanding "the human form Divine" by studying the body "as God made it."[6] But this faction was definitely in the minority. But times have changed.

In the modern era, respect is shown toward the cadaver at all stages of dissection. This includes before a student makes their first cut upon a whole body, to afterwards, when dissected remains are boxed up, cremated, and then either buried or returned to families. Today, many schools hold introductory orientations prior to students entering the gross lab. During one such orientation seminar that I was permitted to observe in the fall of 2021, first-year students were instructed not to refer to the dead as 'cadavers,' but as *donors* – the term cadaver now apparently being considered inconsiderate of power relations, or disrespectful to the living families of the dead and their conception of bodily autonomy.

Although concerted effort was taken to soften the emotional impact of the students' impending, all-important, yet 'unnatural' encounter with the dead body, faculty reminded them that the best way to honor a donor's gift was to take full advantage of the exceptional opportunity they had been given. I should note, at this orientation there was no specific mention of whether students could or could not take photographs in the anatomy lab, just a general mandate that the dead deserved respect at all times during the dissection process, including when 'disposing' of cadaveric refuse.

Indeed, beside each dissecting table staff placed immense lidded containers. On the sides of each, the words, "CADAVER PARTS ONLY," were stenciled in blood red paint. The sole purpose of these 'garbage cans' was the collection of skin, tissue, bone or any other miscellaneous bits removed from the dead. Normal garbage of any kind was forbidden from being placed inside these containers. For following dissection, the contents of these cans would be dumped back into each cadaver's body cavity prior to cremation. Thus, while corporeally fragmented, cadavers left the gross lab as close to complete as when they entered. Once, I observed a student toss a pair of filthy nitrile gloves into one of these bins, only for his absentmindedness or indifference (it wasn't entirely clear) to be thoroughly rebuked by his dissecting team. The student apologized, fished the used gloves out of the red biohazard bag-lined bin barehanded, walked across the lab, and placed them in the proper receptacle.

Modern orientation methods are decidedly more respectful than the ways students were introduced to their cadavers during the era of the dissection photograph. Faculty now strive to engender respect through a focus on personhood. Yet they also need students to maintain and perhaps even deny emotional connectivity. Otherwise, cadaveric utility could suffer. However, during my observations in 2021, the process I witnessed was decidedly oversaturated with a sense of dramatic performance that seemed, at least to me as neutral observer, rather counterproductive. Although it was unquestionably less macabre than ages past, it was no less pleasant, nor less a spectacle then Stewart Elliott's attempts in 1909. For example, once students were inside the gross lab and positioned beside their assigned cadavers, colored shrouds covering the several dozen bodies within were lifted slowly, and in incremental stages, starting at the cadaver's shriveled feet and then moving upwards. Only as a final flourish were the faces of the dead revealed to students. This presented a fascinating divergence. During the era of the dissection photograph, the region most associated with shame or that incited emotional distress was the cadaver's genitals, not the face. What does this say about us as a society, that in the pursuit of instilling a greater sense of personhood into cadaveric bodies, we have somehow lost the ability to gaze into the literal face of humanity?

Instilling this initial 'face to face' encounter with a greater sense of emotional impact, by way of a certain degree of pomp and circumstance, engendered, and indeed insisted upon, a greater emotional reaction by students. Some seemed confused on how to respond under such conditions. Were they supposed to hide their emotions, or, to mirror the dramatic reveal by way of an equally histrionic reaction? Many stole glances at their dissecting partners in an attempt to discern which was the more socially or professionally acceptable response.

Upon seeing their cadaver's face for the first time, the deathly silence and intense stillness of the room was interrupted by faint gasps and fidgeting. A few women from various groups positioned around the room began to audibly cry. One reportedly raced out of the lab and bolted up an empty stairwell to vomit and cry alone. Two fainted. From experience, I can tell you this usually has more to do with students locking their knees while standing than it does with witnessing abject sights. Nevertheless, much like the outward projections of their predecessors a century and a half before them, the majority stood sentinel and showed no major reaction of any kind.

Later in the semester, I posed a simple hypothetical to several dissecting groups (comprised of six students per table). If they were allowed to take photographs with their cadaver, how many of them would? The majority responded quickly that they would not, citing a previous staff announcement that taking photographs of cadavers was strictly forbidden. But this did not exactly answer my question. I understood the rules. But I still wanted to get a sense of what they thought. Were their beliefs and opinions truly aligned with modern ethical standards? Or, was policy suppressing an underlying need; the same need students had almost a century and a half ago and that led to the genesis of dissection photography?

Collectively, the students found photography personally disrespectful to the 'donor' and to their families. Many fell into classic tropes of the 'cadaver as future self,' stating that they would be upset if someone took photos of their bodies, or those of family members, without consent. Yet, when I spoke to some of them individually, many changed their rhetoric.

The students I spoke to one-on-one confessed they would indeed like to take pictures *of* their cadaver, but not necessarily *with* their cadaver. The purpose of the photograph here would be as an educational tool, a study-aid; to help them build up a visual library of the body's inner workings. A few even admitted to having already snuck an image or two of this kind by way of their cellphones. Some blamed the need on their reduced dissection time because of the COVID-19 pandemic. But it wasn't just the lack of knowledge that made them do it. Many expressed frustrations over not building the same sense of community the older students had prior to the start of COVID-19. The pandemic meant they had to dissect by themselves or in smaller groups, never as a full dissecting team, and never as a full class. Thus, the collective experience, the team building, and the identity formation, either never happened, or did not take hold in the way they expected; the way they *wanted*.

This of course then begs the question, if given the opportunity, would modern students take portraits with their cadavers to assist with the formation of their identities? Would a dissection photograph fill the void left behind by a lack of community, or inadvertently widen it? Institutional edicts forbid this behavior. "They violate the ethical norms of our profession that we wish to instill in our students," wrote Yale anatomy professor Lawrence Rizzolo in 2019, after it was discovered that dissection photographs were taken and published in the school yearbook in 2011.[7] Another anatomy professor at Yale, who had taught since the late 1970s, decreed that if he'd been aware of the practice, "he would not have allowed" photography in the dissecting room. This means that either Yale's students had refrained from the practice for over 30 years; or more likely, that the professor was simply unaware of what was really going on in his lab. In either event, the persistence of these images into the 21st century, and possibly right under the nose of departmental staff, only furthers Terry's categorization of dissection photographs as an effective "underground genre."

So, allow me to ask again: If students could take photographs with their cadavers, would they stay true to their word and refute photography of any kind, or, only take photos for educational value? Despite their declarations of evolved ethics and morality, if allowed, or perhaps I should say, if free of consequence, would the modern student resurrect the dissection photograph of old, embrace the abject, and indeed pose *with* their cadavers?

Of course they would.

★★★

Dissection photographs were designed to enhance, reaffirm, or reshape a student's professional identities at a specific transitional time in their lives.

Regardless of mainstream categorizations or social stigmas governing the utility of the dead, American students shaped their photographs, their emblems of identity, to satisfy their evolving needs. "Taboo and science combined," states Terry; a joint effort designed to dramatize experience and identity for themselves, and eventually, for others.[8] Even if these images one day assume a place outside of their realm of abjection, one wonders if they will ever recover from decades of misunderstanding, misclassification, and downright scorn? I for one sincerely hope so.

Over the course of its 50-year reign, dissection photographs evolved, much like the profession and the professionals they depicted. They matured alongside the industry from which they were born. They transformed with each decade's photographic advances, from static formalized group portraiture, to intimate, expressive, and candid snapshots; a vernacular chronicling of the secretive and privileged world of medical schools, its most sacred and profane rites and practices, and the psychological conditioning of its students over death and the dead body. To understand how important and prevalent photography was to these students in the formation of identity, just look at the epic montages, the near organic Modernisme conglutinations of portraits, group shots, and presumably, dissection photographs, that students constructed and hung on the ceilings and walls of their homes and boardinghouses (Figure C.1).

With the eventual ease involved in taking a photograph – the push of a button and the millisecond snap of a camera shutter – students could simultaneously form and fortify more explicit iterations of their professional identities without being mitigated by the critical eye of outsiders. They now spoke to an individualized experience as individualized by the student themselves; an experience complete with its own rituals, conventions, and iconography that built upon, but ultimately deviated from, the symbolism of the past.

Indeed, many of these images parade the macabre and the taboo. To this day they circulate around the world in opposition of social norms and ethical standards, as tangible reminders of the immense chasm between the few who have dissected and the many who have not. But they are also undeniably exploitative. The systemic racism and structures of dehumanization visualized and codified throughout the genre's evolution is an inseparable part of the nation's visual economy, and thus, is inextricably bound to the visual heritage of *all* Americans past and present. Irrespective of whether one is a casual consumer or a curator, regardless of personal feelings of excitement or contempt over these abject images, it is our ongoing responsibility to examine, discuss, and reckon. Not to condemn, censor, or destroy. But to learn, understand, and if need be, atone.

For even in their most explicit abject form, they in no way negate the genre's primary position as pieces of the vernacular history of photography

Figure C.1: Students John David Miller and Paul Stenerson Epperson posing in their boardinghouse room with bones in front of large photographic display. Medical College of Virginia (Richmond, Virginia). Unidentified photographer. Gelatin silver print, circa 1906

Source: Author's collection

and medicine; a combined and dramatized personal experience for thousands upon thousands of medical students of a bygone era, whose relevance, although now largely suppressed, still finds a glimmer of utility today. Even though, as Terry states, these photographs "had done their job, once they had assisted the developing self-images and assuaged the anxieties of fledgling American physicians," our understanding of their importance as an evolving genre within the realm of American visual culture, and the cultures of both medicine and photography, hopefully, has only just begun.[9]

Many modern viewers will likely dismiss these images as nothing more than exploitative grotesqueries. That you have made it this far, and are now at the end of this book, hopefully means that you do not share in this ideology. That even if you are unsure of how you feel about dissection photographs, or more importantly, even if you hate them, you can still acknowledge the genre as an evolving one, and advocate for its preservation and continued scholarly study. For again, dissection photography exists today as an inseparable part of *our* medical heritage, and that fact should not be hidden or dismissed due to personal feelings over their abject subject matter.

To fully appreciate how the commemorated experiences, as well as the experiences involved in taking photographs, transformed countless medical students around the world on personal, professional, and social levels, I leave you with a poignant message from a medical student, inscribed on the back of his dissection postcard, addressed to his mother:

Dear Mama,

I'm sending you this postcard so you can see that I'm working: learning to fight death next to death itself.

With this, you will have one more reason to remember your son who, together with his portrait, sends his heart.[10]

Acknowledgments

I send *my* heart to the following individuals.

To my dear friend Clare Flemming, simply put: you are the best there is, and ever will be. Your friendship and support mean the world to me. I cannot thank you enough for all that you do. To my partner in crime and cats, Dr. M. Elle Saine, thank you for supporting me through the writing of this book and for always being there.

This book would not have been possible without the assistance of Ben Ziegler and Jim Matthews. My deepest thanks as well to the editors, copyeditors, and designers at Bristol University Press, especially Anna Richardson, Emily Ross, Laura Vickers-Rendell, and Jay Allan.

I am deeply indebted to the expertise and friendship of Theresa Connors, B. Douglas Whitmire, Dr. Dennis DePace, Dave Chichilitti, Dr. Steve Peitzman, Alaina McNaughton, Sabrina Bocanegra, Geoff Shannon, and Steve DeGenaro. A huge thank you as well to Grace Seiberling, for her patience, encouragement, and expertise over the years.

Many thanks also to Susan Daiss, Mark Osterman, Christopher Hoolihan, Brian Spatola, John Troyer, Joanne Murray, Ross MacPhee, and Maria Bella. My thanks to the influential work on dissecting room culture by Michael Sappol and Frederic W. Hafferty. And a huge thank you to dissection photography's early pioneers, James S. Terry, Stanley B. Burns, and especially John Harley Warner and Jim Edmonson, whose revelatory book *Dissection* was the inspiration for my own work.

Finally, nearly every image reproduced in this book came from a private collection located in the United States. As I maintain one of the largest private collections of dissection photographs in the country, several images are from my personal collection. To those collectors interested in preserving images 'as disgusting as they are disturbing,' who allowed me access to their inner sanctums, who shared their passion and collections with me, it was truly an honor. My eternal thanks to each and every one of you.

Notes

Introduction

1. *Ascodecoan*, Yearbook of the Atlanta-Southern Dental College (1922).
2. *Terra Mariae Schools of Medicine, Dentistry, Pharmacy, and Law*, Yearbook of the University of Maryland (1905), 252.
3. *Terra Mariae*, 252.
4. *Terra Mariae*, 252.
5. *Terra Mariae*, 253.
6. *Terra Mariae*, 253.
7. It should be noted that, generally, nursing students did not dissect cadavers. Thus, their lack of formative experiences in the dissecting room excludes them from being considered as primary stakeholders in the creation and evolution of dissection photography. However, the visual culture of nursing did embrace abject photographs of both male and female nurses posed in surgical amphitheaters spattered in blood or joking around with skeletons and skulls in hospitals and boardinghouse rooms just like their medical school counterparts.
8. As many 19th-century schools of medicine and dentistry have since merged with universities or are now extinct, it is impossible to confirm that dissection photographs were taken at *every* American school. Likewise, since many 20th-century images were taken without the involvement by or assumed knowledge of school administrators, it's exceedingly difficult to trace which schools did or did not participate based solely on what is extant in institutional archives.
9. J.H. Warner and J.M. Edmonson, *Dissection: Photographs as a Rite of Passage in American Medicine 1880–1930* (New York: Blast Books, 2009), 7.
10. The two paper-based processes yet to be confirmed to have been used are salted-paper prints and platinum prints. And although extant, collodion printing-out prints (POP) are also quite rare.
11. S.B. Burns and E.A. Burns, *Stiffs, Skulls, and Skeletons: Medical Photography and Symbolism* (Atglen: Schiffer Publishing, 2015), 71.
12. The list of countries I have confirmed participated in the taking of dissection photographs include, but are not limited to: Australia, Belgium, Bulgaria, Canada, China, Egypt, England, France, Germany, Greece, Italy, Japan, Peru, the Philippines, Romania, Russia, Sweden, and Turkey.
13. The classic dissection postcard was a photograph developed and printed on postcard stock, complete with a pre-printed postcard backing, also known as a real photo postcard. These postcards were not made using the lithographic or offset printing process (although a few do exist).
14. "See if you can find me." "Brother," Galveston, Texas, to Julia Taylor, Austin, Texas. Gelatin silver postcard, January 12, 1910. Private collection.

NOTES

15 W.S. Forbes, "History of the First Anatomy-Act of Pennsylvania," *The Philadelphia Medical Journal* 2(13) (November 26, 1898), 1132.

16 Quoted in *Journal of Zoöphily* 7 (March 1898), 30.

17 *The Howler*, Yearbook of Wake Forest University (1926), 254.

18 *Dentos*, Yearbook of the Chicago College of Dental Surgery (1915), 69.

19 Once schools went co-ed, the rules of matriculation appear to have been the same between the sexes. For example, in 1894, the Birmingham Medical College stated: "Women are admitted into this College on the same terms and conditions which govern the admission of men." *The First Annual Announcement of the Birmingham Medical College, Session of 1894–1895* (Birmingham: Birmingham Medical College, 1895), 13.

20 See *T-Wave*, Yearbook of the Tulane University School of Medicine (1982), 46; *The Clinic*, Yearbook of Jefferson Medical College (1969); the infamous "Playdoc" issue of the *Jayhawker*, Yearbook of the Kansas University School of Medicine (1969), and "Playdent" issue of the Yearbook of the University of Southern California Dental School (1972). The latter two books were heavily modeled after issues of *Playboy* and featured foldout centerfolds.

21 See *Dentos*, Yearbook of the Chicago College of Dental Surgery (1914 and 1916).

22 See *Retrospectroscope*, Yearbook of the University of Florida (1965), 23.

23 J.S. Terry, "Dissecting Room Portraits: Decoding an Underground Genre," *History of Photography* 7(2) (April–June 1983), 96.

24 Anonymous physician's personal correspondence with author, December 28, 2014. This doctor, who graduated from an Arkansas-based medical school in 1982, stated that when he was in medical school, there were no cameras at all allowed in the anatomy lab. He was completely unaware the historical practice of dissection photography existed. He also stated that his instructors did not allow medical students to wear gloves during dissection as a means of weeding out those students who could not handle it.

25 Terry, "Dissecting Room Portraits," 96–98.

26 While many dissection photographs still exist in the private sector, the two largest publicly known repositories of such imagery are now identified: The Dittrick Medical History Center, Case Western Reserve University, in Cleveland, Ohio, and the Burns Archive, New York City. Much of this larger collection is now associated with Yale University.

27 Terry, "Dissecting Room Portraits," 98.

28 Warner and Edmonson, *Dissection*, 15.

29 Terry, "Dissecting Room Portraits," 98.

30 Terry, "Dissecting Room Portraits," 98.

31 Warner and Edmonson, *Dissection*, 201.

32 Warner and Edmonson, *Dissection*, 8.

33 Warner and Edmonson, *Dissection*, 15.

34 *The Yearbook*, The Yearbook of Yale School of Medicine (1909), 98.

35 B. Murphy, "How Often Do Physicians and Medical Students Die of Suicide?" *American Medical Association*, June 12, 2019. https://www.ama-assn.org/practice-management/physician-health/how-often-do-physicians-and-medical-students-die-suicide.

36 *Chaff*, Yearbook of the College of Dentistry of the University of California (1897), 12.

Chapter 1

1 R. Rudisill, *Mirror Image: The Influence of the Daguerreotype on American Society* (Albuquerque: University of New Mexico Press, 1971), 10.

2 Rudisill, *Mirror Image*, 12.

3 Terry, "Dissecting Room Portraits," 97–98.

4 Terry, "Dissecting Room Portraits," 96.

DISSECTION PHOTOGRAPHY

5   Confirmation is due to the uncovering of thousands of extant images over the last 40 years since the time of Terry's article.

Chapter 2

1   B. Newhall, *The History of Photography from 1839 to the Present Day*, 4th edn (New York: The Museum of Modern Art, 1981), 68; K.F. Davis, "'A Terrible Distinctness': Photography of the Civil War Era," in *Photography in Nineteenth-Century America*, edited by M. Sandweiss (Fort Worth: Amon Carter Museum, 1991), 171.

2   *Philadelphia Photographer* 1(9) (September 1, 1864), 132.

3   *Philadelphia Photographer* 1(9) (September 1, 1864), 132.

4   According to the extant financial records of the Boston daguerreotype studio of Southworth and Hawes, in 1845 the cost to have a postmortem photograph taken ranged between $10 and $15 ($12 being the most commonly charged), in addition, there was an extra fee for hiring a carriage to transport the men and their equipment to the body in the decedent's home (a cost ranging from 25 to 50 cents). While the financial records are not complete – the plate size is often not listed – on July 15, 1845, a miniature of a deceased child was ordered at a cost of $12, with an additional 50 cents added for a hired carriage to the client's home on Oxford Street. Compare this order with another photograph taken on the same day, for one miniature portrait of a living "Lady in case," at a cost of $5. Or, on May 23, 1846, an order for Mr. Bates of East Boston for "services taking likeness of deceased person," in which the studio charged $12, plus $3 for two extra copies. Meanwhile, on that same day, the famous studio took photographs of renowned poet and foremost intellectual Ralph Waldo Emerson (1803–1882), who had three "miniatures ¼ size," taken at a cost totaling $16. See Southworth and Hawes Manuscript Collection, Box 16, Folder 6: Financial Documents Ledger, Daily Business Transactions, November 16, 1844 – September 17, 1846 and August 4, 1864 – December 26, 1865, 29 and 94, George Eastman Museum, Richard and Ronay Menschel Library Special Collections.

5   A. Trachtenberg, "Likeness as Identity: Reflections on the Daguerrean Mystique," in *The Portrait in Photography*, edited by G. Clarke (London: Reaktion Books, 1992), 175.

6   Terry, "Dissecting Room Portraits," 97.

7   J. Ruby, *Secure the Shadow: Death and Photography in America* (Cambridge, MA: MIT Press, 1995), 1.

8   A. Trachtenberg, *Reading American Photographs: Images as History, Mathew Brady to Walker Evans* (New York: Hill & Wang, 1989), 5.

9   A. Trachtenberg, "Photography: The Emergence of a Keyword," in *Photography in Nineteenth-Century America*, edited by M. Sandweiss (Fort Worth: Amon Carter Museum, 1991), 17.

10   Trachtenberg, *Reading American Photographs*, 5.

11   J. Tagg, *The Burden of Representation: Essays on Photographies and Histories* (Amherst: The University of Massachusetts Press, 1988), 5.

12   A. Bazin, "The Ontology of the Photographic Image," in *What is Cinema?* (Berkeley: University of California Press, 2005), vol 1, 13–14.

13   T.S. Arthur, "American Characteristics: No. V. – The Daguerreotypists," *Godey's Lady Book* (May 1849), 352.

14   A.A.L.M. Velpeau, *A Treatise on Surgical Anatomy; or the Anatomy of Regions, Considered in its Relations with Surgery* 1. Translated by J.W. Sterling (New York: Samuel Wood and Sons, 1830), v.

15   The daguerreotype's initial decline was brought about by collodion on glass, commonly referred to as the ambrotype. Taft stated: "The year 1854 marked the beginning of the decline of the daguerreotype – not that the daguerreotype was immediately superseded, for it was during 1854 and the early part of 1855 the major process practiced, but 1856

NOTES

saw its rapid decline and by 1857 it was a minor branch of the photographic trade." R. Taft, *Photography and the American Scene: A Social History, 1839–1889* (New York: Dover Publications, 1989), 122.

[16] William E. Horner, *Special Anatomy and Histology*, 7th edn, 1 (Philadelphia: Blanchard and Lea, 1851), vii.

[17] *Annual Announcement, Lectures, etc., by the Trustees and Professors of Jefferson Medical College, Philadelphia; for the Year 1832* (Philadelphia: Jefferson Medical Faculty, 1832), 5–6.

[18] M. Sappol, *A Traffic of Dead Bodies: Anatomy and Embodied Social Identity in Nineteenth-Century America* (Princeton: Princeton University Press, 2002), 95.

[19] Sappol, *A Traffic of Dead Bodies*, 71.

[20] For an anatomical text geared toward the family, see W.A. Alcott, *The House I Live in: Or the Human Body, for the Use of Families and Schools* (Boston: C.D. Strong, 1854).

[21] M.S. Gove, *Lectures to Women on Anatomy and Physiology with an Appendix on Water Cure* (New York: Harper and Brothers, 1846), 13.

[22] J.F.W. Lane, *Outlines of Anatomy and Physiology, Translated from the French of H. Milne Edwards* (Boston: Charles C. Little and James Brown, 1841), iii.

[23] See P. Starr, *The Social Transformation of American Medicine: The Rise of a Sovereign Profession and the Making of a Vast Industry* (New York: HarperCollins, 1982), 86.

[24] Sappol, *A Traffic of Dead Bodies*, 70.

[25] J.M. Allen, *The Practical Anatomist: Or, the Student's Guide in the Dissecting-Room* (Philadelphia: Blanchard and Lea, 1856), vi.

[26] T. Dwight, "Our Contribution to Civilization and to Science," in *Proceedings of the Eighth Annual Session of the Association of American Anatomists* (Washington, D.C.: Beresford Printers, 1896), 12.

[27] "The Demiurge," *Aeon Flux*, written by P. Chung, S. De Jarnatt, M. Ferris, and J.D. Brancato, directed by H.E. Baker (MTV, 1995).

[28] Sappol, *A Traffic of Dead Bodies*, 77.

[29] Terry, "Dissecting Room Portraits," 98.

[30] F. Goya, *Los Caprichos* (Madrid: Publisher Not Identified, 1799).

[31] "Self-operating Processes of Fine Art. The Daguereotype [sic]," *The Spectator* 12(553) (February 1839), 114.

[32] Trachtenberg, "Likeness as Identity," 173.

[33] Sappol, *A Traffic of Dead Bodies*, 79.

[34] Arthur, "American Characteristics, the Daguerreotypist," 352.

[35] H.F. Pfister, *Facing the Light: Historic American Portrait Daguerreotypes* (Washington, D.C.: Smithsonian Institution Press, 1978), 12. See curatorial preface by W.F. Stapp; Trachtenberg, "Likeness as Identity," 175.

[36] Quoted in Trachtenberg, "Likeness as Identity," 176.

[37] P.A. Béclard, *Additions to the General Anatomy of Xavier Bichat. Translated from the French* (Boston: Richardson and Lord, 1823), xiii. The famed French anatomist and pathologist, Xavier Bichat, was known to spend particularly long periods of time, without protection, examining decomposing cadavers in the low-ceilinged and humid wards of the Hôtel-Dieu. After examining the process of the putrefaction of the skin involving "an infectious fœtor rising from the macerating vessel," Bichat walked out of the anatomy lab, fainted, and fell down a staircase. He exhibited symptoms of ataxic fever from inhaling the fumes rising from the decaying flesh, would later slip into a coma, and die. M. Husson, *A Treatise of the Membranes in General, and on Different Membranes in Particular by Xavier Bichat, of the Societies of Medicine, Medical and Philomatic of Paris; of those of Brussels and Lyons. A New Edition, Enlarged by an Historical Notice of the Life and Writings of the Author; by M. Husson. Paris, 1802.* Translated by J.G. Coffin (Boston: Cummings and Hilliard, 1813), xvii. For more on the offensive and poisonous aspects of cadavers in the 19th century, see Sappol, *A Traffic of Dead Bodies*, 79.

38 Trachtenberg, "Likeness as Identity," 177; Tagg, *The Burden of Representation*, 12.

39 Trachtenberg, "Likeness as Identity," 176.

40 Trachtenberg, "Likeness as Identity," 176.

41 In fact, the studio took out advertisements boasting: "We take great pains to have Miniatures of Deceased Persons agreeable and satisfactory, and they are often so natural as to seem, even to Artists, in a deep sleep." Quoted in Ruby, *Secure the Shadow*, 53.

42 "Self-operating Processes of Fine Art. The Daguereotype [*sic*]," 114.

43 "Self-operating Processes of Fine Art. The Daguereotype [*sic*]," 114.

44 M.J. Dinius, *The Camera and the Press: American Visual and Print Culture in the Age of the Daguerreotype* (Philadelphia: University of Pennsylvania Press, 2012), 20.

Chapter 3

1 A.L. Benedict, "The Life of a Medical Student," *Lippincott's Monthly Magazine* (September 1896), 389.

2 Comments were made to me during thesis topic presentation, Curtis Theater, George Eastman Museum, December 4, 2015.

3 B.M. Stafford, *Body Criticism: Imagine the Unseen in Enlightenment Art and Medicine* (Cambridge, MA: MIT Press, 1993), 48.

4 C. McGinn, *The Meaning of Disgust* (Oxford: Oxford University Press, 2011), 5, emphasis in original.

5 McGinn, *The Meaning of Disgust*, 142.

6 McGinn, *The Meaning of Disgust*, 24.

7 J. Aud, *Does Your Dogma Bite? Artifacts, Metafacts, and Symbols* (Lincoln, NE: Writers Club Press, 2000); McGinn, *The Meaning of Disgust*, 142.

8 McGinn, *The Meaning of Disgust*, 142.

9 R. Arya, "The Fragmented Body as an Index of Abjection," in *Abject Visions: Powers of Horror in Art and Visual Culture*, edited by R. Arya and N. Chare (Manchester: Manchester University Press, 2016), 109.

10 R. Arya, *Abjection and Representation: An Exploration of Abjection in the Visual Arts, Film and Literature* (Basingstoke: Palgrave Macmillan, 2014), 61.

11 K. Cregan, *The Sociology of the Body* (London: SAGE, 2006), 96.

12 For more on the incorruptible nature of photography, see H.J. Morton, "Photography as an Authority," *The Philadelphia Photographer* 1(12) (December 1, 1864), 180; and H.J. Morton, "Photography as a Moral Agent," *The Philadelphia Photographer* 1(8) (August 1, 1864), 116.

13 Cregan, The Sociology of the Body, 96.

14 Arya, *Abject Visions*, 105.

15 J. Kristeva, *Powers of Horror: An Essay on Abjection*, translated by L.S. Roudiez (New York: Columbia University Press, 1982), 4.

16 J. Childers and G. Hentzi (Eds), *The Columbia Dictionary of Modern Literary and Cultural Criticism* (New York: Columbia University Press, 1995), 1.

17 Kristeva, *Powers of Horror*, 3.

18 Whitney Museum of American Art. *Abject Art: Repulsion and Desire in American Art* (New York: Whitney Museum of Art, 1993), 7.

19 Kristeva, *Powers of Horror*, 4.

20 Kristeva, *Powers of Horror*, 1.

21 Kristeva, *Powers of Horror*, 3.

22 Kristeva, *Powers of Horror*, 4.

23 Kristeva, *Powers of Horror*, 3.

24 E. Ahren, *Death, Modernity, and the Body: Sweden 1870–1940* (Rochester: University of Rochester Press, 2009), 39.

NOTES

25 Arya, *Abjection and Representation*, 61.

26 S. Sontag, *On Photography* (New York: Picador, 1977), 98.

27 Arya, *Abjection and Representation*, 61.

28 Arya, *Abject Visions*, 105.

29 Cregan, *The Sociology of the Body*, 100.

30 Sappol, *A Traffic of Dead Bodies*, 217.

31 *The Howler*, Yearbook of Wake Forest University (1922), 17.

32 Terry, "Dissecting Room Portraits," 97.

33 Arya, *Abjection and Representation*, 61; Arya, *Abject Visions*, 108. Photographically speaking, we may partially attribute this inability to the dimensional limitations of visual processes. After all, regardless of size, clarity, or how explicit a photograph is, it is still purely representational.

34 Piece of Peritoneum Dissected from Cadaver. Human Tissue, 1923. 1984.952. Museum of Osteopathic Medicine.

35 Letter from Paul, Hancock, Georgia to Miss Margaret Gault, Newport, Pennsylvania, March 14, 1918. Private collection.

36 Letter from Paul to Miss Margaret Gault.

37 This theory admittedly has its limitations. It discusses the body as object in the aftermath of dismemberment or abstraction, not the levels of objectification at play *during* these processes.

38 Quoted in Arya, *Abject Visions*, 109.

39 Arya, *Abject Visions*, 109. The distinction between images of the partial or fully dissected cadaver and the whole cadaver factors into our understanding of, or confusion over, the material status of what 'exactly' we are viewing.

40 Arya, *Abject Visions*, 105.

41 Arya, *Abjection and Representation*, 2.

42 McGinn, *The Meaning of Disgust*, 161.

43 McGinn, *The Meaning of Disgust*, 161.

44 McGinn, *The Meaning of Disgust*, 201.

45 Quoted in Cregan, *The Sociology of the Body*, 101.

46 Cregan, *The Sociology of the Body*, 101.

Chapter 4

1 B. Newhall, *Photography: A Short Critical History* (New York: The Museum of Modern Art, 1938), 74.

2 "Photography in Medical Science," *Lancet* 22 (January 1859), 89.

3 For more information on Alison Gernsheim's work see her two-part work "Medical Photography in the Nineteenth Century," *Medical & Biological Illustration* 11(2) (April 1961), 85–92.

4 Terry, "Dissecting Room Portraits," 96.

5 D. Chandler, "An Introduction to Genre Theory" (1997). http://www.aber.ac.uk/media/Documents/intgenre/chandler_genre_theory.pdf.

6 Regardless of the reason, in the case of the George Eastman Museum, only two dissection photographs are currently known to be part of the world-famous photography collection. These images, both from the same unknown schools, and taken by unidentified photographers, went unknown and uncatalogued until I identified them in 2015. The two images in question are: 2010.1312.0041 and 2010.1312.0019.

7 A.D. Coleman, *The Grotesque in Photography* (New York: The Ridge Press, 1977), 10.

8 Chandler, "An Introduction to Genre Theory," 3.

9 Quoted in Chandler, "An Introduction to Genre Theory," 3.

10 Warner and Edmonson, *Dissection*, 15.

11 Quoted in Chandler, "An Introduction to Genre Theory," 4.

12 S. Dotterer and G. Cranz, "The Picture Postcard: Its Development and Role in American Urbanization," *Journal of American Culture* 5(1) (spring 1982), 44. Per statistics quoted in Dotterer and Cranz, in the United States alone in 1906, 770,500,000 postcards were mailed. By 1909 this number skyrocketed to 968,000,000.

13 Quoted in Chandler, "An Introduction to Genre Theory," 2.

14 "For the Family." Gelatin silver postcard, circa 1910. Private collection.

15 "Don't suppose you ever have such horrid dreams." R.E.M. Michigan, to Miss [?], Romeo Michigan. *Student Dream*. Gelatin silver postcard, circa 1908. Private collection.

16 Chandler, "An Introduction to Genre Theory," 3.

17 *Yale Medical Annual 1898*, Yale University School of Medicine (1898), 32–33.

18 E.F. Wheeler, "She Saunters Off Into Her Past," draft of typescript autobiography, unpublished, 1946, X.2002.2, 83. Legacy Center, Drexel University College of Medicine.

19 C. Dickens, *A Christmas Carol* (London: Bradbury & Evans, 1858), 17.

20 [W.C.T.?], Indianapolis to Hortense Eads, Omaha, Nebraska. Gelatin silver postcard, June 29, 1909. Private collection.

21 "Chuck it to the bottom of the trunk." Will to Grace. Photograph by Tyler. Gelatin silver postcard. Private collection.

22 "A Student's Dream." "Charles" Louisville, Kentucky to Miss Lulu M. Clevenger, Parker City, Indiana. Gelatin silver postcard, January 6, 1910. Private collection.

Chapter 5

1 Warner and Edmonson, *Dissection*, 194.

2 Quoted in Chandler, "An Introduction to Genre Theory," 2, emphasis in original.

3 Terry, "Dissecting Room Portraits," 96.

4 Terry, "Dissecting Room Portraits," 96.

5 Warner and Edmonson, *Dissection*, 197.

6 Warner and Edmonson, *Dissection*, 197.

7 Warner and Edmonson, *Dissection*, 197–198.

8 For a more thorough exploration of Vesalius and the iconographic shifts inherent to his work, see J. Sawday, *The Body Emblazoned: Dissection and the Human Body in Renaissance Culture* (New York: Routledge, 1996), 63–72.

9 See C. Waldby, *The Visible Human Project: Informatic Bodies and Posthuman Medicine* (London: Routledge, 2000), 66.

10 Warner and Edmonson, *Dissection*, 197.

11 Quoted in Chandler, "An Introduction to Genre Theory," 3.

12 Terry, "Dissecting Room Portraits," 96.

13 S. Warren, *Affecting Scenes; Being Passages from the Diary of a Physician*, vol 2 (New York: Harper and Brothers, 1837), 94–95.

14 Terry, "Dissecting Room Portraits," 96.

15 Sappol, *A Traffic of Dead Bodies*, 128.

16 Terry, "Dissecting Room Portraits," 96.

17 Sappol, *A Traffic of Dead Bodies*, 124.

18 Sappol, *A Traffic of Dead Bodies*, 45.

19 Benedict, "The Life of a Medical Student," 389.

20 W.E. Aughinbaugh, *I Swear By Apollo: A Life of Medical Adventure* (New York: Farrar & Rineheart, 1938), 40–41. Aughinbaugh kept a small photo album, now in the collection of the New York Academy of Medicine. In addition to several clinical photographs of patients exhibiting various diseases, the album also contains several dissection photographs from his time in medical school at Columbian University (now George Washington) in Washington, D.C.

NOTES

[21] See "Lynching Postcards Barred," *Chicago Tribune*, August 18, 1908. The article references bans in Hopkinsville, Kentucky. See also, "Bar Lynching Postcards," *The York Dispatch*, September 5, 1908. The article, whose subtitle reads "Texas Inspectors Close Mails to Representations of White Domination," references bans in Austin, Texas. Per the article, the ruling had less to do with a postcard showing "five negroes hanging on a tree lynched last July in Sabine County," and more to do with an "objectionable" verse written on the back, which decreed: "An emblem of white supremacy. A lesson taught in the white man's school. That this is land of the white man's rule."

[22] *The Commercial Appeal* (Memphis), March 7, 1900.

[23] Terry, "Dissecting Room Portraits," 96.

[24] Terry, "Dissecting Room Portraits," 96–97.

[25] Sappol, *A Traffic of Dead Bodies*, 82.

[26] Without question, the most notable and photographed resurrectionist/janitor during the era of the dissection photograph was 'Chris' Baker, the African American janitor of the Medical College of Virginia. For more on Baker, see Chapter 11.

[27] *The University of Texas Medical Branch at Galveston: A Seventy-five Year History by the Faculty and Staff* (Austin: University of Texas Press, 1967), 38. See p. 38 for a reproduction of the described image showing students in the University of Texas anatomy lab along with Professor William Keiller (1861–1931), who is seated in the foreground in striped pants.

[28] *The Farmer and Mechanic*, January 24, 1899.

[29] *The News and Observer*, January 19, 1899.

[30] *The News and Observer*, January 19, 1899.

[31] *Nashville Banner*, February 12, 1912.

[32] A. Flexner, *Medical Education in the United States and Canada* (New York: The Carnegie Foundation, 1910), 233.

[33] W.E.B. Du Bois (Ed), *The Health and Physique of the Negro American* (Atlanta: Atlanta University Press, 1906), 102.

[34] *Atlanta Constitution*, March 22, 1898.

[35] Du Bois, *The Health and Physique of the Negro American*, 98, emphasis in original.

[36] Du Bois, *The Health and Physique of the Negro American*, 98. For a brief summary of the Medical College of Georgia's purchasing and use of enslaved labor to rob graves for medical dissection, see the story of Grandison Harris, found in D.R. Berry, *The Price For Their Pound of Flesh: The Value of the Enslaved, from Womb to Grave, in the Building of a Nation* (Boston: Beacon Press, 2017), 170–172.

[37] *Public Laws and Resolutions of the State of North Carolina Passed by the General Assembly at the Session of 1903* (Raleigh: Published by Authority, 1903), 1055–1056.

Chapter 6

[1] *Ottumwa Tri-weekly Courier* (Ottumwa, Iowa), November 6, 1900.

[2] *Ottumwa Tri-weekly Courier*, November 6, 1900.

[3] *Ottumwa Tri-weekly Courier*, November 6, 1900.

[4] *Ottumwa Tri-weekly Courier*, November 6, 1900.

[5] H. Montgomery, "Resurrection Times," *The Georgia Review* 43(3) (fall 1989), 532.

[6] R. Richardson, *Death, Dissection and the Destitute* (Chicago: University of Chicago Press, 2000), 30–31.

[7] Richardson, *Death, Dissection and the Destitute*, 31.

[8] Warner and Edmonson, *Dissection*, 22.

[9] Sappol, *A Traffic of Dead Bodies*, 78.

[10] Warner and Edmonson, *Dissection*, 33.

[11] *Chaff*, Yearbook of the College of Dentistry of the University of California (1897), 16.

[12] *Anamnesis*, Yearbook of Jefferson Medical College (1910), 183.

DISSECTION PHOTOGRAPHY

[13] See *Fall River Globe*, November 25, 1901.

[14] *The Howler*, Yearbook of Wake Forest University (1905), 70.

[15] *Chaff*, Yearbook of the College of Dentistry of the University of California (1906), 72.

[16] *The Howler* (1905), 70.

[17] Letter from Franklin A. Wilson, Bowdoin College to Charles P. Stetson, Yale University, April 6, 1852, Charles P. Stetson Letters, M312.1, Series 1, Box 1, Folder 2. George J. Mitchell Department of Special Collections and Archives, Bowdoin College Library.

[18] *The Montgomery Times* (Montgomery, Alabama), July 6, 1910.

[19] *Jambalaya*, Yearbook of Tulane University (1907), 74.

[20] E. Cisney-Smith "The Personal History and Background Diary of Elizabeth Cisney-Smith," Isabel Smith Stein Collection on Elizabeth Cisney-Smith, WM.2007.002, Box 2, Folder 2. Legacy Center, Drexel University College of Medicine.

[21] Cisney-Smith, "The Personal History and Background Diary of Elizabeth Cisney-Smith."

[22] Cisney-Smith, "The Personal History and Background Diary of Elizabeth Cisney-Smith."

[23] *The Howler*, Yearbook of Wake Forest University (1918), 103.

[24] *Jambalaya*, Yearbook of Tulane University (1904), 94.

[25] *The Quax*, Yearbook of Drake University (1904), 85.

[26] *Corks and Curls*, Yearbook of the University of Virginia (1911), 87.

[27] *Videodrome*. Directed by D. Cronenberg, Universal Pictures, 1983.

[28] *Jambalaya*, Yearbook of Tulane University (1915), 158.

[29] *Synapsis*, Yearbook of the Philadelphia College of Osteopathic Medicine (1925), 95.

[30] *1901*, Yearbook of Jefferson Medical College (1901), np.

[31] *The Chironian* 15 (October 16, 1898), 18.

[32] Warner and Edmonson, *Dissection*, 15.

[33] *The Yearbook*, Yearbook of Yale University School of Medicine (1908), 96.

[34] *Bones, Molars, and Briefs*, Yearbook of the University of Maryland (1897), 156.

[35] *Jambalaya*, Yearbook of Tulane University (1930), 7, 107.

[36] See *Baltimore Sun*, December 3, 1896.

[37] *Nebraska State Journal*, November 25, 1896.

[38] *The Yale Clinic: The Annual and Graduate Directory of the Medical Department of Yale University* (New Haven: Yale University, 1904), 68.

[39] *Dentos* (1914), 115.

[40] *Terra Mariae*, 58.

[41] "Brotherhood of Man." Wake Forest College Medical School. Gelatin silver postcard, circa 1910. Private collection. Perhaps the intent behind the cadaver's strange transformation was a visual nod to the cadaveric reformations of the glossy mezzotints of the famous 'flayed angel' of Jacques Fabien Gautier d'Agoty's *Suite de l'Essai d'anatomie en tableaux imprimés* (1745).

[42] "Here we toil ..." Gelatin silver postcard, circa 1909. Private collection.

[43] *Anamnesis*, 183.

[44] *Bones, Molars, and Briefs* (1897), 158.

[45] *Bones, Molars, and Briefs* (1897), 158.

[46] *The Sun* (New York), February 18, 1901.

[47] W.C. Barrett, "The Study of Anatomy," *Dominion Dental Journal* 9 (Toronto: The Nesbitt Publishing Company, 1897), 341.

[48] Barrett, "The Study of Anatomy," 341.

[49] C. Heath, *Practical Anatomy: A Manual of Dissections*, edited by W.W. Keen (Philadelphia: Henry C. Lea, 1870), 15.

[50] A. Hertzler, *The Horse and Buggy Doctor* (Lincoln, NE: University of Nebraska Press, 1938), 174.

[51] For a dissection photograph with this caption written on the mount, see Burns and Burns, *Stiffs, Skulls and Skeletons*, 20.

NOTES

52 Richardson, *Death, Dissection and the Destitute*, 31.

53 *Chaff* (1897), 3.

54 *Terra Mariae* (1905), 57.

55 *Asodecoan*, Yearbook of the Atlanta-Southern Dental (1918), np.

56 *Dentos*, Yearbook of the Chicago College of Dental Surgery (1922), 191.

57 *Jambalaya* (1915), 128.

58 *Terra Mariae* (1905), 58.

59 *Jambalaya* (1915), 129.

60 *Jambalaya*, Yearbook of Tulane University (1905), 61.

61 *Yale Medical Annual 1898*, 32.

62 *Yale Medical Annual 1898*, 32.

Chapter 7

1 Ruth J. Abram Collection, WMCP – 1879, MS #252, Box 1. Legacy Center, Drexel University College of Medicine.

2 Cisney-Smith, "The Personal History and Background Diary of Elizabeth Cisney-Smith."

3 B. Zimmerman, "When Legs and Arms Won: The Culture of Dissection and the Role of the Camera at the Woman's Medical College of Pennsylvania," *Nursing Clio*, August 16, 2018. https://nursingclio.org/2018/08/16/the-culture-of-dissection-and-the-role-of-the-camera-at-the-womans-medical-college-of-pennsylvania/. Although women do appear in paintings and photographs as nurses and other supportive roles, they are rarely figured as occupying positions of authority in the dissecting room. Naturally, there are exceptions to the rules. For an illustration of an allegorical female dissector holding a knife over a prone female cadaver see the frontispiece to Johann Adam Kulmus's *Tabulae anatomicae* (1732), titled, "The Human Body and the Library as Sources of Knowledge."

4 See A. Cunningham, *The Anatomist Anatomis'd: An Experimental Discipline in Enlightenment Europe* (Farnham: Ashgate, 2010), 142–143.

5 Zimmerman, "When Legs and Arms Won."

6 E.H. Cleveland, *Introductory Lecture on Behalf of the Faculty to the Class of the Female Medical College of Pennsylvania, for the Session of 1858–1859* (Philadelphia: Merrihew & Thompson, printers, 1858), 6.

7 Wheeler, "She Saunters Off Into Her Past," 87.

8 *The Lichonian* (New York: Published by the Students of the Long Island College of Medicine, 1935), 39.

9 Cleveland, *Introductory Lecture*, 6.

10 D.H. Agnew, *Lecture Introductory to the One Hundred and Fifth Course of Instruction in the Medical Department of the University of Pennsylvania: Delivered Monday, October 10, 1870* (Philadelphia: R.P. King's Sons, printers, 1870), 18. Agnew would later resign his teaching position at the Pennsylvania Hospital rather than lecture to an audience that included students from WMCP.

11 D. King, *Quackery Unmasked: Or, a Consideration of the Most Prominent Empirical Schemes of the Present Time* (Boston: David Clapp, printers, 1858), 214–215.

12 "Beauty with Brains," unidentified newspaper article, Clara Marshall Papers, WMCP Acc #292. Legacy Center, Drexel College of Medicine.

13 "Beauty with Brains," unidentified newspaper article, Clara Marshall Papers, WMCP Acc #292.

14 See "Material in Box" index, June 1, 1904, WMCP Board of Corporators: Executive Committee Minutes, Box 9. Legacy Center, Drexel University College of Medicine.

15 E.H. Cleveland, *Valedictory Address of the Graduating Class of the Woman's Medical College of Pennsylvania, at the Sixteenth Annual Commencement, March 14, 1868* (Philadelphia: Published by the WMCP Corporators, 1868), 11.

DISSECTION PHOTOGRAPHY

16 Cleveland, *Valedictory Address*, 11.
17 Cleveland, *Valedictory Address*, 11.
18 Cleveland, *Valedictory Address*, 11.
19 Cleveland, *Valedictory Address*, 11.
20 *The Woman's Medical College of Georgia and Training School for Nurses, First Annual Announcement. Session of 1889 and 1890* (Atlanta: American Book and Job Print, 1889), 4.
21 For an account of a dissection photograph taken using an artist's model, see "Sleep with Dead Too Gruesome," *Knoxville Sentinel*, March 2, 1908.
22 See Zimmerman, "When Legs and Arms Won."
23 Warner and Edmonson, *Dissection*, 129. For images in which the primary focus is the skeleton, see *Dissection*, 127–142.
24 Unidentified newspaper article, Clara Marshall Papers, WMCP, Acc #292. Legacy Center, Drexel College of Medicine.
25 Scrapbook of Ida Scudder, circa 1925–1929, Acc. #334. Legacy Center, Drexel University College of Medicine.
26 Scrapbook of Ida Scudder, circa 1925–1929, Acc. #334.
27 Scrapbook of Laura Heath Hills, WM-126. Legacy Center, Drexel University College of Medicine.
28 D.A. Segal, "A Patient So Dead: American Medical Students and Their Cadavers," *Anthropological Quarterly* 61 (January 1988), 21. According to Segal, ORCA was the name of a whale at a well-known aquatic amusement park. As told to him by the medical students, the name was meant as a humorous and generic name to symbolize all whales, "much as Smokey might indicate a bear or Elsie a cow," see Segal, "A Patient So Dead," 25.
29 M.T. McGavran, "Life and Work of Mary T. McGavran" (nd), MS ACC-169, Mary Theodora McGavran Papers, 31–32. Legacy Center, Drexel University College of Medicine.
30 Minutes of Faculty Meetings, Woman's Medical College of Pennsylvania, 1850–1864, February 24, 1853, 48. Legacy Center, Drexel University College of Medicine.
31 Dean's Report, Minutes of Faculty Meetings, Woman's Medical College of Pennsylvania, 1850–1864, December 31, 1862. Legacy Center, Drexel University College of Medicine.
32 Dean's Minutes – Rough Copies, April 27, 1875, Acc. #92. Legacy Center, Drexel University College of Medicine.
33 Cisney-Smith, "The Personal History and Background Diary of Elizabeth Cisney-Smith."

Chapter 8

1 Quoted in Sappol, *A Traffic of Dead Bodies*, 3.
2 Stewart Elliott to Ada S. Elliott, Denton, Texas. Gelatin silver postcard, May 1909. Private collection.
3 For a thorough examination of centuries of Vesalian portraiture, see M.H. Spielmann, *The Iconography of Andreas Vesalius* (London: John Bale, Sons & Danielsson, 1925).
4 See Sotheby's, *Important Daguerreotypes from the Stanley B. Burns, MD. Collection, New York 5 October 2017* (New York: Sotheby's, 2017), 34, 43, 45.
5 S.B. Burns, *A Morning's Work: Medical Photographs from The Burns Archive and Collection 1843–1939* (New Mexico: Twin Palms Publishers, 1998), np.
6 For a reproduction of this image, see Warner and Edmonson, *Dissection*, 114.
7 See, for example, the 'All-Star Operation" at Johns Hopkins Hospital taken on October 5, 1904. At the time, Hopkins was considered a leading institution of medical education and surgery.
8 *Thirty-Seventh Annual Announcement of the Medical Department of the University of Vermont* (Burlington: University of Vermont, 1890), 8.
9 *Yale Medical Annual 1898*, 33.

NOTES

[10] Terry, "Dissecting Room Portraits," 96.

[11] Muybridge was likely hired to document the school's brand-new dissecting room as it had been recently "refitted and furnished with every possible convenience." *Annual Announcement of Lectures at Toland Hall, Medical Department of the University of California, San Francisco, California* (San Francisco: Cubery & Co., 1875), 11.

[12] W. Fergusson, *A System of Practical Surgery*, 3rd edn (London: John Churchill, 1852), 17.

[13] S.D. Gross, *A System of Surgery; Pathological, Diagnostic, Therapeutic, and Operative*, 6th edn (Philadelphia: Henry C. Lea's Son & Co., 1882), 442.

[14] Gross, *A System of Surgery*, 442.

[15] Gross, *A System of Surgery*, 442. Today, students utilize scalpels in dissection much less than they did in Gross' era. Modern anatomists recommend that the scalpel be used solely for the initial incisions for piercing and removing the skin. After those cuts are completed, tweezers and forceps are to be used to separate and reveal delicate structures.

[16] H.L. Hunt, *Plastic Surgery of the Head, Face and Neck* (Philadelphia: Lea & Febiger, 1926), 31.

[17] For an account of the Memphis Hospital College of Medicine shipping cadavers to schools in Nashville in "four large ironbound casks," marked "meat," see *Commercial Appeal*, March 7, 1900.

[18] *Annual Announcement of Lectures at Toland Hall, Medical Department of the University of California, San Francisco, California*, emphasis in original.

[19] *The Vindicator* (Bloomfield Missouri), January 7, 1882.

[20] See University of Pennsylvania Department of Medicine waiver, Clara Marshall Papers. Legacy Center, Drexel University College of Medicine.

[21] WMCP Faculty Minutes, January 1874 – May 1874. Acc #92, Box 2, February 7, 1874. Legacy Center, Drexel University College of Medicine.

[22] A. Worcester, "Reminiscences," *OnView: Digital Collections & Exhibits*, https://collections.countway.harvard.edu/onview/item.

[23] McGavran, "Life and Work of Mary T. McGavran," 11.

[24] J. Godman, *Contributions to Physiological and Pathological Anatomy: Containing the Observations Made at the Philadelphia Anatomical Rooms during the Session of 1824–25* (Philadelphia: Carey and Lea, 1825), 20.

[25] Godman, *Contributions to Physiological and Pathological Anatomy*, 19–20.

[26] C.G. Raue, C.B. Knerr, and C. Mohr (Eds), *A Memorial of Constantine Hering* (Philadelphia: Press of Globe Printing House, 1884), 88.

[27] *The Daily Republican*, March 21, 1890. Perhaps one the most famous instances involving death by a contaminated scalpel involved Dr. Jakob Kolletschka, Professor of Forensic Medicine in Vienna in 1847. Kolletschka frequently conducted autopsies aided by students. During one such investigation, the famed anatomist received an accidental puncture to his finger from the errant blade of one of his pupils. Infection set, and he died shortly after; the scalpel wound "foul with cadaveric particles." W.J. Sinclair, *Semmelweis: His Life and Doctrine: A Chapter in the History of Medicine* (Manchester: Manchester University Press, 1909), 48–49. The threat of imminent death at the hands of a slip and cut of the hands, and the legends associated with such a death were not confined to the 19th century. In 1903, newspapers reported that Nicholas Senn, Chief Surgeon of Rush Medical College in Chicago, cut his right and suffered terribly from the resulting blood poisoning; see the *Salt Lake Telegram*, November 29, 1903.

[28] *Reidsville Review*, January 27, 1903.

[29] *The Morning Post*, January 24, 1903.

[30] See *The Charlotte Observer* (Charlotte, North Carolina), March 21, 1903.

[31] T.L. Stedman (Ed), *Twentieth Century Practice: An International Encyclopedia of Modern Medical Science by Leading Authorities of Europe and America* (New York: W. Wood and Company, 1895), vol 15, 597.

DISSECTION PHOTOGRAPHY

[32] *Yorkville Enquirer*, January 31, 1903.

[33] *Yorkville Enquirer*, January 31, 1903.

[34] *Yale Medical Annual 1898*, 33.

[35] *Yale Medical Annual 1898*, 33.

[36] C. Bell, *Institutes of Surgery: Arranged in the Order of the Lectures Delivered in the University of Edinburgh* (Philadelphia: A. Waldie, 1840), v.

[37] Sappol, *A Traffic of Dead Bodies*, 77.

[38] Stafford, *Body Criticism*, 47.

[39] C. Helman, *Body Myths* (London: Chatto & Windus), 117–118.

[40] Stafford, *Body Criticism*, 47.

[41] Stafford, *Body Criticism*, 47.

[42] Stafford, *Body Criticism*, 47.

[43] F.P. Mall, "On the Teaching of Anatomy as Illustrated by Professor Barker's Manual," *Bulletin of the Johns Hopkins Hospital* 16 (1905), 30.

[44] Mall, "On the Teaching of Anatomy," 30.

[45] C. Heath, *Practical Anatomy: A Manual of Dissections*, edited by W.W. Keen (Philadelphia: Henry C. Lea, 1870), 13.

[46] Flexner, *Medical Education in the United States and Canada*, 216.

[47] Flexner, *Medical Education in the United States and Canada*, 188.

[48] Godman, *Anatomical Investigations*, vii.

[49] W.R. Grant, *An Introductory Lecture to the Course Anatomy and Physiology in the Department of Pennsylvania College, Philadelphia. Delivered Tuesday, November 4th 1845* (Philadelphia: Published by the Class, 1845), 14–15.

[50] Hertzler, *The Horse and Buggy Doctor*, 173.

[51] Bell, *Institutes of Surgery*, v.

[52] Bell, *Institutes of Surgery*, v.

[53] E.J. Chaisty, *The London Dissector, or Guide to Anatomy; for the Use of Students: Comprising a Description of the Muscles, Vessels, Nerves, Lymphatics, and Viscera of the Human Body, as They Appear on Dissection; with Directions for Their Demonstration. From the Last London Edition* (Philadelphia: Edward Barrington and George D. Haswell, 1842), 2.

[54] In addition to its use in dissections, Samuel Gross also recommended the scalpel be held like a writing pen when performing a great variety of surgical operations, such as a lithotomy, the extirpation of tumors, hernia operations, and the removal of cataracts, see Gross, *A System of Surgery*, vol 1, 443.

[55] O. Zuckerkandl, *Atlas and Epitome of Operative Surgery*, edited by J.C. DaCosta (Philadelphia: W.B. Saunders), 18, 25.

[56] Zuckerkandl, *Atlas and Epitome of Operative Surgery*, 18, 25.

[57] D.M. Fox and C. Lawrence, *Photographing Medicine: Images and Power in Britain and America since 1840* (New York: Greenwood Press, 1988), 50.

[58] Allen, *The Practical Anatomist*, 27.

[59] Warner and Edmonson, *Dissection,* 121.

[60] F. Holroyd, Baltimore, Maryland to Robert Mc F. Holroyd, Athens, West Virginia. Gelatin silver postcard, 1906. Author's collection.

[61] Heath, *Practical Anatomy*, 13.

[62] Flexner, *Medical Education in the United States and Canada*, 190, 197, 237.

[63] E. Lemoine-Luccioni, *La Robe: Essai psychanalytique sur le vêtement* (Paris: Seuil, 1983), 15.

[64] Grant, *An Introductory Lecture*, 6, original emphasis.

[65] *The Aesculapian*, Yearbook of the Atlanta College of Physicians and Surgeons (1911), np.

[66] *The Howler*, Yearbook of Wake Forest University (1911), 43.

[67] *Chaff*, Yearbook of the College of Dentistry of the University of California (1909), 158.

[68] *Chaff* (1909), 51.

NOTES

[69] H. Marsh, "The Medical Student and His Environment," *The British Medical Journal* 2(2024) (October 14, 1899), 1013.

[70] Marsh, "The Medical Student and His Environment," 1013.

[71] Oscar in nursing uniform. "Aunt S.," Yonkers, New York to Paul Appleman, Sebec, Maine. Gelatin silver postcard, October 7, 1907. Private collection.

[72] Marsh, "The Medical Student and His Environment," 1013.

[73] *Thirty-Second Annual Announcement of the New York Homeopathic Medical College and Hospital, Session of 1891–92* (New York, 1891), 22.

[74] *The Aesculapian*, Yearbook of Atlanta College of Physicians and Surgeons (1912), 92.

[75] Fergusson, *A System of Practical Surgery*, 3.

[76] Heath, *Practical Anatomy*, 13–14.

[77] In either situation, such positioning bore aesthetic similarities to that of the anatomical textbook.

[78] *Dentos*, Yearbook of the College of Dentistry of the University of California (1923), 101.

[79] *Chicago Tribune*, September 29, 1895.

[80] Warner and Edmonson, *Dissection*, 13.

[81] *Boston Medical and Surgical Journal* 12 (May 13, 1835), 226.

[82] *Boston Medical and Surgical Journal* 12 (May 13, 1835), 226.

[83] *The Hahnemannian Institute* 7 (November 1899), 37.

[84] *The Hahnemannian Institute* 7 (November 1899), 37.

[85] *Class Record of Hahnemann Medical College 1906* (Philadelphia: Hahnemann Medical College, 1906), np.

[86] *The Yearbook*, Yearbook of Yale University School of Medicine (1910), 58.

[87] *The Lancet* 1 (December 27, 1829).

[88] *The Chironian* 15 (December 15, 1898), 48.

[89] *Sodecoan*, Yearbook of the Southern Dental College (1917), np.

[90] Warner and Edmonson, *Dissection*, 47.

[91] See First Class of the American School of Osteopathy. Cabinet Card, circa 1893. Photo by Parcell Studios of Kirksville, MO. Acc. 2007.09. Museum of Osteopathic Medicine.

[92] "Scalpel in eyes." Snapshot. Gelatin silver print, 1961. Private collection.

[93] In the 1830s, bellows – a device used to blow air into a fire – were commonly used to inflate a cadaver's lungs. By the 1890s, its utility had increased. Anatomists recommended its use for a host of investigative procedures, such as examining the perineum space (space between the scrotum and anus) on male cadavers, to inflate a flaccid abdominal wall on women who bore many children, and to inflate intestines to look for Peyer's patches, see D.J. Cunningham, *Manual of Practical Anatomy*, 2nd edn (Edinburgh: Young J. Pentland, 1896), vol 1, 481.

[94] Helman, *Body Myths*, 117–118.

[95] Medical students with 'gruesome instruments.' Gelatin silver print, circa 1906. Private collection.

[96] See *T-Wave* (1982), 30.

[97] "Nero." Gelatin silver print, April 1915. Private collection.

[98] *Asodecoan* (1922).

[99] See *The Howler*, Yearbook of Wake Forest University (1917), 111.

[100] "Of more use while dead than living." Wake Forest College Medical School. Gelatin silver postcard, 1910. Private collection; Warner and Edmonson, *Dissection*, 121.

[101] No one stands on dissecting tables to dissect. This position is very rarely encountered in dissection photographs and is usually only done when large groups of students pose together; the table here serving as a riser so students could position themselves at varying heights.

DISSECTION PHOTOGRAPHY

[102]   *Evening Telegraph*, June 8, 1866. Probst's victims included: Christopher Deering, age 38; his wife Julia Deering, age 45; their son John, age 8; their son Thomas, age 6; their daughter Anna, age 4; their daughter Emily, age 2; niece Elizabeth Dolan, age 25; and their farmhand, Cornelius Carey, age 17.

[103]   From "Charley," Minnesota to Joe Klein, Grants Pass, Oregon. Gelatin silver postcard, 1910. Private collection.

[104]   "Appear Wicked." Gelatin silver print, circa 1925. Author's collection. By the first few decades of the 20th century, the hammer's use as an essential tool in the dissecting room may have been considered outdated and "wicked." However, in the 19th century its use was recommended in the popular student manual, *The Dublin Dissector*, for the removal of the cranium to expose the brain.

Chapter 9

[1]   H. Gercke, "Stripped to the Bones," in *Skin*, edited by H. Hatry (Heidelberg: Kehrer Verlag, 2005), 8–9.

[2]   J. Elkins, *Pictures of the Body: Pain and Metamorphosis* (Stanford: Stanford University Press, 1999), 42, 47.

[3]   For a fascinating discussion on these concepts as they apply to first-year medical students, see F.W. Hafferty, *Into the Valley: Death and the Socialization of Medical Students* (New Haven: Yale University Press, 1991), 98–112.

[4]   Elkins, *Pictures of the Body*, 117.

[5]   For an exceptional work on the concept of the formless, see Y.-A. Bois and R.E. Krauss, *Formless: A User's Guide* (New York: Zone Books, 1999).

[6]   For more examples of this subgenre, see S.B. Burns and S. Cleary-Burns, *Deadly Intent: Crime and Punishment, Photographs from the Burns Archives* (Brooklyn: Powerhouse Books, 2008).

[7]   I have limited my interpretation of this aspect of photographic and cadaveric transformation to paper-based prints since, to date, only one non-paper-based dissection photograph – a tintype of a daguerreotype – is believed extant.

[8]   Hafferty, *Into the Valley*, 104.

[9]   Hafferty, *Into the Valley*, 99.

[10]   Flexner, *Medical Education in the United States and Canada*, 186.

[11]   Hafferty, *Into the Valley*, 104.

[12]   M. Vimal and A. Nishanthi, "Food Eponyms in Pathology," *Journal of Clinical and Diagnostic Research* 11(8) (2017), EE01–EE06.

[13]   H.W. Davenport, *Fifty Years of Medicine at the University of Michigan 1891–1941* (Ann Arbor: The University of Michigan Medical School, 1986), 137.

[14]   Arya, *Abjection and Representation*, 61; Arya, *Abject Visions*, 108.

[15]   *Thoroughbred*, Yearbook of the University of Louisville (1929), 78.

[16]   P.A. Béclard, *Elements of General Anatomy, or, a Description of Every Kind of Organs Composing the Human Body*, translated by J. Togno (Philadelphia: Carey and Lea, 1830), 110.

[17]   Hafferty, *Into the Valley*, 98.

[18]   *Yale Medical Annual 1898*, 32.

[19]   Although minor outliers, such as photographs of executed criminals and those of Civil War dead, did exist before the genre of dissection photography, collectively, an argument could be made that these images did not maintain the same visceral effect. Audiences were ultimately unaccustomed to seeing the bodies of the dead in such an unfiltered, and inglorious, final state.

[20]   J.L. Gihon, "Curious Photographic Experiences," *The Philadelphia Photographer* 8(95) (November 1871), 351.

NOTES

21 "Posing, Lighting, and Expression: On Skylight Construction," *The Philadelphia Photographer* 10 (September 1, 1873), 281.

22 Hafferty, *Into the Valley*, 98.

23 From Lewis, Chicago, Illinois to Jay Forbes, Crook, Colorado. Gelatin silver postcard, December 10, 1913. Private collection.

24 Hafferty, *Into the Valley*, 98.

25 An exception to this statement does exist in the form of injecting cadavers with various colorants (red and blue) to make them appear more 'lifelike.' However, alterations of this kind would be highly mitigated by prolonged exposure to the freezing conditions of cadaver storage chambers, or rendered irrelevant once the body was skinned.

26 T.S. Eliot, *Four Quartets* (Orlando: Harcourt, 1943), 14.

27 B. Lavédrine, *Photographs of the Past: Process and Preservation* (Los Angeles: The Getty Conservation Institute, 2009), 115–118.

28 Elkins, *Pictures of the Body*, 62.

29 Elkins, *Pictures of the Body*, 62.

30 Hafferty, *Into the Valley*, 98. Although in the 1930s, artists and photographers of the Surrealist movement, such as Hans Bellmer, would take advantage of such anthropomorphisms, these purposeful endeavors seem anathema to the intended outcomes of student-orchestrated dissection photographs.

31 Lavédrine, *Photographs of the Past*, 44–145.

32 Lavédrine, *Photographs of the Past*, 138.

33 Mall, "On the Teaching of Anatomy," 40.

34 Mall, "On the Teaching of Anatomy," 40.

Chapter 10

1 *The Yale Clinic*, 72.

2 Flexner, *Medical Education in the United States and Canada*, 297.

3 G.W. Paschal, *History of Wake Forest College, Volume II 1865–1905* (Wake Forest: Wake Forest College, 1943), 336.

4 Flexner, *Medical Education in the United States and Canada*, 280.

5 Worcester, "Reminiscences."

6 WMCP Minutes of the Board of Corporators, vol 1857–1874, September 15, 1864.

7 WMCP Minutes of the Board of Corporators, vol 1857–1874, March 20, 1874.

8 WMCP Executive Committee Minutes, vol 1876–1887, October 3, 1877.

9 *Philadelphia Photographer* 10 (August 1873), 281.

10 *Thirty-Seventh Annual Announcement of the Medical Department of the University of Vermont* (Burlington: University of Vermont, 1890), 3.

11 *First Annual Announcement of the Birmingham Medical College*, 9.

12 *Philadelphia Photographer* 10, 278.

13 Flexner, *Medical Education in the United States and Canada*, 294.

14 See WMCP Minutes of the Board of Corporators, September 28, 1880.

15 *Richmond Dispatch*, October 29, 1893.

16 We know from extant photographs that the rooms of Egyptian Hall, MCV's medical building, were quite small. For example, the MCV dissecting room, located on the top floor, although equipped with a decent sized skylight, had a low ceiling and was less than three dissecting tables long. When posing for photographs, students frequently had to rearrange the furniture in the room. A single table was placed in the center, horizontal to the camera, while the others were pushed out of the way until they hugged opposite sides of the room.

17 *Richmond Dispatch*, October 29, 1893.

DISSECTION PHOTOGRAPHY

18 *Scarab*, Magazine of the Medical College of Virginia (March 1954), 3.

19 *Scarab* (March 1954), 3.

20 W.H. Taylor, *De Quibus: Discourses and Essays* (Richmond: The Bell Book and Stationery Company, 1908), 93.

21 *X-Ray*, Yearbook of the Medical College of Virginia (1916), 213.

22 *The Times Dispatch*, April 12, 1936.

23 Warner and Edmonson, *Dissection*, 139.

24 See M. Fox-Amato, *Exposing Slavery: Photography, Human Bondage, and the Birth of Modern Visual Politics in America* (New York: Oxford University Press, 2019), 160–214.

25 *Richmond Dispatch*, October 29, 1893.

26 Fox-Amato, *Exposing Slavery*, 188.

27 Fox-Amato, *Exposing Slavery*, 190.

28 Fox-Amato, *Exposing Slavery*, 191.

29 WMCP General Photo Collection, P-1756. Legacy Center, Drexel College of Medicine.

30 The image's student photographer, Alice Evans, ingeniously stood in a location in which to show off each of the relevant components of this taboo environment, from the students, janitor, cadaver, and prep table in the foreground, to the background where the college's new Gregory Furnace was installed in the fall of 1892 for the cremation of cadaveric refuse. Both the crematorium door and the small fireplace below are visible in her photo.

31 "What do you know about this?" Undated. Gelatin silver print, circa 1907. Private collection.

32 Located in Kansas City, Missouri, the school was original founded in 1881 as a department within the Kansas City Medical College. It is now known as the University of Missouri-Kansas City School of Dentistry (UMKC).

33 Warner and Edmonson, *Dissection*, 82.

Chapter 11

1 E.V. Neale, *The Analogy of Thought and Nature* (London: Williams and Norgate, 1863), 12.

2 "How the Jubilee Year of Photography was Observed in Germany," *The Photographic Times and American Photographer* 19(423) (October 25, 1889), 534.

3 L. Holden, *A Manual of Dissection of the Human Body*, edited by J. Langton, 5th edn (Philadelphia: J. Blakiston, Son & Co., 1885), 263, 239, 264.

4 *The Western Druggist* 14 (April 1892), 147.

5 *The Pacific Medical and Surgical Journal and Press*, edited by Henry Gibbons (San Francisco: Thompson, Mahon & Co., 1866), vol 8, 103.

6 G.B. Ayers, *How to Paint Photographs in Watercolor and in Oil: Also, How to Retouch Negatives* (Philadelphia: Benerman & Wilson, 1871), 89.

7 A.S. Southworth, "Suggestions for Ladies Who Sit for Daguerreotypes," *The Lady's Almanac* (1854), quoted in J.L. Severa, *My Likeness Taken: Daguerreian Portraits in America* (Kent, OH: The Kent State University Press, 2005), xv.

8 *The American Amateur Photographer* 7 (October 1895), 465.

9 *Collier's: The National Weekly* 47 (April 29, 1911), back cover.

10 *Collier's: The National Weekly* 47 (April 29, 1911), back cover; *The Saturday Evening Post* 183(45) (May 6, 1911), 64; *The Photographic Times* 43(12) (December 1911), x.

11 Taft, *Photography and the American Scene*, 403.

12 *X-Ray*, Yearbook of the Medical College of Virginia (1918), 127–128.

13 Fox and Lawrence, *Photographing Medicine*, 50.

14 Fox and Lawrence, *Photographing Medicine*, 51.

15 Fox and Lawrence, *Photographing Medicine*, 51.

NOTES

[16] Warner and Edmonson, *Dissection*, 122.

[17] *Dentos*, Yearbook of the Chicago College of Dental Surgery (1924), 217.

[18] Burns and Burns, *Stiffs, Skulls and Skeletons*, 90.

[19] "Dr's to be?" "Frank," Baltimore, Maryland to Marjorie White, Pateros, Washington. Gelatin silver postcard, October 23, 1913. Private collection.

[20] J. Shapiro, *The Inner World of Medical Students* (Oxon: Radcliffe Publishing, 2009), 69.

[21] Burns and Burns, *Stiffs, Skulls and Skeletons*, 80.

[22] *Asodecoan* (1918), np.

[23] *Speculum*, Yearbook of the Texas College of Osteopathic Medicine (1974), 76.

[24] *The Druggists' Circular and Chemical Gazette* 23 (1879), 199.

[25] Clarence E. Lauderdale, Buffalo, NY, to Charles Howell Ward, Rochester, NY, February 1896, Charles Howell Ward Papers, A.W22. Rare Books, Special Collections, and Preservation, River Campus Libraries, University of Rochester. After graduation, Lauderdale went on to become a Contract Dental Surgeon for the US Army, stationed in the Philippines, see *The Dental Forum* 2(1) (December 1908), 23.

[26] Clarence E. Lauderdale, Buffalo, NY, to Charles Howell Ward, Rochester, NY, February 1896, Charles Howell Ward Papers, A.W.22.

[27] D. Batchelor, *Chromophobia* (London: Reaktion Books, 2000).

[28] Warner and Edmonson, *Dissection*, 24.

[29] Warner and Edmonson, *Dissection*, 8.

[30] Hafferty, *Into the Valley*, 98.

[31] Quoted in D.G. Faust, *This Republic of Suffering: Death and the American Civil War* (New York: Vintage Books, 2008), 57.

[32] Faust, *This Republic of Suffering*, 57.

[33] Quoted in J. Troyer, *Technologies of the Human Corpse* (Cambridge, MA: Massachusetts Institute of Technology, 2020), 12.

[34] B.T. Doyle and H.H. Swaney, *Lives of James A. Garfield and Chester A. Arthur with a Brief Sketch of the Assassin* (Washington, D.C.: Rufus H. Darby, 1881), 164.

[35] Doyle and Swaney, *Lives of James A. Garfield and Chester A. Arthur with a Brief Sketch of the Assassin*, 166.

[36] Doyle and Swaney, *Lives of James A. Garfield and Chester A. Arthur with a Brief Sketch of the Assassin*, 164.

[37] J.N. Gannal, *History of Embalming, and of Preparations in Anatomy, Pathology, and Natural History; Including an Account of a New Process for Embalming*, translated by R. Harlan (Philadelphia: Judah Dobson, 1840), 19.

[38] G.H. Michel, *"The Scientific Embalmer:" A Treatise on Judicial Embalming, Throwing Light on Very Important Questions Which Had So Far Remained Obscure* (Cleveland: Dr. G.H. Michel & Co., 1913).

[39] Michel, *"The Scientific Embalmer,"* 33–34.

Chapter 12

[1] *Ness County News*, May 28, 1892.

[2] "The beginning of the end." "Earl" to Unknown. Chicago College of Dental Surgery. Chicago, Illinois. Gelatin silver postcard, circa 1910. Private collection.

[3] See *Dentos* (1914), 106. Interestingly, this image not only found use as a postcard, but was reproduced in the college's 1914 yearbook, *Dentos*.

[4] Hafferty, *Into the Valley*, 104.

[5] Wheeler, "She Saunters Off Into Her Past."

[6] Quoted in D.C. Humphrey, "Dissection and Discrimination: The Social Origins of Cadavers in America, 1760–1915," *Bulletin of The New York Academy of Medicine* 49 (September 1973), 819.

DISSECTION PHOTOGRAPHY

[7] J.C. DaCosta, *Selections from The Papers and Speeches of John Chalmers DaCosta* (Philadelphia: W.B. Saunders, 1931), 209.

[8] E.F. Horine, *Daniel Drake (1785–1852): Pioneer Physician of the Midwest* (Philadelphia: University of Pennsylvania Press, 1961), 87–88. At the time of his actions, Drake was in direct violation of strict Kentucky laws against anatomical education.

[9] *Annual Circular of the Trustees and Faculty of the Medical College of the State of South Carolina, with a Catalogue of the Students and List of the Graduates, Session 1865-'66* (Charleston: Medical College of the State of South Carolina, 1866), 8.

[10] *Announcement of the Session of 1867–68, Medical College of the State of South Carolina* (Charleston: Medical College of the State of South Carolina, 1866), 7.

[11] *X-Ray*, Yearbook of the Medical College of Virginia (1917), 133.

[12] *X-Ray* (1917), 139.

[13] *Corks and Curls*, Yearbook of the University of Virginia (1898), 53.

[14] See Warner and Edmonson, *Dissection*, 26. The 1900 example of this epigraph is in a private collection. *Dissection* incorrectly lists this school as the College of Physicians and Surgeons (Baltimore).

[15] Warner and Edmonson, *Dissection*, 26.

[16] Du Bois, *The Health and Physique of the Negro American*, 98.

[17] Du Bois, *The Health and Physique of the Negro American*, 98.

[18] *Jambalaya* (1930), 26; "Louisiana 'Civilization'," *The Colored American Magazine* 1(3) (August 1900), 151.

[19] William Maccall, *National Missions: A Series of Lectures* (London: Trübner and Co., 1855), 104–105.

[20] Romans 8:3.

[21] Naturally, such notions overlook Christ *choosing* to die, his sacrifice, his agency and role as martyr apparently separated morally and legally from the concept of *suicide*, or martyrdom as a form of mental illness or automutilation.

[22] Peter 3:18.

[23] C.W. Bynum, *The Resurrection of the Body in Western Christianity, 200–1330* (New York: Columbia University Press, 1995), 43.

[24] Wheeler, "She Saunters Off Into Her Past," 90.

[25] Wheeler, "She Saunters Off Into Her Past," 90.

[26] It is unclear whether these photographs included dissection scenes as none of Wheeler's photos are known to exist at this time.

[27] Wheeler, "She Saunters Off Into Her Past," 90.

[28] *Caduceus*, Yearbook of the University of Nebraska College of Medicine (1930), 20.

[29] *Caduceus* (1930), 20.

[30] Ezekiel 37: 1.

[31] *X- Ray* (1916), 94.

[32] "If you love me." Toledo Ohio. Gelatin POP, December 1919. Private collection.

[33] The lack of parody associated with this latter tradition seems surprising. Most schools eventually installed crematory ovens in their basements to incinerate refuse from the dissecting room.

[34] Matthew 27:33. An alternative, but much less common placement of the skull and crossbones configuration was on top of the cadaver's groin or on a nearby stool.

[35] Sappol, *A Traffic of Dead Bodies*, 76.

[36] See Sappol, *A Traffic of Dead Bodies*, 96.

[37] *The Aesculapian* (1911), np.

[38] *The Hahnemannian Monthly* (June 1915), 402.

[39] *Jambalaya* (1905), 58.

[40] Shapiro, *The Inner World of Medical Students*, 57.

NOTES

[41] Shapiro, *The Inner World of Medical Students*, 50.

[42] "SHE RESTS IN PIECES." Baltimore Medical College. Gelatin silver print, 1908. Author's collection.

[43] A.R. Brunsman, Kirksville, Missouri to Miss Edna Brunsman, Greenview, Illinois. Gelatin silver postcard, April 7, 1914. Private collection.

[44] Warner and Edmonson, *Dissection*, 93.

[45] Warner and Edmonson, *Dissection*, 100.

[46] "Peace to his Ashes." University of Maryland Dental School. Gelatin silver print, November 21, 1908. Private collection.

[47] Warner and Edmonson, *Dissection*, 97.

[48] See Warner and Edmonson, *Dissection*, 11, 20.

[49] Warner and Edmonson, *Dissection*, 104.

[50] "She May Have Seen Better Days." Southern Homeopathic Medical College. Gelatin silver print, circa 1897. Private Collection.

[51] Warner and Edmonson, *Dissection*, 97.

[52] P. Mitchell, *The Purple Island and Anatomy in Early Seventeenth-Century Literature, Philosophy, and Theology* (Cranbury: Rosemont Publishing & Printing Corp., 2007), 428.

[53] "Toney the florist." Hospital College of Medicine. Gelatin silver print, circa 1900. Private collection.

[54] Richardson, *Death, Dissection and the Destitute*, 76, emphasis in original.

[55] Mitchell, *The Purple Island*, 428.

[56] Mitchell, *The Purple Island*, 428.

[57] Richardson, *Death, Dissection and the Destitute*, 76.

[58] Richardson, *Death, Dissection and the Destitute*, 76, emphasis in original.

[59] R.T. Wright, *Medical Students of the Period: A Few Words in Defence of Those Much Maligned People, with Digressions on Various Topics of Public Interest Connected with Medical Science* (Edinburgh: William Blackwood and Sons, 1862), 135.

[60] J.J. Walsh, "Catholic Universities in the United States," *Studies: An Irish Quarterly Review of Letters, Philosophy, and Science* 7(27) (September 1918), 418.

[61] For example, see *Jambalaya* (1904), 61–62.

[62] In 1873, the commencement exercises of MCV were opened by Rev. Dr. Minnegerode, pastor of St. Paul's Episcopal Church, see *Richmond Dispatch*, March 5, 1873.

[63] Howard University. "Howard University Third Anniversary Commencement" (1870). *Howard University Commencement Programs*. 1. https://dh.howard.edu/hugradpro/1

[64] *Bones, Molars, and Briefs*, Yearbook of the University of Maryland (1899), 77.

[65] *Souvenir of the Sioux City College of Medicine and Hospitals* (Sioux City: George H. Davis, 1904), np.

[66] *Eighteenth Annual Announcement of the Birmingham Medical, Dental, and Pharmaceutical Colleges, Announcement 1911–1912* (Birmingham: Birmingham Medical College, 1912), 12.

[67] Paschal, *History of Wake Forest College, Volume II 1865–1905*, 326.

[68] *The Cincinnati Medical Advance* 2(1) (May 1874), 41.

[69] Quoted in Paschal, *History of Wake Forest College, Volume II 1865–1905*, 322–323.

[70] Quoted in Paschal, *History of Wake Forest College, Volume II 1865–1905*, 323.

[71] *Bones, Molars, and Briefs* (1899), 143.

[72] J. Bell, *An Introductory Lecture Delivered at the Opening of the Thirty-First Session of the Medical College of Ohio. November 4, 1850* (Cincinnati: Printed, Daily Commercial Office, 1850), 20.

[73] *The American Homeopathist* 25 (September 15, 1899), 284.

[74] *The American Homeopathist*, 284.

[75] *The American Homeopathist*, 284.

DISSECTION PHOTOGRAPHY

[76]   Paschal, *History of Wake Forest College, Volume II 1865–1905*, 326.

[77]   *The Arrow of Pi Beta Phi* 26 (1909), 14–15. Ruth J. Abram Collection, MS #252, Box 3. Legacy Center, Drexel University College of Medicine.

[78]   McGavran, "Life and Work of Mary T. McGavran," 83.

[79]   *Asodecoan* (1922).

[80]   "Pray for Ghouls," *The St. Joseph Herald,* August 11, 1889.

[81]   *The Daily Journal of Commerce* (Kansas City, Missouri), February 20, 1878.

[82]   *The Arrow of Phi Beta Capa* (1909), 16. Ruth J. Abram Collection, MS #252, Box 3, emphasis in original.

[83]   N. Rogers, *An Alternative Path: The Making and Remaking of Hahnemann Medical College and Hospital of Philadelphia* (New Brunswick: Rutgers University Press, 1998), 124.

[84]   *The Medic,* Yearbook of the Hahnemann Medical College (1928), 45.

[85]   *Chaff* (1897), 32. It's possible this was an inside joke as Herrington was from Fresno, California, see *Chaff,* Yearbook of the College of Dentistry of the University of California (1898), 20.

[86]   Walsh, "Catholic Universities in the United States," 416.

[87]   Walsh, "Catholic Universities in the United States," 416.

[88]   T. Lewis, "Editor's Table," *Harper's New Monthly Magazine* 8 (April 1854), 690.

[89]   Montgomery, "Resurrection Times," 532.

[90]   Ezekiel 37:5–6.

[91]   "Women with the Scalpel," *Oakland Daily Times,* March 8, 1881.

[92]   Sappol, *A Traffic of Dead Bodies,* 76.

[93]   Quoted in Sappol, *A Traffic of Dead Bodies,* 74.

[94]   Baker's mother had been the first laundress at MCV.

[95]   W. Lawrence, *Lectures on Comparative Anatomy, Physiology, Zoology, and the Natural History of Man,* 9th edn (London: Henry G. Bohn, 1848), 6.

[96]   *The Wilmington Messenger,* May 23, 1897.

[97]   W. Wells, "Medical Education at Chapel Hill," *The Bulletin of the School of Medicine of the University of North Carolina* 2 (April 1955), 4. For published examples of UNC's outdoor dissections, see Warner and Edmonson, *Dissection,* 66–67, and Burns and Burns, *Stiffs, Skulls and Skeletons,* 77, which includes an image of the school's dissecting 'shack.'

[98]   G. Laderman, *The Sacred Remains: American Attitudes Toward Death, 1799–1883* (New Haven: Yale University Press, 1996), 64.

[99]   Walsh, "Catholic Universities in the United States," 416–417.

[100] "Brotherhood of Man," Wake Forest College Medical School. Gelatin silver postcard, circa 1910. Private collection.

[101] *X-Ray,* Yearbook of the Medical College of Virginia (1915), 268.

[102] *X-Ray* (1917), 139.

Chapter 13

[1]   *The Howler* (1911), 89.

[2]   The No. 2 Kodak camera, introduced in 1889 was larger than the original Kodak released a year earlier. It came loaded with 60 3.5-inch diameter images on Eastman's new transparent film. Photographers had the choice of processing their own prints and negatives or shipping the camera back to Kodak for processing and reloading. The discovery and confirmation that WMCP student Alice Evans used a No. 2 Kodak Camera to take her photographs, rather than simply using a circular mask or cut-out, was the result of my grant funded research, "Monochromatic Cadavers: Cyanotype Dissection Photographs and the Birth of Amateur Photography at The Woman's Medical College of Pennsylvania," conducted as the M. Louise Gloeckner, M.D. Research Fellowship, during the summer and fall 2016, at the Legacy Center: Archives and Special Collections,

NOTES

Drexel University College of Medicine, Philadelphia, Pennsylvania. Results and analysis of this research were first published and presented to the public at the *Photo History/ Photo Future Conference*, Rochester Institute of Technology, Rochester New York, April 20–22, 2018.

[3] In this specific context, that the dissector and photographer were both women are inconsequential. Also inconsequential in this context, is that the final print of Randolph is a cyanotype; other than the process' existence reflects students' acceptance of novel printing papers at the dawn of the era of the amateur photographer.

[4] To date, no other dissection photographs taken with a No. 2 Kodak camera, nor its predecessor camera, have been confirmed to exist. Their rarity likely resulted from the camera's expense and limited release. For example, Evans' No. 2 Kodak camera, introduced in 1889, was one of less than 20,000 manufactured. Upon release it cost $32.50. This amounts to well over $1,000 today.

[5] *Dentos* (1924), 30.

[6] *The Howler* (1911), 46.

[7] *The Aesculapian*, Yearbook of the Atlanta College of Physicians and Surgeons (1913), np.

[8] *X-Ray* (1917), 139.

[9] *Dentos*, Yearbook of the Chicago College of Dental Surgery (1912), 51, 62, 69.

[10] *Terra Mariae* (1905), 243.

[11] *The Medic*, Yearbook of the Hahnemann Medical College (1930), 24.

[12] Inscription found on the back of photograph of Dr. Anna Broomall. Attributed to Alice Evans, circa 1895. WMCP General Photo Collection, P-297. Legacy Center, Drexel University College of Medicine.

[13] Scrapbook of Clarence Waring, HMC 1919–1923. Private collection.

[14] Scrapbook of Ruby Inouye Shu, Ruby Inouye Shu Papers, 2016.003. Legacy Center, Drexel University College of Medicine.

[15] M.T. Henry, "Dr. Ruby Inouye Shu (1920–2012)," *Historylink.org*, April 11, 2021. https://www.historylink.org/File/10053.

[16] *X-Ray* (1918), 162, emphasis in original.

[17] Hafferty, *Into the Valley*, 113.

[18] *Bones, Molars, and Briefs* (1899), 116.

[19] *Bones, Molars, and Briefs* (1899), 116.

[20] "Who's Who and Why?" Gelatin silver print, circa 1918. Private collection.

[21] "Aphrodite." Gelatin silver print, circa 1922. Private collection.

[22] J. Hawes, "Response to the Toast, 'The Country Doctor,' at the Colorado State Medical Banquet," *The Journal of Materia Medica* 32 (October 1894), 146.

[23] *Yale Medical Annual 1898*, 60.

[24] *X-Ray* (1917), 98.

[25] *Jambalaya* (1915), 158.

[26] E. Blackwell, *Pioneer Work for Women* (New York: E.P. Dutton and Co., 1914), 58.

[27] Blackwell, *Pioneer Work for Women*, 58. Presumably, Blackwell was not just referencing the mere sight of a dissected body – and likely its exposed genitals since she also mentions trying not to laugh – but the subsequent process of its dissection.

[28] I.G. Drooz, *Doctor of Medicine* (New York: Dodd, Mead and Company, 1949), 27.

[29] Sappol, *A Traffic of Dead Bodies*, 78.

[30] McGavran, "Life and Work of Mary T. McGavran," 8.

[31] Blackwell, *Pioneer Work for Women*, 60.

[32] For a collection of photomechanical reproductions of student-made pen and ink cartoons of students as devils, see "An Initiation," by J.J. Kocher (Class of 1906), in *Class Record of Hahnemann Medical College 1906*; *Chaff* (1906), 57; *Anamnesis* (1910). The devil persona frequently changed depending on the stakeholder most victimized in the given context.

DISSECTION PHOTOGRAPHY

In the first example listed here, students were the victims, and so they reimagined their cadavers, in the form of devils, returning to dissect them. The second example references fraternities, and shows what are presumed to be upperclassmen, reimaged as devils, boiling first years in a massive cauldron as part of some kind of hazing ritual.

33 *Corks and Curls*, Yearbook of the University of Virginia (1901), 99; *Corks and Curls*, Yearbook of the University of Virginia (1903), 26.

34 *X-Ray* (1917), 98.

35 *X-Ray* (1917), 133.

36 Bynum, *The Resurrection of the Body in Western Christianity, 200–1330*, 292.

37 For an example of cadavers hanging from hooks, see Burns and Burns, *Stiffs, Skulls and Skeletons*, 82.

38 *X-Ray* (1917), 133.

39 *Mount Union Times*, September 11, 1903. "We adopt the grim skull and cross bones as the symbol of our loathing for the former, and show our love for the latter."

40 J. Milton, *Paradise Lost, A Poem in Twelve Books* (Glasgow: R. & A. Foulis), 8.

Conclusion

1 *Abel's Photographic Weekly* 30 (July 15, 1922), 63.

2 Faust, *This Republic of Suffering*, 61.

3 Faust, *This Republic of Suffering*, 62.

4 Lewis, "Editor's Table," 690.

5 Dwight, "Our Contribution to Civilization and to Science," 12.

6 J.E. Tuel, "Medical Science," *Journal of Medicine and Science* 3(7) (June 1897), 210.

7 M. Peryer, "Cadaver Photos, Lewd Captions Found in YSM Yearbooks," *Yale News* 13 (February 2019).

8 Terry, "Dissecting Room Portraits," 98.

9 Terry, "Dissecting Room Portraits," 98.

10 "Sends his heart." Alejandro to his mother. Gelatin silver postcard, circa 1908. Private collection.

References

1901, Yearbook of Jefferson Medical College (1901).

Abel's Photographic Weekly 30 (July 15, 1922).

The Aesculapian, Yearbook of the Atlanta College of Physicians and Surgeons (1911).

The Aesculapian, Yearbook of the Atlanta College of Physicians and Surgeons (1912).

The Aesculapian, Yearbook of the Atlanta College of Physicians and Surgeons (1913).

Agnew, D.H. *Lecture Introductory to the One Hundred and Fifth Course of Instruction in the Medical Department of the University of Pennsylvania: Delivered Monday, October 10, 1870* (Philadelphia: R.P. King's Sons, printers, 1870).

Ahren, E. *Death, Modernity, and the Body: Sweden 1870–1940* (Rochester: University of Rochester Press, 2009).

Alcott, W.A. *The House I Live in: Or the Human Body, for the Use of Families and Schools* (Boston: C.D. Strong, 1854).

Allen, J.M. *The Practical Anatomist: Or, the Student's Guide in the Dissecting-Room* (Philadelphia: Blanchard and Lea, 1856).

The American Amateur Photographer 7 (October 1895).

The American Homeopathist 25 (September 15, 1899).

Anamnesis, Yearbook of Jefferson Medical College (1910).

Announcement of the Session of 1867–68, Medical College of the State of South Carolina (Charleston: Medical College of the State of South Carolina, 1866).

Annual Announcement, Lectures, etc., by the Trustees and Professors of Jefferson Medical College, Philadelphia; for the Year 1832 (Philadelphia: Jefferson Medical Faculty, 1832).

Annual Announcement of Lectures at Toland Hall, Medical Department of the University of California, San Francisco, California (San Francisco: Cubery & Co., 1875).

Annual Circular of the Trustees and Faculty of the Medical College of the State of South Carolina, with a Catalogue of the Students and List of the Graduates, Session 1865–'66 (Charleston: Medical College of the State of South Carolina, 1866).

Arthur, T.S. "American Characteristics: No. V. – The Daguerreotypists," *Godey's Lady Book* 38 (May 1849).

Arya, R. *Abjection and Representation: An Exploration of Abjection in the Visual Arts, Film and Literature* (Basingstoke: Palgrave Macmillan, 2014).

Arya, R. "The Fragmented Body as an Index of Abjection," in *Abject Visions: Powers of Horror in Art and Visual Culture*, edited by R. Arya and N. Chare (Manchester: Manchester University Press, 2016).

Ascodecoan, Yearbook of the Atlanta-Southern Dental College (1918).

Ascodecoan, Yearbook of the Atlanta-Southern Dental College (1922).

Atlanta Constitution, March 22, 1898.

Aud, J. *Does Your Dogma Bite? Artifacts, Metafacts, and Symbols* (Lincoln, NE: Writers Club Press, 2000).

Aughinbaugh, W.E. *I Swear By Apollo: A Life of Medical Adventure* (New York: Farrar & Rinehart, 1938).

Ayers, G.B. *How to Paint Photographs in Watercolor and in Oil: Also, How to Retouch Negatives* (Philadelphia: Benerman & Wilson, 1871).

Baltimore Sun, December 3, 1896.

"Bar Lynching Postcards." *The York Dispatch*, September 5, 1908.

Barrett, W.C. "The Study of Anatomy," *Dominion Dental Journal* 9.

Batchelor, D. *Chromophobia* (London: Reaktion Books, 2000).

Bazin, A. "The Ontology of the Photographic Image," in *What is Cinema?* (Berkeley: University of California Press, 2005), vol 1.

Béclard, P.A. *Additions to the General Anatomy of Xavier Bichat. Translated from the French* (Boston: Richardson and Lord, 1823).

Béclard, P.A. *Elements of General Anatomy, or, a Description of Every Kind of Organs Composing the Human Body.* Translated by J. Togno (Philadelphia: Carey and Lea, 1830).

Bell, C. *Institutes of Surgery: Arranged in the Order of the Lectures Delivered in the University of Edinburgh* (Philadelphia: A. Waldie, 1840).

Bell, J. *An Introductory Lecture Delivered at the Opening of the Thirty-First Session of the Medical College of Ohio. November 4, 1850* (Cincinnati: Printed, Daily Commercial Office, 1850).

Benedict, A.L. "The Life of a Medical Student," *Lippincott's Monthly Magazine* (September 1896).

Blackwell, E. *Pioneer Work for Women* (New York: E.P. Dutton and Co., 1914).

Bois, Y.-A. and R.E. Krauss. *Formless: A User's Guide* (New York: Zone Books, 1999).

Bones, Molars, and Briefs, Yearbook of the University of Maryland (1897).

Bones, Molars, and Briefs, Yearbook of the University of Maryland (1899).

Boston Medical and Surgical Journal, 12 (May 13, 1835).

Burns, S.B. *A Morning's Work: Medical Photographs from The Burns Archive and Collection 1843–1939* (New Mexico: Twin Palms Publishers, 1998).

REFERENCES

Burns, S.B. and S. Cleary-Burns. *Deadly Intent: Crime and Punishment, Photographs from the Burns Archives* (Brooklyn: Powerhouse Books, 2008).

Burns, S.B. and E.A. Burns. *Stiffs, Skulls, and Skeletons: Medical Photography and Symbolism* (Atglen: Schiffer Publishing, 2015).

Bynum, C.W. *The Resurrection of the Body in Western Christianity, 200–1330* (New York: Columbia University Press, 1995).

Caduceus, Yearbook of the University of Nebraska College of Medicine (1930).

Chaff, Yearbook of the College of Dentistry of the University of California (1897).

Chaff, Yearbook of the College of Dentistry of the University of California (1898).

Chaff, Yearbook of the College of Dentistry of the University of California (1906).

Chaff, Yearbook of the College of Dentistry of the University of California (1909).

Chaisty, E.J. *The London Dissector, or Guide to Anatomy; for the Use of Students: Comprising a Description of the Muscles, Vessels, Nerves, Lymphatics, and Viscera of the Human Body, as They Appear on Dissection; with Directions for Their Demonstration. From the Last London Edition* (Philadelphia: Edward Barrington and George D. Haswell, 1842).

Chandler, D. "An Introduction to Genre Theory" (1997). http://www.aber.ac.uk/media/Documents/intgenre/chandler_genre_theory.pdf

The Charlotte Observer, March 21, 1903.

Chicago Tribune, September 29, 1895.

Childers, J. and G. Hentzi (Eds). *The Columbia Dictionary of Modern Literary and Cultural Criticism* (New York: Columbia University Press, 1995).

The Chironian 15 (October 16, 1898).

The Chironian 15 (December 15, 1898).

The Cincinnati Medical Advance 2(1) (May 1874).

Cisney-Smith, E. "The Personal History and Background Diary of Elizabeth Cisney-Smith," Isabel Smith Stein Collection on Elizabeth Cisney-Smith, WM.2007.002, Box 2, Folder 2. Legacy Center, Drexel University College of Medicine.

Class Record of Hahnemann Medical College 1906 (Philadelphia: Hahnemann Medical College, 1906).

Cleveland, E.H. *Introductory Lecture on Behalf of the Faculty to the Class of the Female Medical College of Pennsylvania, for the Session of 1858–1859* (Philadelphia: Merrihew & Thompson, printers, 1858).

Cleveland, E.H. *Valedictory Address of the Graduating Class of the Woman's Medical College of Pennsylvania, at the Sixteenth Annual Commencement, March 14, 1868* (Philadelphia: Published by the WMCP Corporators, 1868).

The Clinic, Yearbook of Jefferson Medical College (1969).

Coleman, A.D. *The Grotesque in Photography* (New York: The Ridge Press, 1977).

Collier's: The National Weekly 47 (April 29, 1911).

Commercial Appeal, March 7, 1900.

Corks and Curls, Yearbook of the University of Virginia (1898).

Corks and Curls, Yearbook of the University of Virginia (1901).

Corks and Curls, Yearbook of the University of Virginia (1903).

Corks and Curls, Yearbook of the University of Virginia (1911).

Cregan, K. *The Sociology of the Body* (London: SAGE, 2006).

Cunningham, A. *The Anatomist Anatomis'd: An Experimental Discipline in Enlightenment Europe* (Farnham: Ashgate, 2010).

Cunningham, D.J. *Manual of Practical Anatomy*, 2nd edn (Edinburgh: Young J. Pentland, 1896), vol 1.

DaCosta, J.C. *Selections from the Papers and Speeches of John Chalmers DaCosta* (Philadelphia: W.B. Saunders, 1931).

Daily Journal of Commerce, February 20, 1878.

The Daily Republican, March 21, 1890.

Davenport, H.W. *Fifty Years of Medicine at the University of Michigan 1891–1941* (Ann Arbor: The University of Michigan Medical School, 1986).

Davis, K.F. " 'A Terrible Distinctness': Photography of the Civil War Era," in *Photography in Nineteenth-Century America*, edited by M. Sandweiss (Fort Worth: Amon Carter Museum, 1991).

"The Demiurge," *Aeon Flux*, written by P. Chung, S. De Jarnatt, M. Ferris, and J.D. Brancato, directed by H.E. Baker (MTV, 1995).

The Dental Forum 2(1) (December 1908).

Dentos, Yearbook of the Chicago College of Dental Surgery (1912).

Dentos, Yearbook of the Chicago College of Dental Surgery (1914).

Dentos, Yearbook of the Chicago College of Dental Surgery (1915).

Dentos, Yearbook of the Chicago College of Dental Surgery (1916).

Dentos, Yearbook of the Chicago College of Dental Surgery (1922).

Dentos, Yearbook of the Chicago College of Dental Surgery (1923).

Dentos, Yearbook of the Chicago College of Dental Surgery (1924).

Dickens, C. *A Christmas Carol* (London: Bradbury & Evans, 1858).

Dinius, M.J. *The Camera and the Press: American Visual and Print Culture in the Age of the Daguerreotype* (Philadelphia: University of Pennsylvania Press, 2012).

Dotterer, S. and G. Cranz. "The Picture Postcard: It's Development and Role in American Urbanization," *Journal of American Culture* 5(1) (spring 1982).

Doyle, B.T. and H.H. Swaney. *Lives of James A. Garfield and Chester A. Arthur with a Brief Sketch of the Assassin* (Washington, D.C.: Rufus H. Darby, 1881).

Drooz, I.G. *Doctor of Medicine* (New York: Dodd, Mead and Company, 1949).

The Druggists' Circular and Chemical Gazette 23 (1879).

REFERENCES

Du Bois, W.E.B. (Ed). *The Health and Physique of the Negro American* (Atlanta: Atlanta University Press, 1906).

Dwight, T. "Our Contribution to Civilization and to Science," in *Proceedings of the Eighth Annual Session of the Association of American Anatomists* (Washington, D.C.: Beresford Printers, 1896).

Eighteenth Annual Announcement of the Birmingham Medical, Dental, and Pharmaceutical Colleges, Announcement 1911–1912 (Birmingham: Birmingham Medical College, 1912).

Eliot, T.S. *Four Quartets* (Orlando: Harcourt, 1943).

Elkins, J. *Pictures of the Body: Pain and Metamorphosis* (Stanford: Stanford University Press, 1999).

Evening Telegraph, June 8, 1866.

Exudate, Yearbook of Jefferson Medical College (1912).

Fall River Globe, November 25, 1901.

Farmer and Mechanic, January 24, 1899.

Faust, D.G. *This Republic of Suffering: Death and the American Civil War* (New York: Vintage Books, 2008).

Fergusson, W. *A System of Practical Surgery*, 3rd edn (London: John Churchill, 1852).

First Annual Announcement of the Birmingham Medical College, Session of 1894–1895 (Birmingham: Birmingham Medical College, 1895).

Flexner, A. *Medical Education in the United States and Canada* (New York: The Carnegie Foundation, 1910).

Forbes, W.S. "History of the First Anatomy-Act of Pennsylvania," *The Philadelphia Medical Journal* 2(13) (November 26, 1898).

Fox, D.M. and C. Lawrence. *Photographing Medicine: Images and Power in Britain and America since 1840* (New York: Greenwood Press, 1988).

Fox-Amato, M. *Exposing Slavery: Photography, Human Bondage, and the Birth of Modern Visual Politics in America* (New York: Oxford University Press, 2019).

Gannal, J.N. *History of Embalming, and of Preparations in Anatomy, Pathology, and Natural History; Including an Account of a New Process for Embalming.* Translated by R. Harlan (Philadelphia: Judah Dobson, 1840).

Gercke, H. "Stripped to the Bones," in *Skin*, edited by H. Hatry (Heidelberg: Kehrer Verlag, 2005).

Gernsheim, A. "Medical Photography in the Nineteenth Century," *Medical & Biological Illustration* 11(2) (April 1961).

Gihon, J.L. "Curious Photographic Experiences," *Philadelphia Photographer* 8(95) (November 1871).

Godman, J. *Contributions to Physiological and Pathological Anatomy: Containing the Observations Made at the Philadelphia Anatomical Rooms during the Session of 1824–25* (Philadelphia: Carey and Lea, 1825).

Gove, M.S. *Lectures to Women on Anatomy and Physiology with an Appendix on Water Cure* (New York: Harper and Brothers, 1846).

DISSECTION PHOTOGRAPHY

Grant, W.R. *An Introductory Lecture to the Course Anatomy and Physiology in the Department of Pennsylvania College, Philadelphia. Delivered Tuesday, November 4th 1845* (Philadelphia: Published by the Class, 1845).

Gross, S.D. *A System of Surgery; Pathological, Diagnostic, Therapeutic, and Operative*, 6th edn (Philadelphia: Henry C. Lea's Son & Co., 1882), vol 1.

Hafferty, F.W. *Into the Valley: Death and the Socialization of Medical Students* (New Haven: Yale University Press, 1991).

The Hahnemannian Institute 7 (November 1899).

The Hahnemannian Monthly (June 1915).

Hawes, J. "Response to the Toast, 'The Country Doctor,' at the Colorado State Medical Banquet," *The Journal of Materia Medica* 32 (October 1894).

Heath, C. *Practical Anatomy: A Manual of Dissections*. Edited by W.W. Keen (Philadelphia: Henry C. Lea, 1870).

Helman, C. *Body Myths* (London: Chatto & Windus, 1992).

Hertzler, A. *The Horse and Buggy Doctor* (Lincoln, NE: University of Nebraska Press, 1938).

Holden, L. *A Manual of Dissection of the Human Body*, 5th edn. Edited by J. Langton (Philadelphia: J. Blakiston, Son & Co., 1885).

Horine, E.F. *Daniel Drake (1785–1852): Pioneer Physician of the Midwest* (Philadelphia: University of Pennsylvania Press, 1961).

Horner, W.E. *Special Anatomy and Histology*, 7th edn (Philadelphia: Blanchard and Lea, 1851).

"How the Jubilee Year of Photography was Observed in Germany." *The Photographic Times and American Photographer* 19(423) (October 25, 1889).

Howard University. "Howard University Third Anniversary Commencement" (1870).

The Howler, Yearbook of Wake Forest University (1905).

The Howler, Yearbook of Wake Forest University (1911).

The Howler, Yearbook of Wake Forest University (1917).

The Howler, Yearbook of Wake Forest University (1918).

The Howler, Yearbook of Wake Forest University (1922).

The Howler, Yearbook of Wake Forest University (1926).

Humphrey, D.C. "Dissection and Discrimination: The Social Origins of Cadavers in America, 1760–1915," *Bulletin of The New York Academy of Medicine* 49 (September 1973).

Hunt, H.L. *Plastic Surgery of the Head, Face and Neck* (Philadelphia: Lea & Febiger, 1926).

Husson, M. *A Treatise of the Membranes in General, and on Different Membranes in Particular by Xavier Bichat, of the Societies of Medicine, Medical and Philomatic of Paris; of those of Brussels and Lyons. A New Edition, Enlarged by an Historical Notice of the Life and Writings of the Author; by M. Husson. Paris, 1802.* Translated by J.G. Coffin (Boston: Cummings and Hilliard, 1813).

Jambalaya, Yearbook of Tulane University (1904).

REFERENCES

Jambalaya, Yearbook of Tulane University (1905).

Jambalaya, Yearbook of Tulane University (1907).

Jambalaya, Yearbook of Tulane University (1915).

Jambalaya, Yearbook of Tulane University (1930).

Jayhawker, Yearbook of the Kansas University School of Medicine (1969).

Journal of Zoöphily 7 (March 1898).

King, D. *Quackery Unmasked: Or, a Consideration of the Most Prominent Empirical Schemes of the Present Time* (Boston: David Clapp, printers, 1858).

Kristeva, J. *Powers of Horror: An Essay on Abjection.* Translated by L.S. Roudiez (New York: Columbia University Press, 1982).

Laderman, G. *The Sacred Remains: American Attitudes Toward Death, 1799–1883* (New Haven: Yale University Press, 1996).

The Lancet 1 (December 27, 1829).

Lane, J.F.W. *Outlines of Anatomy and Physiology, Translated from the French of H. Milne Edwards* (Boston: Charles C. Little and James Brown, 1841).

Lavédrine, B. *Photographs of the Past: Process and Preservation* (Los Angeles: The Getty Conservation Institute, 2009).

Lawrence, W. *Lectures on Comparative Anatomy, Physiology, Zoology, and the Natural History of Man*, 9th edn (London: Henry G. Bohn, 1848).

Lemoine-Luccioni, E. *La Robe: Essai psychanalytique sur le vêtement* (Paris: Seuil, 1983).

Lewis, T. "Editor's Table," *Harper's New Monthly Magazine* 8 (April 1854).

The Lichonian (New York: Published by the Students of the Long Island College of Medicine, 1935)

"Louisiana 'Civilization'." *The Colored American Magazine* 1(3) (August 1900).

"Lynching Postcards Barred." *Chicago Tribune*, August 18, 1908.

Maccall, W. *National Missions: A Series of Lectures* (London: Trübner and Co., 1855).

Mall, F.P. "On the Teaching of Anatomy as Illustrated by Professor Barker's Manual," *Bulletin of the Johns Hopkins Hospital* 16 (1905).

Marsh, H. "The Medical Student and His Environment," *The British Medical Journal* 2(2024) (October 14, 1899).

McGavran, M.T. "Life and Work of Mary T. McGavran" (nd), Mary Theodora McGavran Papers, MS ACC-169. Legacy Center, Drexel University College of Medicine.

McGinn, C. *The Meaning of Disgust* (Oxford: Oxford University Press, 2011).

The Medic, Yearbook of the Hahnemann Medical College (1928).

The Medic, Yearbook of the Hahnemann Medical College (1930).

Michel, G.H. *"The Scientific Embalmer:" A Treatise on Judicial Embalming, Throwing Light on Very Important Questions Which Had So Far Remained Obscure* (Cleveland: Dr. G.H. Michel & Co., 1913).

Milton, J. *Paradise Lost: A Poem in Twelve Books* (Glasgow: R. & A. Foulis, 1750).

Mitchell, P. *The Purple Island and Anatomy in Early Seventeenth-Century Literature, Philosophy, and Theology* (Cranbury: Rosemont Publishing & Printing Corp., 2007).

Montgomery, H. "Resurrection Times," *The Georgia Review* 43(3) (fall 1989).

Montgomery Times, July 6, 1910.

The Morning Post, January 24, 1903.

Morton, H.J. "Photography as a Moral Agent," *The Philadelphia Photographer* 1(8) (August 1, 1864).

Morton, H.J. "Photography as an Authority," *The Philadelphia Photographer* 1(12) (December 1, 1864).

Mount Union Times, September 11, 1903.

Murphy, B. "How Often Do Physicians and Medical Students Die of Suicide?" *American Medical Association*, June 12, 2019. www.ama-assn.org/practice-management/physician-health/how-often-do-physicians-and-medical-students-die-suicide

Nashville Banner, February 12, 1912.

Neale, E.V. *The Analogy of Thought and Nature* (London: Williams and Norgate, 1863).

Nebraska State Journal, November 25, 1896.

Ness County News, May 28, 1892.

Newhall, B. *Photography: A Short Critical History* (New York: The Museum of Modern Art, 1938).

Newhall, B. *The History of Photography from 1839 to the Present Day*, 4th edn (New York: The Museum of Modern Art, 1981).

News and Observer, January 19, 1899.

Ottumwa Tri-weekly Courier, November 6, 1900.

The Pacific Medical and Surgical Journal and Press. Edited by Henry Gibbons (San Francisco: Thompson, Mahon & Co., 1866), vol 8.

Paschal, G.W. *History of Wake Forest College, Volume II 1865–1905* (Wake Forest: Wake Forest College, 1943).

Peryer, M. "Cadaver Photos, Lewd Captions Found in YSM Yearbooks," *Yale News* 13 (February 2019).

Pfister, H.F. *Facing the Light: Historic American Portrait Daguerreotypes* (Washington, D.C.: Smithsonian Institution Press, 1978).

Philadelphia Photographer 1(9) (September 1, 1864).

Philadelphia Photographer 10 (August 1873).

The Photographic Times 43(12) (December 1911).

"Photography in Medical Science." *Lancet* 22 (January 1859).

"Playdent," Yearbook of the University of Southern California Dental School (1972).

"Posing, Lighting, and Expression: On Skylight Construction." *Philadelphia Photographer* 10 (September 1, 1873).

"Pray for Ghouls." *The St. Joseph Herald*, August 11, 1889.

REFERENCES

Public Laws and Resolutions of the State of North Carolina Passed by the General Assembly at the Session of 1903 (Raleigh: Published by Authority, 1903).

The Quax, Yearbook of Drake University (1904).

Raue, C.G., C.B. Knerr, and C. Mohr (Eds). *A Memorial of Constantine Hering* (Philadelphia: Press of Globe Printing House, 1884).

Reidsville Review, January 27, 1903.

Retrospectroscope, Yearbook of the University of Florida (1965).

Richardson, R. *Death, Dissection and the Destitute* (Chicago: University of Chicago Press, 2000).

Richmond Dispatch, March 5, 1873.

Richmond Dispatch, October 29, 1893.

Rogers, N. *An Alternative Path: The Making and Remaking of Hahnemann Medical College and Hospital of Philadelphia* (New Brunswick: Rutgers University Press, 1998).

Ruby, J. *Secure the Shadow: Death and Photography in America* (Cambridge, MA: MIT Press, 1995).

Rudisill, R. *Mirror Image: The Influence of the Daguerreotype on American Society* (Albuquerque: University of New Mexico Press, 1971).

Ruskin, J. *Modern Painters* (New York: John Wiley, 1862).

Salt Lake Telegram, November 29, 1903.

Sappol, M. *A Traffic of Dead Bodies: Anatomy and Embodied Social Identity in Nineteenth-Century America* (Princeton: Princeton University Press, 2002).

The Saturday Evening Post 183(45) (May 6, 1911).

Sawday, J. *The Body Emblazoned: Dissection and the Human Body in Renaissance Culture* (New York: Routledge, 1996).

Scarab, Magazine of the Medical College of Virginia (March 1954).

Segal, D.A. "A Patient So Dead: American Medical Students and Their Cadavers," *Anthropological Quarterly* 61 (January 1988).

"Self-operating Processes of Fine Art. The Daguereotype [*sic*]." *The Spectator* 12(553) (February 1839).

Severa, J.L. *My Likeness Taken: Daguerreian Portraits in America* (Kent, OH: The Kent State University Press, 2005).

Shapiro, J. *The Inner World of Medical Students* (Oxon: Radcliffe Publishing, 2009).

Sinclair, W.J. *Semmelweis: His Life and Doctrine: A Chapter in the History of Medicine* (Manchester: Manchester University Press, 1909).

"Sleep with Dead Too Gruesome." *Knoxville Sentinel*, March 2, 1908.

Sodecoan, Yearbook of the Southern Dental College (1917).

Sontag, S. *On Photography* (New York: Picador, 1977).

Sotheby's. *Important Daguerreotypes from the Stanley B. Burns, MD. Collection, New York 5 October 2017* (New York: Sotheby's, 2017).

Souvenir of the Sioux City College of Medicine and Hospitals (Sioux City: George H. Davis, 1904).

Speculum, Yearbook of the Texas College of Osteopathic Medicine (1974).

Spielmann, M.H. *The Iconography of Andreas Vesalius* (London: John Bale, Sons & Danielsson, 1925).

Stafford, B.M. *Body Criticism: Imagine the Unseen in Enlightenment Art and Medicine* (Cambridge, MA: MIT Press, 1993).

Starr, P. *The Social Transformation of American Medicine: The Rise of a Sovereign Profession and the Making of a Vast Industry* (New York: HarperCollins, 1982).

Stedman, T.L. (Ed). *Twentieth Century Practice: An International Encyclopedia of Modern Medical Science by Leading Authorities of Europe and America* (New York: W. Wood and Company, 1895), vol 15.

The Sun, February 18, 1901.

Synapsis, Yearbook of the Philadelphia College of Osteopathic Medicine (1925).

Taft, R. *Photography and the American Scene: A Social History, 1839–1889* (New York: Dover Publications, 1989).

Tagg, J. *The Burden of Representation: Essays on Photographies and Histories* (Amherst: The University of Massachusetts Press, 1988).

Taylor, W.H. *De Quibus: Discourses and Essays* (Richmond: The Bell Book and Stationery Company, 1908).

Terra Mariae Schools of Medicine, Dentistry, Pharmacy, and Law, Yearbook of the University of Maryland (1905).

Terry, James S. "Dissecting Room Portraits: Decoding an Underground Genre," *History of Photography* 7(2) (April–June 1983).

Thirty-Second Annual Announcement of the New York Homeopathic Medical College and Hospital, Session of 1891–92 (New York: New York Homeopathic Medical College, 1891).

Thirty-Seventh Annual Announcement of the Medical Department of the University of Vermont (Burlington: University of Vermont, 1890).

Thoroughbred, Yearbook of the University of Louisville (1929).

The Times Dispatch, April 12, 1936.

Trachtenberg, A. *Reading American Photographs: Images as History, Mathew Brady to Walker Evans* (New York: Hill & Wang, 1989).

Trachtenberg, A. "Photography: The Emergence of a Keyword," in *Photography in Nineteenth-Century America*, edited by M. Sandweiss (Fort Worth: Amon Carter Museum, 1991).

Trachtenberg, A. "Likeness as Identity: Reflections on the Daguerrean Mystique," in *The Portrait in Photography*, edited by G. Clarke (London: Reaktion Books, 1992).

Troyer, J. *Technologies of the Human Corpse* (Cambridge, MA: Massachusetts Institute of Technology, 2020).

Tuel, J.E. "Medical Science," *Journal of Medicine and Science* 3(7) (June 1897).

T-Wave, Yearbook of the Tulane University School of Medicine (1982).

REFERENCES

The University of Texas Medical Branch at Galveston: A Seventy-five Year History by the Faculty and Staff (Austin: University of Texas Press, 1967).

Velpeau, A.A.L.M. *A Treatise on Surgical Anatomy; or the Anatomy of Regions, Considered in its Relations with Surgery.* Translated by J.W. Sterling (New York: Samuel Wood and Sons, 1830).

Videodrome. Directed by D. Cronenberg, Universal Pictures (1983).

Vimal, M. and A. Nishanthi. "Food Eponyms in Pathology," *Journal of Clinical and Diagnostic Research* 11(8) (2017).

The Vindicator, January 7, 1882.

Waldby, C. *The Visible Human Project: Informatic Bodies and Posthuman Medicine* (London: Routledge, 2000).

Walsh, J.J. "Catholic Universities in the United States," *Studies: An Irish Quarterly Review of Letters, Philosophy, and Science* 7(27) (September 1918).

Warner, J.H. and J.M. Edmonson. *Dissection: Photographs as a Rite of Passage in American Medicine 1880–1930* (New York: Blast Books, 2009).

Warren, S. *Affecting Scenes; Being Passages from the Diary of a Physician*, vol 2 (New York: Harper and Brothers, 1837).

Wells, W. "Medical Education at Chapel Hill," *The Bulletin of the School of Medicine of the University of North Carolina* 2 (April 1955).

The Western Druggist 14 (April 1892).

Wheeler, E.F. "She Saunters Off Into Her Past." Draft of typescript autobiography, unpublished, 1946, X.2002.2, 83. Legacy Center, Drexel University College of Medicine.

Whitney Museum of American Art. *Abject Art: Repulsion and Desire in American Art* (New York: Whitney Museum of Art, 1993).

The Wilmington Messenger, May 23, 1897.

The Woman's Medical College of Georgia and Training School for Nurses, First Annual Announcement. Session of 1889 and 1890 (Atlanta: American Book and Job Print, 1889).

"Women with the Scalpel." *Oakland Daily Times*, March 8, 1881.

Worcester, A. "Reminiscences," *OnView: Digital Collections & Exhibits.* https://collections.countway.harvard.edu/onview/item

Wright, R.T. *Medical Students of the Period: A Few Words in Defence of Those Much Maligned People, with Digressions on Various Topics of Public Interest Connected with Medical Science* (Edinburgh: William Blackwood and Sons, 1862).

X-Ray, Yearbook of the Medical College of Virginia (1915).

X-Ray, Yearbook of the Medical College of Virginia (1916).

X-Ray, Yearbook of the Medical College of Virginia (1917).

X-Ray, Yearbook of the Medical College of Virginia (1918).

The Yale Clinic: The Annual and Graduate Directory of the Medical Department of Yale University (New Haven: Yale University, 1904).

Yale Medical Annual 1898, Yale University School of Medicine (1898).

The Yearbook, Yearbook of Yale University School of Medicine (1908).

The Yearbook, Yearbook of Yale University School of Medicine (1909).

The Yearbook, Yearbook of Yale University School of Medicine (1910).

Yorkville Enquirer, January 31, 1903.

Zimmerman, B. "When Legs and Arms Won: The Culture of Dissection and the Role of the Camera at The Woman's Medical College of Pennsylvania." *Nursing Clio*, August 16, 2018. https://nursingclio.org/2018/08/16/the-culture-of-dissection-and-the-role-of-the-camera-at-the-womans-medical-college-of-pennsylvania/

Zuckerkandl, O. *Atlas and Epitome of Operative Surgery*. Edited by J.C. DaCosta (Philadelphia: W.B. Saunders, 1898).

Index

References to figures appear in *italic* type. References to endnotes show both the page number and the note number (229n10).

A

abjection
  about 12, 36–37
  of cadavers 37–38, 172, 193, *193*
  dissection photography and 48, 49
  objectification and 45
  scalpels as agents of 101, 106
  viscera and 35
  women, refusal of by 89, 90
Abjection and Representation: An Exploration of Abjection in the Visual Arts, Film and Literature (Arya) 39
Abject Visions: Powers of Horror in Art and Visual Culture (Arya) 44
accidents, dissecting room *See* dissecting rooms
acts, anatomical (legislation, laws)
  about 5, 62
  grave robbing, banning of 62
  North Carolina 66–67, 70
  passing of 7, 65
  Pennsylvania 94
  Texas 65
Aeon Flux 29
African Americans
  cadavers of 166–167, 170, 173–176, 195
  dehumanization of 6, 42, 53, 57, 129–130, 170, 187, 204
  desecration of (graves / bodies) 64, 65, 173
  janitors 6, 153, 154–157, 174, 179, 194–195, 227n26
  physicians 68, 174
  students, dissection photographs of 69, *69*
  training hospitals for 7, 67–68
Agnew, David Hayes 88, 229n10
albumen prints
  about 18, 32, 120, 147, 200
  examples of *18*, *25*, *60*, *121*
  fading in 145–146
Allen, J.M. 28, 112

amateur photographers *See* photographers, student amateur
American School of Osteopathy (Kirksville, MO) 43, 90, *91*, 103, 123, 151
anatomical acts *See* acts, anatomical (legislation, laws)
anatomical legislation *See* acts, anatomical (legislation, laws)
"The Anatomist" (Brodnax) 196–197
anatomy
  as a discipline 59
  dissection's role in advancing 24, 26
  illustrations / paintings 58–59
Anatomy Lesson of Dr. Nicolaes Tulp (Rembrandt) 58, 99
animals *See* dissection
anthropodermic bibliopegy 43
antisepsis 121
  See also hygiene
archives *See* dissection photography
Arthur, T.S. 30
Arya, Rina 12, 35, 39, 43, 44–45
asepsis 121
  See also hygiene
Asper, Guy P. 80
Atlanta College of Physicians and Surgeons 202
Atlanta-Southern Dental College *See* Southern Dental College (Atlanta, GA)
Atlanta University 68
Aughinbaugh, William E. 63, 226n20
axes *See* instruments, cutting

B

Baker, 'Chris' 154–157, *156*, 179, 194, 195, 227n26
Baltimore College of Dental Surgery 164, 170, 175
bandages 71, 96, 144, 147, 165, 179
Barrett, W.C. 81

255

DISSECTION PHOTOGRAPHY

Barthes, Roland 24
Bassett, Henry Linn 75
Bataille, Georges 36, 136
Batchelor, David 166
Bazin, André 24
Béclard, P.A. 139, 141, 163
Belcher, Harriet Gilliland 85
Bell, Charles 106, 109–110
Bellevue Hospital Medical College of
    New York City 114, *114*, 192
bellows 126, 233n93
Benedict, A.L. 33, 63
Bichat, Xavier 223n37
bigotry
    epigraphs, dissecting table 4–5, 129, 170,
        175–176
    institutional 6, 189–190
    See also dehumanization; racism; sexism
Bird (doctor) 105
Birmingham Medical College (AL) 152,
    185, 221n19
Birnbaum, Henry F. 94
Blacks *See* African Americans
Blackwell, Elizabeth 207, 208, 241n27
blood 99, 112, 134, 158–159, 160, 161,
    163, 220n7
    See also fluids
bodies *See* cadavers; corpses
*Body Criticism: Imagine the Unseen in
    Enlightenment Art and Medicine*
    (Stafford) 34
Borden, Lizzie 130
Boston Medical and Surgical Journal 122
Brady, Matthew 21, 141
Brodnax, John W. 196–197
Broomall, Anna 203, 241n12
brotherhoods 78–79
Brunsman, A.R. 182
buckets 129, 156, 179
Burns, Stanley B. 4, 50, 99
Bynum, Caroline Walker 178

C

cabinet cards 3, 20, 41, 111, 123
cadavers
    abjection of 37–38, 172, 193, *193*
    acquisition of 94
    African American 166–167, 170,
        173–176, 195
    bandages, wrapping of in 71, 96, 144, 147,
        165, 179
    color of in photographs 160–162,
        166–168, *167*
    commodification of 95, 165, 197
    criminals 67, 70, 183–184, 211, 234n19
    dehumanization of 6, 71, 73–74, 129
    donation programs 181, 183
    flaying of 49, 79, 133, 139, 141, 147, 164,
        165, 183

naming of 92–94, 230n28
objectification of 42–45, 46–47, 82, 83–84
personhood 36, 42, 44, 84, 93, 133–134,
    213–214
posing of 16, 19, 38–39, 96–97, *97*, 179,
    193, *193*
race of, determining 166–168
respect for 89, 90, 213–215
storage of 165
suicide victims 104, 137, 183–184
swollen (edema) 138
    See also corpses; dead, the;
    dissection; embalming
Camera Lucida (Barthes) 24
camera obscura 23
cameras *See* camera obscura; No. 2 Kodak
    box camera
Carlisle, Mr. 143
Cartes-de-visite photographs 3, *25*, 65
Catholics 146, 176, 185, 190
    See also Christ; Christianity; God; souls
censorship 34, 48, 216
Chaillé, Stanford E. 181
Chandler, Daniel 50, 52, 54
Charles (student) 56
Charles Lentz and Sons 122
Charley (student) 131
Charlotte (student) 105
Chicago College of Dental Surgery 78, 121,
    164, 172, 201, 202
children, photos of 31–32, 79, 141–142
Christ 177–181, 182, 183, 238n21
Christianity 30, 145–146, 177–179, 182,
    185, 186, 188, 190, 195–196
    See also Catholics; God; souls
Chromophobia (Batchelor) 166
Cisney-Smith, Elizabeth 74, 86, 95
Cleveland, Emeline H. 89
clinical detachment
    development of 5–6, 62–63, 72
    evidence of, dissection photograph
        as 15
    and objectification of cadavers 42–45
Coleman, A.D. 51
collections *See* dissection photography
collodion process 26, 30, 106, 200,
    220n10, 222n15
commercial photographers *See*
    photographers, commercial
communicable diseases, contracting of 103
consent 23, 49, 203, 214–215
contagious diseases *See* communicable
    diseases, contracting of
*Contributions to Physiological and Pathological
    Anatomy* (Godman) 104
Corner, G.W. 192
corpses
    cadavers, compared to 37–38
    discoloration of 168–170

256

INDEX

postmortem photography, preparations of for 142–143

rituals for 39–40

See also cadavers; dead, the

counterculture 15–17, 48, 51–52

COVID-19 pandemic 215

Cregan, Kate 35–36, 39, 47

crime scene photographs 136–137

criminals 67, 70, 183–184, 211, 234n19

Cuenca, Alex 181–182

cultural traditions *See* traditions, cultural

cutting instruments *See* instruments, cutting

cyanotype photographs 19, 157, *199*, 200

D

daguerreotypes 26, 30–32, 161, 222n15

dark humor *See* humor, gallows

Davidson (student) 105

dead, the

as photographic subjects 22

respect due to 29, 89, 90, 213–215

See also cadavers; corpses; postmortem photography (memorial portraits)

death

cultural perceptions of 33–34, 144

religion and 176–178

Death, Dissection and the Destitute (Richardson) 72

deceased, photographs of the *See* postmortem photography (memorial portraits)

decomposition

abjection and 36, 37, 107

cadavers, slowing process of in 38, 139, 147

discoloration and 134, 143, 167, 168–169

measures against 147

photographs of 15, 21, 47–48

postmortem photographs 'halting' 31–32, 33, 143–144

risks from 102–103, 105, 223n37

De Humani corporis fabrica (Vesalius) 58–59

dehumanization

of African Americans 6, 42, 53, 57, 129–130, 170, 187, 204

of cadavers 6, 71, 73–74

desecration

of cadavers 42, 64

of graves 65, 173

See also cadavers; grave robbing

detachment *See* clinical detachment

Dinius, Marcy 32

diseases *See* communicable diseases, contracting of

disgust 33–35, 44, 45–47, 144, 206

dissecting kits

modern medicine, as symbols of 121–123

in photographs *25*, *97*, 97–98, 100, 120–121, *121*

See also instruments, cutting; scalpels

"Dissecting Room Portraits: Decoding an Underground Genre" (Terry) 10

dissecting rooms

accidents 102–105, 231n27

buckets 129, 156, 179

conditions of 149–152, *150*

etiquette 115–116

as initiation zone 40–41

lighting 149, 152–153

outdoor 103, 151–152, 196

racial segregation of 70

See also epigraphs, dissection table

dissection

as abject 49

anatomy, role in advancing 24, 26

of animals 138

as butchery 163–165

risks faced during 102–105, 223n37, 231n27

as ritual of trespass 40–41, 62, 72

as taboo 24, 27–28, 29–30

as training tool 81, 82–83

Dissection: Photographs of A Rite of Passage in American Medicine 1880–1930 (Warner and Edmonson) 11, 51, 57–58, 166

dissection photography

archives / collections 10, 85, 221n26, 225n6, 226n20

history of 2–3, 7–9, 16–17

See also photographers, commercial; photographers, student amateur; postcards; Stage I period (circa 1880–1930); Stage II period (circa 1895–1930); Stage III period (circa 1905–1925); *Student Dream* photographs; *individual schools (e.g., Woman's Medical College of Pennsylvania)*

dissectors (student manuals) 109–110

donors 213

Douglas, Mary 39, 47

Drake, Daniel 173, 238n8

dreams 55–56

See also Student Dream photographs

Drooz, Irma Gross 207–208

Dr. S. 189

dry plate photography 19, 21, 148, 160, 161–162

Dunn, Rose M. 103–104

Dwight, Thomas 29, 212

E

Eakins, Thomas 163

Eastman Kodak Company 18, 162, 200, 240n2

See also No. 2 Kodak box camera

écorché 142

edema (swollen cadavers) 138

Edmonson, James M. 11, 57–58

Edwards, H. Milne 27–28

Eichelberger, Agnes 88, 92

Eliot, T.S. 145
Elkins, James 133, 135, 145–146
Elliott, Ada S. 96, 97, 98, 120
Elliott, Stewart 96, *97*, 98, 117, 120, 214
Elsie (student) 54
embalming
  colors, 'life-like' 161, 168–170, 235n25
  death process, halting of 38
  effects of 134
  fluids 37, 78, 108, 153, 158–159, 168, 169
  funeral home rituals 39–40
  hygiene and 106
  as modernized preservation method
    108–109, 121–122
  See also cadavers; dissection
Emerson, Ralph Waldo 222n4
entrails *See* viscera
entrance requirements 12–13
epigraphs, dissection table
  about 182–185
  Black students 69, *69*
  examples of 123, 164, 190, *191*, 196
  introduction of 42
  racism and 4–5, 129, 170, 175–176
  See also dissecting rooms
Epperson, Paul Stenerson *217*
ethics 9, 11, 21, 78, 89, 187, 190, 214–216
Evans, Alice 85, 198–200, *199*, 201, 203,
    236n30, 240n2
*Exposing Slavery: Photography, Human Bondage,
  and the Birth of Modern Visual Politics in
  America* (Fox-Amato) 157
eye contact 111

F

Fabrica (Vesalius) *See De Humani corporis
  fabrica* (Vesalius)
facial hair 77, 80
fading (of photographs) 145–146, 147, 148
Fasciculus medicinae 59
Faust, Drew Gilpin 168, 212
Female Medical College of Pennsylvania
    (Philadelphia, PA) 151
Fergusson, William 101–102, 110, 120
fetuses, photos of 141–142
Fiske, John 53
Fiterman, Morris 190
flaying 49, 79, 133, 139, 141, 147, 164,
    165, 183
  See also cadavers
flesh *See* skin
Flexner Report 68, 108, 150, 153
Flint Medical College of New Orleans
    University (New Orleans, LA) 68
fluids
  bodily 35, 44, 100, 138, 163, 166
  preservative (embalming) 37, 78, 108, 138,
    153, 158–159, 168, 169
formation, identity *See* identity formation

formless *(informe)* 136
The Four Quartets (Eliot) 145
Fox, Daniel M. 111, 163
Fox-Amato, Matthew 156–157
Freedman's Hospital 68
Friedenberger, Katrina 157
Funderburk, K. 190
funeral homes 39–40

G

gallows humor *See* humor, gallows
Gannal, J.N. 169
Gardner (photographer) 141
Garfield, James A. 168–169
gelatin, animal 148
gelatin silver prints
  adoption of 19, 20, 26
  examples of *46, 66, 69, 97, 114, 124, 126,
    127, 150, 156, 158, 167, 175, 191, 193, 217*
  fading in 146, 147–148
gender segregation *See* segregation, gender
genitalia 9, 100, 121, 125, 126, 157, 193,
    210, 214, 241n27
genres, photography
  about 50, 52, 54
  dissection photography as 49–52, 57–58, 60
  See also portraiture; postmortem
    photography (memorial portraits); *Student
    Dream* photographs
George Eastman Museum 34, 225n6
Gercke, Hans 133
ghosts 30, 55, 181, 191
Gihon, James L. 142–143
gloves, 19, 102, 106, 107, 123, 213, 221n24
God 34, 37, 171–173, 176–178, 181–182,
    196, 207–210, 211
  See also Catholics; Christianity; souls
Godman, John 104–105
Goodchild, Trevor 29
Goode, William Ashby 184
Gove, Mary S. 27
Grant, William R. 109, 115, 116
grave robbing
  dissection and 29, 68–69, 173
  dissection photography and 61, 64, 65–66
  end of 5, 7, 62
  by female schools 94
  and student identity 62–63, 65
  See also resurrectionists
Greenwood, C.J. 210
Gross, Samuel David 102, 110, 116,
    163, 232n54
The Gross Clinic 163
Grosz, Elizabeth 44

H

Hafferty, Frederic 137–138, 143–144,
    167–168, 205
Hahnemann, Samuel 104

INDEX

Hahnemann Medical College (Philadelphia, PA) 78, 181, 189–190, 194, *194*, 202, 203

hammers *See* instruments, cutting

Harrower, J. William 1–2, 202

Hart, Charles 184

Harvard University (Boston, MA) 29, 150–151, 212

hatchets *See* instruments, cutting

Haughton, Samuel 6

hazing rituals 76–78, 86, 241n32

Heath, C. 81

Henfield, John 175

Hering, Constantine 104–105

Herrington, William 190, 240n85

Hertzler, Arthur 81

Hills, Laura Heath 92

Holden, L. 161

Homeopathic Medical College *See* University of Michigan, Homeopathic Medical College

Horner, William E. 26

Howard University College (Washington, D.C.) 68, *69*, 185

The Howler (Wake Forest yearbook) 6, 129, 198 *See also* Wake Forest College Medical School (Chapel Hill, NC)

human remains, objects made from 43

humor, gallows

  limits to 180–181

  skeletons and 92, 124, *124*

  students' use of 73, 82, 83, 90, *91*, 179

  tableaus (Stage III) and 19, 53, 54, 60, 79, *124*, 125, 128–129

Hunter, William 72

hygiene

  hazards 102–105

  practices, improvement of 121–122

  precautionary measures 106

I

identity formation

  occupation (work) and 14

  scalpels, role in 98, 100–101

  of students 12, 14–15, 16, 53, 65, 75–76, 82–83

illustrations, anatomical 58–59

imago Dei 171, 172–173, 177, 181

incoming students *See* students

infectious diseases *See* communicable diseases, contracting of

informe (formless) 136

instruments, cutting

  images of 25

  unconventional 16, 19, *127*, 127–130, 131, 234n104

  See also dissecting kits; scalpels

I Swear by Apollo: A Life of Medical Adventure (Aughinbaugh) 63, 226n20

Ives, Frederic E. 161–162

J

janitors

  African American 6, 153, 154–157, 174, 179, 194–195, 227n26

  dissection photographs with *66*, *156*, 156–157, *175*

  grave robbing by 62, 65, 94

  See also resurrectionists

Japanese Americans 203–204

Jefferson Medical College (Philadelphia) 26, 72, 74, 75, 149, *150*, 188

Jesus *See* Christ

Jews 176, 189, 190

Johns Hopkins School of Medicine (Baltimore, MD) 107, *167*, 230n7

Johnson, David J. 94

K

Kansas City Dental College (Kansas City, MO) 159, 236n32

Keen, W.W. 81

Keiller, William 65, 227n27

Kentucky School of Medicine (Louisville, KY) 174, *175*

Keokuk Medical College (Iowa) 103

King, Dan 88

Kirksville College of Osteopathic Medicine (MO) 182

Klein, Joe 131

knives *See* scalpels

Kolletschka, Jakob 231n27

Kristeva, Julia 12, 36, 37, 45, 134

L

Landes, H.H. 1–2

Lane, J.F.W. 27–28

Lauderdale, Clarence E. 165–166, 237n25

Lawrence, Christopher 111, 163

Lawrence, William 195

Leeds School of Medicine (United Kingdom) *60*

legislation *See* acts, anatomical (legislation, laws)

Leibfreid, Frederick 120, *121*

Lemoine-Luccioni, Eugénie 115

Leonard Medical School of Shaw University (Raleigh, NC) 67–68

Lewis (student) 144

Lewis, R.H. 67

Lewis, Tayler 190, 212

lighting

  challenges with (poor) 42, 134, 139, 149, 152, 157, 160

  magnesium flash 21, 24, 65, 157–159, 162, 201

  postmortem photography 142

  See also photography

Locke, John 191

DISSECTION PHOTOGRAPHY

Long Island College of Medicine
  (New York, NY) 87
Louisville National Medicine College
  (Louisville, KY) 68
lynching
  legalization of 130, 174
  photographs 23, 48, 51, 64, 183, 227n21

M

Maccall, William 177
magnesium flash 21, 24, 65, 157–159,
  162, 201
Mall, Franklin P. 107–108, 119
Manual of Dissection of the Human Body
  (Holden) 161
manuals *See dissectors* (student manuals)
Marsh, Howard 117–119
Martineau, Harriet 173
Maurer Photo Company 4
McElwee, Lucien Claude 68
McGavran, Mary T. 94, 103–104, 188, 208
McGinn, Colin 34, 46
MCV *See* Medical College of Virginia
  (MCV) (Richmond, VA)
The Meaning of Disgust (McGinn) 34
meat eating 164
Medical College of Pennsylvania
  (Philadelphia, PA) 168
  See also Woman's Medical College of
  Pennsylvania (WMCP) (Philadelphia, PA)
Medical College of the State of South
  Carolina 173, 174
Medical College of Virginia (MCV)
  (Richmond, VA)
  Baker, 'Chris' 154–157, *156*, 179, 194,
    195, 227n26
  dissecting room conditions 174,
    179, 235n16
  dissection photography *46*, *156*, *217*
  epigraphs, dissection table 183
  nicknames, student 202
  students 163, 204, 207, 210
medical portraiture *See*
  illustrations, anatomical
Meharry Medical College of Walden
  University (Nashville, TN) 67, *69*
memorial portraits *See* postmortem
  photography (memorial portraits)
Michel, Gustav H. 169
Miller, John David *217*
*Mirror Image: The Influence of the Daguerreotype
  on American Society* (Rudisill) 14
Montgomery, Horace 72
moral character 186–187
Muybridge, Eadweard 50, 101, 231n11

N

Neale, Edward 160
Neale, Steve 54

necrophilia 30
New York Homeopathic Medical College
  (New York City, NY) 119, 123
New York University *See* Bellevue Hospital
  Medical College of New York City
nicknames
  cadavers 92–94, 230n28
  janitors 155
  professors 181
  students 164, 202
Nicol, Rachel 'Jennie' Jane 188, 189
nightmares *See* dreams; *Student
  Dream* photographs
No. 2 Kodak box camera 160, 199, *199*,
  203, 240n2, 241n4
  See also Eastman Kodak Company
North Carolina Anatomy Act 66–67, 70
North Carolina Medical School 105
Northwestern University (Evanston, IL) 90,
  128, 129
Northwestern University Dental School
  (NUDS) 128, 131
NUDS *See* Northwestern University Dental
  School (NUDS)

O

objectification
  and abjection 45
  of cadavers 42–45, 46–47, 82, 83–84
  of female bodies 88
obstetrical manikins 99–100
O'Connor, Erin 50
open-air dissecting rooms *See*
  dissecting rooms
orthochromatic plates 160, 162
outdoor dissecting rooms *See*
  dissecting rooms
Outlines of Anatomy and Physiology (Lane) 28

P

paintings, anatomical *See*
  illustrations, anatomical
panchromatic film / plates 162
Parker, Mary 95
Patterson, Ellen 'Ellie' 157
Paul (student) 44
Pennsylvania Anatomy Act 94
Perkins, A.M. 179
personhood 36, 42, 44, 84, 93, 133, 213–214
petroleum jelly 147
Philadelphia College of Osteopathic
  Medicine 75, 150
Philadelphia School of Anatomy
  (Philadelphia, PA) *18*
photographers, commercial 18, 19, 41–42
photographers, student amateur
  agency of 38–39
  commemorating dissecting room
  experiences 28–29

260

INDEX

dissection photographs by 18–20, 198–200, *199*
non-dissection photography 187
single-dissector photographs 118, *199*, 200, 202–203, 205–206, 209
transgressive posing techniques *124*, 124–130, *126*, *127*
See also postcards; *Student Dream* photographs; students
photographs *See* cabinet cards; crime scene photographs; postcards; postmortem photography (memorial portraits); single-dissector photographs; *Student Dream* photographs
photography
about 136
advancements in 21
business of 41–42
See also albumen prints; collodion process; cyanotype photographs; daguerreotypes; dry plate photography; gelatin silver prints; lighting; salted-paper prints; stereographs; tintypes; wet plate photography
poetry 181–182, 196–197, 198
portraiture
dissection photography as subgenre of 15, 50–52, 58
popularity of, rise in 21–22
See also postmortem photography (memorial portraits)
portraiture, medical *See* illustrations, anatomical
postcards
circulation of 4, 96, 144, 159
examples of *97*
messages written on 4, 54, 55–56, 96, 112–113, 118, 124, 127, 131, 144, 159, 164, 182, 218
real photo 20, 38, 112–113, 118, 182, 220n13
Student Dream 55–56
transgression of, double 53, 164, 172
postmortem photography (memorial portraits)
about 22, 23–24, 30–32, 50–51, 144–145
corpses, preparing of 142–143
costs of 222n4
Powers of Horror: An Essay on Abjection (Kristeva) 36, 37
The Practical Anatomist (Allen) 28, 112
Probst, Anton 130, 234n102
professional photographers *See* photographers, commercial
Pulte Medical College (Cincinnati, OH) 153
pus *See* fluids

Q

Quackery Unmasked (King) 88
quacks 14, 27
Queen's University (Ontario, Canada) 53

R

racial segregation *See* segregation, racial
racism
institutional 6, 67, 68, 170, 176, 204
United States, in the 156–157, 174–176, *175*, 216
Randolph, Anna Moon 198–200, *199*, 241n3
religion *See* Catholics; Christ; Christianity; God; Jews; souls
Rembrandt 58, 99
The Republic of Suffering: Death and the American Civil War (Faust) 212
requirements, entrance *See* entrance requirements
respect (for the dead) 29, 89, 90, 213–215
resurrectionists 61, 62, 65, 154–157, *156*, 194, 227n26
See also grave robbing
resurrections 177–178, 179, 190, 191
Richardson, Ruth 72, 82, 184
rites of passage
African American students 70
dissection as 7, 10, 14, 15, 82, 107–108
dissection photography as 3, 16, 19, 52–53
scalpels as 98
rituals
corpses 39–40
dissection 46–47, 72
grave robbing 62–63
hazing 76–78, 86, 241n32
of trespass, dissection as 40–41, 62
Rizzolo, Lawrence 215
Rogers, Naomi 189
Ruby, Jay 22
Rudisill, Richard 14
Rush Medical College (Chicago, IL) 149, 165

S

salted-paper prints 145, 220n10
Sappol, Michael 27, 29, 30, 40, 62, 65, 180
scalpels
abject, as agents of the 101, 106
handling of 101–102, 110–111, 115–116, 232n54
identity, role in 98, 100–101
in photographs *97*, 97–98, 109, 111–112
transgressive use of in photos *124*, 124–130, *126*, *127*
See also dissecting kits; instruments, cutting
Scarlett, Mary J. 94
Schurman, Henry 80
Scrooge, Ebenezer 55
Scudder, Ida 92
Secure the Shadow, Death and Photography in America (Ruby) 22
segregation, gender 67, 68, 83, 188
segregation, racial
medical institutions 67–69, 70, 156–157, 176
United States, in the 42, 79, 129–130, 174

DISSECTION PHOTOGRAPHY

Senn, Nicholas 231n27
septicemia 105
sexism 6, 87–89
Shu, Ruby Inouye 203–204
single-dissector photographs 118, *199*, 200,
    202–203, 205–206, 209
skeletons
    dancing with 179–180
    dressing up of 16
    posing of *124*, 124–125
skin
    about 133, 134–135
    of cadavers 139, 140, 163–164, 166–168
    fading of in photographs 145–148
    postmortem photographs 142–143
Smith, Augustus Edwin 74
Sontag, Susan 38
souls
    bodies as vessels of 171, 172–173
    existence of 177–178, 192, 195–197, 206
    images capturing/conjuring 30, 32
Southern Dental College (Atlanta, GA) 123,
    164, 188, 190
Southworth, Albert Sands 152, 153, 161
Southworth and Hawes 32, 222n4
specimenhood 42
Speight, F.W. 129, 130
Stafford, Barbara Maria 34, 107
Stage I period (circa 1880–1930) 18, *18*, 42,
    53, 85–86, 100, 194, 200
Stage II period (circa 1895–1930) 18–19, 53,
    85–86, 91–92, 200
Stage III period (circa 1905–1925) 19–20,
    53, 54, 98, 106, *193*, 193–194
    See also Student Dream photographs
Stam, Robert 57, 59
Starling Medical College (Columbus,
    OH) 184
State University Medical Department
    (San Francisco, CA) 101
stereographs 3, *5*, 48, 101, 141
Stiff Law *See* North Carolina Anatomy Act
Streeter, G.L. 138
Student Dream photographs 3–4, 19, 54–55,
    124–125, *124*, 142, 181
student photographers *See* photographers,
    student amateur
students
    African American 69, *69*, 70
    behavior of 71, 72, 209–210
    brotherhoods 78–79
    as 'butchers' 163–165
    clinical detachment 5–6, 15, 42–45,
    62–63, 72
    deaths of 105
    as the dissected in photographs *124*,
    124–125, 128
    grave robbing rituals 62–63, 65
    hazing rituals 76–78, 86, 241n32

health of 205–206
identity formation of 12, 14–15, 16, 53,
    65, 75–76, 82–83
incoming 73, 75, 78, 80, 86, 123
moral character of 186–187
nicknames 164, 202
nursing 92, 118, 180, 220n7
religion 172, 178, 180–182, 185–188, 192
respect (for cadavers) 89, 90, 213–215
responses (to cadavers) 207–208
selection (of cadavers) 84
single-dissector photographs 118, *199*, 200,
    202–203, 205–206, 209
suicide risks 13
training of 81, 82–83, 107–108, 115–116,
    117–118
    See also photographers, student amateur
subgenres, photography *See* genres,
    photography; *Student Dream* photographs
suicide
    Christ's death as 238n21
    medical students 13
    victims 104, 137, 183–184
superstitions 23, 31, 32, 61, 188–189
surgical knives *See* scalpels
A System of Surgery (Gross) 102

T

tableaus
    gallows humor of 19, 54, 124–125, *193*,
    193–194
    props, use of in 57, 79, 97–98, 120, 141–142
    religious 180–181, 196
    as unsettling 11, 58, 163, 172
    See also Stage III period (circa 1905–1925);
    Student Dream photographs
Taft, Robert 162, 222n15
Tagg, John 24
Taylor, Charles E. 185, 186
Taylor, Julia 4
Taylor, P. Richard 176
Taylor, William H. 155
Terra Mariae (University of Maryland
    yearbook) 2
Terry, James S.
    on codes of behavior 42, 216
    on dissection photography 10–11, 15, 16,
    50, 58, 59–60, 215, 217
    on grave robbing 61–62, 64–65
    on postmortem photography 22
Texas Anatomy Act 65
Texas College of Osteopathic Medicine (Fort
    Worth, TX) 150, 164–165
Thomas, Charles Hermon 94
tintypes 31, 32, 106, 234n7
tools *See* dissecting kits; instruments,
    cutting; scalpels
Trachtenberg, Alan 24, 30, 31
traditions, cultural 80

262

INDEX

A Traffic of Dead Bodies: Anatome and Embodied Social Identity in Nineteenth-Century America (Sappol) 27
Tulane Medical College (New Orleans, LA) 75, 83
Tulane University 77, 82, 128, 181, 207

U

University of Alabama (Mobile, AL) 138
University of California (San Francisco, CA) 73, 82, 103, 116, 190
University of Georgia (Augusta, GA) 68–69
University of Louisville (KY) 182, 183
University of Maryland School of Medicine
  class portraits 82–83, 164, *167*, 182
  cultural traditions 80
  dissecting room 78–79, 82, 123
  dissection photography 1–2
  exams 205
  hazing rituals 77
  nicknames, student 202
  religion 185, 186
  Terra Mariae (yearbook) 2
University of Michigan, Homeopathic Medical College 5, 71, 73–74, 138
University of North Carolina (UNC) (Chapel Hill, NC) 66, 103
University of North Carolina School of Medicine (Raleigh, NC) 196
University of Pennsylvania (Philadelphia, PA) 88, 103, 115, 120, *121*
University of Texas Medical Department 4, 65
University of Vermont 99–100, 152
University of Virginia (Charlottesville, VA) *66*, 75, 175, 209
Uno, Kazuko 203–204

V

Vaseline (petroleum jelly) 147
Velpeau, A.A.L.M. 26
Vesalius, Andreas 58–59, 87, 98
violence
  dissection photographs 125, 126, 130, 133
  hazing rituals 77, 80, 86
  postmortem 29, 64
viscera 35, 126, 134, 139, 141, 145, 158
Vogel, Hermann Wilhelm 161–162

W

Wake Forest College Medical School (Chapel Hill, NC)
  dissecting rooms 73, 150
  dissection photography 79
  The Howler 6, 129, 198

racism at 6, 187
religion 185, 186, 187, 196
Walsh, James J. 185
Walters, Theo A. 159
Walton, Israel 157
Waring, Clarence 203
Warner, John Harley 3, 11, 57, 166–167
Warren, Samuel 61
Weaver, Rufus Benjamin 181, *194*, 194–195
Wetmore, S.W. 161
wet plate photography 19, 20, 160, 162
Wheeler, Edith Flower 55, 87, 173, 178, 238n26
Whitehead, Richard Henry *66*, 66–67
Wilson, Franklin 73
WMCP *See* Woman's Medical College of Pennsylvania (WMCP) (Philadelphia, PA)
Woman's College of Medicine (New York, NY) 192
Woman's Hospital of Philadelphia 151
Woman's Medical College of Georgia and Training School for Nurses 90, 227n36
Woman's Medical College of Pennsylvania (WMCP) (Philadelphia, PA)
  about 74, 85
  cadavers, acquisition of 94
  communicable diseases, contracting 103
  dissecting rooms 151
  dissection photography 85–86, *86*, 198–200, *199*
  hazing rituals 86
  racism 204
  religion 188
  sexism 6, 87–89
women
  anatomy text designed for 27
  cadavers, respect for 89, 90, 92
  dissection photographs 85–87, *86*, *91*, 157
  gender segregation 67, 68, 83, 188
  photographers 198–200, *199*
  physicians 88, 89, 203–204, 207, 208
  sexism toward 6, 87–89, 229n10
  training hospitals for 7, 74, 85–86
Woodward, John F. 154

Y

Yale University
  dissection photography 215
  dissection rooms 84
  hazing rituals 76–77, 78
  hygiene measures 106
yearbooks
  about 8
  The Howler (Wake Forest) 6, 129, 198
  Terra Mariae (University of Maryland) 2
Young Men's Christian Association (Y.M.C.A.) 185